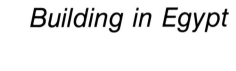

Building in Egypt

Building in Egypt

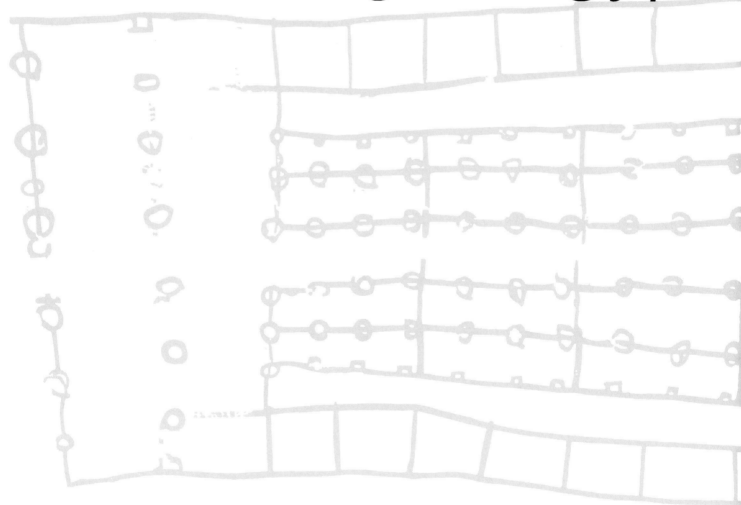

New York Oxford   OXFORD UNIVERSITY PRESS 1991

DIETER ARNOLD

Pharaonic Stone Masonry

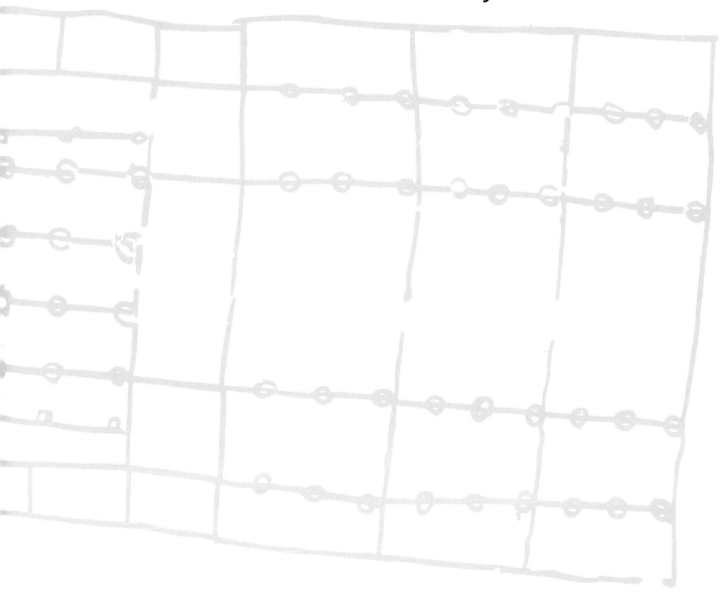

Oxford University Press

Oxford   New York   Toronto
Delhi   Bombay   Calcutta   Madras   Karachi
Petaling Jaya   Singapore   Hong Kong   Tokyo
Nairobi   Dar es Salaam   Cape Town
Melbourne   Auckland

and associated companies in
Berlin   Ibadan

Published by Oxford University Press, Inc.,
198 Madison Avenue, New York, New York 10016-4314

Oxford is a registered trademark of Oxford University Press

Library of Congress Cataloging-in-Publication Data
Arnold, Dieter, 1936–
Building in Egypt : pharaonic stone masonry / Dieter Arnold.
p. cm.   Includes bibliographical references.
ISBN 0-19-506350-3
ISBN 0-19-511374-8 (Pbk.)
1. Building, Stone—Egypt—History.
2. Egypt—History—To 332 B.C.   I. Title.
TH1201.A77   1991   622′.35′0932—dc20   90-6929

9 8 7 6 5 4 3

Printed in the United States of America
on acid-free paper

Acknowledgments

I would like to express my gratitude to the Metropolitan Museum of Art, New York, which has enabled me in many ways to carry out this study and to make use of the splendid collection of Egyptian builder's tools, the vast files of site and object photos in the Egyptian Department, and the services of the Thomas J. Watson Library. I would like to thank Bill Barrette for taking numerous new photos and the Photo Studio of the museum for producing prints from old negatives. I also thank the German Archaeological Institute in Cairo and its director, Rainer Stadelmann, for permission to make use of its rich collection of excavation photos. I also wish to thank my former students at the Egyptological Institute of the Vienna University, who kindly helped me during the years 1979 to 1984 to collect basic material for this study.

Gerhard Haeny, I. E. S. Edwards, Peter Grossmann, Jean Jacquet, Martin Isler, Christian Hölzl, Rainer Stadelmann, and Denys Stocks have over many years generously discussed different aspects of the subject with me.

Barbara Porter kindly revised my English manuscript, and Adela Oppenheim took charge of the proofreading.

I would also like to express my gratitude to Oxford University Press and its editors for publishing this book.

New York   D. A.
October 1989

Contents

Building in Egypt

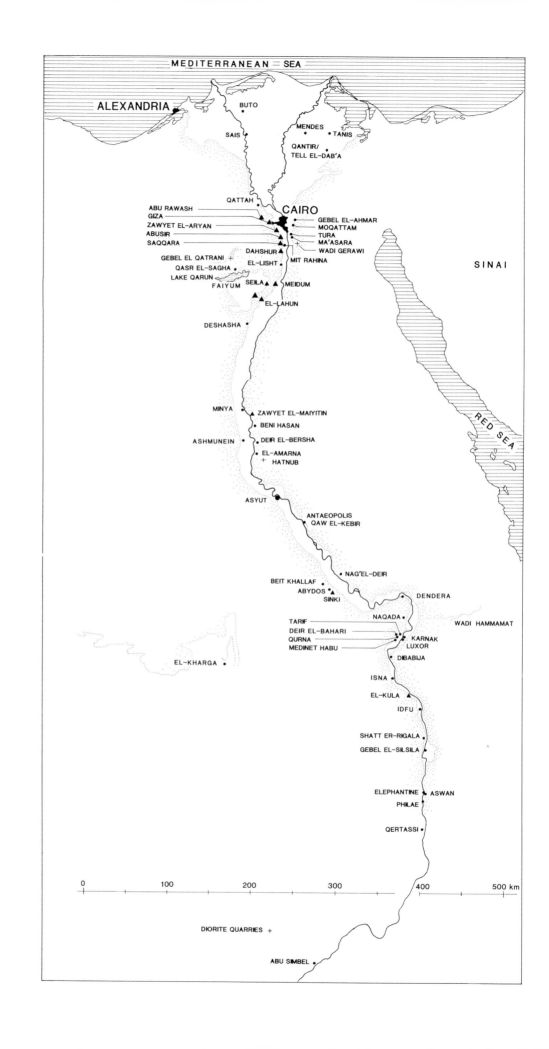

Introduction

Although the view is widely held, Egyptian stone architecture does not have its roots in the worldwide megalithic building activities of Neolithic cultures, which go back at least to the fifth millennium B.C.[1] In Neolithic Egypt—from ca. 5200 (or 4800) to ca. 3200 (or 3000) B.C.—the common building materials were pisé, mudbrick, reed, and wood; there was no stone architecture. Why the use of stone for structural or other important parts of building started only in the first two dynasties is an unanswered question. In the Third Dynasty (ca. 2700 B.C.), true stone architecture appeared cometlike with the mortuary complex of King Djoser at Saqqara. The existence of other primitive forerunners of this type is possible, but they remain beyond our grasp.

This comparatively late appearance of stone building when brick architecture was already flourishing had important consequences for the development of Egyptian building forms. Practically all principal features of Egyptian architecture, such as the battered walls, the Egyptian cornice, screen walls, false doors, and the different types of columns, were distinctive marks of building in a different material, which was translated into stone. This process of translation also influenced the new building dimensions, which were comparable with those of brick architecture and did not—at least during a transitional period—surpass human proportions. The construction methods of brick building were applied at first to building in stone. Small, regular blocks were set in a pattern of brick bonding, frequently in rows that inclined inward and were joined with a lot of mortar. Both these characteristics of brick building soon disappeared, however. Just a few generations after King Djoser, in the reigns of Snofru, Cheops, and Chephren, pyramids and pyramid temples of gigantic dimensions were erected with blocks weighing up to 200 tons.

We know the reason neither for the sudden rise of stone architecture nor for its immediate development into superhuman dimensions. We can only refer to similar phenomena in societies of comparative cultural level or ideology, such as the pre-Columbian cultures of America, assuming that early societies under divine rulership and strong governmental organization tend to manifest and immortalize their ideology in architecture that dwarfs individuals by its monumental dimensions. This the ancient Egyptians certainly carried through in an exemplary way. They not only turned their conception of kingship and the netherworld into stone, but also animated these stone replicas by rituals and magic spells written on the walls. They also linked the buildings to phenomena such as the rise of the original hill from the primeval waters and the daily orbit of the sun. Only a proper conjuration in stone seems to have been a guarantee for the functioning of the Egyptian universe.

To achieve this ambitious goal, a considerable part of the population of Egypt, either directly or indirectly, was continually occupied in building projects all over the country. The erection of the pyramids of the Old Kingdom and the gigantic temples of Amenhotep III and Ramesses II of the New Kingdom are only the most eminent peaks of this activity. Hundreds of thousands of cubic meters of limestone and sandstone, alabaster, granite, and basalt were quarried from the cliffs along the Nile Valley and the surrounding deserts. Hundreds of boatloads of timber had to be imported from the Lebanon. Large quantities of tools and equipment had to be produced, from primitive stone axes to wooden sledges 30 meters long and huge boats for the transport of stones weighing several hundred tons. Mountains of sand and Nile mud had to be moved for the fabrication of brick. Finally, all this vast amount of material had to be brought to the construction site and lifted into position. For this purpose, thousands of people had to be conscripted according to complicated procedures, and steered to the many building projects. These people had to be trained, fed, and clothed. The gigantic apparatus was masterminded and then enforced by the pharaoh with his priests and officials. Conscription on such a level was not done without pressure, but the process was certainly backed by some of the population.

This enormous building activity lasted about 3000 years and has left innumerable monuments in various states of preservation, from practically intact temple halls as those of Sety I at Abydos, to mere foundation trenches that can be interpreted only by architectural historians.

Numerous tools and other relics connected with construction work have been excavated. Records from papyri and representations of technical procedures in the wall decoration of tombs contribute further to our understanding of Egyptian building operations. This material is a unique source of information about an early civilization that worked predominantly with stone tools and mounted its building projects without true pulleys or cranes and with a restricted use of wheels.

The technical aspects of Egyptian architecture have long been neglected in favor of historical reviews of Egyptian architecture and studies of its religious function. The last comprehensive, classical documentation of Egyptian building methods, *Ancient Egyptian Masonry* by Somers Clarke and

Reginald Engelbach (*CEAEM*), is now sixty years old. New material has changed the picture since then. Also, studies of construction methods of preclassical, Greco-Roman, medieval, and Inca architecture have made considerable progress and provide comparative material.[2] This book also tries to combat speculative literature on how the ancient Egyptians solved certain technical problems. Such studies, often filled with unproved theories, obscure our outlook.

In our age of specialization, this book can be considered neither comprehensive nor final; in fact, some of its subjects may already be outdated by continuing fieldwork. The work is also understandably tinged by the author's long-term occupation with the architecture of the Middle Kingdom; numerous examples in the text date to this period.

This study concentrates on the technical aspects of Pharaonic building activities to the fifth century B.C. Architecture after this time represents a changing technical world that must be considered in the context of the architecture and technology of the Greeks and Romans.[3] Also, the book's technical emphasis precludes a comprehensive description of the forms of the structural components of Egyptian buildings, such as columns, doors, and drains.

Sources cited frequently in the notes are given in abbreviated form. These abbreviations are listed with the full citations in the Bibliography.

NOTES

1. C. Renfrew, in *Archaeology, Myth and Reality* (readings from *Scientific American*) (San Francisco, 1982), 47–55; G. Daniel, in *Archaeology, Myth and Reality,* 56–66; Roger Joussaume, *Dolmens for the Dead* (Ithaca, N.Y., 1988), 23, 129.

2. For example, Shaw, *Minoan Architecture;* Martin, *Architecture grecque;* Graziano Gasparini and Luise Margolies, *Inca Architecture* (Bloomington, Ind., 1980); Friedrich Wilhelm Deichmann and Peter Grossmann, *Nubische Forschungen* (Berlin, 1988), 95–167; John Fitchen, *The Construction of Gothic Cathedrals: A Study of Medieval Vault Erection* (Chicago, 1961).

3. These aspects have recently been discussed by scholars more involved in that sector: J.-C. Golvin and J. Larronde, *ASAE* 68 (1982): 165–190; Golvin and Larronde, *ASAE* 70 (1984–1985): 371–381; J.-C. Golvin and R. Vergnieux, *Hommages à François Daumas* (Montpelier, Vt. 1988), 299–320; Golvin and Goyon, *Karnak,* with a valuable retrospective of the building techniques of the New Kingdom.

CHAPTER I   *Preparations*

PLANS[1]

On the walls of the rock tombs and temples of the New Kingdom, Egyptian artists drew accurate and detailed elevations of pylons, chapels, palaces, private houses, and other buildings. Such artists were certainly capable of drawing architectural plans and elevations for building purposes as well, but few drawings of this type have survived; in fact, no true building plan as executed by an architect for construction purposes has been preserved.

Building without ground plans is unthinkable to us. But were they really of the same importance to ancient Egyptian builders? Perhaps a rough sketch and drawings of some architectural details were sufficient. We know that Egyptian architects tried to develop their ideas on the basis of ancient prototypes that must have been familiar to them. Was this knowledge based on scholarly studies of existing buildings or on records written by architects about their buildings, similar to those of classical architects, as mentioned in the preface of Vitruvius's book 7?

The layout of Egyptian buildings shows that whole cubit measurements were preferred for overall inside and outside measurements. Obviously fractions of cubits such as palms and fingers—or, according to another system, half-cubits—could not always be avoided.[2] One may therefore assume that the original plan of a building was developed with the help of a grid, the squares of which represented 1 cubit. No such plan has survived, but a papyrus with a construction drawing of a shrine for a carpenter (Table 1.1, no. 11) suggests how such plans must have looked.[3] We also know from numerous examples of construction grids drawn over the vertical faces of walls to be decorated or over blocks of stone to be shaped into statues or columns (fig. 2.26)[4] that the Egyptians were experts in working with the grid system.

In using the grid system, however, did the Egyptians also understand the method of drawing to a certain scale—were the squares in the grid of the plan intentionally drawn as a fraction of the real cubit? And did the archi-

TABLE 1.1. PLANS AND ARCHITECTURAL DRAWINGS

Object	Date	Location	Bibliography
1. Curve coordinates for arch or vault; ostrakon (fig. 1.1)	Djoser(?)	Cairo	B. Gunn, *ASAE* 26 (1926): 197–202; *CEAEM*, 52–53, figs. 53, 54
2. Plan of garden or temple; paving slab (fig. 1.2)	Mentuhotep	MMA 22.3.30	Arnold and Winlock, *Mentuhotep*, 23, fig. 9; *CEAEM*, 57–59, figs. 59, 60
3. Plan of a building; paving slab(?)	Senwosret I	MMA 14.3.15	Arnold, *Senwosret I* I, 98, fig. 47
4. Plan of temple of Heliopolis (Hathor?); slate tablet	Dynasty 12(?)	Turin 2682	H. Ricke, *ZÄS* 71 (1935): 111–133
5. Sketch of a building; ostrakon	Amenemhat III	Berlin	Alan Gardiner, *The Ramesseum Papyri* (Oxford, 1955), fig. 2
6. Sketch plan of a tomb (Theban tomb no. 71?); ostrakon	Eighteenth Dynasty	Cairo CG 66262	W. C. Hayes, *Ostraka and Name Stones* (New York, 1942), 15, pl. 7
7. Sketch plan of a house; ostrakon	Eighteenth Dynasty	Cairo?	Unpublished
8. Plan of an estate; wooden panel (fig. 1.3)	Eighteenth Dynasty	MMA 14.108	N. De Garis Davies, *JEA* 4 (1917): 194–199; *CEAEM*, 56–57, fig. 57
9. Sketch plans of houses, scratched into floor	Eighteenth Dynasty	Amarna	J. D. S. Pendlebury, *The City of Akhenaten* III (London, 1951), pl. 36 [4–5]
10. Plan of a pillared chapel; ostrakon	Eighteenth/Nineteenth Dynasty	BM 41228	S. R. K. Glanville, *JEA* 16 (1930): 237–239
11. Elevation of a shrine; papyrus "from Ghurab"	Eighteenth Dynasty	University College, London	Petrie, *Ancient Egypt* (1926): 24–27; *CEAEM*, 46–48, fig. 48
12. Plan of a large temple; graffito in a quarry (fig. 1.4)	Amarna Period?	Sheikh Said	N. De Garis Davies, *Ancient Egypt* (1917): 21–25
13. Plan of the tomb of Ramesses IV; papyrus (fig. 1.5)	Ramesses IV	Turin 1885	H. Carter and A. Gardiner, *JEA* 4 (1917): 130–158; *CEAEM*, 48–51, fig. 49
14. Plan of the tomb of Ramesses IX; ostrakon from Biban el-Muluk	Ramesses IX	Cairo CG 25184	G. Daressy, *Ostraca* (Cairo, 1901), 35, pl. 32; *CEAEM*, 51, fig. 50
15. Plan of room with four pillars; ostrakon	Ramesside?	Cairo CG 51936	R. Engelbach, *ASAE* 27 (1927): 72–75; *CEAEM*, 51, fig. 51
16. Plan of staircase and door; ostrakon from Biban el-Muluk	Ramesside?	Cairo	*CEAEM*, 52, fig. 52

tects cover their construction sites with such a grid of cubit squares in order to construct the actual outlines of the walls? Construction lines preserved on the foundations or pavement of buildings seem not to favor this possibility.

There is no doubt that the elevation of a building was also constructed with the help of such a grid. But until now no surveys have been carried out that are accurate enough to determine the elevation proportions.[5] The only plans that have survived are not real building plans as we would expect them, but were created for slightly different purposes.

Six ground plans (Table 1.1, nos. 2, 3, 5, 6, 7, 9, 12) drawn on paving slabs or similar surfaces apparently were preliminary drafts. The sketches, consisting of lines representing walls and dots marking columns, were made either during the planning of a building or later, perhaps in a discussion to recall a building.

Other ostraka (Table 1.1, nos. 1, 10, 15, 16) show details of constructions to be carried out. They were sketched free hand but with all the necessary details. Measurements were attached to them so that the masons or builders could work from these instructions, which may have been prepared by their superiors. Because these sketches were on cheap material, they were not intended as permanent records but were to be thrown away after completion of the task.

A third group (Table 1.1, nos. 8, 13, 14) is apparently made up of demonstration objects for the client (who could have been even the king), students, or others. They are carefully executed and adorned with pleasing but unnecessary details, including landscape (a nearby river, trees, surrounding desert). They may contain, as in the example of the Turin Papyrus, eloquent labeling, with description even of the wall decoration and the essential measurements. These plans were plain enough to be easily understood but did not contain sufficient information for the builders.

Finally, the inventory list of the Ra-Harakhty temple of Heliopolis was a kind of temple plan drawn on a slab of stone (Table 1.1, no. 4).[6] It was apparently made as a votive to the god or as a document to be kept in the archives, not so much to represent the building but rather its features and contents.

Because the Egyptians were great model builders, one would not be surprised to see real architectural models as well. But we are not sure that ancient architects made as much use of models as do architects today.[7] Besides the many "soul houses," or models made for funerary use, we actually know very little about real architectural models. The famous granite base of a model of the entrance part of the temple of Heliopolis, from the time of Sety I, was certainly made as a votive for the gods.[8]

The only model-like object preserved is the representation of a royal tomb of the late Middle Kingdom from the valley temple of the pyramid of Amenemhat III at Dahshur (fig. 1.6).[9] Carved from limestone, it shows the main corridors and chambers in an abbreviated fashion. The corridors, for example, were shortened in order to fit them into the dimensions of the block (with an extended part for the entrance corridor). There are enough details to show the function of a sliding block in front of the antechamber

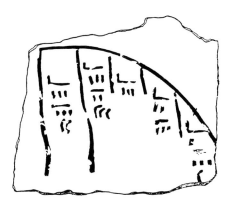

Fig. 1.1 Third Dynasty ostrakon from Saqqara, with sketch for the construction of a vaulted roof.

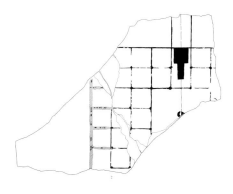

Fig. 1.2 Paving slab from the temple of Mentuhotep at Deir el-Bahari, with the plan for a garden or temple. (MMA acc. no. 22.3.30)

Fig. 1.3 Wooden panel of the Eighteenth Dynasty, with the plan for an estate. (MMA acc. no. 14.108)

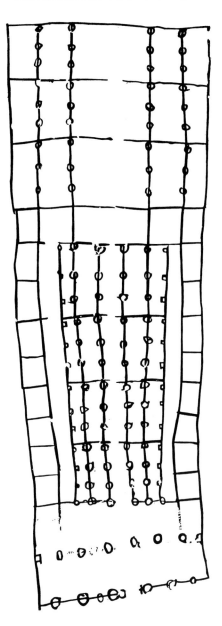

(set in as a block of wood) and the closing of the roofing block of the burial chamber, as is found in the pyramid at Hawara. Since the model is not inscribed or made in an attractive way, it was probably not votive; but its actual purpose remains unknown.

A corridor system northeast of the Cheops Pyramid was for a long time considered to be a nearly full-scale model of some parts of the Cheops Pyramid[10] until Mark Lehner made it clear that it is an unfinished and separate tomb, perhaps the original tomb for Queen Hetepheres.[11]

MEASURING

Measuring Distances · The art of measuring probably came into existence in ancient Egypt together with the invention of writing and counting in general. That units and instruments for measuring distances existed as early as the First Dynasty can be deduced from the canon of proportions on the palette of Narmer[12] and the cubit system used for the layout of the so-called mastaba of Menes at Naqada.[13] All later buildings clearly attest the use of an exact measuring system, but only from the New Kingdom are actual cubit rods preserved. They differ only slightly in length, being about 52.5 centimeters long.[14] Howard Carter's calculations of 52.3 centimeters[15] are contradicted by measuring existing buildings, all of which seem to be built according to a cubit of 52.5 centimeters,[16] with the usual discrepancies that have to be expected in such work.

For practical reasons, builders may also have used 2-cubit rods, one example being preserved, or even longer ones. In the mastaba of Ptahshepses at Abusir, builders may have used an otherwise unknown measurement of a foot (*tb.t*), the length of which remains uncertain.[17] Also unknown is the extent to which measuring ropes were used in building.[18]

Exact measuring depended on a clear marking of the points to be measured. Marks on buildings are preserved in great numbers. The discovery of wooden pegs hammered into the ground for measuring is rare;[19] however, their frequent use is shown in the famous representations of the "stretching of the cord" during the foundation ceremonies for temples,[20] where they are pounded with elongated wooden hammers. Several examples of wooden pegs that could have been used for that purpose have been

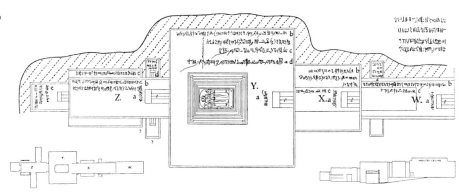

Fig. 1.5 Papyrus with the plan for the tomb of Ramesses IV. (Turin 1885)

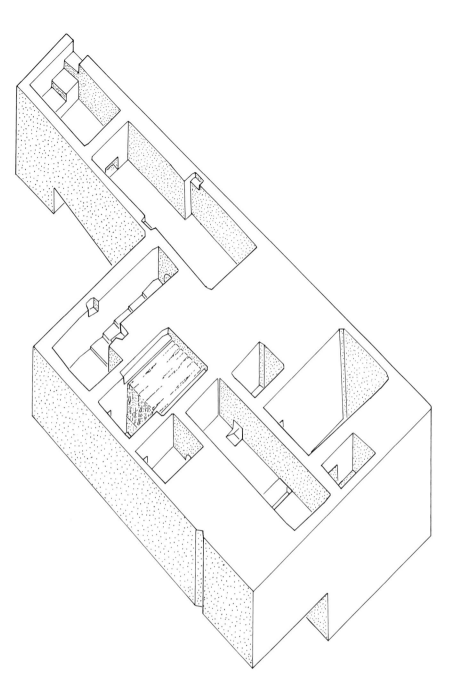

Fig. 1.6 Limestone model of an unidentified royal tomb, found in the valley temple of the pyramid of Amenemhat III at Dahshur.

found in situ.[21] Many round holes cut into the bedrock around the foundations of pyramids and temples may have served for inserting measuring pegs.[22] Other marks were scratched with chisels and flint tools into the surface of pavement blocks and column bases[23] or were indicated by a red brush line.

Measuring the Inclination[24] · The faces of pyramids, mastabas, pylons, and many stone-built walls were inclined, and the Egyptian builders seem to have developed a simple and exact method to calculate this inclination, or *sqd*,[25] without knowing our system of working with the 90-degree divi-

Fig. 1.7 The Egyptian method of expressing the inclination (*sqd*).

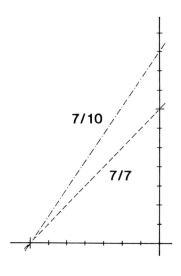

7/10

7/7

Fig. 1.8 System of measuring lines preserved in the foundation trenches of mastaba 17 at Meidum.

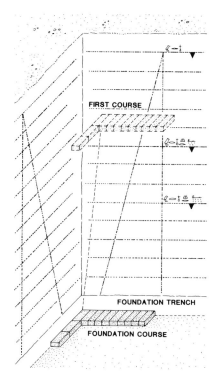

FIRST COURSE

FOUNDATION TRENCH

FOUNDATION COURSE

sion of a quadrant. This method was apparently used in brick buildings from the First Dynasty on and is attested for the first time in the mastaba no. 17 at Meidum. From the Rhind Mathematical Papyrus we know[26] that the *sqd* was defined as the relation between the horizontal setback of the wall and the vertical rise of 1 cubit (fig. 1.7).[27] The setback could be 1 cubit (that is, an inclination of 45 degrees) but was more often only part of a cubit. The papyrus reference to setbacks of 5 ½₅ palms and 5 palms 1 finger suggests already rather sophisticated calculations.

It is not easy for us to recognize the proportion originally intended by measuring existing buildings whose walls are frequently distorted by settling and destruction, certainly resulting in errors of calculation of one finger or more. The problem is increased by the use of fractions of cubits, such as half- and quarter-cubits. This may be shown by the inclination of some pyramids of the Twelfth Dynasty:

Amenemhat I	7 p : 5 p
Senwosret I	7 p : 8 p
Senwosret III	7 p : 10.5 (!) p
Amenemhat III	
(Dahshur)	7 p : 10 p
(Hawara)	7 p : 8 p (?)

Petrie's observations about mastaba no. 17 of Meidum (see n. 26) shows what method was used to transfer the calculated *sqd* to the building (fig. 1.8). Outside the four corners, L-shaped brick walls were built from bedrock up to the intended ground level (the *nfrw;* see p. 17) of the mastaba. On the plastered and whitewashed inner faces of these walls, the builders drew construction lines. In red are the vertical lines marking the corners of the mastaba at ground level (now destroyed). Horizontal lines were drawn at distances of 1 cubit and numbered from the ground level to probably 13 cubits (*ḥr nfrw*). The actual inclination lines were drawn in black starting at the foot point of the mastaba corners at ground level with a slope of ¼ to 1 cubit, a ratio of 1 cubit to 4 cubits. Due to a change of plan, the mastaba was enlarged by 1 cubit so that a second, black line 1 cubit in front of the older one was made.

How the men laying the bricks transferred these markings to the walls is not known. Since the mastaba walls are too long to be checked by the human eye (52.5 × 105.0 meters) and too long for stretching a cord (which would sag in the center),[28] most probably wooden frames sloping in the correct manner were set up at the corners and at some places in between that could be used for stretching the cord. Alexander Badawy suggested that similar L-shaped walls with inclination lines could have been used for pyramid building as well.[29] This method could have been applied to only the first few courses above ground. Farther up, no room would have been free for the erection of such walls because the corner area of a pyramid was not left open, and the corner blocks of each course would certainly have been the first blocks to be laid to guarantee exact measurements for the whole course. How the corner blocks were measured and put in position in such an accurate way as to serve as guiding blocks for the direction, height, and inclination of the whole course is unknown.

One example, from a different period and location, is a construction sketch for the inclination of a pyramid at Meroë.[30] Basically it still preserves the old method used for mastaba no. 17 at Meidum, containing horizontal parallels, a vertical line, and the *sqd*. Again, the sketch is drawn on a wall at some distance from the building itself.

At one Old Kingdom example, the queen's pyramid GIa at Giza,[31] the inclination line of the core steps is drawn against the core masonry, near the corner. It was probably not meant for cutting down the extra stock of these blocks to the actual indicated batter, but only as a help for the construction (fig. 1.13).

Examples for the method used at Meidum are also found at later buildings. At Mendes, the corners of the foundation pit for the platform of the famous naos show white gypsum stripes on which, in fine black lines, the exact outline of the platform is indicated.[32] In the foundation trench of the pyramid of Amenemhat III at Dahshur, De Morgan found the corners "strengthened" by brick walls; however, these walls may have been the background for the construction sketches of the surveyors of the pyramid.[33]

Normally, building stones were set with extra stock at the front faces. Such bossed front faces would have prevented the construction of an exact inclination. One has to assume, therefore, that vertical flat grooves or channels that permitted the transfer of the batter from one course to the next were cut during the positioning of the blocks. This could easily be achieved by the method shown in fig. 1.9.

Leveling · Egyptian buildings were normally erected on accurately leveled foundations or pavements, as were the individual wall blocks. Irregularities in height were always compensated for by horizontal steps, never by sloping planes. This can be observed in existing buildings and deduced by the leveling lines, frequently painted in red on the faces of walls and core masonry and occasionally still accompanied by numbers indicating the height "above zero" (see p. 17).

The only instrument for leveling known to the Egyptians was the square level (figs. 1.10, 6.4, 6.6); more complicated instruments, such as those using water, were first invented by the Romans.[34] With this simple tool, it was apparently possible to achieve amazing results. One has to remember, however, that the ancient Egyptians were provided with the experience of many generations of surveyors trained in the irrigation of the fields and the surveying of channels and canals.

It has been established that the foot of the casing of the Cheops Pyramid was leveled so exactly that the difference between the north and south sides is only 2 centimeters.[35] This was, however, an exception since acquaintance with Egyptian buildings teaches us that quite frequently differences of up to 1 palm or even more were accepted. We do not know, of course, how much of this inaccuracy is actually the result of later settling of the foundations.

Field tests with a square level carried out in 1987 at Lisht[36] showed that up to a distance of 40 to 45 meters, a difference in height of 1 centimeter can be recognized with some difficulty (fig. 1.10). From one station, a distance of 80 to 90 meters could therefore be covered by reading in two

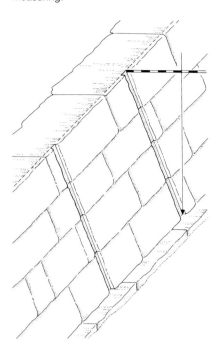

Fig. 1.9 Establishing the inclination of an undressed wall in grooves prepared for measuring.

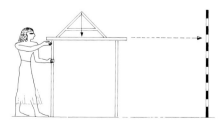

Fig. 1.10 Use of the square level for establishing equal levels.

Fig. 1.11 Bench mark from the
Mentuhotep temple at Deir el-Bahari.

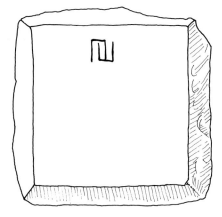

directions. Since the Egyptians were not able to increase the effectiveness of the human eye,[37] they were forced to level longer distances by working in small steps.[38]

Egyptian surveyors not only transferred the results of their measuring to the vertical walls of core masonry, but also marked levels on the ground. Such bench marks consisted of square limestone slabs with a cross mark in the center (fig. 1.11).[39] They were set at pavement level in front of the foot of a wall, from which the height of the wall could easily be determined. In the causeway of Mentuhotep, they were also used to mark the slope of the pavement of the road.[40] Similar rectangular limestone slabs were found inserted into the granite floor of the sloping pyramid passage of Senwosret I.[41] The surface of the slabs is worn so much that one can no longer see any traces of cross marks. They probably existed and were used to determine not only the slope of the passage, but also the horizontal distance. This may be deduced from the fact that the distance to the center of the slabs is 10 cubits, but only if measured horizontally.

In the outer court of the same pyramid, a network of thin brick walls was uncovered,[42] which were explained by the excavators as leveling walls. They were erected on the surface of the construction site surrounding the pyramid after the work was completed. Their tops were all at the same level—the level aimed at for the surface of the outer court. After that, filling material could be spread over the area up to the level of these walls or slightly higher in order to achieve a completely level outer court.

In recent years, the question has been raised again about the extent to which the ancient Egyptians could have made use of water for leveling purposes.[43] Lehner, especially, thought that the flat ditches surrounding the pyramids of Cheops and Chephren were actually leveling installations from the time of the construction of the pyramids. He assumed that tree trunks set into holes in these ditches were sawed down to the level of the water in the trenches so that they could thereafter be used as bench marks. Yet the ditches were too large to be filled with water, which had to be carried up from the valley and would have dried out and disappeared in the many crevices of the bedrock. Furthermore, the ditches are so similar to that of the pyramid of Illahun, which was certainly used as a drainage channel, that they might have had the same function.[44]

Constructing the Right Angle · Egyptian monumental buildings were generally constructed with precise right angles. For short distances, this could certainly be achieved by using the set square. In the interior apartments of the pyramid of Amenemhat III, for example, there was not much room for other tools. The method is described by Engelbach, who claims that in none of his experiments did the error from the right angle exceed 1 minute of arc (fig. 1.12A).[45] The base leg of the square is placed on the line with its outer corner against the intersection point of the intended perpendicular, and the position of the other leg is marked. The measurement is repeated with the square flipped over the intersection point and the extended leg again marked. If there is any difference between the two marks, a bisection between them would produce the correct direction of the perpendicular.

We are not sure, however, if this method is accurate enough for the determination of the right angle of larger structures, such as pyramids, temples, and towns.

Another simple method would have been constructing a perpendicular to a given base line at a given point on that line by drawing two arcs with the help of measuring cords (fig. 1.12B). But evidence for this method from ancient Egypt is also missing. Modern surveyors even doubt that measuring cords could have been used for drawing an arc because of the elasticity of the ropes.

The application of the "sacred triangle" would have been a revolutionary improvement in surveying, but it is not clear when Egyptian surveyors discovered and used the "Pythagoras." No written sources exist on that subject, so we can only infer its application from buildings that show the typical proportion (3 : 4 : 5). Jean-Philippe Lauer is convinced that this proportion can be found in the pyramid temples of the Old Kingdom.[46] W. Meyer-Christian claims to have measured it in the Djoser complex.[47] One must suspect, however, that such proportions were not always intended but were the coincidental result of building on rectangular plans. Dorner even doubts that methods based on creating such triangles would have been precise enough, for example, for laying out the quadrangle of the Cheops Pyramid.[48]

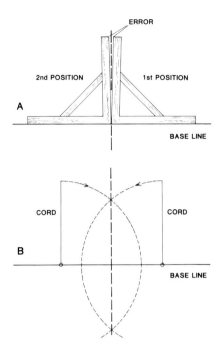

Fig. 1.12 Constructing a right angle (A) by using the set square and (B) by drawing arcs with cords.

Orientation · Frequently the ancient Egyptian architects had to achieve an exact orientation of a building on the four cardinal points. Although in general Egyptian temples were not oriented with great accuracy, no efforts were spared to orient the pyramids as closely as possible. The mean errors of the east and west sides of the casing could generally be reduced to less than 1 degree:

Djoser	3°	east of north
Meidum	0°24′25″	west of north
Bent Pyramid	0° 9′12″	west of north
Cheops	0° 5′30″	west of north
Chefren	0° 5′26″	west of north
Mycerinus	0°14′ 3″	east of north
Sahura	1°45′	west of north (surveyors' error, see p. 237)
Neferirkara	0°30′	east of north[49]

If Petrie's measurements are correct, the passages of the pyramids of Cheops and Chefren are far closer to the north–south direction than is the casing. From that he concludes that a redetermination of the north was made before the finishing of the casing.[50] The north–south orientation of burial chambers and coffins was equally essential and was frequently achieved to a high degree, in spite of the problems of working underground and without a magnetic compass.

The questions of how this accuracy was achieved and what methods and instruments were involved have often been studied but remain unanswered because, to quote I. E. S. Edwards, "Egyptian texts giving information on the method of orienting buildings are few in number, late in date and formal in character. They refer invariably to the foundation ceremonies of temples performed by the king."[51] These ceremonies were carried out by the king, (a priestess impersonating?) the goddess Seshat, and a priest impersonating the god Thoth. The king and the goddess are depicted wielding wooden mallets over stakes that are connected to one another by an endless cord, the king "looking at the sky, observing the stars and turning his gaze towards the Great Bear."[52] Because this action could only have been a symbolic one, the actual and more accurate orientation would have either preceded or followed the ritual. From this evidence, it seems likely that astral observations were made, most probably of the stars in the Great Bear, and some authors have shown that such a determination was within reach of Pharaonic surveyors.[53] Since the "stride of Ra" and the "shadow" are also mentioned in connection with the "stretching of the cord" ceremonies,[54] one might assume that solar observations were made as well, especially in orienting a temple whose axis was not arranged north–south but east–west. An example is the temple of Ramesses II of Abu Simbel, which is oriented in a way that the rays of the sun reached the four statues of the sanctuary at the solstices.

Again, authors have demonstrated that the measuring of the shadow—cast by a kind of gnomon and perhaps even clarified by a shadow definer—was within the technical reach of the ancient Egyptians. M. Isler recently proposed such a method and substantiates his theory by practical experiments and the reference to similar methods used in ancient India and China.[55] He suggests the Indian method of marking the crossing points of the shadow on a circle run around a gnomon. The marking would have been done in the forenoon and the afternoon of the same day. The two crossing marks indicate the east–west direction. Borchardt has shown that for these observations, the *mrḫt* bar and the *b*ʿy palm-rib with a V-shaped slot were used.[56]

Isler also showed how the relatively short line achieved by this method could have been extended without a greater loss in accuracy with the help of an endless cord around two poles, suggesting that this operation is actually depicted in representations of the "stretching of the cord" ceremony.

CONSTRUCTION LINES AND SETTING MARKS

The most obvious and common construction line marked on the top surface of the foundations or on pavement slabs is the middle axis of a building, indicated either by a red brush line or by a more accurate and durable incision in the stone.[57] In addition to that and in order to achieve accurate alignments of blocks and walls, the Egyptian builders used an elaborate system of other construction lines.

Setting Lines · To mark the exact position of the foot of a wall,[58] setting lines were normally scratched into the leveled surface of the pavement slabs or foundation blocks.[59] Often, they are repeated on the top surface of wall blocks. These lines together with others marking the axis of rooms and corridors,[60] practically repeat the floor plan of a building in full scale on the foundation platform.

Leveling Lines · These horizontal lines are drawn in red color (ocher) on the front face of core masonry (fig. 1.13). Sometimes a single line was sufficient, but frequently more lines were needed and were drawn in equal distances of 1 cubit.[61] Small triangles were attached to the line and, with their tops, showed the direction of measuring. To avoid repeated counting and confusion, the number of cubits from the ground line was written above or below the corresponding lines, often with 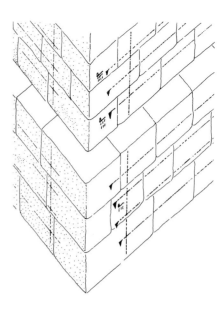 "cubit."[62] The ground or zero line, called *nfrw* (fig. 1.14), was not always the lowest line and could occasionally be the top line. Whether it made a difference to write the numbers inside the triangles or outside them is not clear.[63]

Fig. 1.13 Leveling lines at a pyramid corner, with levels every three cubits.

George A. Reisner observed at Giza that the triangles were drawn in vertical rows about 2 meters from the ends of the corner.[64] The 3-cubit mark was always filled in solid with the red paint. The vertical distance of the leveling lines was not always very consistent with irregularities up to 10 centimeters. The zero mark would have been just about level with the top of the foundation platform. Since the Mycerinus temple was unfinished, a second leveling line would have been expected at the level of the top of the pavement (placed against the granite casing), but it was never drawn. Reisner thought that the 3-cubit line was the one carried across the whole building and that it was used because of its convenient height as the actual working level, from which the other cubit marks were fixed by dead measurement up and down.

It is possible that such lines were called sm^{3c}. At the pyramid of Niuserra, a graffito marks a horizontal line as "1 cubit above the sm^{3c}."[65] In this case, the next line below is not the base line but is 1 cubit higher. Also, vertical sm^{3c} are known from the same pyramid where "46 cubits from the sm^{3c}" are mentioned with a triangle pointing sideward. Reisner collected the following Egyptian technical terms:

Zero	*nfrw*
Zero line	*m tp n nfrw*
Above zero	*ḥr nfrw*[66]
Below zero	*md ḥr n nfrw*

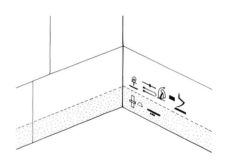

Fig. 1.14 The pavement level (*nfrw*) in the Mastabat el-Fara'un.

From the inscriptions in the antechamber and burial chamber of the Mastabat el-Fara'un,[67] one may learn additional terms:

Level of the pavement	*nfrw*
Area above the true pavement	*ḥr st³m³ᶜ*
Area below, covered by paving slabs	*ḥr st³m³ᶜ*
Area under the ground	*jmjw t³*

The observations of Jéquier, Borchardt, and Maragioglio[68] have shown that the zero line is not the dressed rock surface below but the pavement that is now missing. Borchardt also observed a system of leveling lines on the core masonry of the pyramid of Niuserra with a zero line at the same level as that of the court pavement.[69] We may assume therefore that, quite naturally, the foot of the pyramid at court level was considered zero.

Rowe noted leveling lines on the axis of the north side of the Meidum pyramid[70] with numbers counting 6 and 8 cubits above the middle of the passage opening, which seems to have functioned as another zero, being

Fig. 1.15 Whitewashed vertical band for red face line in the construction shaft of the pyramid at Zawyet el-Aryan.

itself already 36 cubits above the foot of the pyramid. Unfortunately, these few remains do not completely reveal the measuring line system of pyramids, but they seem to indicate that the vertical height was carefully measured from 1 cubit to the next and from one core step to the next, probably following vertical lines such as the axis of the pyramid.

The vertical lines mentioned were used not only for horizontal measuring, but also for marking directions. As an example we have the vertical red lines on white gypsum bands at the south and west sides of the shaft of the unfinished pyramid at Zawyet el-Aryan (figs. 1.15, 1.16).[71] Together with the now missing line down the east side of the shaft, they defined the basic measuring grid for the orientation of the shaft and its ramp.

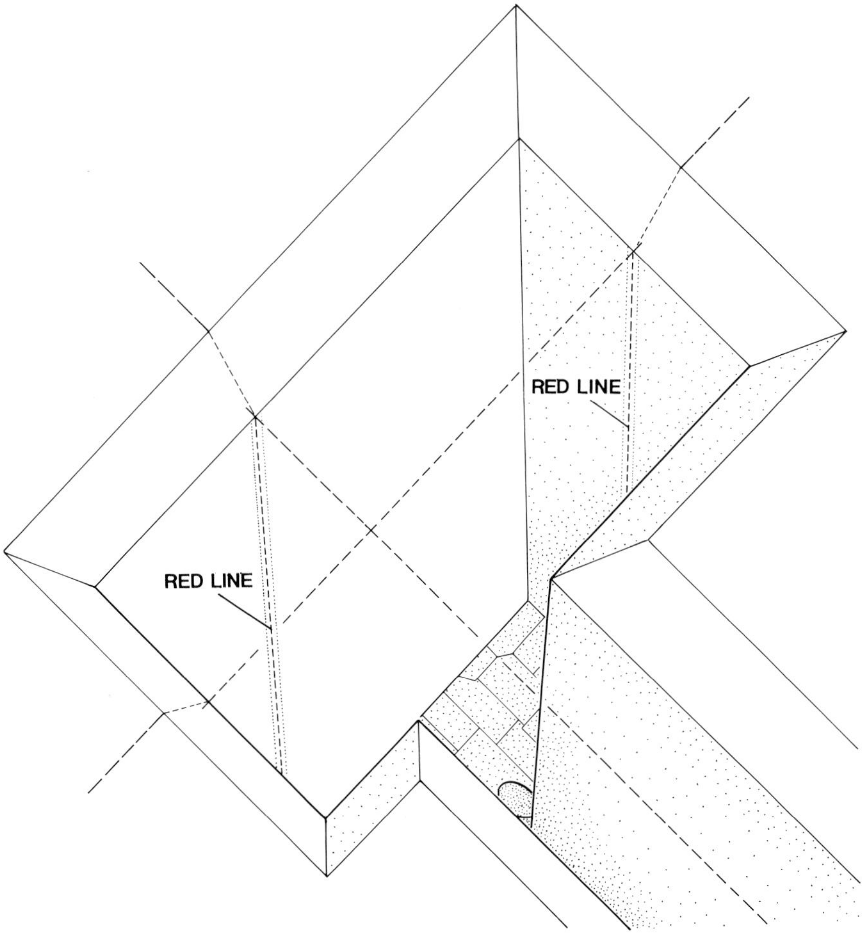

RED LINE

RED LINE

Fig. 1.16 System of vertical orientation lines in the construction shaft of the pyramid at Zawyet el-Aryan.

Inclination Lines · Inclination lines were painted in red or black on the surface of walls that had to be built in an L-shape next to the corners of a mastaba or perhaps a pyramid.[72] Hölscher mentions a case in which the line of inclination was scratched directly on the side face of a block of the masonry.[73]

Setting Marks for Columns and Pillars · When columns and pillars were not made of one block but composed of several ones, it was important to set the upper blocks exactly in plumb line with the intended center of the column or pillar. This center was generally marked with a cross scratched into the foundation or base (fig. 1.17).[74] When the column was constructed in half drums, it was relatively easy to transfer the center by a plumb line or channel up to the next course (fig. 1.18).[75] Since the drums were set with extra stock,[76] the actual outline of the column, with appropriate planning, could be carved later. As an additional precaution, a vertical groove could be applied on all four sides along which more plumb lines could be brought down to the ground. Such grooves seem to appear on the unfinished columns in the first court of the Karnak temple.[77] Such lines would also have helped when a column made of full drums had to be erected without the possibility of lowering a plumb bob in the center. On the top face of the

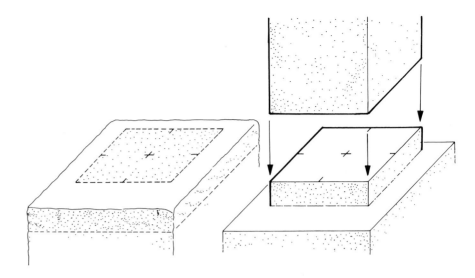

Fig. 1.17 Setting marks for pillars in the Mentuhotep Temple at Deir el-Bahari.

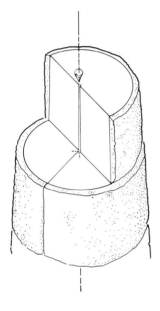

Fig. 1.18 Centering undressed half-drums of columns with the help of a plumb line.

Fig. 1.19 Setting marks on the abacus of the columns in the hypostyle hall at Karnak.

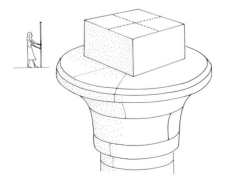

abacus, two cross lines often indicate the center of the column below as well as that of the architrave above (fig. 1.19).[78]

Distance Marks · As has been shown at the beginning of the previous section, the exact distance between two walls erected with extra stock was measured out before building ensued (at least during the Middle Kingdom) in the following way. From the center of the room, marked along the axis by a scratched line, measurements were taken sideways with measuring rods. The necessary distance was gained by cutting small sockets for setting black marks. This procedure was sometimes repeated hundreds of times all over the walls, producing a pattern consisting of short black marks arranged in long vertical files. The stonecutters could thereafter remove the extra stock between these marks.

Positioning Marks · Written instructions on blocks and walls for the builders are quite frequent, especially in cases where the correct delivery and positioning of a stone block were essential. In tomb corridors and chambers, the available room was so narrow that a misguided block could become a serious obstacle. The exact preparation of the blocks according to their size and shape, the planning of the sequence of delivery and setting, and a reliable system of numbering would help to prevent such accidents.

Numbering systems giving the cardinal points or name of the courses and the numbers of the blocks are known from the roofing blocks of the burial crypts of Djoser,[79] Cheops,[80] Mentuhotep Nebhepetra,[81] and the kings and queens of the Twelfth Dynasty at Dahshur (fig. 1.20).[82] In the pyramid of Amenemhat III at Dahshur, the burial chambers and the nearby corridors had to be filled with masonry. Since these blocks had to follow the complicated size and shape of the vaulted chambers that held the sarcophagi, they were all prefabricated and numbered aboveground before they were placed. They carry the numbers of the courses (sm^3); indications of placements, such as above, below, in front, and behind; and the number of the stone in the course. The last information was, however, frequently overlooked, either because of negligence or because the masons were clever enough to recognize which blocks could be misplaced without endangering the whole arrangement.

We also know several cases where the joints were marked by writing the same hieroglyph (such as ⸢ ⸣ ⸣ ⸣ ⸣) on the blocks at the side of the joints (fig. 1.21).[83] This system required a full-scale construction of the corresponding building aboveground and a drawing or sketch of it in the hands of the people underground as a guide line. This method could also be used for work aboveground—for example, for the construction of a roof with roofing slabs of complicated shapes, such as that of the *chapelle blanche*,[84] where each slab had its specific place, or even in pavements[85] that were assembled mosaic-like from irregularly cut basalt slabs.

Information for the delivery of a stone to the correct construction site was also indicated. It is, however, generally not very detailed but only gives indications like pyramid, pyramid temple, solar boat, mastaba.[86]

Another type of construction drawing is preserved near the entrance to

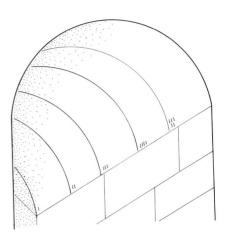

Fig. 1.20 Numbering system for roofing beams in tombs of the Twelfth Dynasty.

Fig. 1.21 Marking joints in tomb no. 5124 of the Imhotep Mastaba at Lisht.

Fig. 1.22 Construction drawing for the
vault of the crypt at the entrance to the
tomb of Ramesses VI.

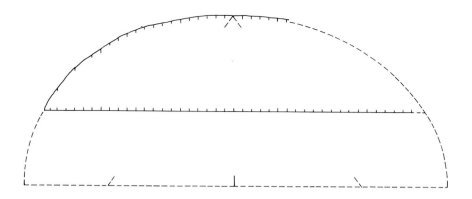

the tomb of Ramesses VI (fig. 1.22),[87] apparently made for the construction of the vault of the crypt of his tomb. It is drawn in full scale on the leveled and whitewashed rock surface. From this master drawing, prepared by a skillful architect or mathematician, the stonecutters could easily take the measurements and transfer them to their working place at the roof of the crypt. The drawing is the more remarkable, since it represents a true ellipse constructed on a triangle of the proportions 3 : 4 : 5, using distance units of 2 palms.

NOTES

1. See, in general, *CEAEM*, 47–57; L. Borchardt, *ZÄS* 34 (1896): 69–76. Much useful information on this subject is in Alexander Badawy, *Ancient Egyptian Architectural Design* (Berkeley and Los Angeles, 1965).

2. Arnold, *Qasr el-Sagha*, pl. 27; Arnold, *Amenemhet III* I, 63.

3. W. M. Flinders Petrie, *Ancient Egypt* (1926): 24–27. The use of similar grids in Minoan architecture is suggested by D. A. Preziosi, *AJA* 71 (1967): 193, and *AJA* 72 (1968): 171.

4. See p. 47.

5. Z. Wysocki, *MDAIK* 40 (1984): 339, fig. 6, 343, fig. 9; Wysocki, *MDAIK* 43 (1987): 273, fig. 8. For elevations, see Wysocki, *MDAIK* 40 (1984): 341, figs. 7, 8.

De Lubicz carried out a study of a grid for the elevation of the pylons of Luxor (*Temple* II, pl. 67; *Temple* III, 262–264). His results are confused, however, by prejudiced ideas. For the proportion system of the Roman temple of Kalabsha, see Karl Georg Siegler, *Kalabsha* (Berlin, 1970); Siegler, *MDAIK* 25 (1969): 139–153.

6. H. Ricke, *ZÄS* 71 (1935): 111–133.

7. Even from medieval building only one example of a model has survived, that of the late Gothic church of St. Maclou at Rouen (John Fitchen, *The Construction of Gothic Cathedrals: A Study of Medieval Vault Erection* [Chicago, 1961], 5).

8. Alexander Badawy, *A Monumental Gateway for a Temple of King Sety I*, Miscellanea Wilbouriana 1 (New York, 1972).

9. Arnold, *Amenemhet III* I, 86–88, pls. 66, 67; Edwards, *Pyramids*, 277, figs. 60, 61, depicts two limestone objects in the shape of a stepped and a true pyramid. Their purpose is unknown, however.

10. Petrie, *Pyramids and Temples*, 50, pl. 3; Maragioglio, *Piramidi* IV, pl. 9 [6].

11. Mark Lehner, *The Pyramid Tomb of Queen Hetep-heres I and the Satellite Pyramid of Khufu*, Sonderschrift des Deutschen Archäologischen Institutes Kairo, no. 19 (Mainz, 1985), 45–50.

12. K. H. Meyer, *SAK* 1 (1974): 247–265.

13. L. Borchardt, *ZÄS* 36 (1898): 87–105.

14. Richard Lepsius, *Die alt-aegyptische Elle* (Berlin, 1865), 13–17.

15. H. Carter, *JEA* 3 (1916): 150; Petrie, *Pyramids and Temples*, 181 (52.37 centimeters).

16. Arnold and Winlock, *Mentuhotep*, 30; Borchardt, *Neuserre*, 155–156.

17. *Ptahshepses*, 83, graffito no. 18. In the Eighteenth Dynasty, another unit, the *nbjw*, of 1¼ or 1⅓ cubits, or about 65 centimeters, appears occasionally (Alan Gardiner, *Egyptian Grammar*, 3rd ed. [London, 1973], 199). Petrie excavated two cubit rods at Kahun, which are 67.13 and 68.275 centimeters long and subdivided into seven divisions. He suggested an Asiatic origin (*Kahun*, 27; *Illahun, Kahun and Gurob 1889–90* [London, 1891], 14). See also p. 283, n. 4.

18. L. Borchardt, *ZÄS* 42 (1905): 70–72; L. Schenkel, in *LÄ* IV, 115.

19. Arnold and Winlock, *Mentuhotep*, 9, 12, fig. 4.

20. R. Engelbach, *JEA* 20 (1934): 183–184; Friedrich Wilhelm von Bissing and Hermann Kees, *Das Re-Heiligtum des Königs Ne-woser-Re II Bl.1;* more examples are in B. Letellier, in *LÄ* II, 912–914. For another explanation of the pegs, see M. Isler, *JARCE* 26 (1989): 202–206.

21. Arnold and Winlock, *Mentuhotep*, figs. 2b, 9, 22.

22. M. Lehner, *JARCE* 20 (1983): 8–9, figs. 2, 3.

23. De Lubicz, *Temple* II, pls. 83–85; Siegler, *Kalabsha*, 19, 45; Arnold, *Amenemhet III* I, 27, 58, 76, pl. 58, foldout 1.

24. See, in general, L. Borchardt, *ZÄS* 31 (1893): 9–17; Lauer, *Observations*, 85–97; Lauer, *Mystère*, 342.

25. *WB* IV, 309, 20 ("die Böschung einer Pyramide"); B. Gunn, *JEA* 15 (1929): 176, n. 1.

26. W. M. Flinders Petrie, *Medum* (London, 1892), 12, pl. 8.

27. Lauer, *Hist. Mon.* I, 262–264; Lauer, *Observations*, 93–97; Lauer, *Mystère*, 342–343; Arnold, *Amenemhet III* I, 13.

28. The consequences of this for the Cheops Pyramid are studied by M. Isler, *JARCE* 20 (1983): 27–32. One would not expect, however, that the builders of the pyramid would have tried to stretch a cord over a distance of 230 meters, the base length of the pyramid.

29. A. Badawy, *JEA* 63 (1977): 52–58.

30. F. Hinkel, *ZÄS* 108 (1981): 105–124.

31. Maragiglio, *Piramidi* IV, 78, pl. 12 [10].

32. D. Hansen, *JARCE* 6 (1967): 7, pl. 9, fig. 7.

33. De Morgan, *Dahchour* I, 88, fig. 205. No construction lines were recorded.

34. The Greek builders still used the square level (see Coulton, *Greek Architects*, 46, nn. 70–71). For Roman instruments, see Vitruvius, *The Ten Books on Architecture* VIII.5.1–13. The inventor of the real bubble is considered to be Robert Hooke (1635–1703).

35. R. Engelbach, *ASAE* 25 (1925): 169–170; Borchardt, *Grundkanten;* J. H. Cole, *Determination of the Exact Size and Orientation of the Great Pyramid of Giza* (Cairo, 1925); Dorner, "Absteckung," 74–77. The error in level of the four corners of the Meidum pyramid is 12 centimeters and that of the Bent Pyramid, 4.6 centimeters, possibly indicating a gradual improvement of leveling methods.

36. Together with Martin Isler. We fixed a 2-meter horizontal rod on two poles and leveled it with the help of the square level.

37. The Romans improved human vision by use of a tube, a "telescope" without lenses (*Paulys Real-Encyclopädie der classischen Altertumswissenschaft* V, 1073–1079 [s.v. "Dioptra"]; suppl. VI [Stuttgart, 1935], 1287–1289).

38. Dorner mentioned to me that a greater number of shorter sightings would not add one error to the other but equalize them.

39. Arnold and Winlock, *Mentuhotep*, 27, fig. 10, pl. 21a.

40. Arnold, *Jnj-jtj.f*, 34.

41. Arnold, *Senwosret I* I, 68, pls. 44d, 89.

42. Arnold, *Senwosret I* II (forthcoming).

43. The idea is old (*CEAEM*, 62; Edwards, *Pyramids*, 267; M. Lehner, *JARCE* 20 (1983): 7–25). Lehner, too, seems to have abandoned the idea.

44. Petrie, *Lahun II*, pls. 4 (top), 5.

45. *CEAEM*, 67–68; M. Isler, *JARCE* 26 (1989): 191–206.

46. J.-P. Lauer, *BIFAO* 77 (1977): 55–78; Lauer, in *Acts of the First International Congress of Egyptology* (Berlin, 1979), 423–424; Lauer, *Téti*, 51–55; Lauer, *Ounas*, 66–71.

47. W. Meyer-Christian, *MDAIK* 43 (1986): 195–203.

48. Dorner, "Absteckung," 111–114.

49. Zbynek Žába, *L'Orientation astronomique dans l'ancienne Égypte, et la précession de l'axe du monde* (Prague, 1953), 11–12.

50. Petrie, *Pyramids and Temples*, 126.

51. Edwards, *Pyramids*, 265.

52. Ibid., 266.

53. Borchardt, *Grundkanten*, 9–14; *CEAEM*, 68; Žába, *L'Orientation astronomique dans l'ancienne Égypte*; J.-P. Lauer, *Observations*, 99–124; Lauer, *BIFAO* 60 (1960): 171–183; Edwards, *Pyramids*, 263–268; G. Goyon, *RdÉ* 22 (1970): 85–98; Dorner, "Absteckung."

54. Borchardt, *Grundkanten*, 13, n. 2; Siegler, *Kalabsha*, 45; Maragioglio, *Piramidi* IV, 100–102.

55. M. Isler, *MDAIK* 48 (1992) 45–55.

56. L. Borchardt, *ZÄS* 37 (1899): 10–17, and *ZÄS* 48 (1910): 9–17.

57. Borchardt, *Neuserre*, 99; De Lubicz, *Temple* II, pls. 83–85; M. Verner, *ZÄS* 115 (1988): 79.

58. Arnold, *Mentuhotep*, pls. 17a–c; *Karnak-Nord* IV, fig. 7.

59. W. Kaiser, *MDAIK* 40 (1984): pl. 58c.

60. Arnold, *Amenemhet III* I, foldout 1.

61. For examples, see *LD* Text I, 119, 132, 133, 176; Junker, *Giza* I, 96–99; *Ptahshepses*, 82–84.

62. Borchardt, *Sahure*, 86–92; Borchardt, *Re-Heiligtum*, 63; *Ptahshepses*, no. 15.

63. *Festschrift Ricke*, 7, fig. 3; A. Barsanti, *ASAE* 7 (1906): 275, mark no. 36.

64. Reisner, *Mycerinus*, 76–77.

65. Borchardt, *Niuserre*, 154.

66. *Ptahshepses*, 81.

67. Jéquier, *Le Mastabat Faraoun*, 5; L. Borchardt, *OLZ* 34 (1931): 402; Maragioglio, *Piramidi* VI, 156, pl. 17.

68. Ibid.

69. Borchardt, *Neuserre*, 154, fig. 129.

70. Rowe, "Meydum," pl. 10.

71. A. Barsanti, *ASAE* 7 (1906): 262–265, figs. 2, 4.

72. For the methods used, see pp. 12–13.

73. U. Hölscher, *MDAIK* 12 (1943): 146, fig. 5.

74. Arnold, *Mentuhotep*, 18, fig. 9; Arnold, *Senwosret I* I, pl. 84.

75. U. Hölscher, *MDAIK* 12 (1943): 149, fig. 8.

76. *CEAEM*, fig. 162.

77. Ibid., fig. 162.

78. Ibid., figs. 155, 161.

79. B. Gunn, *ASAE* 35 (1935): 62–65, pls. 1–3.

80. Vyse, *Pyramids* I, pls. between 278 and 279, 284 and 285; Petrie, *Pyramids and Temples*, 212.

81. Unpublished data.

82. De Morgan, *Dahchour* II, 44, figs. 99, 100, 103; 72, figs. 120, 121.

83. Borchardt, *Sahure*, 94–95; Felix Arnold, *Control Notes and Team Marks: The South Cemeteries of Lisht* II (New York, 1990), 35–38. An example from Meroitic building: F. Hintze, *Wissenschaftliche Zeitschrift der Humboldt-Universität zu Berlin, Gesellschafts- und Sprachwissenschaftliche Reihe* 17 (1968): 676, fig. 17.

84. Lacau and Chevrier, *Sésostris Ier*, pl. 4.

85. Borchardt, *Sahure*, 93–96, pl. 13.

86. Several types of pyramids (Petrie, *Meydum and Memphis*, pl. 6 [15–18, 20–24]; Rowe, "Meydum," pl. 6; De Morgan, *Dahchour* II, figs. 64, 65); mortuary temples (Arnold, *Control Notes*); sun temple (Ricke, *Sonnenheiligtum* II, figs. 4 [15], 5 [22–26], 6 [19–21]); solar boat (*Festschrift Ricke*, figs. 6.a, b, e); mastaba (Junker, *Giza* X, 77, fig. 35 [10]).

87. G. Daressy, *ASAE* 8 (1907): 237–241.

CHAPTER II

Production of Stone

QUARRYING

Soft Stone[1] · In dressing stone, the different methods and types of tools used divide the softer sandstones and limestones from the harder ones, which have to be treated with the true "hard" stones, such as granite, quartzite, and diorite. In quarrying, however, the traditional division between the "soft" sandstone and limestone and the "hard" granite, quartzite, and diorite seems to be more appropriate (Table 2.1).

Limestone and sandstone were the great building stones of ancient Egypt. Limestone was typically used for constructions dating from the Third Dynasty to the Middle Kingdom and the early New Kingdom. Sandstone began to be used in the Eleventh Dynasty but became a common building stone from the Eighteenth Dynasty on.

Ancient limestone quarries can be found in numerous places between Cairo and Esna, the more important ones on the east bank of the Nile (fig. 2.1). Since a complete survey on this material will be published by Rosemarie Klemm and Dietrich Klemm, here only the provisional listing by James A. Harrel will be presented (following his terminology and numbering system) (Table 2.2).[2] This wide distribution of limestone sources normally shortened the transport distances to 60 kilometers or less.

Sandstone, originally the building material of Upper Egypt,[3] appears everywhere between Esna and the Gebel Barkal. The most famous quarries are on both sides of the Nile at Gebel Silsila, with many smaller quarries up to Aswan and farther to Qertassi, where the stone for several Nubian temples was extracted. Since the Eighteenth Dynasty, sandstone was also used for buildings in Memphis and other Lower Egyptian towns. The problems of transportation were not so serious, however, in spite of the long distances, because the quarries of Gebel Silsila (fig. 2.2) were so close to the river that the transport ships could practically sail into the harborlike quarry bays. The sandstone here is less dense and more porous and whitish gray to brown, whereas sandstone from Shatt er-Rigala and Aswan-West

Fig. 2.1 Exhausted limestone quarries of the New Kingdom El-Babein near Minya, with traces of the stepwise removed blocks.

TABLE 2.1. EGYPTIAN BUILDING STONES AND THEIR PROPERTIES

	Hardness (MOH)	Weight* (kg/l)	Compressive strength (kg/qcm)	Strokes until destruction (DIN 52107)
Dense limestone	4?	2.65–2.85	800–1800	8–10
Porous limestone		1.7–2.6	200–900	—
Calcareous sandstone				
Nubian sandstone	–8	2.0–2.65	300–1800	5–10
Quartzite	6–8	2.6–2.8	1200–2000	8–10
Alabaster (calcite)	2–3	2.7		
Granite	6–8	2.6–3.2	1600–2400	10–12
Aswan granite		2.679		
Syenite		2.6–2.8		
Diorite	5–6	2.75–2.87	1700–3000	10–15
Basalt	6–8	2.8–3.3	2500–4000	12–17
Dolerite		2.93–3.05		

*Specific gravity.

Fig. 2.2 Sandstone quarry of the Gebel Silsila (east bank).

TABLE 2.2.   ANCIENT LIMESTONE QUARRIES, BY GEOLOGIC FORMATION

Various formations of the Mokattam Group of Late Middle Eocene age [except where otherwise indicated by brackets]

15 Abu Rowash [Upper Cretaceous Matulla or Wata Fm.]
16 Giza Gizehensis Member of Mokattam Fm.
17 Tura Gebel Hof Fm.
18 Ma'sara Observatory Fm.
20 Saqqara [Middle Eocene "Ravine Beds"]
21 Helwan Observatory Fm.
23 Medinet Madi (Faiyum) Observatory Fm.
25 El-Hiba (southeast of El-Fashn) Observatory Fm.

Samalut Formation of the Mokattam Group of Middle Eocene age

26 El-Bahnasa (Oxyrhynchos)
27 El-Sawayta (northeast of Samalut)
28 El-Siririya (opposite Samalut)
29 El-Babein (near Beni Khalid)
30 Gebel El-Teir (southeast of Samalut)
31 Tihna el-Gebel (northeast of Minia)
33 Zawyet el-Amwat (Zawyet el-Sultan)
34 Beni Hasan
35 El-Sheikh Timay (south of Beni Hasan)

Minia Formation of Early Middle Eocene age [except where otherwise indicated by brackets]

36 El-Sheikh Abada (Antinoupolis)
37 Deir Abu Hennis (northeast of Mallawi)

38 Tuna el-Gebel [Samalut Fm.]
39 Deir Bersha (Wadi el-Nakhla)
41 El-Sheikh Said
42 El-Amarna
44 Meir
45 Deir el-Amir Tadros (Gebel Abu Foda)
46 El-Maabda (opposite Manfalut)
47 Deir el-Gabrawi (near El-Maabda)
48 Arab el-Atiat (near El-Maabda)

Durunka Formation of the Thebes Group of Lower Eocene age

51 Asyut (Stabl Antar)
52 Deir Durunka (south of Asyut)
54 Deir Rifa (south of Asyut)
55 El-Hammamiya (north of Qaw el-Kebir)
56 Qaw el-Kebir (Antaeopolis)
57 Deir el-Ganadla (opposite El-Badari)
58 Wadi Sarga (opposite El-Badari)
59 Gebel el-Haridi (north of Akhmim)
60 El-Salamuni
61 El-Manshah (Ptolemais Hermiou)
62 El-Madfuna (Abydos)

Serai Formation of the Thebes Group of Lower Eocene age

63 Qurna (near Wadi Biban el-Muluk)
64 El-Gebelein

Tarawan Formation of Paleocene age

65 El-Dibabiya (opposite El-Gebelein)
66 Zarnikh (opposite Esna)

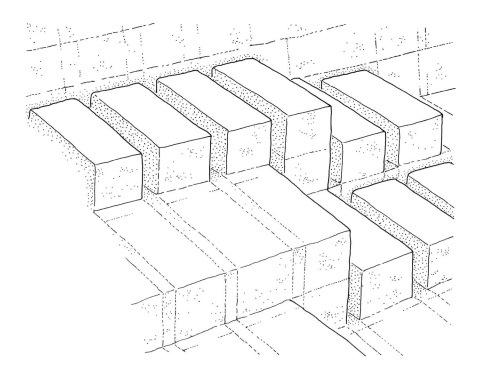

Fig. 2.3 System of separating blocks by trenches in limestone quarries.

tends to be denser, and thus harder to dress, and darker in color.[4] James Harrel's list of sandstone quarry sites is presented in Table 2.3.

Limestone and sandstone could normally be quarried in open quarries from the top or front of the cliffs. But very often, stone of good quality had to be followed into the mountain and cut out from deep, covered galleries. Frequently, both methods had to be combined, and open and covered quarry sites occur together.[5] R. Klemm assumes that working in underground galleries or open quarries was a matter of chronological develop-

TABLE 2.3. ANCIENT SANDSTONE QUARRIES, BY GEOLOGIC FORMATION

Various formations of the Nubia Group of Upper Cretaceous age

North of Aswan	*South of Aswan*
Quseir Formation	*Abu Aggag Formation*
67 El-Mahamid (north of El-Kab)	79 Debod (10.5 km south of Aswan)
68 El-Kab	80 Qertassi (40 km south of Aswan)
69 El-Keijal (southeast of El-Kab)	81 Tafa (Taifa) (46 km south of Aswan)
70 El-Kilh (northeast of Edfu)	82 Beit el-Wali (50 km south of Aswan)
71 Hieraconpolis	*Sabaya Formation*
72 Gebel Serag (southeast of Edfu)	83 Qurta (114 km south of Aswan)
73 El-Hosh (north of Shatt er-Rigala)	84 Tumas (209 km south of Aswan)
74 Wadi Shatt er-Rigala (opposite Silwa Bahari)	85 Abu Simbel (280 km south of Aswan)
75 Nag el-Hammam (south of Shatt er-Rigala)	
76 Gebel el-Silsila	
Umm Barmil Formation	
77 Gebel El-Hammam (northeast of Aswan)	
Abu Aggag Formation	
78 El-Waresab (El-Kubaniya)	
2 Aswan	

ment, the underground galleries being the older ones used in the Old and Middle Kingdoms and the open quarries the later ones of the New Kingdom.[6] Working in open quarries was easier because there were fewer problems with lighting or dust, and many more stones could be worked on at the same time. The front of the quarries of Beni Hasan is said to be wider than 5 kilometers.

The opening of a new quarry site was an official event, frequently commemorated by rock stelae of the king or the responsible officials; the stelae were sometimes dated and might include an inscription noting the purpose of the work.[7] The first step of work was the removal of the covering of bad rock, rubble, and sand. Then the tops of the stones to be removed were marked by a succession of indentations with a chisel or with red ocher in a double line that indicated the separation trench between the blocks (fig. 2.3). These trenches were about 3 palms wide for ordinary blocks, but had to be wider when larger blocks were extracted; separation trenches would likewise be proportionally deeper.[8] By the large (3 × 3 meters wide) blocks in the famous quarry close to the Chephren pyramid, the trenches are 60 centimeters wide, enough for a stonecutter to stand or kneel in the trench (fig. 2.4). They descend 30 to 40 centimeters below the cleavage surface along which the blocks had to be split off. Before the removal of the blocks, the trenches must have exceeded 1 meter in depth. Since the blocks had to

Fig. 2.4 Bottom of a large-scale open limestone quarry north of the Chephren Pyramid, with stumps of removed blocks.

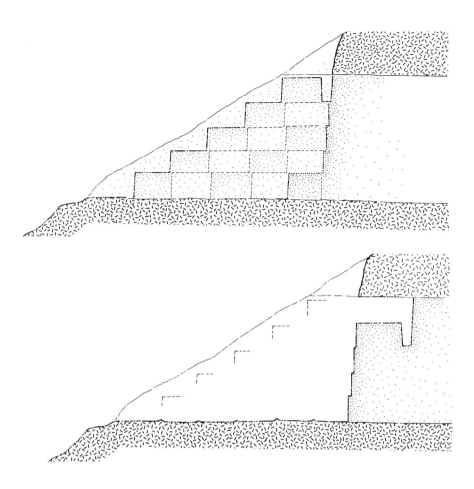

Fig. 2.5 System of changing from an open to a covered quarry.

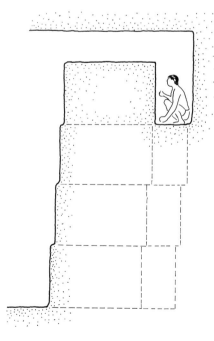

Fig. 2.6 Starting work in a covered quarry directly under the ceiling.

be dragged out from the front, cutting straight front lines in vertical steps was the project's aim.

Covered quarries developed when good stone disappeared under heavy layers of unusable material, too thick to be removed from the top (fig. 2.5). The front of such quarries appears huge, with gates many meters high giving access to underground halls and galleries, some of which were several hundred meters long, with their ceilings carried by square pillars.[9] The blocks cut in covered quarries had to be detached first from the top. A flat corridor was therefore cut first; it ran directly below the ceiling along the line of blocks to be exploited (fig. 2.6).[10] This tunnel is just high enough for a stonecutter to squat or kneel there and not much deeper than the depth of the block to be separated. It could be reached by a ladder in the shape of slots cut into the vertical rock face, similar to the steps cut by mountaineers of the older generation into a wall of ice. From the floor of the tunnel, a vertical trench was cut that separated the block from the rear and then the trenches between the single blocks. Finally, the block had to be lifted from its base from the front. After that, the stone could be thrown down on the floor of the quarry, by now covered by stone chips, which softened its fall. After the top line of blocks had been detached in this way, the second course from the top could be attacked. The stonecutter had more standing room now. But when cutting the rear trench, he automatically worked slightly in front of the rear face, thus reducing the depth of his block because he had to keep clear of the back wall with his hands and tools. This explains the slightly stepped front face of all exploited quarry walls.[11] Such end walls naturally do not preserve the ladder slots because the original front has been removed. At freestanding (outside) corners, holes are sometimes preserved, cutting through the edge, which were probably used for fixing ropes.[12] They correspond to similar holes in the quarries of Carrara.[13] The detachment of blocks was not always carried out in a straight line, but the layout of a quarry often afforded corners and steps, producing rather irregularly shaped ground plans.

The question as to what kind of tools were used to cut the separation trenches and to lift the blocks from their beds has not been answered satisfactorily because of the contradiction between the tool marks left on the quarry walls and the tools actually found in ancient Egypt. According to R. Klemm, who has visited and studied most of the "soft" stone quarry sites in Egypt,[14] a chronological development of tool marks can be observed. Curved but somewhat irregular lines in one direction appear in Old and Middle Kingdom sites (fig. 2.7); longer lines that alternate in the direction of work after each layer of blows (herringbone pattern) characterize the early New Kingdom (fig. 2.8); and very regular, closely set longish lines, all hewn from the same direction, are known from Ramesside to the end of Pharaonic times (fig. 2.9).[15]

R. Klemm concludes from these marks that "softer copper chisels" were used during the Old and Middle Kingdoms and "harder bronze chisels" came into use in the New Kingdom, suggesting an improvement in the hardness of tools after the Middle Kingdom. The tool marks indicate, however, the introduction of differently shaped tools, pointed chisels driven by mallets, from the New Kingdom on. The situation is further confused by the fact that "harder bronze tools" were not an invention of the New Kingdom, but were already in use during the Middle Kingdom. Furthermore, the only known metal chisels suitable for working in stone (the round bar chisels; fig. 6.10 and Table 6.1) are not pointed, however, but show a flat, wide cutting edge. They were used for cutting the walls of rock tombs (fig. 2.10), for example, and have left those typical wide, bandlike marks. In consequence, one would have to assume that pointed stone picks or axes were used during the Old and Middle Kingdoms. The type of tool used from the New Kingdom on, however, has still to be found.

Since Joseph Röder has shown that wedges and fins were not used before Ptolemaic quarrying,[16] one has to assume that the blocks were pried out of their bed with the help of wooden levers. Reisner assumed that wooden beams, 16 × 16 centimeters in section, were put into long rectangular excisions near the bottom of the trench and the trench was watered so that the swollen wood could have done the lifting (figs. 2.10, 2.11).[17] These excisions actually exist and can be seen in the quarry of Qaw el-Kebir (fig. 2.12). In the same way, no vertical wedges could have been used to separate the blocks from their neighbors. This separation could have been achieved only by cutting vertical trenches.

These observations would again be in accord with the assumption that even "soft" stones were not only dressed but also quarried mainly with

Fig. 2.7 Marks of stone picks in quarries of the Old and Middle Kigdoms.

Fig. 2.8 Marks of stone picks in quarries of the early New Kingdom.

Fig. 2.9 Marks of stone picks in quarries from Ramesside times to the Thirtieth Dynasty.

Fig. 2.10 Marks of huge, flat chisels in the soft limestone walls of the tomb of Mentuhotep at Lisht, early Twelfth Dynasty.

Fig. 2.11 Excisions for detaching a block with the help of beams at the pyramid temple of Mycerinus.

Fig. 2.12 Excisions for detaching a block with the help of beams in the quarry of Qaw el-Kebir.

stone tools, an assumption that would not deny, of course, that metal chisels existed and were occasionally used for special purposes.

Hard Stone · As we have seen, quarrying even the softer stones was carried out with stone tools. Quarrying true "hard" stones would naturally have required stone tools; the methods used, however, were completely different. In spite of the existence of several quarries of granite, quartzite, basalt, and diorite, only those of granite have been sufficiently studied,[18] and some observations on quartzite quarries have been published.[19]

After limestone and sandstone, granite was the most common stone used in Egyptian architecture, starting with the First Dynasty.[20] An early peak of granite quarrying was reached during the Old Kingdom, when—according to Röder—45,000 cubic meters of stone must have been removed from the quarries of Aswan. Also in the Middle Kingdom, granite was much used for sarcophagi, casing, and blocking tomb corridors and burial chambers. The most voluminous quarrying took place, however, during the Eighteenth and Nineteenth Dynasties, when dozens of huge obelisks, some of them over 30 meters high, and numerous colossal statues were produced.

During the earlier periods, huge boulders of granite, scattered on the

Fig. 2.13 Method of separating a granite block by pounding out trenches.

ground, were a ready source of the stone.[21] Soon actual quarrying was necessary, but it was always performed in open quarries, never in covered galleries. From unfinished monuments and the quarry surface at Aswan, Reginald Engelbach recognized the method used, so-called pounding (fig. 2.13). It consisted of bruising off small flakes of granite by bringing down rhythmic and regular bounces of roundish dolerite balls, weighing up to 5 kilograms (fig. 6.16). Not only were the dolerite balls still found at the site, but they have left clear marks on the stone itself, completely different from those of stone picks.

The famous unfinished obelisk in the quarries southeast of Aswan is a unique source of information on the methods used for the extraction of large granite monuments and the problems with which the ancient engineers were confronted. The date of the obelisk is not known, but it is assumed to be the Thutmoside period. The obelisk is 41.75 meters long and if completed would have weighed 1168 tons. The work was discontinued when cracks in the rock convinced the engineers that the obelisk could not be extracted unbroken (fig. 2.14).[22]

To separate such a block from the bedrock, its surface first had to be cleaned of rotten material, perhaps sometimes by heating it with fire and cooling it suddenly with water until a spotless piece of granite was exposed. Now from the top surface on all four (or at least three) sides, a separating trench had to be dug. This trench was about 75 centimeters (10 palms) wide and divided into working sections 60 centimeters long, the minimum space for a squatting or kneeling worker. These working sections were marked by vertical red lines on the walls of the trenches. One working section was again subdivided into four quadrants, which indicate that the worker assumed four positions, kneeling in one quadrant and working in the opposite one while his basket and reserve tools were stored in the free squares. From time to time, he changed position in order to relax his knees and to produce level surfaces. Nevertheless, those slightly sunken quadrants, 30 × 30 centimeters wide, can still be discovered on unfinished hardstone surfaces.

Fig. 2.14 The unfinished obelisk in the granite quarries of Aswan.

As Engelbach has shown, a foreman measured the progress of work by lowering cubit rods into the working holes and marking the wall with red paint at the upper end of the rod (fig. 2.15).[23] Thus a vertical chain of triangles that pointed upward was marked on the face of each working area. This system worked only with a wall high enough for these marks. Otherwise, one would have to measure in the opposite direction—that is, downward from the surface level, the *nfr*. As in soft-stone working, the separation trenches had to be carried deeper than the intended cleavage level. From the bottom of these trenches, the awkward work of undercutting the block or obelisk had to be carried out.

Larger monuments such as obelisks had to be completely undertunneled (fig. 2.16) so that the block was resting on only a few ledges or on artificially added masonry. Then the block could be broken from its bed with the help of a series of huge levers set into the trench behind the stone. Since it would have been too difficult to lift an obelisk out of its quarry hole,[24] the front of the hole had to be opened as well so that the block could be levered or pushed out more easily and rolled down over its long sides to the transport ramp.

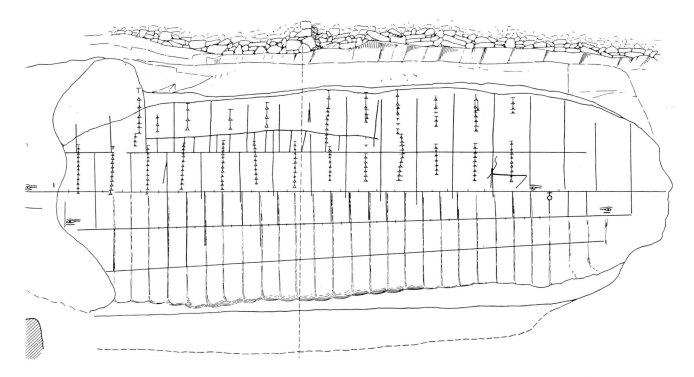

Fig. 2.15 Rear face of a granite quarry at Aswan, with traces of the working sections covered with the control marks of the supervisors.

In the trenches of the unfinished obelisk on each of the long sides, about fifty workers could be placed at the same time. These men did not need special training and were certainly prisoners of war or people condemned to "be sent to the granite," apparently thought as a severe punishment (see n. 62, p. 55).

Since the specialists for granite treatment were more available in the quarries, the blocks were roughly dressed there. The transport scenes from the causeway of Unas and the temple of Hatshepsut indicate that columns, architraves, and obelisks were dressed to their final shape in the quarry, excluding, of course, polishing and inscribing the surface. But there are a few examples of monuments, left in quarries, that had already been inscribed there.[25]

For a long time, Egyptologists believed that granite was quarried with the help of wooden wedges inserted into wedge holes (made with copper chisels), since long chains of wedge holes could still be seen in the quarries of Aswan. This theory was abandoned for two reasons. First, Röder showed that no such wedge holes could be dated before 500 B.C. Second, most specialists seem to agree that wooden wedges, after being watered, would not be able to break granite.[26] This new finding contradicts the remarks of Petrie,[27] who described what he thought to be wedge marks on the floor of the fourth construction chamber of the Cheops Pyramid. But it clearly fits into our new picture of stoneworking in ancient cultures, such as stone production in ancient Peru.[28] And it accords with the results of experiments carried out by Antoine Zuber, Jean-Pierre Protzen, and Denis Stocks,[29] who have demonstrated that quarrying hard stones with stone tools was a difficult and time-consuming activity, but one that apparently

Fig. 2.16 Using levers to break an undertunneled block from the ground.

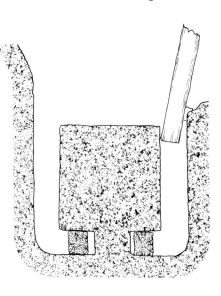

Production of Stone | 39

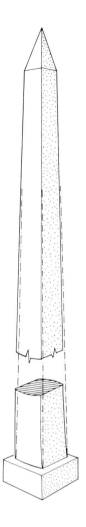

Fig. 2.17 Irregularities in the faces of the Luxor obelisks resulting from grinding methods.

did not create real problems. We are told in the inscription of the base of the obelisk of Hatshepsut[30] that quarrying and moving the pair of 30-meter-high obelisks in front of Pylon V of Karnak took only seven months.

In quarrying obelisks, occasionally a slight carelessness resulted in irregularities of the monument (fig. 2.17). For example, the two obelisks of the Luxor temple (one of them now in Paris) do not have regular planes but are slightly bowed, such that the opposite sides are convex and concave when seen in an elevation, and are convex when seen in section. Martin Isler explained these irregularities by the measuring and polishing system used.[31] The longitudinal curves seem to be the result of the sagging of the measuring cord that was stretched over the stone when it was still lying in the quarry. The swelling of the surface (seen in section) might result from the motion of the polishing stones, which tend to take slightly more stone off along the edges than from the center. One cannot help but wonder that the creators of the older obelisks of the Twelfth and Eighteenth Dynasties apparently knew and avoided that danger.

Cutting quartzite in the quarries of Gebel el-Ahmar (fig. 2.18) and Aswan (the two major sources of this stone) must have been a more serious task, one that seems to have necessitated different methods. Perhaps this is the reason for the relatively late employment of quarried quartzite in Egyptian architecture. Although sculpture in quartzite was created since Djedefra,[32] probably worked from stones collected on the surface, the first architectural features that probably needed quarrying are the eighteen pillars in the court of the pyramid temple of Pepy II at Saqqara.[33]

The extent to which dolerite balls were used for pounding quartzite is not clear. The traces on the surface of quarried sites at Gebel el-Ahmar that were depicted by Engelbach (fig. 2.19)[34] indicate that the methods used must have been somewhat different because the walls of the quarry are not as vertical as those of granite quarries, but show steps as deep as 1 foot. The front of these steps is banded by many horizontal grooves that consist (seen from nearby) of files of punctuated strikes, apparently produced by a pointed stone pick. Engelbach suggested that a trench was cut into the rock by hacking closely set, long files of small holes into the surface, thus producing narrow ridges in between that could be jarred off by heavy blows of a stone hammer. This would explain why the walls were not vertical but quite inclined. The heavy stone picks would not reach the innermost edge of the preceding level and would automatically move the next level to be cut farther in front. It would not explain, however, the foot-high steps.

In any case, there seem to be no clear indications for the pounding method, and we must assume that chiseling was employed. This work could have been achieved only by experienced laborers, who probably were not numerous enough to produce huge quantities of quartzite. Still, the sepulchral chamber of Amenemhat III at Hawara and the statues of Memnon were made of that stone, and their manufacture certainly required a sizable number of such people.

No observations have been made or published on the quarrying methods of basalt. Ancient basalt quarries were near Abu Rowash, at the desert road between Cairo and the Red Sea, and the Gebel Qatrani west of the Faijum.

Fig. 2.18 Separation trenches and stepped tool marks in the quartzite quarries of Gebel el-Ahmar.

Fig. 2.19 Tool marks in the quartzite quarries of Gebel el-Ahmar.

DRESSING

Soft Stone[35] · For some time, the observation of ancient tools, their traces on the stone surface of unfinished monuments, and occasional tests of the hardness of Egyptian copper or bronze tools[36] made it clear that Egyptian masons and sculptors were able to cut softer stones with copper tools but had to use stone tools for dressing hard stones. The line distinguishing the two was between limestone, sandstone, and alabaster on one side and granite, quartzite, and basalt on the other.

A series of tests carried out recently by Denys Stocks[37] seems to lower this border line drastically. He produced by ancient casting methods bronze chisels of 3 to 15 percent tin and different grades of hardness that he achieved by cold hammering in the range of VPN (Vickers Pyramid Number) 132–247. He used the chisels on nine different Egyptian stones, from soft sandstone to the hardest granodiorite. The result was that he could cut red sandstone with ease, soft limestone with infrequent sharpening of the tools, and alabaster (calcite) with frequent sharpening of the tool. The harder variations of limestone and sandstone—not to mention the still harder stones—immediately ruined the tools. Stocks concluded that these stones could be dressed only with stone tools and that the use of metal tools,

Fig. 2.20 Stone masons dressing and checking the blocks with a cord, as depicted in the tomb of Rekhmira.

at least until the introduction of iron at the very end of Pharaonic stone building, was much less frequent than had been thought.

This rather important finding is contradicted, however, by two other major sources available to us. First, the stonecutters shown in the tomb of Rekhmira obviously used copper chisels, driven with wooden mallets (fig. 2.20).[38] Second, the toolmarks left on numerous unfinished or unsmoothed limestone blocks from the Old[39] and Middle Kingdoms[40] show such a distinctive rectangular shape with very sharp inner corners that it is difficult to believe that they were produced by stone tools (fig. 2.21). Stocks assumes that it is possible to differentiate between the grooves cut by metal chisels and those cut by stone chisels.[41] Since copper would tend to be worn off at the corners, the chisel would soon develop a more rounded cutting edge, as can actually be seen in existing copper chisels. The stone chisel would tend to flake off more in the center, producing a half-moon-shape concave edge. The grooves would therefore have either a more concave center when a copper chisel was used or a more pronounced outer edge when stone was used. In both cases, a wooden mallet would have driven the chisel, producing a typical elongated groove with a series of smaller steps in it.

One problematic aspect of this theory has to be kept in mind. A large number of copper chisels are preserved, in spite of their great value, but stone chisels with a cutting edge of the expected shape are relatively rare. Furthermore, there is strong evidence that the huge roofing blocks of the boat pit of Cheops were dressed with copper chisels. The excavators report: "Very small fragments of corroded copper were found sticking to the different sides of the blocks. These fragments are apparently broken edges of the tools which were used for dressing the surfaces of these blocks. They were chemically and physically examined."[42]

One might assume that at least during the Old and Middle Kingdoms the first step of stone production—that is, the cutting of the blocks from the bedrock—was carried out with stone mauls or picks. This procedure produced only roughly squared blocks. In some rare cases, a huge chisel may have been used; 2.5-centimeter-wide grooves on some undressed blocks may be evidence of its use.[43] In this rough shape, the blocks were transported to the storage area near the construction site for further treatment.

Blocks intended to be built into foundations and core masonry, which did not need further dressing, could be left waiting, sometimes up to three years, until they were used.[44] The other blocks that needed dressing could not be left too long, for the stone would dry fast and its hardness would increase considerably. Of the six sides of a block, first the lower face and then at least one side face had to be dressed and smoothed. These were the sides that came into direct contact with the already existing masonry. The second side face could be dressed at the same time or later, when the block was set.

It was not unusual to dress these side faces in the Greek manner of anathyrosis,[45] to ensure the close fitting of one block to another. In order to achieve closer contact, a short copper saw was used, either a real tool with a wooden handle[46] or just a sheet of metal, as Lauer has suggested.[47]

Fig. 2.21 Chisel marks from the pyramid of Senwosret I at Lisht.

Since the vertical joints were frequently filled with mortar, especially in the hollowed central part, occasionally a vertical groove was provided for filling in the liquid mortar.[48]

The rear face of the stones was rarely treated, since the contact with the blocks behind was never close (figs. 2.22, 2.23, 2.28). The upper surface was frequently dressed only after the setting of the block and only when the height of the neighboring blocks was known and the cord could be stretched to produce a regular, straight line. Quite often, steps had to be cut into the upper surface for the setting of the blocks above (fig. 4.83).

The last face to be dressed was the front because it was left with extra stock in order to protect it from damage during the setting. It was also easier to produce a flat surface when a whole wall could be worked over. This was done first with chisels or pounders and then with grinding stones. Because some time might have elapsed between extracting the stone from the quarry and the final dressing of the surface, the stone would probably have dried out and become more difficult to work.

For the determination of the final surface, the Egyptians used several methods, which are described in the section on bosses in Chapter 4 (pp. 132–141). Very often, the outer surface of Egyptian walls is sprinkled with half-moon-shape incisions and scratches. These are the ends of chisel

Fig. 2.23 Rear part of the funerary chapel of the Meidum pyramid, which was left undressed because builders' debris covered the pyramid casing.

marks where the mason's chisel had cut so much behind the line of the intended surface that the marks could not be effaced.[49]

The final rubbing or grinding was carried out with sandstone grinding stones or perhaps with sand. Liquid plaster or grout was frequently filled into cracks and irregularities and was rubbed flat, producing a smooth surface of uniform color,[50] especially when the wall had to be carved by sculptors. Other walls were often left with a chiseled surface.

To test the flatness of the surface, it could be touched with a true surface (a wooden board) covered with red paint. The color would stick to the protruding areas, which then had to be treated again. This last smoothing was occasionally forgotten, so that the red paint remained.[51] Another tool, which probably was more frequently used, was the boning rod (fig. 6.8). Two equally long rods were connected at their tops by a string that could thus be stretched over the surface to be tested. A third rod of the same length could be held under the string to measure the right distance. The procedure is shown in the tomb of Rekhmira (fig. 6.7),[52] and many original boning rods are preserved. Larger surfaces, such as the face of a pylon or of a pyramid, could be measured with boning rods by following the horizontal joints, which seem to have been dressed back to the intended surface,[53] and measuring the protuberances of the stone surface in between.

Straight rods or boards of 3 to 4 meters in length could also have been used, and they would have reached over several courses and blocks. Uvo Hölscher, based on his observations of the unfinished Pylon I of Karnak,[54] shows that after the footline of the walls, the upper front edge of each following course had also been measured and marked by a bandlike anathyrosis (contact band). The lower front edge of each following block had

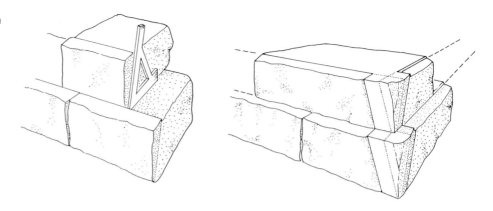

Fig. 2.24 Obtaining the inclination of an undressed wall.

to be pushed exactly against this marking. The angle of the slope could be constructed with a kind of builder's square, with one leg marking the inclination (fig. 2.24). The inclination could be determined for each stone individually or for only the corner blocks. This is the state in which the surface of the pyramid of Mycerinus is found (fig. 2.30).

The preparations for the equally inclined corner torus would have been rather laborious because its exact shape had to be constructed on the surface of the extra stock along the edge (fig. 2.25). The task would have been even more complicated when the torus was tapering. The problem of calculating the slowly diminishing size of the torus could have been solved with the help of a full-scale drawing from which the measurements could be transferred. If the builders understood the use of reduced scales, the prototype could also have been at a smaller scale.

The same method would have been used for the construction of the tapering of columns. If the column was made of drums or half-drums, the center of the column could be determined by plumbing up along a vertical line in the center of the column (fig. 1.18). From this center, the circle of the following diameter could be constructed; but it had to be taken from a full or otherwise scaled model.[55]

The dressing of a monolithic column certainly was more difficult, and we

Fig. 2.25 Preparations for the cutting of the corner torus of Pylon I at Karnak.

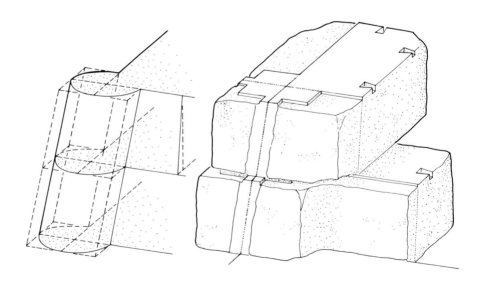

have no information about the methods used. The first step, apparently, was to draw the outlines of a column on the sides of a quadrangular block that was the size of the intended column. Such blocks, which were never shaped into columns, are known.[56] That the production was carried out in the quarries can be gathered from reliefs showing the transport of finished columns from Aswan to Saqqara (fig. 6.37). The dressing of the columns was probably done in the same manner as the sculpting of other monuments. Achieving accuracy was difficult, however, if we consider that granite columns nearly 11 meters long had to be manufactured.[57] On a portion of a 6.30-meter-long shaft of the granite columns of Sahura, the mean diameter tapers 11.4 centimeters, with an error of only 8 millimeters.[58]

Engelbach suggested that the granite columns of Sahura were dressed in a horizontal position with the help of ring-shaped facing surfaces, probably with the aid of templates. He described methods of measuring the progress of work with vertical facing surfaces, which actually could be observed on unfinished columns. It is clear, however, that the production of a true circle—even with a taper—was a question of careful and repeated measuring and checking, especially of the two end faces of the column.

One method that was certainly not used was the rotation of the column shaft suspended from axles at the two ends; this method would have required deep sockets for the rotation axles, sockets for which we have no evidence. By viewing such column shafts, one can see that their diameter is not always a true circle. This observation, the heavy weight of such column shafts, and the missing drill holes for inserting a fulcrum-shaft axle rule out the possibility that the column shafts were hung in a horizontal position and rotated. This method would not have functioned in cutting columns in rock-hewn tombs and temples. Unfinished tombs, such as those of Amarna, show that the work was carried from the ceiling down to the floor and that the capitals of the columns were already complete before the floor was reached.[59]

Decorated capitals for columns were produced in the same way as other sculpture (fig. 2.26). A block slightly larger than the intended capital was cut into a perfect rectangular shape. Then on several of its sides, the parallel projections of its top and side views were constructed and drawn, apparently with the help of a grid. The sculptor probably had models or model drawings of capitals in pocket-size from which he could work. Such models as well as drawings of intended capitals are preserved (fig. 2.27).[60] We know examples of full-size drawings as well, scratched into the flattened surfaces of standing architecture. On the pylon of the temple of Philae, a huge drawing of a column was found, and on the walls of the temple of Edfu, the full-scale drawing of the cornice—probably of the pylon of the temple—was executed.[61]

Hard Stone · The dressing of hard stones, which were used abundantly in the Egyptian building industry, was certainly a problem for the ancient masons, and the work in granite quarries was used as a punishment for criminals.[62] Because of this difficulty, Egyptian masons avoided working in hard stones as much as possible and restricted the dressing of such material

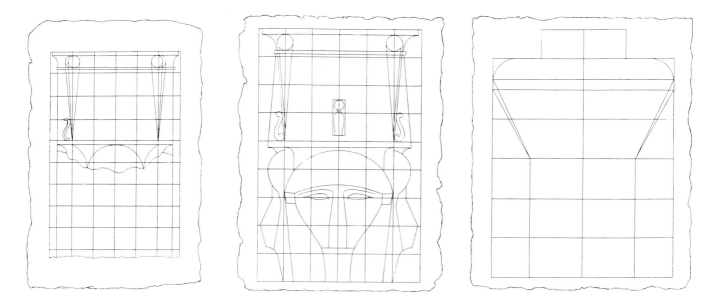

Fig. 2.26 Tracings for capitals on blocks in the quarry of Gebel Abu Fedah.

to an absolute minimum and to visible parts of the blocks only. The underside and the rear of blocks, which came into contact with bedrock, were often left rough, and the bedrock was cut accordingly to take into account the protuberances of the granite (figs. 2.22, 2.28).[63]

Although the tools used for that work are still the subject of discussion in Egyptology,[64] general agreement has now been reached. We know that hard stones such as granite, granodiorite, syenite, and basalt could not have been cut with metal tools. The tests conducted by Stocks seem to indicate that even hard limestone, sandstone, and alabaster would fall into this category. First, no marks of metal tools have been observed on these stones. Second, all known types of copper chisels do not—even after cold hammering[65]—have any effect on these stones; in fact, the tools suffer so much damage that they could not have been used for that work. In addition, near the pyramid of Senwosret I, layers of stonecutters' debris could be studied,[66] and the presence of granite dust indicated that the material was worked there. In these layers, no traces of greenish discoloration from copper could be detected; however, there was a large amount of broken or chipped dolerite, granite, and flint from tools. We have to assume that these were the instruments used for dressing hard stones.

This picture is completed by the presence of huge quantities of spherical balls of dolerite (fig. 6.16) and elongated mauls or axes (figs. 6.12–6.14) all over Pharaonic construction sites. Surface traces also offer clear proof that the rough work of dressing down a surface was carried out primarily by the pounding method. By bouncing the dolerite balls, which weighed up to 6 kilograms or more, at a certain angle and rhythm, the surface of a stone like granite was bruised and ground down to powder.[67] It is difficult to imagine, however, how this method was applied to inclined, vertical, or even overhanging planes. The method seems to be very time-consuming. But the building inscription of the obelisks of Hatshepsut[68] assures us that both obelisks were made in only seven months, a time that seems to have

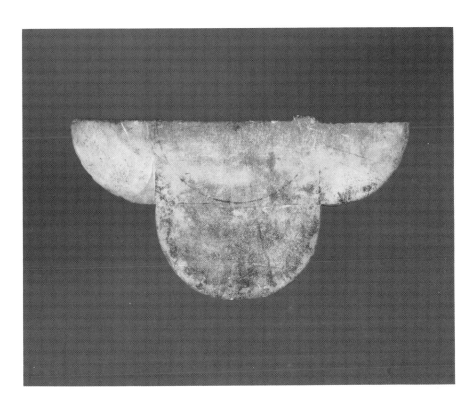

Fig. 2.27 Sculptor's model of a composite capital. (MMA acc. no. 12.182.6)

amazed even the Egyptians. It could probably have been achieved by several teams working day and night and taking over from one another without interruption. This method was certainly not restricted to ancient Egypt. The stonecutters of the Inca dressed their granite, porphyry, and andesite with practically the same tools,[69] and the methods of much older Mesoamerican cultures, such as the Olmecs, cannot have been different.

Besides pounding, the Egyptian workers in hard stone had two more available methods, which were taken over directly from the production of stone vessels. The first is drilling. In architecture, it was used mainly for producing holes for pivots, door bolts, and nails (fig. 6.20) and is attested by the discovery of drilling cones from the Third Dynasty.[70] There are also indications, that even larger projects, such as producing a granite sarcophagus, were carried out by drilling (fig. 2.29). Because the consumption of metal would have been enormous, the drilling method would have been restricted to the production of sarcophagi and architectural features that could otherwise not have been made.

The other method, again attested from the Third Dynasty on, is the sawing of hard stone, such as hard alabaster and granite (figs. 6.22–6.24). We know from some examples that the lid of a sarcophagus was occasionally sawed from the same block as the bottom part of the sarcophagus with tools up to 2.40 meters long. In architecture, strictly speaking, the use of saws can be shown for the final treatment of joint faces in casing blocks of Shepseskaf (fig. 6.23), Unas, and Senwosret I. But again for reasons of metal consumption, the sawing of stone was restricted to special and rare cases. One may also assume that the marks at the foot of vertical joints, very often visible on the surface of foundation blocks or paving slabs, were unintentionally produced by sawing down the joints. Sawing stone not only was carried on until Roman times,[71] but remains the primary method of quarrying and producing stone today.

For more accurate, fine, and detailed work, such as the production of sharp inside corners or decorative elements (decorations and inscriptions), we have again to assume that stone scrapers and chisels were used, not metal tools. Stocks also carried out some experiments with flint and chert chisels.[72]

The last step of surface treatment in hard stone was polishing. This was certainly done with grinding stones like quartzite, sandstone, or other grained materials in connection with quartzite sand. The method would have been identical to that used for softer stones; only the choice of grinding stones and the number of grinding phases with different materials would have been different.

The testing of the flatness of the surface was the same. In one example, a

sunken band had been run over the surface of a granite block in order to avoid any twisting in the dressing of the face, perhaps because the block surface was too large to be tested otherwise.[73]

Comparing soft- and hard-stone building blocks in unfinished monuments, one has the impression that a piece of hard stone was often chosen individually from the material in the quarry and dressed down to its final shape on the spot. Only the final steps, such as polishing, would have been carried out at the construction site or on the wall. Apparently, the specialists for hard stone remained in the quarries and were not among the builders and masons available at the construction site. Thus the columns and cornices for the temple of Unas were sent in their final shape, if we may trust the wall reliefs in the Unas causeway.[74] The single obelisk of Thutmosis III at Karnak (Lateran) was even inscribed before it was set up in the temple.[75] This might also be the reason why granite wall blocks, whose surface was already flattened, often still show handling bosses. This might indicate that the dressing was carried out in the quarry, and the handling bosses would have been used during transport. The casing blocks of the pyramid of Mycerinus, however, are still covered with extra stock and heavy handling bosses and would have been dressed only at the end of the work (fig. 2.30).

NOTES

1. See, in general, *CEAEM*, 12–22; D. Klemm and R. Klemm, *SAK* 7 (1979): 118–140; R. Klemm, in *LÄ* v, 1276–1279; Engelbach, *Aswan Obelisk;* Petrie, *Antaeopolis,* 15–16; *Paulys Real-Encyclopädie der classischen Altertumswissenschaft* II. series III (Stuttgart, 1929), 2241–2293 (s.v. "Steinbruch"); R. J. Forbes, *Studies in Ancient Technology* VII (Leiden, 1966), 167–177. For the ancient names of building stones, see Kurt Sethe, *Die Bau- und Denkmalsteine der alten Aegypter und ihre Namen,* Ab-

handlungen der Berliner Akademie der Wissenschaften, Phil. hist. Klasse (Berlin, 1933), 864–912; J. R. Harris, *Lexicographical Studies in Ancient Egyptian Minerals* (Berlin, 1961); *LÄ* I, 129–130 (s.v. "Alabaster"); *LÄ* III, 301–303 (s.v. "Kalkstein"), 382–383 (s.v. "Sandstein"); *LÄ* V, 1276–1283 (s.v. "Steinbruch").

2. J. A. Harrel, *Newsletter of the American Research Center in Egypt* 146 (1989): 3–5.

3. See, in general, Lucas and Harris, *AEMI*, 55–57.

4. D. Klemm and R. Klemm, *SAK* 7 (1979): 132–137, pls. 10, 11.

5. H. Sourouzian, *MDAIK* 39 (1983): 207, pl. 48. Shaw points out that in the open quarry of Zakro blocks were extracted in steps but in the quarries below ground of Knossos in vertical layers (*Minoan Architecture*, 39).

6. R. Klemm, *ZÄS* 115 (1988): 42.

7. For example, Vyse, *Pyramids* III, 93–98, on the quarries of Tura and Ma'sara.

8. Trenching was also used in Minoan Crete (Shaw, *Minoan Architecture*, 32–35, figs. 23–28 [toolmarks suggest that bronze picks were used]), in Anatolia (Naumann, *Architektur*, 38–39, figs. 18–19 [Bogazkoy]), and on the Easter Islands (Mulloy, "Easter Islands," 6, pl. 2 [with crude basalt picks]).

9. Petrie, *Antaeopolis*, pl. 19 [2–3]; R. Klemm, *ZÄS* 115 (1988): 41–51.

10. Petrie, *Antaeopolis*, pl. 20 [1–3].

11. Ibid., pl. 20 [4–5].

12. *CEAEM*, figs. 17, 18.

13. Mannoni, *Marble*, fig. 100.

14. R. Klemm, *ZÄS* 115 (1988): 42; Klemm, in *LÄ* V, 1274–1275.

15. Klemm, *Steine der Pharaonen*, fig. 32, for the chisels; figs. 38.1–38.3, for the tool traces. Also see Golvin and Goyon, *Karnak*, 96, 97 top left.

16. J. Röder, *Archäologischer Anzeiger* 3 (1965): 523.

17. Reisner, *Mycerinus*, 70.

18. See, in general, *CEAEM*, 23–33; Engelbach, *Aswan Obelisk*, 23–27; Engelbach, *Problem of the Obelisks*, 32–51; Forbes, *Studies in Ancient Technology*, 169–172. On granite, see J. Röder, *Archäologischer Anzeiger* 3 (1965): 461–551; Lucas and Harris, *AEMI*, 57–74; Klemm, *Steine der Pharaonen*, 30; M. Pillet, *BIFAO* 36 (1936): 71–84; H. Chevrier, *RdÉ* 23 (1971): 71–72; Zuber, "Travail des pierres dures," 161–180, 195–215; S. Clarke, *Ancient Egypt* (1916): 110–113. On Roman quarrying at Mons Claudianus, see J. Röder, *MDAIK* 18 (1962): 98–116, and *MDAIK* 22 (1967): 140–155, 184–190.

19. D. Klemm and R. Klemm, *SAK* 7 (1979): 120–121; Klemm and Klemm, *MDAIK* 40 (1984): 209–212, figs. 1, 2, pl. 11.

20. On the granite pavement in the tomb of King Den at Abydos, see Petrie, *Royal Tombs* II, 9.

21. See Reisner, *Mycerinus*, 71.

22. Engelbach, *Aswan Obelisk*, 7.

23. *CEAEM*, fig. 29.

24. For another detailed description of the production of an obelisk and the problems of the curvature, see M. Isler, *JEA* 73 (1987): 137–147.

25. Klemm, *Steine der Pharaonen*, figs. 39, 40.

26. Zuber succeeded in breaking a block of granite with wetted sycamore wedges of 5 centimeters depth ("Travail des pierres dures," 202). The procedure afforded constant wetting for one day and one night. For late Roman cutting of granite with wedges, see M. Azim, in *Karnak* VI, 113–114.

27. Petrie, *Pyramids and Temples*, 93–94.

28. J.-P. Protzen, *Scientific American* (February 1986): 80–88; Protzen, *Journal of the Society of Architectural Historians* 44 (1985): 173–177, figs. 15–20.

29. Zuber needed twelve days (!) to cut the six wedge holes necessary for detaching a small granite block ("Travail des pierres dures," 201–202). D. Stocks, *Popular Archaeology* (April 1986): 24–29, and *Popular Archaeology* (July 1986): 25–29.

30. *BAR* II, sec. 318.

31. M. Isler, *JEA* 73 (1987): 137–147.

32. H. W. Müller, *ZÄS* 91 (1964): 129–133.

33. Jéquier, *Pepi II* III, 23–24, fig. 9.

34. *CEAEM*, figs. 31–33.

35. See, in general, *CEAEM*, 96–116; Engelbach, *Aswan Obelisk*, 25–27.

36. *CEAEM*, 25; Lucas and Harris quote experiments by which the temper of copper could be increased by hammering from 136 to 257 and from 171 to 275 on the Brinell Scale, according to the percentage of tin in the alloy of 9.31 percent and 10.34 percent (*AEMI*, 220). R. M. Cowell stresses that arsenic increases the hardness achieved by cold working (W. V. Davies, *Tools and Weapons*, vol. I, *Axes* [catalogue of the Egyptian Antiquities in the British Museum] [London, 1987], 97). Zuber was able to cut limestone of medium hardness with a bronze chisel (8 to 12 percent tin) that was shaped by cold hammering. The same tool had no effect on granite ("Travail des pierres dures," 170).

37. D. Stocks, *Popular Archaeology* (July 1986): 25–28.

38. *Rekhmire*, pl. 62. The blade of the tools is orange to red.

39. Reisner, *Mycerinus*, 88.

40. Arnold, *Amenemhet III* I, 79, n. 183–185.

41. Private communication.

42. Zaki Nour, *Cheops Boats*, 34–39.

43. Arnold, *Amenemhet III* I, pls. 9d, 33b; see also fig. 2.10, p. 35.

44. In the court foundations of the pyramid of Senwosret I, blocks with the delivery date of year 12 and 13 are lying side by side, and at some distance lies one of the year 19.

45. For details, see p. 123.

46. Such as D. Stocks used (*Popular Archaeology* [April 1986]: 29, top fig.).

47. Lauer, *Hist. Mon.*, 253. On many more monuments, traces along the front edge show incisions made by saws; see pp. 266–267.

48. Arnold, *Amenemhet III* I, 81, fig. 39.

49. Ibid., pl. 11b.; Frank Teichmann, in Erik Hornung, *Das Grab des Haremhab im Tal der Könige* (Bern, 1971), fig. 12.

50. F. Teichmann, in *Das Grab des Haremhab*, 33–35, figs. 13, 14.

51. For example, Petrie, *Meydum and Memphis*, 17; Petrie, *Labyrinth*, 54; Arnold, *Amenemhet III* I, 79c.

52. *Rekhmire*, 58, pl. 62; Charles K. Wilkinson and Marsha Hill, *Egyptian Wall Paintings* (New York, 1983), 95 (MMA no. 31.6.20), 96 (MMA no. 31.6.27). D. Stocks has studied the use of boning rods in a detailed article in the *Manchester Archaeological Bulletin* 2 (1987): 42–50.

53. Stocks rightly points out that for huge surface dressing the use of true planes would have been insufficient and that boning rods would have worked better (*Manchester Archaeological Bulletin* 2 [1987]: 45–46).

54. U. Hölscher, *MDAIK* 12 (1943): 146–149, figs. 4–8. A good example for an undressed column in the first court of Karnak is in H. Chevrier, *RdÉ* 23 (1971): pl. 5.

55. H. Chevrier, *RdÉ* 23 (1971): fig. 8.

56. W. M. Flinders Petrie, *A Season in Egypt 1887* (London, 1888), pl. 25; *Description de l'Égypte* IV, pls. 62.3–5; R. Klemm, *ZÄS* 115 (1988): 50, fig. 7.

57. E. P. Uphill, *The Temples of Per Ramesses* (Warminster, 1984), 19–20.

58. R. Engelbach, *ASAE* 28 (1928): 144–152.

59. Walter Wreszinsky, *Von Kairo bis Wadi Halfa* (Halle, 1927), pl. 19; Ludwig Borchardt, *Allerhand Kleinigkeiten* (Leipzig, 1933), pl. 11 [2–3].

60. For model capitals, see C. C. Edgar, *Sculptors' Studies and Unfinished Works* (Cairo, 1906), 49–50, pl. 20; E. Young, *BMMA* n.s., 22 (March 1964): 256. For blocks with outlines of capitals, see *Description de l'Égypte* IV, pl. 64 [3–5]; Petrie, *Season in Egypt 1887*, pl. 25.

61. L. Borchardt, *ZÄS* 34 (1896): 69–76; Karl Georg Siegler, *Kalabsha* (Berlin, 1970), 18–21.

62. For example, for officials who forced priests to compulsory work, see H. Goedicke, *ÄA* 14 (1967): 22–23.

63. For example, the granite casing of the pyramids of Chephren and Mycerinus.

64. Petrie, *Pyramids and Temples*, 173–177; *CEAEM*, 25; Lucas and Harris, *AEMI*, 65–74. Reisner stresses that the granite blocks of the pyramid of Mycerinus do not show any traces of metal tools except those made by the Arab stonecutters of the twelfth to thirteenth centuries A.D. (*Mycerinus*, 71).

65. See n. 36.

66. Fill of builders' debris in the entrance cut to the pyramid and between the causeway and the mastaba of Imhotep (unpublished data).

67. A detailed description of the method is in *CEAEM*, 26–27, figs. 25–29, and Engelbach, *Aswan Obelisk*, 12–13.

68. Studies by J.-P. Protzen, *Scientific American* (February 1986): 80–88; Protzen, *Journal of the Society of Architectural Historians* 44 (1985): 161–182.

69. Protzen discovered quartzite hammerstones and river cobbles or other materials like granite and olivine basalt with a hardness of at least 5.5 Moh and a weight of some hundred grams up to 8 kilograms. He also observed that along the edges of the blocks the tool scars are much finer and suggests that a smaller stone hammer, probably weighing only 0.6 kilogram, was applied for cutting the more accurate features.

70. Petrie, *Pyramids and Temples*, 173; Hölscher, *Chephren*, 77–79; Borchardt, *Neuserre*, 142–143; *CEAEM*, 202–204; Lucas and Harris, *AEMI*, 42–44, 66–71, 423–426.

71. Vitruvius, *The Ten Books on Architecture* II.7.1, and Pliny, *Natural History* XXXVI.9–10, mention the cutting of stone with toothed saws.

72. D. Stocks, *Popular Archaeology* (July 1986): 26, figs. 1, 3.

73. Petrie, *Pyramids and Temples*, 83 (granite block over the doorway in the burial chamber of Cheops).

74. S. Hassan, *ZÄS* 80 (1955): 136–139, fig.; G. Goyon, *BIFAO* 69 (1971): pls. 3–5.

75. Engelbach, *Problem of the Obelisks*, 108–109. The pyramidion of the unfinished obelisk of Sety I, left in the quarries of Aswan-West, already was decorated on three sides.

CHAPTER III   *Transport of Stone*

CARRYING

Building material such as sand, gravel, mud, bricks, timber (fig. 3.1), and stones often had to be transported overland for long distances from canals and harbors up to the desert edge or through the fields to the construction site. The simplest method, and the traditional one, was to carry these materials on the shoulders of men or on the backs of donkeys. Representations of this kind of transport are frequent. In the tomb of Rekhmira,[1] for example, we see workers carrying three bricks hanging in slings on each side of a shoulder pole, or another man who carries five bricks piled up on his shoulder, in the same way as it is done today on Egyptian construction sites.

The number of bricks carried by one man at the same time depended on the brick size, and one may expect that only one brick of the larger size could be carried on one side.[2] We have reports, however, that Asian porters were able to carry up to 150 kilograms as far as 10 kilometers a day over terrible roads. Heavier loads, such as middle-size stones, could be laid over two poles or hung from them in slings to be carried by two or more people. This would be comparable with the way the sacred barks were carried. The bark of Amun was carried on four poles by up to forty priests.[3] And I remember seeing similar transport exercises by modern workers reconstructing the temple of Hatshepsut who were carrying heavy stones hanging from poles.

The discovery of a wooden handbarrow in the southern tomb of Djoser (fig. 3.2)[4] seems to indicate that such devices were not uncommon. It was 3 meters long and would have carried an object 0.6 × 1.9 meters wide at its base. Another, more primitive handbarrow was also found in the complex of Djoser.[5]

John Fitchen quotes an Indian source that states that 300 to 400 people could be united to carry heavy blocks of stone in a gigantic cribwork of bamboo trunks. In two or three hours, the stone could be moved over a

Fig. 3.1 Carrying a heavy load: relief from a late Eighteenth Dynasty tomb at Saqqara (Haremhab?). (Bologna, Museo Civico B 1889)

distance of 1 kilometer.[6] We also know that the builders of the Inca used similar methods.[7] But there is no evidence for such cribworks in ancient Egypt or for the existence of bamboo in general.

Since the Egyptians were accustomed to outfitting their desert expeditions with several hundred donkeys to carry water and equipment,[8] one may be sure that donkeys were also used on a larger scale for carrying building material. A donkey today is capable of carrying up to 100 kilograms over short distances. And the sight of these animals packed with a heavy basket full of soil was certainly as familiar to the ancient Egyptian builders as it is to us. Horses and camels were not used for carrying in Pharaonic Egypt, and cattle were used only for pulling.

MOVING HEAVY MONUMENTS

There are few ancient cultures in which so many heavy monuments were erected as in ancient Egypt and whose construction necessitated transport over such great distances (fig. 3.3).[9] The list in Table 3.1 is a much abbreviated record of the volume that was actually moved over the 2000 years of monumental stone building in Pharaonic Egypt.

This list shows that the technique of transport must have improved over the years. During the Old Kingdom, the enormous size of the buildings required speed and a great number of building blocks rather than blocks of great dimensions. For example, the pyramids of the Fourth Dynasty would

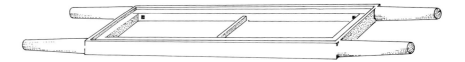

Fig. 3.2 Wooden handbarrow of the Third Dynasty from the southern tomb of Djoser.

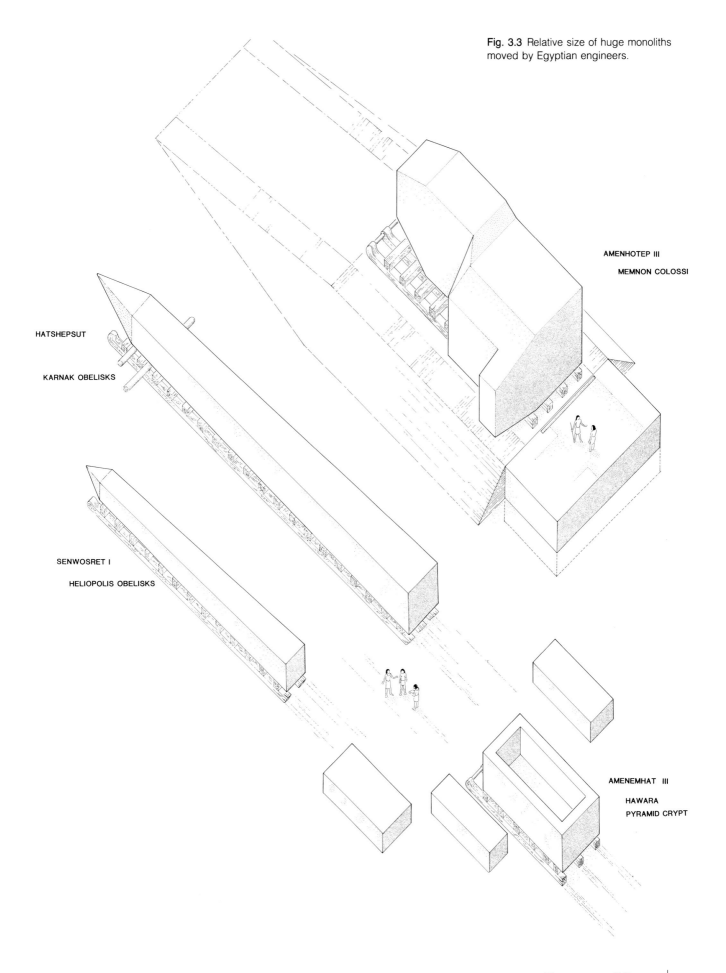

Fig. 3.3 Relative size of huge monoliths moved by Egyptian engineers.

AMENHOTEP III

MEMNON COLOSSI

HATSHEPSUT

KARNAK OBELISKS

SENWOSRET I

HELIOPOLIS OBELISKS

AMENEMHAT III

HAWARA
PYRAMID CRYPT

Fig. 3.4 Oversize wall blocks in the funerary temple of Mycerinus.

TABLE 3.1. HEAVY MONUMENTS TRANSPORTED IN ANCIENT EGYPT

Reign	Object	Comment	Dimensions (m)	Weight (tons)
Cheops	Pyramid chamber	Granite beams	1.3 × 1.8 × 8	50–60
Chephren	2 sphinxes	Valley temple	L. 8.4	80
	Pillars	Valley temple	1 × 1.5 × 4	14–19
Mycerinus	Wall blocks	Mortuary temple	3 × 5, 3 × 8	100–220
Niuserra	Roof blocks	Pyramid chamber	L. 5	90
Senwosret I	2 obelisks	Heliopolis	H. 20.42	120
	Colossus	Djehutihotep	H. 6.83	58
Amenemhat III	2 colossi	Biahmu	H. 11.7	ca. 100
	Burial crypt	Hawara	3 × 3.5 × 8	110
Thutmosis I	2 obelisks	Karnak	H. 20.016	143–173
Thutmosis II	2 obelisks	Pylon 4, Karnak	H. ca. 28	?
Hatshepsut	2 obelisks	Karnak	H. 29.5	323
Thutmosis III	2 obelisks	London, New York	H. 21.18	193
	Obelisk	Vatican	H. 25.31	331
	Obelisk	Istanbul	H. 28.95	380
	Obelisk	Pylon 7, Karnak	H. 28.98	?
	Obelisk	Lateran	H. 32.15	455–510
	Obelisk	Aswan, unfinished	H. 41.75	1168
	2 colossi	Pylon 7, Karnak	H. 11.00	?
	Sphinx	Mit Rahina	L. 8.6	80
Amenhotep III	2 colossi	Qurna	H. 17.3 + 5.7	700
Sety I	Obelisk	Rome	H. 22.84	263
Ramesses II	2 obelisks	Luxor, Paris	H. 24.94	227
	Colossus	Mit Rahina	H. 14	
	Colossus	Ramesseum	H. 19.3	1000
	3–4 colossi	Tanis	H. 21–28	1000
Amasis	"Green naos"	Sais	L. 10	580
Psametik II	Obelisk	Monte Citorio	H. 21.79	230

have consumed at least 9 million cubic meters of limestone, mortar, and sand,[10] which had to be delivered quickly in small quantities. The heaviest blocks known to have been brought from Aswan to Giza were the fifty-six granite blocks, weighing 54 tons each, for the chamber and roof construction of the crypt of Cheops; one of the granite blocks in the mortuary temple of Mycerinus weighed 28 tons.[11] Only a few blocks of local limestone in the same temple had the excessive weight of up to 200 tons, but they did not have to be moved very far (fig. 3.4).[12]

Blocks of huge dimensions, weighing up to 90 tons, were also found in the gable-roof constructions of the pyramids of the Fifth and Sixth Dynasties. Due to the limited space available, their transportation and positioning must indeed have been difficult. Also during the Middle Kingdom, some oversized blocks had to be transported over long distances. A pair of granite obelisks for Senwosret I, weighing about 120 tons each, were shipped from Aswan to Heliopolis. And the burial chamber of Amenemhat III, made of one 110-ton block of quartzite, had to be moved from Gebel el-Ahmar to the pyramid of Hawara. Since it was probably impossible to sail such a load upstream, it had to be hauled first overland on the east bank to a point upstream where the Nile could be crossed (probably near el-Wasta). From there, canals could be followed into the Faiyum.

The two colossal statues of the same king, weighing 11 to 13 tons and made for his sanctuary of Biahmu, would have traveled the same way. We also should remember that the famous colossus of the nomarch Djehutihotep first had to be brought down from its quarry, Hatnub, a distance of 12 kilometers through the desert until it could be loaded on a boat and shipped downstream to its destination at the city of Hermopolis, 20 kilometers on the other side of the river (fig. 3.5). This statue weighed about 58 tons.

The New Kingdom was the great period of moving large numbers of colossal monuments, such as the small obelisks of Thutmosis I (143 tons),

Fig. 3.5 Pulling a colossal statue on a sledge, as depicted in the Twelfth Dynasty tomb of nomarch Djehutihotep at Bersheh.

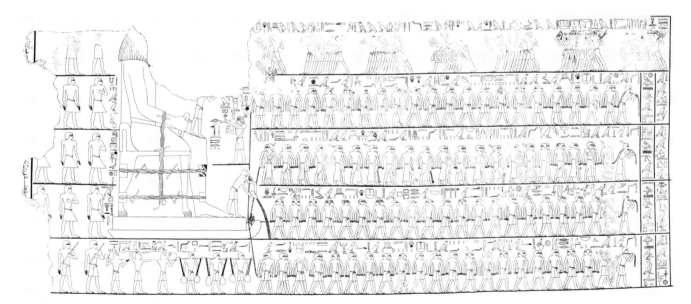

the gigantic obelisks of Hatshepsut (323 tons), and the still taller "Lateran" obelisk of Thutmosis III (455 tons). No higher obelisks could be removed from the quarries or transported and erected, and the mention of 100-cubit obelisks (52.5 meters) of Hatshepsut certainly was a fairy tale.[13]

The major technical feat of the later Eighteenth Dynasty was the production and transportation of the two colossal statues of Amenhotep III ("Memnon"). They weighed at least 700 tons each and had to be moved 700 kilometers overland from Gebel el-Ahmar to Qurna (fig. 3.6),[14] since no boats with such loads could have been sailed or pulled upstream.

The transportation activity of the Eighteenth Dynasty was surpassed in the reign of Ramesses II, when not only his 1000-ton statue for the Ramesseum was moved from Aswan to Qurna, but also a great number of other colossal statues (albeit of smaller sizes) and many obelisks were placed all over the country. At Tanis, fragments of up to four granite colossi were found that could even have surpassed the size of that in the Ramesseum and certainly weighed about 1000 tons.[15]

After the decline of the New Kingdom, short revivals took place in the reigns of King Amasis and Nectanebo II when the "green naos" was produced at Aswan and transported by 2000 workmen over a three-year period down to Sais.[16] Pliny reports how an obelisk (now unknown) for Ptolemy II Philadelphos was transported to Alexandria:

> A canal was dug from the river Nile to the spot where the obelisk lay; and two broad vessels, loaded with blocks of similar stone a foot square—the cargo of each amounting to double the size and consequently double the weight of the obelisk—were put beneath it; the extremities of the obelisk remaining supported by the opposite sides of the canal. The blocks of stone were removed and the vessel, being thus gradually lightened, received their burden.[17]

We cannot tell if this also was the Pharaonic method of loading obelisks. The Ptolemies certainly used Greek engineers, who might well have surpassed their original teachers by further technological inventions. Still, the method described has such a "prehistoric" appearance that it might indeed have been a Pharaonic practice.

Overland transport of such large monuments was always involved, either from the quarry to the loading stage or from the harbor to the construction site. We also know that only rollers and sledges were available to the Pharaonic builders, that workers were available in great numbers, and that time was not an overriding concern. With all these indications, the scene for moving an obelisk or a colossal statue is set, exactly as represented in the relief of nomarch Djehutihotep of Bersheh (fig. 3.5). Issues such as how many workmen were necessary to move such monuments and how they were to be used are more difficult to address, not only for modern scholars but also for the ancient engineers, as we can learn from the exchange of letters between the scribe Hori and his colleague.[18]

Answers cannot be provided only by pure arithmetic but by modern engineers working under similar conditions. Chevrier, for example, records from Karnak the removal of a block weighing 5 to 6 tons with the help of a sledge.[19] He had the surface of the track watered under the sledge, with the result that the friction was reduced to almost zero and the load could easily be pulled by six workers. He calculated, therefore, that under similar conditions the load of 1 ton could be moved by one man. This result is close to the representation in the tomb of Djehutihotep, in which 172 men are pulling the colossus of 58 tons with a pulling force of one-third ton per man. The account of Herodotus that 2000 men pulled the "green naos" of 580 tons would also lead to an estimate of one-third ton per man.

A ratio of one-half ton per man has been calculated by scholars studying prehistoric European methods to move megalithic monuments.[20] They estimate that on slopes, the minimum size of the hauling party would increase rapidly. For a gradient of 9 degrees, for example, nine men per ton would be required compared with two men on flat ground. These favorable results are gained by pulling loads on sledges over wet ground. The friction and the required pulling power increase when rollers are used or even more when the load is dragged directly over the ground. An experiment carried out in 1979 at Bougon, France, showed that a 32-ton block could be moved on rollers made of oak on rails of oak beams.[21] One

Fig. 3.7 One of the carcasses of draft animals thrown into the builders' debris of the Mentuhotep temple at Deir el-Bahari.

hundred seventy men were needed to pull in front and thirty to work with levers from behind to move the block, with an average pull of 160 kilograms per man. In one morning the monument could be moved about 40 meters on flat ground. A rope of linen cords was placed around the block, with four pulling ropes, each 100 meters long. A major problem apparently was maintaining the intended direction. The uneven underside of the block and irregularities of both the rollers and the rails frequently knocked the block off course, so that it had to be levered back into place regularly.

Reports of similar activities in modern times prove that the normal pull of a man is not more than 50 to 60 kilograms, sometimes even less.[22] This result therefore seems to support the idea that such monuments could be moved better on sledges. Certainly, oxen were used as well for pulling with a much greater force distributed over a smaller area (fig. 3.7).[23] Thus one would estimate that 1000 men or about 200 oxen would have been needed to move the 1000-ton colossus of Ramesses II on a sledge. How such great numbers of men or animals could be arranged and kept under control and what kind of ropes could be used, however, are separate questions.

That large numbers of workmen are not pure imagination may be learned from numerous expedition records documented in the rock inscriptions of the Wadi Hammamat and elsewhere.[24] Here is not the place to discuss the question of which numbers represent the actual workers and which ones a system of calculating the work power or efficiency.[25] Totals like 8368 (Ramesses IV) and 17,000 (Senwosret I) are certainly not the numbers of workmen, as so many were not necessary to work in the Wadi Hammamat nor could they be supplied with food and water in such a place, which is 100 kilometers from the Nile River. There is no reason, however, to doubt the correctness of an inscription at the Gebel Silsila mentioning that 3000 men with 40 boats were working to produce and transport the building material for the temple of Medinet Habu.[26] That this kind of work was not highly esteemed by those who had to carry it out is shown by numerous listings in the Kahun and Reisner Papyri of people fleeing such compulsory work.[27]

One should also keep in mind that besides these huge projects—which were, after all, quite exceptional—the routine work of normal temple building was going on. With fewer workmen, a limited number of relatively small blocks had to be produced and moved over a longer period. Some ostraka, apparently from the construction office of the Ramesseum, allow us to get a small glimpse into that kind of work.[28] They are accounts of the stones arriving from the quarries of Gebel Silsila in the boats of various captains (fig. 3.8).

BOAT OF NEMETI

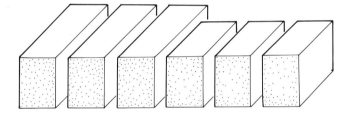

Fig. 3.8 Reconstruction of the cargo of sandstone blocks of three barges, traveling from the quarries of Gebel Silsila to the Ramesseum.

BOAT OF PAIABU

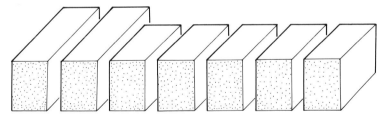

BOAT OF KHAY

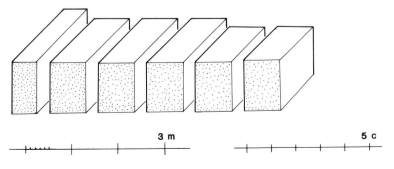

3 m   5 c

Transport of Stone | 65

Checklist of those stones loaded in the (quarry?)

Ship of Pentepu		Ship of Tauy		Ship of Khay	
3c × 2c × 1c	*2*	3c × 2c × 1¹/₂c	*2*	2¹/₂c × 2c × 1¹/₂c	*3*
3c × 1¹/₂c × 1¹/₂c	*1*	2¹/₂c × 2c × 1¹/₂c	*5*	3c × 2c × 1c	*1*
3c × 1c × 1c	*1*			2c × 2c × 1¹/₂c	*2*
2c × 2c × 1¹/₂c	*1*				
3c × 2c × 1¹/₄c	*1*				
Total: *7* [*sic*]		Total: *7*		Total: *6*	

Total altogether: 64 stones delivered by 10 ships.[29]

From these lists, we learn that each boat carried from five to seven blocks, weighing altogether about 15 to 20 tons, and that sixty-four such blocks probably arrived daily at the construction site. The dimensions of the blocks are those of normal wall blocks.

LIFTING STONES[30]

Since Pharaonic times, the monumental character and enormous size of Egyptian buildings and the building material used in them have awed visitors, many of whom have left inscriptions on the walls of such places. Later in Greek times, Herodotus visited the pyramids and discussed with his guides the ancient construction methods.[31] The discussion of how the pyramids could have been built seems, however, to be never-ending and continues to produce fantasies. In this respect, Egyptology shares the fate of other archaeological fields that deal with monumental architecture. But although Egyptian builders accomplished great feats in moving and lifting enormous weights, everything was achieved with the relatively simple building methods that are well attested for Pharaonic Egypt.

The Egyptian builders used three basic methods to lift a weight: by pulling it up an inclined plane; by lifting it with ropes and primitive devices; and by levering. These methods were still used for the construction of the temples of Ptolemaic and Roman times, when engineers outside Egypt had developed complicated cranes, capstans, and the "great wheel" (working on the principle of a treadmill).

Use of the first method, inclined planes or construction ramps, is well attested in Pharaonic Egypt and other cultures with a similar technological standard. They were used whenever possible—that is, when enough room, time, and manpower for their construction were available. The inclined planes offered a simple and safe device to pull up heavy materials like architraves and roofing slabs of temple roofs or the enormous quantity of building material for pylons and pyramids. The ramps were of different quality and technical sophistication, from rough accumulations of debris with a surface of lubricated mud to solid constructions of brick walls with stone pavement(?) or timbered working surfaces and built-in pulling devices. When little material had to be lifted to a modest height, the primitive type was appropriate. But from the experience of Legrain at Karnak,[32] we learn that even the 52-ton architraves of the hypostyle hall of Karnak could be pulled up such a primitive ramp.

The ramp at the pyramid of Amenemhat I at Lisht[33] shows that relatively small ramps could be strengthened internally by crossbeams. These beams were not visible on the surface—as they are frequently shown in modern reconstruction drawings—but well covered by a heavy layer of limestone chip and mortar. However, ramps could not always be used—for example, at the upper parts of pyramids the enormous quantities of materials consumed and the static problems due to such accumulations probably prevented their use.[34] Also in densely built areas like pyramid or temple precincts, space was not always available for the laying out of huge ramps. In such cases, another method would have been applied.

Pulling with ropes, the second method, was probably used to erect monolithic pillars, steles, and even obelisks. The shape of the foundation sockets of pillars in the temple of Harmachis,[35] the mortuary temple of Chephren,[36] and the sun temple of Userkaf[37] attest to this method (fig. 3.9). Reisner reconstructed the maneuver with the help of the shape of these sockets cut into the foundation platform of the mortuary temple of Mycerinus.[38] These sockets are 2 cubits deep and as wide as the granite pillars, with one sloping side that descends 3 to 5 centimeters below the actual bottom of the socket. The pillars, being 4.15 to 4.56 meters long, were dragged on a sledge beside the slope of the sockets with their ends opposite the front third of the socket. Then the pillar was rolled over, perhaps on three beams, perpendicular to the runners of the sledge. By removing the front beam, the pillar could be made to teeter on the middle beam until it revolved and descended the slope of the socket. The pillars weighed 13 to 14 tons but could easily be erected by men standing on the other side or on the top of the opposite walls and pulling with ropes. The bottom of each socket shows a thick layer of plaster, which would have facilitated the final adjustment of the pillar by twisting it. The slope was then filled in either with a single stone or with rubble and plaster. In all the cases cited, already existing adjacent buildings offered the convenient possibility to position men or other pulling devices on top.

Erecting obelisks has always been considered a great technical feat, not only in Pharaonic technology but also later, from Roman times until the nineteenth century, when obelisks were removed from Egypt and reerected in Rome, Istanbul, Paris, London, and New York.[39] For each occasion, another ingenious method for setting up the obelisk was developed. But besides a few traces of the Roman installations for taking down an obelisk,[40] and some specific grooves on the surface of obelisk socles, we have no indications of how the Egyptian engineers solved the problem.

Basically, two methods have been considered by Egyptologists. Engelbach[41] and later Chevrier[42] suggest that the obelisk was pulled up a ramp leading as high as possible directly above the base (fig. 3.10). The force needed to pull the 227-ton Luxor obelisk up the ramp during its erection in Paris was 94 tons. According to Engelbach's calculations, this would have required 2000 men. Around the base, a funnel-like brick construction was filled with sand; by extracting the sand from openings at ground level, the obelisk, with its heavier lower part, would slowly descend with the level of the sand until it reached the base. It would have been guided into a groove, 20 to 30 centimeters wide and 6 to 10 centimeters

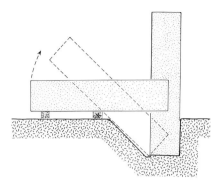

Fig. 3.9 Erecting granite pillars in temples of the Fourth Dynasty.

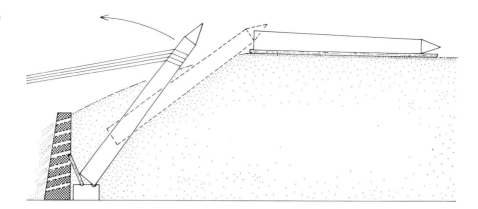

Fig. 3.10 An obelisk descending from the sand construction ramp onto its pedestal, according to Engelbach and Chevrier.

deep, cut along the nearer edge of the base in which the lower edge of the obelisk would catch. By being pulled from the opposite direction with ropes fixed around the upper part of the obelisk, it could be made to pivot over the edge of the groove into the final upright position. While grooves can really be seen on obelisk bases, neither remains of ramps nor the necessary brick constructions have so far been traced.

One objection to such a theory was that in all the models created by its proponents, the ramp ends in front of the sand funnel. Therefore, no platform existed to accommodate the several hundred or even thousand workers who were supposed to pull the obelisk right into the sand funnel. Golvin and Goyon[43] suggested therefore two opposed ramps meeting in the axis between the pair of obelisks. The workmen could work in front of the first obelisk. After the first obelisk had disappeared in its sand funnel, the second of the pair could be pulled over from the opposite side.

For the obelisk to have achieved a nearly vertical position as it glided into the funnel, the height of the ramp would have had to be identical to that of the obelisk. The enormous length of such a ramp would have created serious problems in the temple enclosures, which were densely covered with various buildings and monuments. A ramp of half that height might have served its purpose as well (fig. 3.11); however, the obelisk would have reached the pedestal in an inclined position and would have had to be pulled up into its final position with ropes. The general idea of this method

Fig. 3.11 Erecting an obelisk from a relatively low brick ramp with the help of ropes.

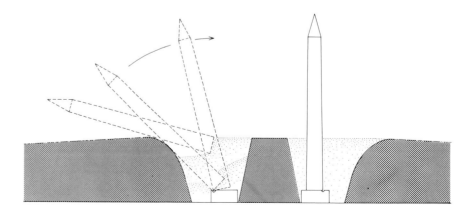

seems convincingly easy, but how the Egyptians were able to calculate the center of gravity of the obelisk and the way of its descent and how they managed to control its movement in order to guide the butt exactly into the groove of the pedestal remain unanswered questions.

Borchardt presented a completely different method.[44] He assumed that the obelisk was pulled with its butt directly over the granite socle so that the lower edge of the obelisk was exactly above and parallel to the groove on the top surface of the socle (fig. 3.12). Two other grooves (running in the direction of the obelisk) were used to fix a crossbeam along the lower edge of the obelisk to serve as a foothold when the obelisk was lifted[45] in order to prevent the lower edge of the obelisk from breaking out of the groove. This crossbeam would be removed after the obelisk was firmly caught in the groove, certainly a difficult and dangerous procedure. The actual lifting operation would have been carried out by alternately levering and supporting with wood and masonry until the obelisk was inclined so much that pulling ropes could be applied.

At this critical point, control of the obelisk's movement was essential. Otherwise the "jump" would twist and remove the obelisk from its intended exact position, as happened with the obelisk of Hatshepsut, which is 20 centimeters distant from the groove and considerably oblique. A large, cross-shape groove on the surface of the foundations of the Lateran obelisk

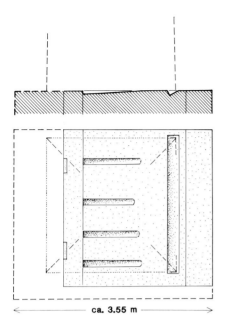

Fig. 3.13 Grooves on the surface of the pedestal of the Luxor obelisk of Ramesses II.

ca. 3.55 m

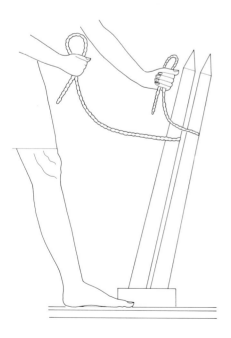

Fig. 3.14 Representation of the (symbolic) erection of an obelisk with ropes by Ptolemaios XII Neos Dionysos.

may have helped achieve the exact orientation of this enormous monument.[46] Since the socle of the obelisk of Ramesses II at Luxor shows four instead of two longitudinal putlog holes, Borchardt suggested a development in the art of erecting obelisks from the Eighteenth to the Nineteenth Dynasty (fig. 3.13).

It is not easy to decide which of these methods were actually used by the Egyptian builders. But we should not overlook the evidence of the inclined sockets on the top of obelisk pedestals. These sockets clearly show that the butt of the obelisk approached its pedestal not at a steep angle but with an inclination of 1 to 10 degrees only. And one should also keep in mind that in temple reliefs showing the king (symbolically) erecting an obelisk, the obelisks are pulled up with ropes (fig. 3.14).[47] Both indications favor the theory of Borchardt. One must admit, however, that the idea of levering up an obelisk is frightening.

In the papyrus Anastasi I, one of the tasks described seems to be an operation related to the moving of a royal monument requiring the removal of sand from a maneuvering chamber. Unfortunately we cannot understand the details well enough:

> Empty the space which has been filled with sand under the monument of thy Lord which has been brought up on the ground from the Red Mountain. It [probably the chamber] makes 30 c stretched upon the ground, and 20 c in breadth, opened from three corridors filled with sand from the river-bank.
> The openings of the 3 corridors have a breadth of 4, 4, 4 c; in height it is 50 c all together . . . in the emptying device (?). Thou art commanded to find out what is before (the Pharaoh) how many men will (it take to) demolish it in six hours (if) apt are their minds (?). But small is their desire to demolish it without their coming a pause. Thou should give a rest to the troops, that they may take their meal—so that the monument may be established in its place(?).[48]

Colossal statues would normally have been quarried and transported in a recumbent position,[49] only to be erected over the socle. That this equally difficult maneuver was carried out in a manner similar to that of erecting obelisks is shown by an elongated groove along the southern side of the socle of the statues of "Memnon."[50] But the famous relief of Djehutihotep (fig. 3.5) shows that such statues could also already have been lifted in the quarry and transported in an upright position.

A related problem might have been the erection of the enormous flagpoles standing in the front niches of pylons, flagpoles that could have reached a height of 60 meters and a weight of 5 tons. They could not have been lifted without proper scaffolding and ropes. We do not know how the ropes for all these maneuvers were applied or what kind of pulling or lifting devices besides pure manpower the Egyptian engineers really had. Representations and models of Pharaonic sailing boats suggest, however, that they understood how to handle complicated systems of ropes to hoist or lower sails and heavy masts.[51]

Hölscher believed that the Egyptians possessed lifting devices that are generally considered to be later inventions of Greek engineering. But Reisner had already showed that this hypothesis was based on false observations.[52] However, one cannot completely rule out the possibility that Egyp-

Fig. 3.15 Lifting water with a *shaduf*, as depicted in the Theban tomb of Ipui (reign of Ramesses II).

Fig. 3.16 Pulley wheel from a tomb of the late Twelfth Dynasty at Lisht.

Fig. 3.17 Ramesside pulley wheel from Deir el-Medineh.

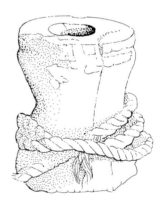

Fig. 3.18 Saite pulley wheel from the Step Pyramid at Saqqara.

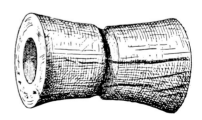

tian builders might have used a shear-leg device similar to the A-shape ship masts of the Old Kingdom as a kind of pulley. The existence of the *shaduf*, an instrument to lift water, at least from the New Kingdom on (fig. 3.15),[53] might indicate that Egyptian technicians could have developed a similar system to move stones. One also has to consider the existence of round and deep holes all over construction sites, first seen by Borchardt in the sun temple of Niuserra,[54] which might well have served as anchorages for such instruments. One has especially to consider the four round brick foundations along the ascending ramp at the pyramid of Senwosret I (figs. 3.42, 3.43), which certainly held poles or perhaps even revolving axles for an instrument to pull up the stones.

But the oldest true pulley found in Egypt possibly dates to the late Twelfth Dynasty and was probably not used to gain mechanical advantage but just to change the direction of pull (fig. 3.16).[55] Larger examples are known from the New Kingdom[56] and Saite times (figs. 3.17, 3.18).[57] Their existence already in the Old Kingdom is contradicted by the discovery of instruments that seem to be the primitive forerunners of pulleys (fig 6.45). The revolving beams inserted into the side walls of the portcullis chamber of the Cheops Pyramid suggest, however, that the engineers of the Fourth Dynasty already had some basic knowledge of changing the direction of pull and reducing the tractive force.

The third way to lift stones is by levering (fig. 3.19). Levers were generally used in building to move a block in a sideways direction. But by supporting a block with two small pillars (or beams) near its center and using levers or sets of levers from opposite sides, a block could be rocked up by alternately lifting one side and raising the support being released at that

Transport of Stone | **71**

Fig. 3.19 About fifteen excavation workers lift the granite altar of Amenemhat I at Lisht, weighing about 10 tons, with a single lever.

moment. The process of levering up one small side of a block and setting supports of wood or stone under it and then lifting the other end seems to be a relatively easy matter. In a practical experiment with a 32-ton block, three huge lever beams were used to lift the block in steps of 50 centimeters, apparently without any problem.[58] Petrie calculated that by this method the huge granite blocks for the roofing of the relieving chambers above the burial crypt of Cheops could have been lifted easily in one year by a crew of only sixty to seventy people.[59] According to Legrain, 150 workers were needed to lift the 180-ton obelisk tip of Hatshepsut with six levers only on top of the rollers.[60]

Fitchen suggested that the capstone of pyramids was raised with levers from one course of core masonry to the next.[61] The placement of the pyramidion on top of the last two courses would have been complicated but feasible. The restricted space near the top of the pyramid could have been enlarged by ledges on top of the casing blocks or by wooden scaffolding. However, since all core and casing blocks had to be lifted into place from outside, there would have been no need for treating the pyramidion differently.

Much thought has also been given to the use of rockers (figs. 6.29, 6.30) as a lifting device, especially in pyramid building. We have to admit that the evidence for the use of such an instrument is rather weak. The old question of how the pyramids were built concerns, of course, the problem of lifting. We can only suppose that all the previously mentioned methods were used at a certain point during 800 years of pyramid building or at certain stages of construction of one pyramid. But at what point one method or another was used can only—if at all—be determined by detailed technical studies of some of the thirty major pyramids. Before this is accomplished, the most ingenious and scrupulous system developed on the drawing board is nothing but one more example of unprovable speculation.[62]

LOWERING STONES

While lifting strained mainly the muscles of the workmen, lowering created the additional problems of slowing down the movement, preventing accidents, and maneuvering in narrow spaces. This last problem did not exist for bringing down the blocks from quarries to the loading sites. In many cases, the transport workers—in crews of two to four people—could just roll and lever the blocks down a steep slope of stone chip or down a roughly prepared slideway.[63] In other cases, real transport ramps would have been constructed, and the blocks packed on sledges or stone boats to be lowered down with the help of ropes held by larger teams of workmen.[64]

The lowering of blocks, sarcophagi, and other objects through sloping passages could be much improved by inserting crossbeams into the side walls for fixing the ropes. Putlog holes for such beams can still be seen in pyramids of the Old[65] and Middle Kingdoms[66] and in many private tombs (fig. 3.20).[67] After removing the beams, the putlog holes were closed or at least intended to be closed with patches and plaster. Blocks that had to be moved more frequently, such as slabs covering the entrance of a subterranean crypt, could have been provided with handles for opening and closing maneuvers.

More solid installations were necessary for the lowering of the three to four heavy portcullis slabs in the pyramids of Cheops[68] and Mycerinus.[69] Before the burial, the portcullises were waiting in a small chamber above the corridor. From there, they could be lowered with a system of ropes wound around round beams. The ropes could be handled from the corridor in front of the portcullises. The putlog holes are still visible. Since the

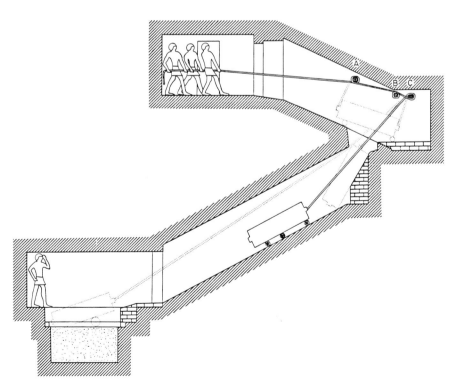

Fig. 3.20 Lowering the sarcophagus lid in the tomb of Ibi, reconstructed from putlog holes.

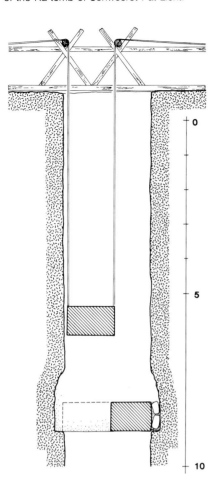

Fig. 3.21 Lowering ceiling blocks, suspended from three ropes, into the shaft of the Ka-tomb of Senwosret I at Lisht.

maneuvering chambers could not be closed in a safe way after lowering the slabs, the whole system was abandoned in later pyramids.

Vertical lowering of heavy blocks was already carried out in the First Dynasty, when, for example, the portcullises of the royal tombs at Saqqara had to be put in place.[70] And in the Third Dynasty tombs of Beit Khallaf, portcullises of 6 to 7 tons were lowered into shafts 25 meters deep.[71] To do so, solid wooden constructions had to be built on top of the mastaba. A later example is the Ka-pyramid of Senwosret I, where the construction shaft had to be closed by an intermediate stone ceiling consisting of two blocks, weighing 5 tons each (fig. 3.21).[72] These blocks preserved three deep grooves cut through the short sides, made for the fastening of heavy ropes, by which the blocks were lowered 10 meters into the shaft. Each block was lowered with three ropes, which must have been about 50 meters long. Since the blocks could not be tilted over the edge of the shaft and be adequately controlled, they had to be suspended from scaffolding above the opening of the shaft and lowered from crossbeams.

Since the Third Dynasty, numerous sarcophagus lids with drill holes for ropes are known (fig. 3.22).[73] These holes were needed for lids whose top surface fitted flush into the rim of the sarcophagus chest. The lid could therefore not be lowered with the help of levers or ropes slung around handles, but could only be inserted vertically from ropes. Since the drill holes are always arranged in pairs, one rope could be guided in a U-shape and thereafter easily pulled out again. Stone slabs could also be lowered with the help of wide straps. We do not know the kind of straps used; however, we can still see the wide and flat mortises cut into the stones that permitted the straps to be easily removed after the placement of the stones.[74]

In the tomb of Imhotep at Lisht, the shape of the scaffolding for lowering the granite sarcophagus and its lid can be reconstructed with the help of putlog holes in the floor and side wall of the crypt (fig. 3.23). Also interesting is the method of sliding down used to position the sarcophagus of a vizier at Lisht. It was first positioned on five crossbeams above the sarcophagus pit. Ropes suspended from scaffolding near the head end were attached to the sarcophagus, and all crossbeams were removed except the last one, which was probably round. The head end of the sarcophagus was then lowered with the help of ropes until it touched the floor of the pit, and the sarcophagus was pushed over rollers running on poles inserted in the floor into the actual sarcophagus niche (fig. 3.24).

Another method of lowering heavy blocks or sarcophagi into deep shafts has been described frequently, but has actually never been attested by direct observation (fig. 3.25). The procedure was to refill a finished shaft with clean, soft sand; put the stone on top; and remove the sand regularly from all four sides or from below through a second shaft connected with the first one. As the sand slowly sank, the load would be lowered. This maneuver would have afforded careful sideways propping to prevent the stone from sliding askew. The Egyptians clearly knew of this possibility, as is shown by their use of the caisson technique (fig. 5.1) and by another invention also made at least in the late Twelfth Dynasty.

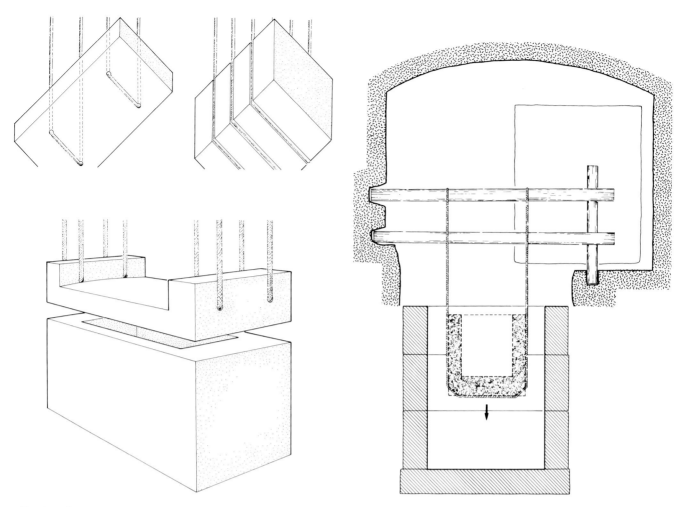

Fig. 3.22 Drill holes and grooves for lowering blocks of stone on ropes.

Fig. 3.23 Scaffolding for lowering the sarcophagus of Imhotep at Lisht into its pit, reconstructed from putlog holes.

The first example of this invention is found in the pyramid of Amenemhat III at Hawara (fig. 3.26),[75] and it was later rediscovered for the tomb of King Khendjer and his nameless neighbor at Saqqara (fig. 3.27),[76] and in the Saite tomb shafts of the Twenty-sixth Dynasty (fig. 3.28).[77] In all these examples, the huge lid of a sarcophagus resting on four to six pillars of masonry was kept raised until the burial. For the lowering procedure, the weight was transferred to four wooden beams carrying the four bosslike handles on the lid. These beams were not placed on the rim of the sarcophagus, like the masonry pillars, but to the side of it in a vertical, chimneylike channel filled with clean sand. These channels could be reached and emptied through a system of underground tunnels or shafts, so that the supports would slowly sink with their heavy load so deeply into their shafts that the lid finally rested on the rim of the sarcophagus.

These sand-filled shafts could be arranged in groups of two, at either the long or the short sides of the rectangular sarcophagus, depending on the position of the handles of the lid. The three oldest known examples of the Middle Kingdom were operated through corridors starting in the antechamber of the crypt. In the Saite examples, the sand was removed

Fig. 3.24 (*overleaf*) Method of lowering the sarcophagi of vizier Mentuhotep at Lisht into the sarcophagus niche, reconstructed from putlog holes.

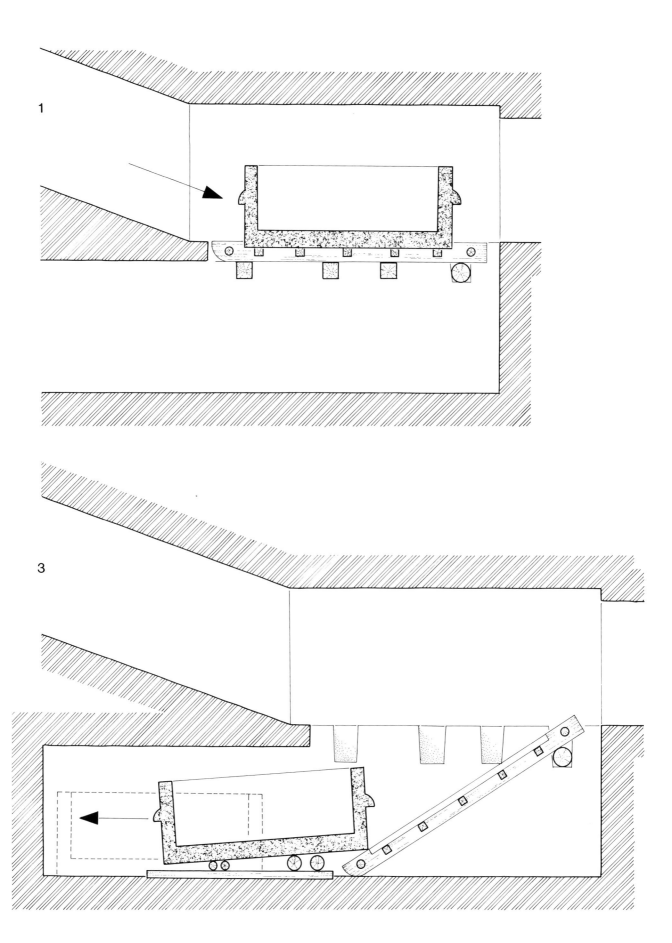

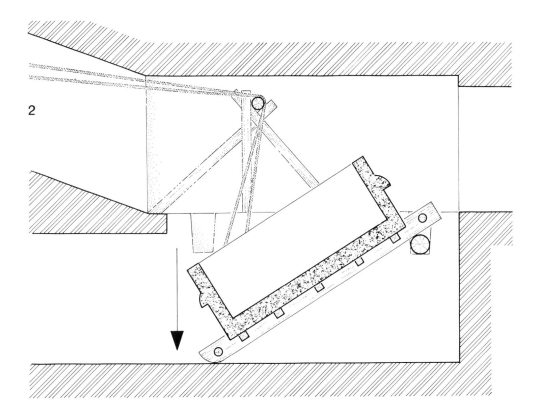

2

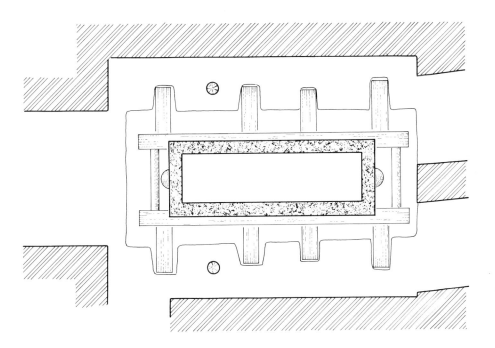

PLAN

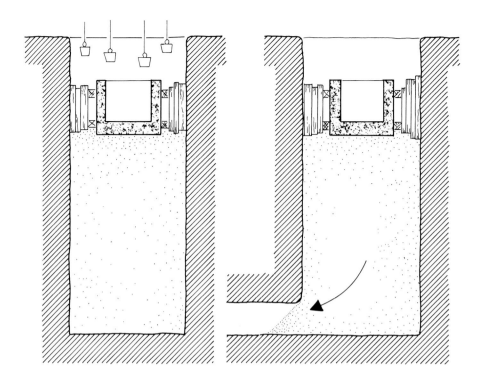

Fig. 3.25 Lowering heavy blocks of stone into sand-filled shafts by removing the sand from below the blocks.

through an open shaft in the center of the long or short side of the sarcophagus. The method might indeed be even older. It could have been used as well for the lowering of smaller stone lids with four handling bosses. In this case, brick chambers holding the sand would have been constructed at the small sides of the sarcophagus, with shafts for the supports to be lowered in sand. The supports would carry the lid on its four bosses.[78] But we have many examples where the lid is not stored above but behind the sarcophagus, from where it could be pulled or rolled over the sarcophagus.[79]

Fig. 3.26 Method of closing the roof of the crypt of Amenemhat III at Hawara by removing sand from below the pillars carrying the roof.

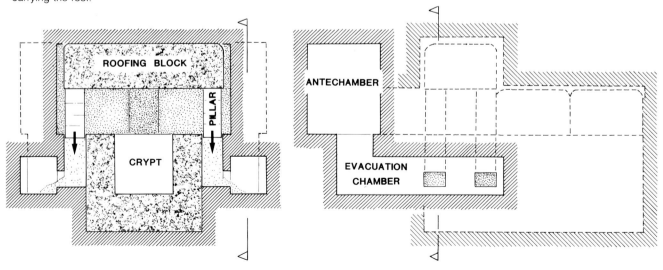

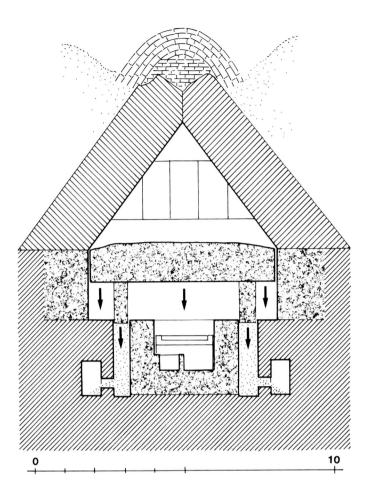

Fig. 3.27 Method of closing the roof of the crypt of King Khendjer.

0   10

The downward movement of blocks could not always be kept under control. For example, the blocking plugs of sloping tomb corridors usually filled the section of the corridor so exactly that no room was left for fixing ropes to the plugs. In the pyramid of Senwosret I, the six or seven granite plugs (some of them being 8.5 meters long and weighing 20 tons) certainly slid down the corridor with some speed, as their ends were smashed by the impact. One was provided with a deep horizontal groove at the upper end, possibly to be filled with a sandbag in order to prevent damage.[80]

In other tombs, a steep transport corridor was built separately in order to slide the sarcophagus down into the crypt, avoiding the precarious vertical suspension of a sarcophagus weighing up to 5 tons.[81]

CONSTRUCTION ROADS AND RAMPS

Moving building material and heavy monuments overland was a troublesome job, and therefore the Egyptian builders tried to avoid it as much as possible and to transfer much by water. Nevertheless, considerable distances had to be overcome on land, either from the point of origin of the raw material to the Nile or from the quay to the actual construction site. Some quarries—for example, Gebel el-Qatrani, Hatnub, or the Wadi Ham-

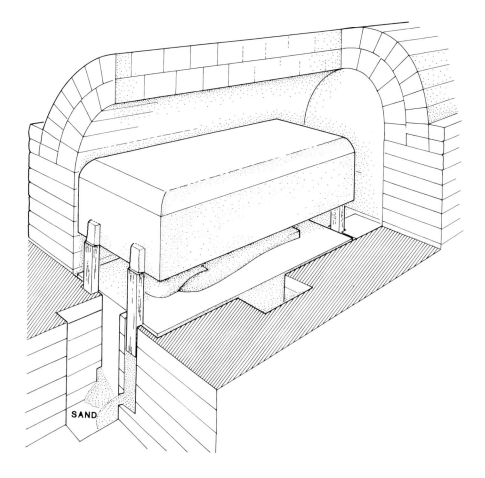

mamat—were up to 100 kilometers from the Nile. Quite often, differences in elevations increased the problems for the transport gangs. Either stones had to be lowered from quarries to the Nile or from the construction plain into corridors and burial chambers, or, even worse, they had to be lifted to the desert plateau or to the height of temple roofs and pyramids.

To facilitate this movement, solid roads and ramps had to be built to prevent the sledges and stones from getting stuck in the dust of the desert or in the cultivation. Such ramps and roads are normally preserved only in unfinished constructions, areas covered in a later phase of building, or in the desert, where they would have disturbed no one. At finished buildings, such ramps and roads were normally removed after the completion of work.

Construction ramps were used in many ancient cultures.[82] In Egypt, depending on the kind of traffic expected, the core, the surface, and the side faces of the ramps could be quite different. A selection of such structures, presented chronologically, gives an impression of the versatility of Egyptian road and ramp building.

Close to the north end of the west side of the unfinished pyramid of Sekhemkhet at Saqqara,[83] a huge construction ramp was partially excavated by Zakaria Ghoneim. It was preserved above the first step of the pyramid. Its slightly sloping side face was rather crudely made of rough

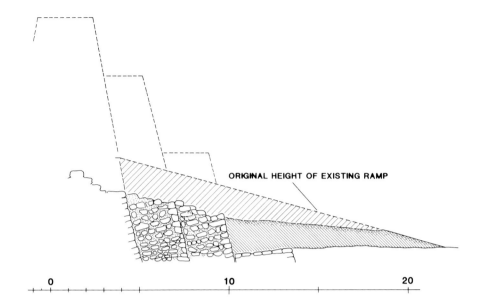

ORIGINAL HEIGHT OF EXISTING RAMP

0   10   20

fieldstones. It approached the pyramid at a right angle from the quarries in the west and led over unfinished masonry directly into the center of the pyramid. The whole extension of the ramp is unknown, and nearly nothing was published about this important discovery or about more ramps observed by the excavator at other sides of the pyramid.

At the small, unfinished pyramid of the Third Dynasty at Sinki (fig. 3.29),[84] four ramps lead from all sides against the inclined faces of the pyramid. Each ramp is 12 meters long and has an angle of about 12 to 15 degrees. These ramps, if completed, would have reached a height of only 6 meters. To raise the material to the top of the pyramid, which was planned to be 12 meters high, considerable additions would have been necessary. Since the ramps cover the lower parts of the third layer, they would have been partially dismantled and rebuilt, similar to the ramp at Saqqara. This defect seems to indicate the still-limited experience in the early period of pyramid building.

From the quarries of the northern pyramid of Snofru at Dahshur (fig. 3.30), two enormous, parallel transport roads lead up to the pyramid plateau. They are not aimed at the center of the pyramid itself, but only at a storage area southwest of the pyramid.[85] Similar roads have left their traces in the desert east of the pyramid, either for the delivery of Tura limestone or, as Stadelmann has suggested,[86] to be used later for the removal of material. At the upper end of the causeway of the Bent Pyramid, a brick-lines road was discovered,[87] which seems to have been the predecessor of the causeway during the building period.

At the pyramid of Meidum (figs. 3.31, 3.32), remains or traces of two construction ramps were observed by Petrie and Ernest Mackay[88] and further studied by Borchardt.[89] One ramp started south of the valley temple and climbed the desert plateau at an angle of 10 to 17 degrees. It was 4 meters wide, made primarily of brick and brick fill, revealing several addi-

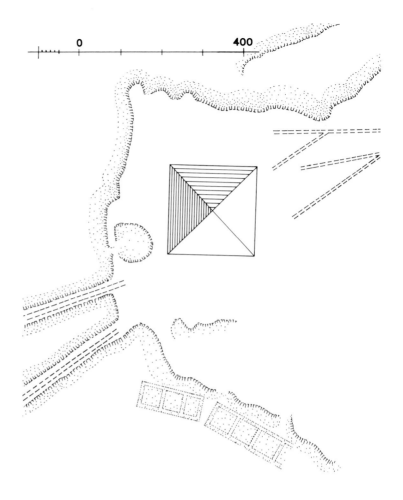

Fig. 3.30 Transport roads leading from the local quarries to the Northern Pyramid of Snofru at Dahshur.

tions in height. The remains of this ramp were seen in connection with some unusual features at the east side of the fifth and sixth steps of the pyramid. There, areas 4.95 and 5.36 meters wide are clearly set backward for a few centimeters. Possibly, the building ramp approaching from the east had been bound 10 to 20 centimeters deep into undressed casing blocks. When the surface was dressed down afterward, such a deep incision could no longer be compensated for.

A similar observation could be made at the south side. Three hundred meters from the foot of the pyramid, another ramp was found. It was only 3.25 meters wide, made of parallel brick walls, with the interior filled with builders' debris, and exactly at its meeting point with the pyramid casing on the sixth step, a vertical groove is visible again, about 3.50 meters distant from the corner.

Since no ramp with nearly vertical retaining walls could stand up to a height of 55 meters, inclined outer layers would have been added from the two sides. But the foot of the pyramid is still surrounded by such huge amounts of debris that no traces of an enlarged base of the ramp could be discovered. One even has to ask if the ramps could really have mounted the pyramid at an angle of 20 degrees, as Borchardt had suggested. More likely, the surface of a structure of such steepness would have been shaped as a staircase.

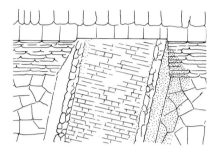

Fig. 3.31 Depression on the front faces of the fifth and sixth steps of the Meidum Pyramid, probably caused by the construction ramp (see fig. 3.32).

Fig. 3.32 Reconstruction of the ramp approaching the sixth step of the Meidum Pyramid.

A huge ramp near the Cheops Pyramid (fig. 3.33) was excavated leading up from the quarries west of the Sphinx to the pyramid plateau, east of the queens' pyramids.[90] The ramp is 5.4 to 5.7 meters wide and was contained by two parallel walls, carefully constructed of rough fieldstones, coated with mortar, and set in sections 10 to 21 meters long. The fill, now removed, contained seal impressions with the name of Cheops. Eighty meters of the ramp are preserved. It was probably used for the delivery of stones to the plateau, probably not for the pyramids but for one of the mastabas of later Fourth Dynasty.[91]

Fig. 3.33 Retaining walls of a huge ramp of the Fourth Dynasty, southeast of the Cheops Pyramid.

Mark Lehner has suggested that a rock cutting northwest of the pyramid of Cheops may indicate the location of the major ramp leading up from the quarries to the actual pyramid ramp, the foot of which he assumes to be at that corner of the pyramid.[92] The position and shape of this ramp has frequently been the subject of both scholarly debate and popular attempts to hypothesize about the construction of the pyramid. All these theories, however, are in vain, since no traces of any ramp survived.

A loading ramp of large blocks of diorite, 1.2 meters high and 8 meters long, together with remains of other ramps are recorded from the diorite quarries of Abu Simbel, used from the time of Cheops on.[93] Since no wagons were used in those times, the purpose of the ramps is unknown.

Reisner[94] and Hermann Junker[95] observed several examples of short ramps, leading to the rooftops of mastabas at Giza (fig. 3.34). These ramps were apparently used for construction as well as for bringing up the coffin and other burial equipment. The shafts were accessible only from the roofs of the mastabas. A funerary procession to the top of a mastaba is also

Fig. 3.34 Example of the ramps leading up to the burial shafts on the roof of mastabas at Giza.

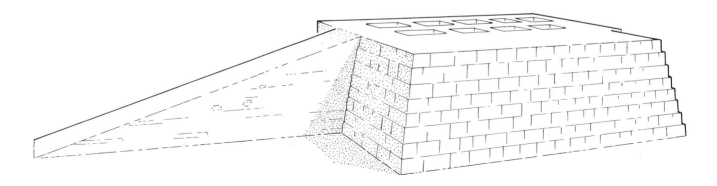

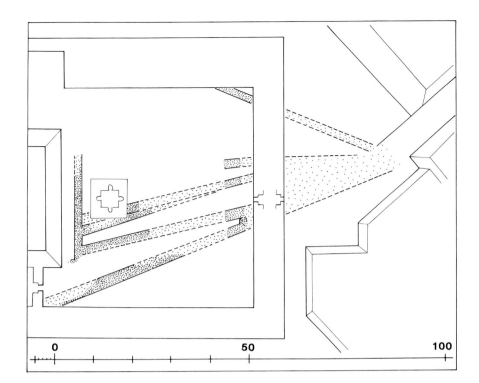

depicted in a tomb relief.[96] These ramps were constructed of bricks, fieldstones, or a mixture of both.

Under the pavement of the court of the sun temple of Niuserra at Abu Ghurab (fig. 3.35), east of the obelisk, Borchardt found five 2.5- to 5-meter-thick brick ramps, which fanned out from the obelisk.[97] Their sides were vertical, and the bricks were set horizontally. But from a red line on the outer face of the obelisk base, Borchardt concluded that the ramps had an inclination of 14 degrees. They interrupt the foundations of the eastern court wall and were certainly construction ramps for the obelisk.

In the burial chambers of the mastabas of Ti[98] and Mereruka (fig. 3.36),[99] ramps were preserved in front of the sarcophagi for hauling up the heavy lids of the huge sarcophagus. For some reason, they were not removed after the burial. They were constructed of stone and had an inclination of 18 degrees.

At Mastabat el-Fara'un, in the desert south of the tomb of Shepseskaf, there were traces of two transport roads, each 1000 meters long.[100] They approached the site from different locations, probably quarries for local limestone such as was used for the gigantic core blocks of the tomb. No details of the roads are recorded, and their traces are obscured now by the numerous tracks covering the desert surface.

Along the south enclosure wall of the court of the temple of Mentuhotep at Deir el-Bahari, a row of eighteen rather carelessly spread acacia baulks were excavated. Their shape suggests reused boat timber.[101] Since their ends seem to reach under the court wall, they might belong to the period of construction of the temple.

At the pyramid of Amenemhat I at Lisht (fig. 3.37), remains of a care-

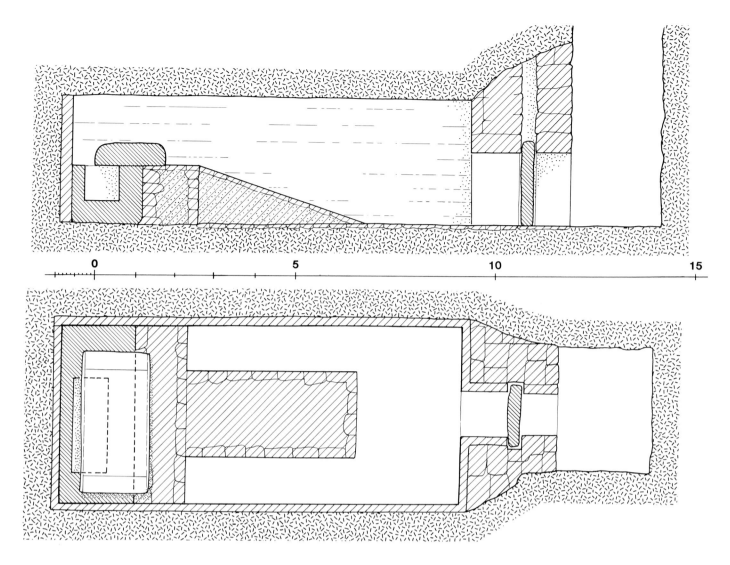

Fig. 3.36 Ramp for lifting the sarcophagus lid in the burial chamber of Mereruka at Saqqara.

fully built construction ramp were excavated; the ramp came up from the area of the valley temple and approached the pyramid near its northeast corner.[102] The surface consisted of mud and mortar into which a row of beams (reused boat timber) was sunk, with their upper surface certainly below the road surface. The ramp was at least 6.5 meters wide, including the brick retaining walls, which were 90 centimeters thick. The ramp was apparently used for delivering building material to the area around the pyramid entrance.

The excavations of the pyramid of Senwosret I at Lisht, conducted by the Metropolitan Museum of Art, New York, revealed numerous remains of transport roads approaching and surrounding the pyramid from all sides.[103] The more or less horizontal transport roads consisted of 5-meter-wide tracks of limestone chip and mortar into which rows of beams (reused boat timber) were inserted in such a manner that their upper face disappeared under the road surface (figs. 3.38, 3.39). Since the reused timber was too short to cover the road, frequently two pieces had to be positioned

together with their ends overlapping in the center. The core and surface of the roads had a cementlike hardness. The edges of the road might occasionally have been contained in wavy walls.

The ramps of a second type, the actual construction ramps for the pyramid, were removed after the completion of the work, and therefore few traces remain (fig. 3.40). They consisted mainly of bricks and Nile mud, retained by side walls of bricks. In one case (at the ramp in the center of the west side), the bricks were laid at an inclination of 12 degrees, which must have been the slope of the ramp (fig. 3.41). Remains of a second ramp approach the pyramid from the south, near the southwest corner. Since both ramps seem to have had a length of only about 50 meters, they could—with a moderate slope—have reached only the lower parts of the 60-meter-high pyramid; otherwise, they would have had an increased angle further up, giving them the appearance of a staircase. Nothing remains of the surface of the ramps, however.

The entrance cut is a downward-sloping ramp or dromos, cut for the construction of the burial apartments. It was used for carrying up the debris and for lowering the blocks for the casing of the chambers. The ramp was 5 meters wide and constructed as a huge brick staircase. The steps were covered with timber as a protective working surface. After the lower parts of the tomb had been finished and a lesser slope of the ramp was therefore desirable, the older staircase was filled with sand and covered with another layer of timber.

Another interesting ramp ascended the pyramid plateau from the south (figs. 3.42, 3.43). It consisted of the usual brick retaining walls and was 3.85 meters wide and raised at an angle of 8 degrees. The core, removed by the excavators, seems to have been filled with builders' debris. Unique were two round brick pillars on both sides of the ramp and halfway up. They

Fig. 3.38 Boat timber reused to reinforce transport roads at the pyramid of Senwosret I.

Fig. 3.39 Slideway with boat timber overlaying inclined bricks of the western ramp of the pyramid of Senwosret I.

Fig. 3.40 (*facing*) Reconstruction of the two major construction ramps of the pyramid of Senwosret I at Lisht.

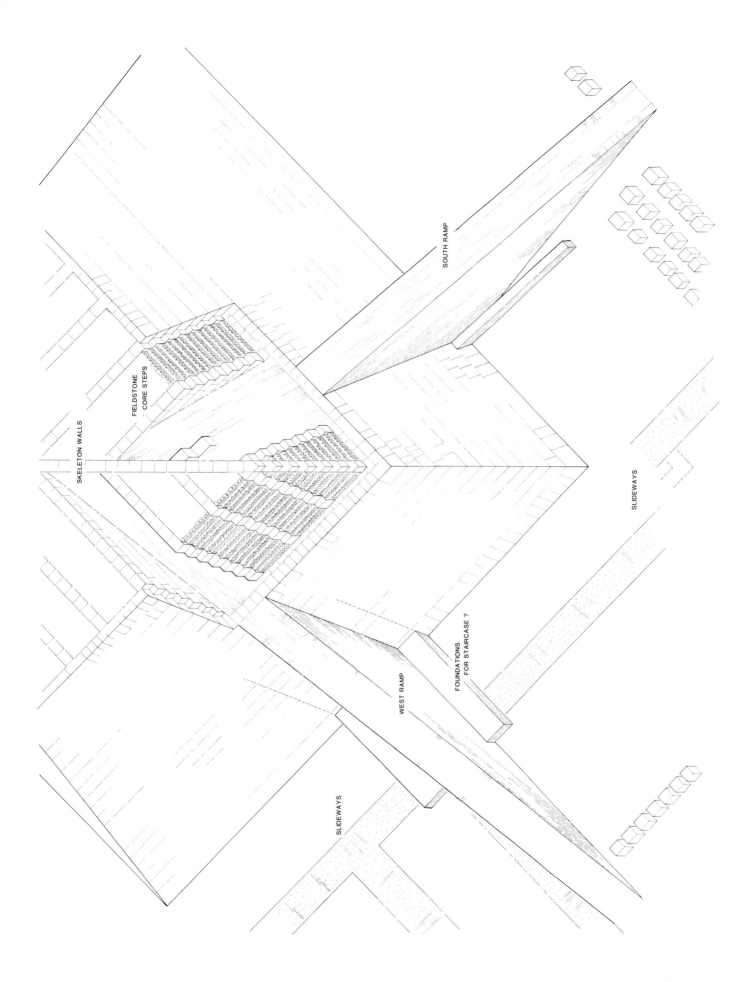

SOUTH RAMP

SLIDEWAYS

FIELDSTONE
CORE STEPS

SKELETON WALLS

WEST RAMP

FOUNDATIONS
FOR STAIRCASE ?

SLIDEWAYS

Fig. 3.41 Inclined brick courses of the western ramp of the pyramid of Senwosret I at Lisht.

were the foundations for vertical wooden posts, which were used to attach the ropes. Similar posts must have been erected at the upper end of the ramp.[104] Unfortunately, it is not known if the arrangement consisted of only these posts or also of a more efficient kind of lifting mechanism.

At the pyramid of Senwosret II at Illahun (fig. 3.44), Petrie discovered the remains of a baulk-covered transport road, 3.6 meters wide, coming up from the local limestone quarry south of the pyramid.[105] Again, the beams—reused boat timber—were set in pairs in order to cover the width of the road.

At the southern short side of the temple Qasr el-Sagha (fig. 3.45), the accumulation of builders' debris seems to indicate an old ramp. It coincides with sockets for timber to be inserted on top of the walls as a protection of

Fig. 3.42 Brick ramp climbing the plateau of the pyramid of Senwosret I from the South Khor.

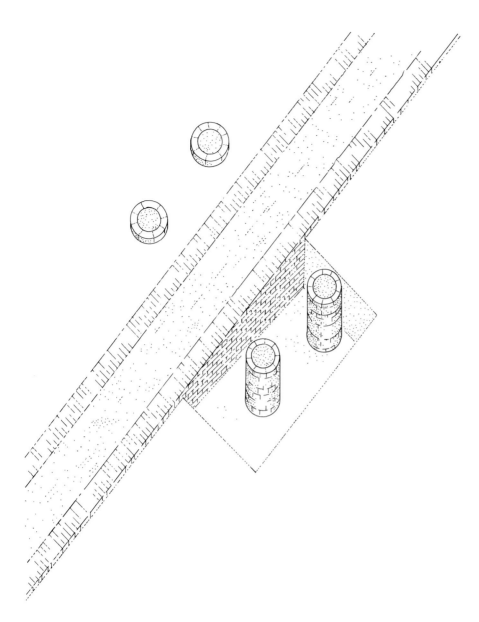

the upper outer edge of the building when the huge ceiling slabs were pulled up the ramp.[106]

From the basalt quarry at the mountain Widn el-Hosan (massif of Gebel el-Qatrani) (fig. 3.46), a 10-kilometer track leads through the desert sand to the quay at the former shores of Lake Qarun. Along the road, heaps of stone are piled up.[107] The road surface has never been excavated. The quay itself is an impressive stone ramp with an L-shape. It might be dated, in connection with the nearby temple and workmen's village, to the late Middle Kingdom.[108]

Another example is provided by a boat slide uncovered 500 to 800 meters northeast of the port of Mirgissa. The excavations of Jean Vercoutter revealed a 77-meter-long part of the slideway, over which the sailors who wanted to avoid the second cataract could pull their boats.[109] This road was originally 2 kilometers long. It consisted of a mud fill, 3.65 meters

Fig. 3.44 Slideway in the quarry of the pyramid of Senwosret II at Lahun. The sledge of Dahshur is added as a scale.

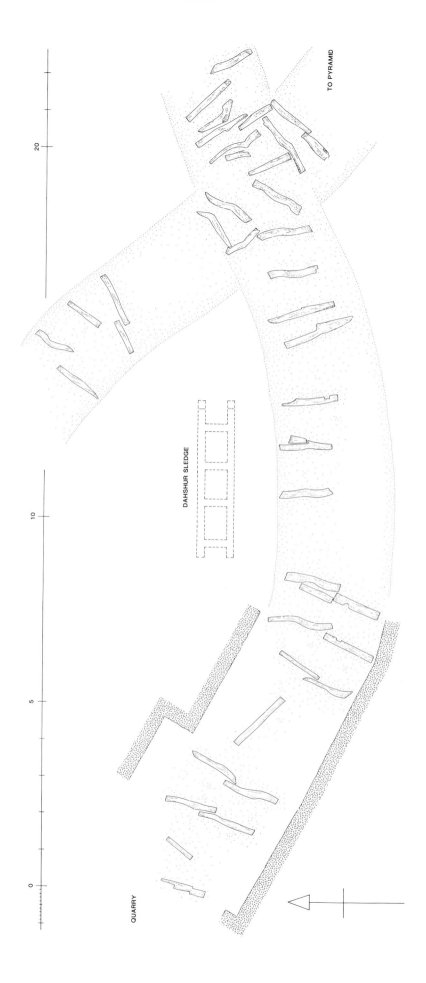

TO PYRAMID

DAHSHUR SLEDGE

QUARRY

20

10

5

0

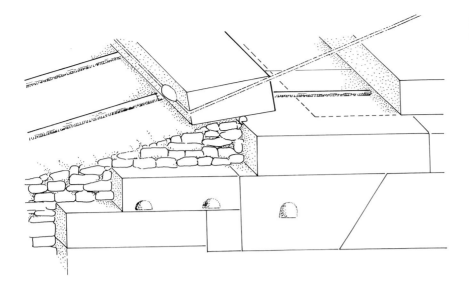

wide and 36 centimeters deep, into which every 20 to 70 centimeters round beams of 5 to 8 centimeters in diameter were inserted. Impressions of the boats, 1.2 to 1.7 meters wide, were left in the mud, which was apparently wetted for the maneuver. The boat slide was dated from the Middle Kingdom to the Second Intermediate Period.

In the limestone quarries of Antaeopolis, Petrie observed a gully filled with limestone chips and apparently used to throw the limestone blocks down a steep slope.[110] He also saw a huge brick ramp, leading from the quarries to the quay. It was made of two parallel brick walls with a fill of loose mud in between. The bricks had the size of 12 × 18 × 37 centimeters and were stamped with the name of Amenhotep III.

Remains of another ramp of bricks with the name of Amenhotep III are preserved south of the mortuary temple of Chephren (fig. 3.47).[111] This

Fig. 3.46 Transport road leading through the desert to the basalt quarry of Gebel Qatrani (west of the Birket Qarun).

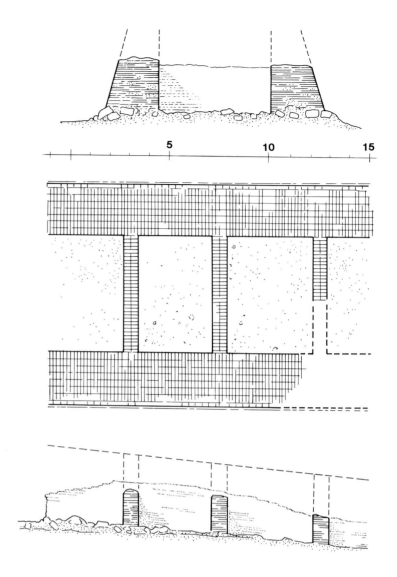

ramp may have been used for the demolition of the temple, which had started under Amenemhat I, who reused blocks in his pyramid.

Remains of an ancient road connecting the alabaster quarries of Hatnub with the plain of Amarna, 17 kilometers away, have recently been investigated.[112] It consisted apparently of two parallel trackways. On the hard and flat desert plateau, the road needed little artificial improvement. In sandy areas, however, tightly packed embankments of fieldstones had to be erected, the deepest of which was about 1 meter.

In the granite quarries south and east of Aswan (fig. 3.48), several transport roads were seen in the nineteenth century. The major one led over several kilometers from the center of the quarries through a flat valley to the quay in the north.[113] It had considerable dimensions and was retained by stone walls. It was apparently the ramp over which such heavy monuments as the obelisks of the New Kingdom were hauled. This main ramp had tributary branches coming from the actual quarry sites. In the quartzite quarries of Gebel Gulab and Gebel Tingar, several tracks lead from the quarries to the river. Their sides are marked by piles of stone (fig. 3.49).[114]

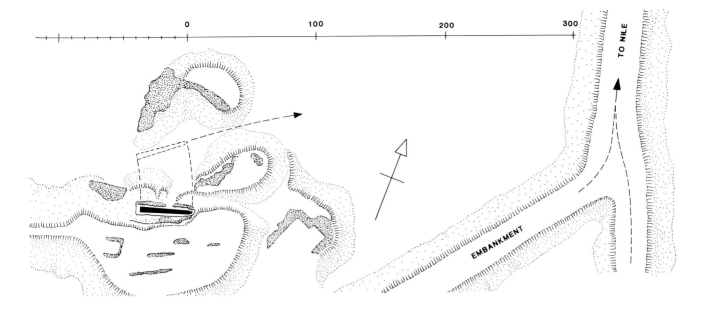

Fig. 3.48 Roads for the transport of obelisks in the granite quarries of Aswan.

From the construction of the Ramesside temple in the lower Asasif, a steep ramp was preserved,[115] consisting of debris made firm with palm logs laid across the fill and retained with a wall of reused blocks from the nearby causeway walls. The sliding had been made easier by putting a layer of mud on the surface and pouring water in front of the blocks.

The first Pylon at Karnak (fig. 3.50) was only built under Nectanebos I[116] but has to be mentioned here, since some of its building methods were carried out in the Pharaonic tradition. When the pylon was excavated in the nineteenth century,[117] it was enveloped by the remains of the construction ramps, which had never been removed because the pylon had been left unfinished. These ramps have since been removed, without any recording,

Fig. 3.49 Transport roads leading to the sandstone quarries in the desert, west of Aswan.

Transport of Stone | 95

Fig. 3.50 Remains of the brick ramp behind the south tower of Pylon I at Karnak.

down to a few remains in the court behind the south tower. It seems that each tower was approached by a ramp from inside and out. These were built of unequally spaced brick walls that leaned against the tower without touching it directly, some connected by cross walls. The space in between was filled with builders' debris. The walls show signs of a regular growth in height at distances of about 1 meter.

The reconstruction of the shape of the ramp has been attempted in various ways. A. Choisy[118] draws a gigantic and rather complicated stair-

Fig. 3.51 Hölscher's reconstruction of the brick ramp at Pylon I at Karnak.

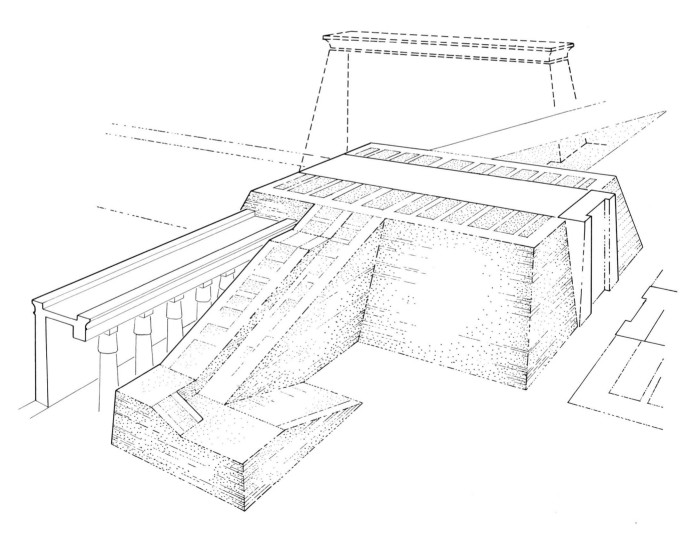

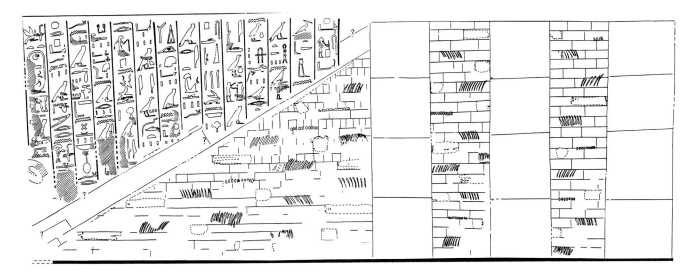

case with a rise that is probably too steep. Uvo Hölscher[119] reconstructed the brick chambers as a sort of massive scaffolding and added the actual ramp from outside (fig. 3.51). To gain the necessary angle, he had to reverse the ramp at 180 degrees. He did not explain how the upper parts of the towers would have been reached. Choisy suggested that the baulk holes, which were cut by modern *fellahin* who built their huts on top of the ramp and against the pylon, might indicate the outlines of the ancient ramp. It would have had a high-rising central part with sharply drooping sides. This shape would suggest a more gently sloping ramp for the lower parts and a kind of staircase in the center for the upper parts.

A detailed drawing of a ramp is shown in the tomb of Rekhmira (fig. 3.52).[120] It ascends with an exaggerated slope a building, the nature of which can no longer be determined.[121] The ramp seems to be made of bricks, laid in alternating courses of headers and stretchers with reed mats in between and with a filling material that is not clearly specified. The top surface of the ramp is drawn as though paved with limestone slabs. A building block is also shown lying on the ramp itself. Stone-paved ramps are not known from elsewhere.

Finally, we have an ancient description of a building ramp preserved in the Papyrus Anastasi I. A scribe, Hori, is testing the capabilities of his colleague Amenemope by asking him difficult questions, such as the number of bricks necessary to build a ramp of the following specifications: "There is to be made a ramp of 730 c, with a breadth of 55 c, consisting of 120 compartments, covered(?) with reeds and beams, with a height of 60 c at its top, at its middle of 30 c, its batter 15 c, middle 10 c, its batter 15 c, its base of 5 c. . . . Each one of its compartments is 30 c (long) and 7 c broad."[122] The explanation of the text and the reconstruction of the ramp leads, however, to discrepancies, since the total of 120 compartments, each 7 cubits broad, does not fit into a total length of 730 cubits, but only into one of 840 cubits. Different attempts have been made to solve the problem,[123] but, to quote Alan Gardiner, "The technicalities of these passages are such that the modern Egyptologist is placed in a far worse quandary than this ancient scribe; so far from being able to supply the answers, he is

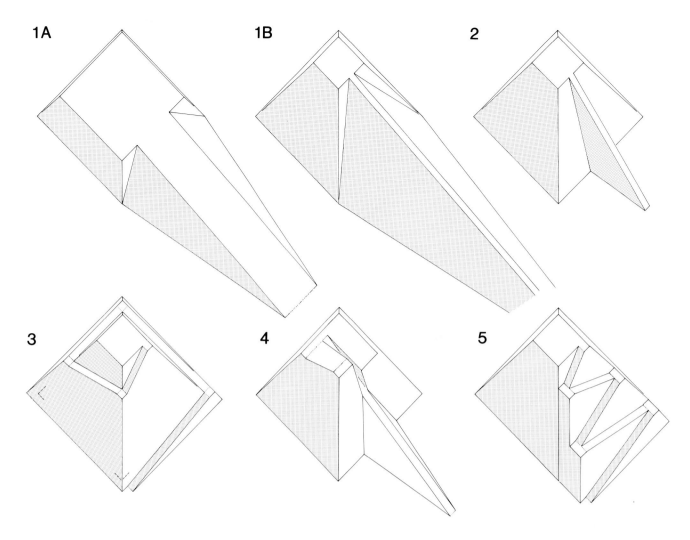

Fig. 3.53 Five of the major theories on pyramid ramps: (1a) the inclined plane growing into (1b) the linear ramp; (2) the staircase ramp; (3) the spiral ramp; (4) the interior ramp; and (5) the reversing ramp on one side of the pyramid.

barely able to understand the questions."[124] The main conclusion for us is that ancient Egyptian scribes and builders seem to have been accustomed to constructions and calculations of this kind, including the amount of material to be provided. The second conclusion is that gigantic ramps such as this one, with its nearly 400-meter length and 30-meter height, were not unthinkable.

PYRAMID RAMPS

The type of ramp used for the construction of the Cheops Pyramid has been the subject of countless studies.[125] They rarely take into account, however, that we do not have the slightest indication of the kind of ramp or ramp systems used for this pyramid. These studies also forget that traces of such ramps have actually been recorded from other pyramids (see the examples in the previous section). These traces indicate that the Egyptian builders did not use the same ramp system for every pyramid project. They developed numerous variations, according to the size of the project, the location of the pyramid and its quarries, and the type of core masonry. For that reason, we have to dismiss all theoretical systems so far proposed as

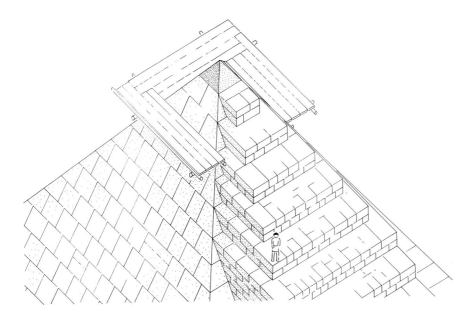

pure imagination. Only detailed studies of each pyramid, based on field observations or excavation, will really contribute to our knowledge. The following notes on pyramid ramps are therefore only a survey of the most probable possibilities without relation to a specific building.

Linear Ramp · The simplest and most obvious construction ramp would be an inclined plane directed against the center of the building (fig. 3.53 [1]).[126] Such inclined planes could be piled up from builders' debris, desert conglomerate, or other useless material, covered by more solid slideways. The slope would not be more than 10 degrees and presumably less.

Such inclined planes, which one would not call true ramps, could be used with advantage for the lower parts of all types of pyramids. They were easy to build and offered the possibility of arranging several parallel slideways, an important factor in the early years of a construction project when enormous masses of material had to be transported simultaneously. Such planes would even permit the use of oxen for pulling heavy blocks on sledges.

In general, it cannot be expected that significant traces of such construction planes could still be found. But we assume that the first example in the previous section, the ramp of the pyramid of Sekhemkhet at Saqqara, belonged to such a type.

Staircase Ramp · Calculations of the dimensions and the material necessary to construct ramps that would reach to the top of the major pyramids have shown that such ramps would have been unrealistic and structurally impossible.[127] The only alternative would have been the reduction of the width of the ramp, which would have necessitated building it from brick or, even better, from ashlar. At the same moment one would have to raise the angle of the ramp over 10 degrees. Such an angle could have been overcome only by the use of steps.[128] Traces of such narrow, short, steep staircase ramps (figs. 3.53 [2], 3.54) may have been identified at Sinki, Meidum,

Fig. 3.55 Reversing ramps on a step pyramid or a stepped pyramid core.

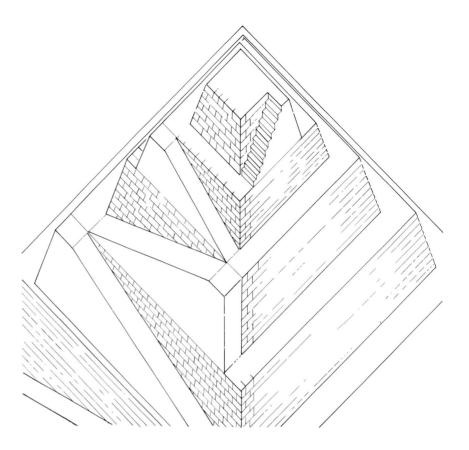

Giza, Abu Ghurab, and Lisht. Naturally, the building stones could not be pulled up the steps but would have been lifted with levers or other devices. This work would have been time-consuming and could have been carried out only for the upper sections of a pyramid when the daily output was no longer so essential. At the pyramid of Meidum, such a ramp may have reached a height of 65 meters.

Spiral Ramp · Some scholars have proposed a system of spiral ramps (fig. 3.53 [3]),[129] starting either from one or from all four corners and mounting the four faces at an increasing angle and decreasing length of its individual sections. Two possibilities were devised: the ramps either could rest on the protuberances of the undressed casing blocks, a rather unsafe footing indeed, or could stand on separate foundations in front of the pyramid and only lean against the sloping faces. Ramps of this type would naturally leave no traces after their removal,[130] and one would even doubt their feasibility. In spite of the ingeniousness of such a device, spiral ramps would have created serious problems. During the whole construction period, the pyramid trunk would have been completely buried under the ramps.[131] The surveyors could therefore not have used the four corners, edges, and foot line of the pyramid for their calculations. Furthermore, at a certain height the sides of the pyramid would no longer be wide enough to provide a ramp from one corner to the next.

Reversing Ramp on One Side of a Pyramid · Ramp systems could also have concentrated on one side of a pyramid (figs. 3.53 [5], 3.55). Ramps parallel to the side would take a zigzag course up the face, either resting on the steps of the still-exposed core masonry, or standing on separate foundations in front of the pyramid and leaning against the sloping casing.[132] Since the amount of material necessary for such a reversing ramp was not overwhelming, one could imagine that the core steps were erected quite frequently with the help of ramps standing on the steps themselves. A new system had to be added later from outside when the casing had to be laid together with the backing and packing stones. The main problem with this quite convincing system is that, despite the fact that stepped pyramids would have been ideal for this construction concept, we have three examples—at Saqqara, Sinki, and Meidum—where stepped pyramids show remains of linear and not reversing ramps.

Interior Ramps · The core masonry of a pyramid could well have served directly for an interior ramp system (fig. 3.53 [4]), cutting through the masonry up to a considerable height of the building.[133] Since these open trenches would have to be filled in after some time, an added exterior ramp would have been necessary. Not much material would have been required, so this exterior ramp could have been comparatively small, perhaps in the shape of a staircase ramp. Petrie suggested for the construction of the upper part of a pyramid a reversing ramp leaning against the pyramid face.[134]

The disadvantage of this system is that the construction trenches would have disturbed the proper building of the core steps and accretion layers. Nevertheless, construction gaps, probably from such interior ramps, could be seen in the core masonry of the pyramids of Sahura, Niuserra, Neferirkara, and Pepy II.[135]

NOTES

1. *Rekhmire*, pl. 59 (upper).

2. Ibid. (lower).

3. Carrying poles could be temporarily attached to shrines (O. Königsberger, *ASAE* 40 [1940]: 247–255).

4. Lauer, *Hist. Mon.*, 240, fig. 67.

5. Firth and Quibell, *Step Pyramid*, pl. 14 [4].

6. Fitchen, *Building Construction*, 172.

7. Arnim Bollinger, *So bauten die Inka* (Diessenhofen, 1979), 148.

8. Jaroslav Černý, Alan Gardiner, and T. Eric Peet, *The Inscriptions of Sinai* I, II (London and Oxford, 1952, 1955), nos. 110, 114 (284 and 500 donkeys!).

9. See, in general, L. Croon, *OLZ* 30 (1927): 757–759. For comparative discussions, see Naumann, *Architektur*, 34–37; Mulloy, "Easter Islands"; J. S. Velson and T. C. Clark, *Transport of Stone Monuments to the La Venta and San Lorenzo Sites,* Contributions of the University of California Archaeological Research Facility, no. 24 (1975), 1–39; Coulton, *Greek Architects*, 141–144; Bollinger, *So bauten die Inka*, 148–150.

10. R. Stadelmann, *MDAIK* 36 (1980): 438–439.

11. Reisner, *Mycerinus*, 72. The block was 1 × 2 × 5 meters.

12. Ibid., 70. These blocks were quarried very close to the construction site and had only to be lifted into the wall. Cutting them into smaller pieces would have produced less volume in stone, hence a less desirable solution for the Egyptian builders.

13. The Northampton stele mentions two obelisks of Hatshepsut of 108 cubits (*Urk.* IV, 425).

14. R. Stadelmann pointed out that the colossi were—contradicting the results of R. Klemm and D. Klemm—not quarried at Aswan but at the Gebel el-Ahmar (*MDAIK* 40 [1984]: 291–296).

15. E. P. Uphill, *The Temples of Per Ramesses* (Warminster, 1984), 129–132.

16. Herodotus, *History* II.175.

17. Pliny, *Natural History* XXXVI.14.

18. Fischer-Elfert, *Anastasi I*, 134–142.

19. H. Chevrier, *RdÉ* 22 (1970): 20–21.

20. R. J. C. Atkinson, *Antiquity* 35 (1961): 292–299.

21. J.-P. Mohen, *Les Dossiers d'Archéologie* 46 (1980): 58–67.

22. Collected by Velson and Clark, *Transport of Stone Monuments to the La Venta and San Lorenzo Sites*, 9–10.

23. For a depiction of oxen pulling stones, see Saleh and Sourouzian, *Kairo*, no. 119; fig. 6.39, p. 278.

Mannoni, *Marble*, 118, fig. 137, shows thirty-four oxen pulling a cart carrying a stone that may have weighed 60 to 65 tons. Ian Dunlop mentions that teams of twenty-six yoke oxen were engaged in hauling up stones for the cathedral of Laon (*The Cathedrals' Crusade* [London and New York, 1982], 52). According to him, one pair of oxen would do 30 kilometers daily (!), pulling 1 cubic meter of stone, which weighs not 15 tons, as he assumes, but only 2 to 2.8 tons. For all this work carts were used. This clearly contradicts R. J. C. Atkinson's view that oxen could not be used for such work (*Antiquity* 35 [1961]: 292–293).

24. J. Couyat and P. Montet, *Les Inscriptions hiéroglyphiques et hiératiques du Ouadi Hammamat* (Cairo, 1912); Georges Goyon, *Nouvelles inscriptions rupestres du Wadi Hammamat* (Paris, 1957).

25. Karl-Joachim Seyfried, *Beiträge zu den Expeditionen des Mittleren Reiches in die Ostwüste* (Hildesheim, 1981).

26. *BAR* IV, sec. 18–19.

27. A. Scharff, *ZÄS* 59 (1924): 40 [P 10024 A]; William C. Hayes, *A Papyrus of the Late Middle Kingdom in the Brooklyn Museum, Papyrus Brooklyn 35.1446*, Wilbour Monographs 5 (New York, 1955), 132.

28. Wilhelm Spiegelberg, *Hieratic Ostraka and Papyri Found by J. E. Quibell, in the Ramesseum, 1895–6* (London, 1898), pls. 17, 18 [134–137]. Another ostrakon of the Nineteenth Dynasty (*Ägyptens Aufstieg zur Weltmacht*, no. 64) lists ships that carried only 2 to 3 blocks (E. Endesfelder, *Forschungen und Berichte* 8 [1967]: 68–69).

Another ostrakon published by Petrie, which he thought was of the same kind, is not necessarily a transport list of ships (*Ancient Egypt* [1915]: 136–137).

29. Spiegelberg, *Hieratic Ostraka and Papyri*, pls. 17, 18 [136a].

30. For comparison, see J. J. Coulton, *Journal of Hellenic Studies* 94 (1974): 1–19. The lifting methods suggested by M. Isler are purely hypothetical (*JARCE* 13 [1976]: 31–41).

31. Herodotus, *History* II.125. He stated that the stones for the pyramids were lifted over steps by the help of either permanently installed or regularly moved installations of short beams or poles.

32. Legrain, *Karnak*, 166–171, figs. 102–107.

33. *BMMA* 9 (October 1914): 220, fig. 16; for the plan, see *BMMA* 17, part 2 (December 1922): fig. 1. See also photos MMA L13–14, 298–302, 359.

34. For the engineering problems, see P. Garde-Hansen, *Ingeniøren* 1 (1974): 1–35.

35. Ricke, *Harmachis*, figs. 9–12.

36. Hölscher, *Chephren*, fig. 61; Maragioglio, *Piramidi* v, pl. 12, figs. 5, 6, 9.

37. Ricke, *Sonnenheiligtum*, fig. 22. For more simple versions of such sockets, see Ricke, *ASAE* 55 (1958): pl. 1b.

38. Reisner, *Mycerinus*, 84–86, figs. 15, 16.

39. On erecting Egyptian obelisks in modern times, see Bern Dibner, *Moving the Obelisks* (Norwalk, Conn., 1952); Gorringe, *Obelisks*, 110–118.

40. For the French excavation at Pylon VII, see *Karnak* VII, 167–197.

41. Engelbach, *Aswan Obelisk*, 36–43, pl. 8; Engelbach, *Problem of the Obelisks*, 66–84.

42. H. Chevrier, *ASAE* 52 (1954): 309–313; Chevrier, *RdÉ* 22 (1970): 33–38. The lifting method suggested by M. Isler does not explain the shape of the grooves on the obelisk bases and must be rejected (*JARCE* 13 [1976]: 31–41). The same argument applies to the theory of Choisy to lower the obelisk by the use of sand bags (*L'Art de bâtir*, 124, fig. 95).

43. Golvin and Goyon, *Karnak*, 131–133.

44. Borchardt, *Amonstempel*, 15–17. For a description of several obelisk bases, see M. Pillet, *ASAE* 22 (1922): 244–248.

45. H. Chevrier assumed that the grooves were used as footholds for beams guiding the obelisk into position (*ASAE* 54 [1952]: 310–311). See also *Karnak* VIII, 155, pl. 2.

46. P. Barguet, *ASAE* 50 (1950): 272, fig. 2.

47. C. M. Zivie, *BdE* 81 (1979): 477–498; *LD* IV, 47b, 48a. The oldest known representations are from the reign of Ramesses II (M. Pillet, *ASAE* 23 [1923]: 122, pl. 25b; Golvin and Goyon, *Karnak*, 136 upper). The Easter Island statues (the largest one is 9.8 meters high and weighs 82 tons, with an unfinished one even 20 meters long) were presumably also lifted by lateral levering and supporting the rising statue by a masonry platform. During the final phase, the levering would have been aided by ropes and restraining cables snubbed around heavy posts anchored in the ground (Mulloy, "Easter Islands," 16–20, figs. 4, 5). This theory is supported by actual reerection work carried out by Mulloy.

48. Alan Gardiner, *Egyptian Hieratic Texts* I (Leipzig, 1911), 18–19, 33–34, pl. 16.6–17; A. Badawy, *ZÄS* 110 (1983): 13–15; Fischer-Elfert, *Anastasi I*, 143–147.

49. The stratification of the bedrock would have made it impossible to quarry blocks of an extraordinary height. See, for example, the preparations for a 20-meter-high limestone statue of a king in a quarry near Minya, which was, of course, outlined in a lying position (Klemm, *Steine der Pharaonen*, fig. 41).

50. L. Borchardt, *ZÄS* 45 (1908): 32–34.

51. For examples, see *CEAEM*, figs. 43–47.

52. Reisner rejects this idea because the holes under the rear edge of the granite casing, considered by Hölscher to be sockets for brackets, were actually lever holes for the core blocks behind (*Mycerinus*, appendix D).

53. For the earliest example in the tomb of Merira at El-Amarna, see Norman De Garis Davies, *The Rock Tombs of El Amarna* I (London, 1903), 41, pl. 32. In general, see K. W. Butzer, in *LÄ* v, 520–521; Norman De Garis Davies, *The Tomb of Neferhotep at Thebes* (New York, 1933), 70–73, pl. 47.

54. Borchardt, *Re-Heiligtum*, 62; Arnold, *Mentuhotep*, 24, n. 36, pls. 10a, c, d, 11d.

55. MMA 15.3.1118.

56. Bernard Bruyère, *Les Fouilles de Deir el Médineh 1933–1934* (Cairo, 1937), 122, fig. 54. Three wooden wheels with grooves for ropes were found at Lisht-North in a tomb dating to the Twelfth Dynasty. They were apparently used for

lowering a limestone slab, which had two drill holes for fixing the ropes (unpublished data).

57. Lauer, *Pyramid à degrés* I, 45, n. 4; 52, fig. 26.

58. J.-P. Mohen, *Les Dossiers d'Archéologie* 46 (1980): 66.

59. Petrie, *Pyramids and Temples*, 212. But since the relieving chambers were apparently not planned from the beginning, the building material for them could not have been loaded on one of the lower courses in order to travel upward.

60. G. Legrain, *ASAE* 5 (1904): 26.

61. Fitchen, *Building Construction*, 238–239.

62. The best studies to consult on this subject are Choisy, *L'Art de Bâtir*, 98–113; L. Croon, in Borchardt, *Entstehung der Pyramide*, 26–31; *CEAEM*, 112–129; W. M. Flinders Petrie, *Ancient Egypt* (1930): 33–39; Leslie Grinsell, *Egyptian Pyramids* (Gloucester, 1947), 51–77; Lauer, *Observations*, 47–63; Lauer, *Mystère*, 261–295; David Macaulay, *Pyramid* (Boston, 1975); Goyon, *Khéops;* Celeste Rinaldi, *Le Piramidi* (Milan, 1983); Edward, *Pyramids*, 262–294. Isler has shown that the Cheops Pyramid could have been built practically without ramps by using staircases provided by the core masonry and construction platforms supported by protruding courses of the casing (*JARCE* 22 [1985]: 129–142; *JARCE* 24 [1983]: 95–112). Those casing courses would still be recognizable by their greater height (fig. 4.102). I cannot detect a serious technical flaw in his method.

63. Mannoni shows such an activity in the quarries of Carrara (*Marble*, fig. 245). For a similar slide near Antaeopolis, see Petrie, *Antaeopolis*, pl. 22 [2].

64. Mannoni, *Marble*, figs. 128–132, 256. The sledges are called *lizzature*. In the Pentelikon quarries, similar procedures could be reconstructed (Martin, *Architecture grecque*, 167, fig. 66).

65. Maragioglio, *Piramidi* III, pls. 13 [8], 14 [6, 7]. Also the famous putlog holes in the ascending gallery of the Cheops Pyramid should be mentioned here.

66. Arnold, *Amenemhet III* I, 25.

67. Kuhlmann and Schenkel, *Ibi*, fig. 90; Bernard Bruyère, *Les Fouilles de Deir el Médineh 1928* (Cairo, 1929), 16, pl. 4. This shaft is 30 meters deep and contained the famous sarcophagus of Ankhnesneferibre, the lowering of which must indeed have been a technical feat.

68. Maragioglio, *Piramidi* IV, pl. 7; Borchardt, *Dritte Bauperiode*, pls. 4, 5, 10.

69. Borchardt, *Dritte Bauperiode*, pl. 12. All pyramids of the Fifth and Sixth Dynasties seem to have sets of three portcullises, which are, however, poorly documented.

70. Emery, *Great Tombs* I, 108, pl. 44; Zaki Saad, *Royal Excavations at Saqqara and Helwan, 1941–1945* (Cairo, 1947), pls. 68, 69, 86.

71. Garstang, *Bet Khallaf*, 9, 11, pls. 7, 17, 18.

72. Arnold, *Senwosret I* I, 74, foldout v.

73. Lauer, *Pyramid à degrés* I, figs. 33, 38; Junker, *Giza* v, fig. 30; D. Arnold, *MDAIK* 23 (1968): pl. 2b; Richard A. Fazzini et al., *Ancient Egyptian Art in the Brooklyn Museum* (New York, 1989), 10. The lid of the Henhenet sarcophagus from Deir el-Bahari in the Metropolitan Museum of Art, New York (MMA acc. no. 07.230.1), is composed of four slabs, which were lowered with the help of six pairs of drill holes (Hayes, *Scepter* I, fig. 98).

74. Remains of straps were found in the boat timber mentioned on p. 86.

75. Arnold, *Amenemhet III* I, 86, n. 210.

76. Jéquier, *Deux pyramides*, pls. 8, 17f.

77. A. Barsanti, *ASAE* 1 (1900): 283–284; Choisy, *L'Art de Bâtir*, 127–128, fig. 98; J.-P. Lauer, *ASAE* 51 (1951): 476, pl. II 2; Vyse, *Pyramids* II, 131, figs. 3–5 (Camp-

bell's Tomb); Barsanti, *ASAE* 1 (1901): 161–163, 230–233; Barsanti, *ASAE* 2 (1901): 97–99; Barsanti, *ASAE* 5 (1904): 69–72; Z. Saad, *ASAE* 41 (1942): 388–389; O. R. Rostem, *ASAE* 43 (1943): 351–356; J.-P. Lauer, *ASAE* 52 (1952): 135, pl. 2.

78. Examples are known since the early Fourth Dynasty (Petrie, *Meydum and Memphis*, pl. 10 [4]; Junker, *Giza*, pls. 10–12).

79. Junker, *Giza* IV, 13, fig. 4.

80. Arnold, *Senwosret I* I, pl. 90F.

81. Pit 5117 of Imhotep at Lisht (unpublished data).

82. Pliny, *Natural History* XXXVI.14; Bollinger, *So bauten die Inka*, 149; Coulton, *Greek Architects*, 144.

83. Zakaria Goneim, *The Buried Pyramid* (London, 1956), fig. 25; Lauer, *Hist. Mon.*, 187–188. For a good photograph, see Lauer, *Observations*, pl. 11b.

84. G. Dreyer and N. Swelim, *MDAIK* 38 (1982): figs. 2ff., pls. 11–14.

85. J. De Morgan, *Carte de la nécropole memphite* (Cairo, 1897), pls. 3, 4; *LD* I, 34–35, text 205–209.

86. R. Stadelmann, *MDAIK* 38 (1982): 384–385.

87. Fakhry, *Sneferu I*, fig. 59. Not mentioned in text.

88. Petrie, *Meydum and Memphis*, 6ff., pls. 1–3; Rowe, "Meydum," pls. 12, 31–34.

89. Borchardt, *Entstehung der Pyramide*, 20–24; Maragioglio, *Piramidi* III, pl. 5.

90. Reisner, *Giza* I, 69, n. 1, 82(e); A. Saleh, *MDAIK* 30 (1974): 137.

91. Mastaba G5230 (end of Fourth Dynasty?) (Reisner, *Giza* I, 69, n. 1, 82[e]).

92. M. Lehner, *MDAIK* 41 (1985): 121, with some more suggestions on construction ramps at Giza.

93. R. Engelbach, *ASAE* 33 (1933): 67, pl. 1 [3]; Engelbach, *ASAE* 38 (1938): 372, pl. 58 [1].

94. G. A. Reisner, in *Studies Presented to F. L. Griffith* (London, 1932), 329, pl. 51a.

95. Junker, *Giza* I, 61; *Giza* VII, 122–123; *Giza* IX, 4–7, figs. 2, 3; 219, fig. 100; 225–226, fig. 102; 233, fig. 105; *Giza* X, 68–69, fig. 33; 85, fig. 36.

96. *LD* II, 35.

97. Borchardt, *Re-Heiligtum*, 59–61, plan. For the date of some of the brick walls, see M. Verner, *BIFAO* 87 (1987): 293–297.

98. Probably unpublished.

99. The Sakkarah Expedition, *The Mastaba of Mereruka* II, OIP, no. 39 (Chicago, 1938), pl. 200A. See also Cecil M. Firth and Battiscombe Gunn, *Teti Pyramid Cemeteries: Excavations at Saqqara* (Cairo, 1926), fig. 19.

100. De Morgan, *Carte de la nécropole memphite*, pls. 5, 6; Maragioglio, *Piramidi* VI, 150.

101. Arnold and Winlock, *Mentuhotep*, 28, pls. 21b, 45.

102. *BMMA* 9 (October 1914): 220, fig. 16. For a plan, see *BMMA* 17 (December 1922): fig. 1. See also photos MMA L13–14, 298–302, 359.

103. Arnold, *Senwosret I* II (forthcoming).

104. A similar installation is preserved in the Greek quarries of Pentelikon, with the only difference being that stones there had to be lowered and not pulled up (Martin, *Architecture grecque*, 167, fig. 66).

105. Petrie, *Lahun II*, 9, 12, pls. 8, 13, 15A–C, 25A [8].

106. Arnold, *Qasr el-Sagha*, 14, 19, fig. 9.

107. Gertrude Caton-Thompson and E. W. Gardner, *The Desert Fayum* (London, 1934), 136–137; Arnold, *Qasr el-Sagha*, 24–25, fig. 13, pl. 18.

108. Arnold, *Qasr el-Sagha*, 26.

109. Jean Vercoutter, *Mirgissa* I (Paris, 1970), 178–180, figs. 3–5; 204–214, figs. 11–20. Brian A. MacDonald kindly draws my attention to the *diolkos*, the transport

installation connecting the Gulf of Corinth with the Aegean Sea. There, cargo, but also warships, could be rolled over the Isthmus of Corinth with the help of wheeled platforms on parallel tracks (B. R. MacDonald, *Journal of Hellenic Studies* 106 [1986]: 191–195).

110. Petrie, *Antaeopolis*, pl. 19 [1].

111. Hölscher, *Chephren*, fig. 59.

112. I. M. E. Shaw, in Barry J. Kemp, *Amarna Reports* IV (London, 1987), 160–163, figs. 13.1–13.5.

113. J. De Morgan et al., *Catalogue des monuments et inscriptions de l'Égypte antique* I (Vienna, 1894), 64; Engelbach, *Problems of the Obelisks*, fig. 26. Also mentioned in Arthur E. P. Weigall, *A Guide to the Antiquities of Upper Egypt* (New York, 1910), 408; *Baedeker's Egypt* (London, 1929), 382. The roads are visible in Engelbach, *Aswan Obelisk*, pl. 4 [4].

114. R. Klemm and D. Klemm et al., *MDAIK* 40 (1984): fig. 2, pl. 11b.

115. A. Lansing, *BMMA* 30, part 2 (November 1935): 15, fig. 16.

116. U. Hölscher, *MDAIK* 12 (1943): 144; Paul Barguet, *Le Temple d'Amon-Re à Karnak* (Cairo, 1962), 46; J.-C. Golvin and R. Vergnieux, *Hommages a François Daumas* (Montpelier, Vt., 1988), 302, n. 10.

117. Legrain, *Karnak*, 35–38, figs. 1, 2, 4, 7, 8, 26–31; Golvin and Goyon, *Karnak*, 105–107.

118. Choisy, *L'Art de bâtir*, 86–93.

119. U. Hölscher, *MDAIK* 12 (1943): 139–149.

120. *Rekhmire*, pl. 60.

121. Clarke and Engelbach suggest three columns, but it could as well be the front of a pylon with niches for the flagpoles (*CEAEM*, 93). U. Verhoeven suggests that the ramp is leading up to a brick kiln (*MDAIK* 43 [1987]: 264).

122. Gardiner, *Egyptian Hieratic Texts* I, 16–17, 31–33, pl. 14.3–14.10; Fischer-Elfert, *Anastasi I*, 121–124.

123. Engelbach, *Problem of the Obelisks*, 90; W.-F. Reineke, *Zur Ziegelrampe des Papyrus Anastasi I, Altorientalische Forschungen* II (Berlin, 1975), 5–9; A. Badawy, *ZÄS* 110 (1983): 12–15; Fischer-Elfert, *Anastasi I*, 124–132.

124. Gardiner, *Egyptian Hieratic Texts* I, p. 31*.

125. See, for example, Goyon, *Khéops;* M. Isler, *JARCE* 22 (1985): 129–142; Isler, *JARCE* 24 (1987): 95–112.

126. Borchardt, *Entstehung der Pyramide*, 20–24; Petrie, *Ancient Egypt* (1930): 35; Lauer, *Observations*, 55–58; Lauer, *Mystère*, 280–283.

127. Goyon, *Khéops*, 71–75.

128. Choisy, *L'Art de bâtir*, fig. 87; D. Arnold, *MDAIK* 37 (1981): fig. 4; M. Isler, *JARCE* 22 (1985): fig. 20.

129. N. F. Wheeler, *Antiquity* 9 (1935): 5–21, 161–189, 292–304; D. Dunham, *Archaeology* 9 (1965): 159–165; Goyon, *Khéops*, 82–86, figs. 24, 73, 85.

130. Goyon takes the brick enclosure wall of the tomb of Khentkaus for the remains of a spiral ramp (*Khéops*, 69). But I see no reason for that.

131. Goyon, seeing this problem, assumed the existence of a narrow shaft in the center of the pyramid to lower a plumb bob (ibid.). Except for a round hole (30 centimeters deep and 15 centimeters in diameter) on top of the Meidum Pyramid (probably serving for a measuring point; see A. Robert, *ASAE* 3 [1902]: 78), no such central shafts have ever been observed on the summit of pyramids.

132. Hölscher, *Chephren*, frontispiece; Choisy, *L'Art de bâtir*, fig. 87 (ramps in form of a staircase); Petrie, *Ancient Egypt* (1930): 36–37 (for the topmost part of the

pyramid only); Grinsell, *Egyptian Pyramids,* 66, fig. 7; August Mencken, *Designing and Building the Great Pyramid* (Baltimore, 1963), 40, fig. 13c.

133. P. Garde-Hansen, *Ingeniören* 1 (1974): 18, 33; D. Arnold, *MDAIK* 37 (1981): 22–23, figs. 3, 4; Edwards, *Pyramids,* 290, fig. 60.

134. Petrie, *Ancient Egypt* (1930): 37, fig. 2.

135. These gaps are generally understood to enable the erection of the core masonry during a period when the work on the crypt and the entrance corridor was not yet completed, work carried out in an open trench.

CHAPTER IV   *Building*

FOUNDATIONS[1]

This chapter on the foundations of Pharaonic stone buildings, although primarily descriptive, is included because of the foundation's close relationship to the more technical aspects of construction. By providing a flat and level building ground, foundations prevent sagging of walls on unstable ground. Although Engelbach has asserted that Egyptian architects were poor layers of foundation,[2] in many cases quite efficient foundations were constructed. The best proof of this is the innumerable buildings still standing after 3000 to 4000 years. What Egyptian architects did not foresee, of course, was the slow but continual rising of the alluvium and the level of both ground water and inundation, factors that contributed to the undermining of the foundations and the final collapse of many of these structures. Another factor,[3] which was generally not disregarded but underrated, was the enormous weight and thrust of a huge building on its building ground; the resulting problems could sometimes become evident even during construction.

The foundations of the oldest known stone buildings in the Third Dynasty are still rudimentary. In the precinct of Djoser, they consist of one course of slabs that serves as both pavement and foundation. At the location of walls, a shallow trench was dug to receive a slab that is slightly thicker than the surrounding masonry. There are already some walls with very deep foundations of rough fieldstones set in mortar.[4] The granite burial chamber of the Step Pyramid is resting on twenty-four peculiar little pillars of rough fieldstone slabs. The sloping layers of the step pyramids of Djoser and Sekhemkhet, and those at Zawyet el-Aryan and Zawyiet el-Maiyitin, do not have any foundations but are resting on inward-inclined steps dug into the conglomerate of the desert in such a way that the outermost step is the lowest and the innermost one the highest.[5] Some of the smaller pyramids—like those at Seila, Zawyet el-Maiyitin, and el-Kula—are built on a leveled rock surface, again without special precautions for foundations.[6]

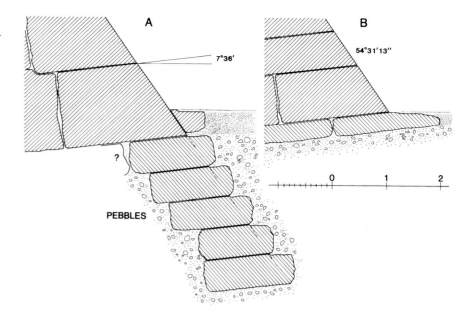

Fig. 4.1 Foundations of the Bent Pyramid at the corners (A) and along the sides (B).

The foundations of the pyramids of the early Fourth Dynasty still consist of only one to three courses of blocks, laid into the foundation trench that was dug into the desert conglomerate or sand without protruding much in front of the base line of the casing.[7] Although no damage can be observed at Meidum and the Red Pyramid, the Bent Pyramid seems to have suffered so heavily from sagging that an outer coat had to be added (figs. 4.1, 5.31),[8] with foundations consisting now of five courses of blocks about 3 meters deep at the corners and one course only along the sides of the pyramid. The Giza pyramids, however, were erected on a solid limestone plateau, so that a rock core could be used and practically no foundations were necessary, except a kind of leveling course underlying the first casing course and sunk into a shallow trench.

The mortuary temple of Mycerinus had to be erected on a sloping plane, and thus needed a solid substructure, according to Reisner:

> It consisted of enormous blocks of limestone, apparently as they came from the quarry but bruised by transport and loosely set together without any binding material. The interstices were filled with masons' limestone chips, debris, or quarry debris. The surface of the bedrock had been dressed but not leveled to take this platform. The platform varied in depth to equalize the irregularity of the bed rock, and produce an approximately level surface. . . . As the top of the upper course was 86 cm below the floor, the depth of the foundation platform was 349 cm.[9]

From this period on, one can observe the custom of embedding the lowest layer of the foundation blocks into a more or less heavy fill of clean desert sand. The strength of that fill varies. Sometimes it is only a means to adjust and level the stones. Sometimes it is a layer half a meter thick. Its purpose was twofold: on the one hand, the equal bedding of the foundation blocks was produced; and on the other hand, the religious intention to establish a temple on a pure "primeval hill" of sand filled in during the foundation ceremonies was achieved.[10]

Quite interesting are the foundations of the Mastabat el-Fara'un. They consist of two separate foundations, one of a layer of huge blocks for the core and the other for the casing, which has the same depth but is constructed of two courses covered by a pavement of fine limestone to carry the casing blocks.[11]

Unusually heavy are the foundations for the crypt of an unknown king of the Fourth Dynasty at Zawyet el-Aryan. The bottom of the construction shaft for the crypt was filled with four layers of huge granite blocks, measuring altogether 4.50 meters.[12] But it seems likely that this result represents a change in plan, according to which the floor of the burial chamber was raised considerably.

In the Fourth Dynasty, foundations for rectangular pillars frequently were prepared as pits of considerable depth cut into the bedrock or desert surface, into which the shaft of the pillar was inserted. In places that consisted of rock, as at Giza, no further additions had to be made.[13] But in less solid ground, a stone box had to be constructed to house the foot of the pillars, as in the valley temple of the Bent Pyramid.[14]

Little is known about foundations of the pyramids and temples of the Fifth and Sixth Dynasties. The pyramid of Niuserra has only one foundation course set into a trench of the desert surface, and it was covered by a thinner leveling course, which continues in front of the pyramid as pavement of the pyramid court; both together measure only 1.20 meters in thickness.[15] The lower temple of the sun temple of Userkaf has a solid foundation platform in what one could call the classic system of the Old and Middle Kingdoms: one subfoundation course and one foundation course, covered by a thinner course of pavement blocks or slabs, altogether 1.13 meters thick.[16] As far as one can see from the surface, the pyramid temples of those dynasties have foundations of up to three courses and not always as a solid platform, but placed only under the main walls and structures.

In the temple of Mentuhotep at Deir el-Bahari, which is built on solid *tafl* bedrock (fig. 5.22),[17] columns and walls rest on separate foundations, which are only one course deep and at the same time serve as the pavement.

The pyramids of the Twelfth Dynasty again had up to three foundation courses of 1-meter-high blocks, set into wide foundation trenches and protruding about 1 to 2 cubits in front of the foot of the casing.[18] Only the pyramid of Illahun could be erected on a rock core, again with only one foundation course. The pyramid of Amenemhat III at Dahshur had a foundation trench reaching 2 cubits in front of the foundation. Against the outer corners of the trench, brick walls were set, which might have been whitewashed and used for drawing the construction lines for the pyramid (see p. 12).

Stone and brick foundations of the Middle Kingdom were not always built on completely leveled ground. At the pyramid sites of Dahshur and Lisht, the bedrock preserved its more or less undulating surface and the foundations occasionally climb down deep into the depressions. This procedure fits well into the picture of a period of rationalization of work.

Foundation trenches walled up with brick retaining walls also exist in the

New Kingdom and later. They seem to have been especially made in alluvial soil to prevent percolating water from carrying away the sand of the foundation trenches.[19] Occasionally, bricks were also used for massive foundations of stone buildings,[20] but this was most likely due to a temporary shortage of stone.

In the foundation trenches of the funerary complexes of Amenemhat I and Senwosret I, we see for the first time the custom of "leveling" the ground by spreading smaller stones or slabs, some of which were reused from older buildings (fig. 4.2).[21] This may be the origin of the unfortunate custom of building up the foundation in several courses of rather small blocks, which was found in some buildings of the New Kingdom, even in huge monuments. A good example is the foundation platform of the Lux-

Fig. 4.3 Clipped section through the foundation platform of the Luxor temple, filled with reused material.

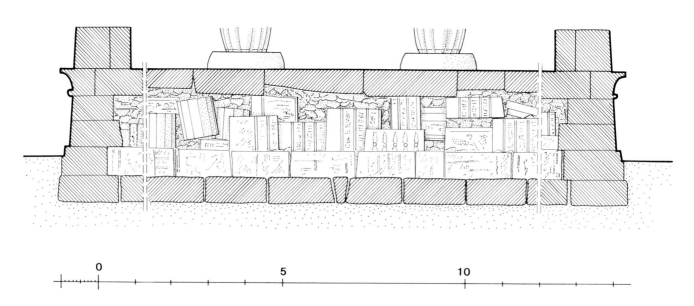

0   5   10

or temple, which consists of a foundation course of newly dressed blocks, several courses of reused blocks, and the final course of paving blocks (fig. 4.3).[22]

Another reason for this method was the availability of reusable material from older buildings. Such blocks—in proportion to the smaller size of the older buildings—had much smaller dimensions (fig. 4.4). Quite frequently, column drums, stelae, and even sculptures were packed into such foundations. These smaller blocks very often do not extend beyond the base of the building that rests on them.[23] Even small pillars of brick were occasionally used as foundations for heavy columns.[24] And they certainly do not add to the stability of the construction, because a slightly uneven placement of such stones leads to uneven pressure and cracking of the overlaying blocks.

The use of older inscribed or decorated blocks certainly was a measure of economy. An afterthought might have been that foundations consisting of blocks "enriched" with the magic of religious texts and pictures might be good for the new structure. Scholars like A. Varille and C. Robichon were even convinced that the exact placement of conspicuous blocks followed certain patterns.[25] This may have occasionally been the case, but it was certainly not carried out in such ingenious programs as conceived by Schwaller de Lubicz.[26]

Foundation trenches regularly contained a clean, specially sieved desert sand in which the foundation blocks were floated.[27] This sand provided protection against the infiltration of ground water and against earthquakes and was furthermore a religious symbol for the primeval hill, on the sand of which a sanctuary should be built.[28] Engelbach reproached the builders of Karnak for not having prepared adequate foundations for their obelisks, because at least eight of those left in place by the Romans eventually fell.[29] Actually, the foundations would have been sufficient were it not for earthquakes and cracks in the shafts of the obelisks, which acceler-

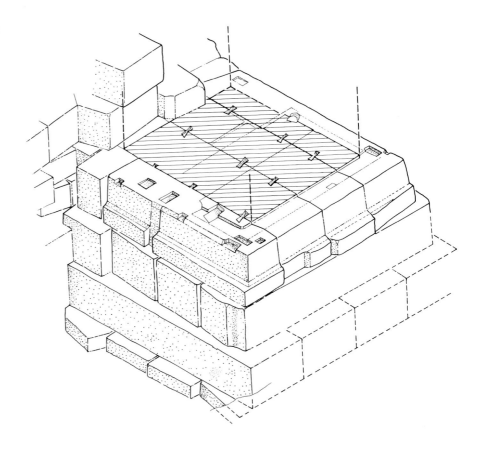

ated their collapse. For example, the obelisks of Amenhotep III in front of Pylon III were standing on a base resting on four courses of four elongated blocks each, and each course laid crosswise, the whole 3.5 meters deep (fig. 4.5).[30]

The general view is that foundations of Pharaonic buildings were made separately for each part of the structure—that is, separate foundations for walls, columns, and so forth—unlike buildings of Ptolemaic and Roman times, which had huge foundation platforms of great depth and many

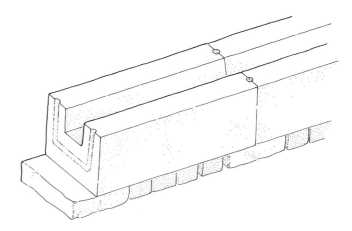

Fig. 4.6 Water drain around the tomb of Mentuhotep at Lisht, with stone foundations under the joints and U-shaped grooves for plaster insulation between the joints.

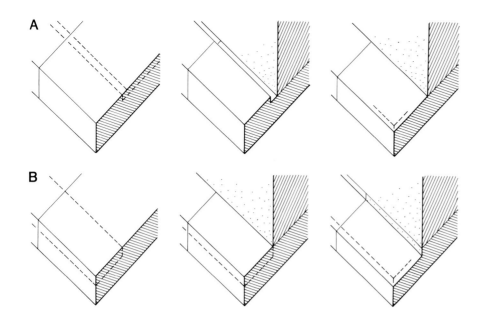

Fig. 4.7 (A) Laying the wall blocks into a sunken bed or socket. (B) Setting the wall blocks on the flattened surface.

courses of well-dressed blocks.[31] This view might be correct if we compare, for example, the foundations of the complex of Djoser with those of the temples of Philae. But contrasting patterns are also evident. Foundation platforms were built—perhaps of slightly lesser dimensions—from the Old Kingdom onward.[32] And it seems that the Kiosk of Trajan on Philae stands on foundation courses that follow each wall, with a fill in the center.[33] Unusual structures, such as drain blocks, required special foundations (fig. 4.6). Foundation slabs were restricted to the area beneath joints. Between the slabs, bricks were laid.

LAYING THE BLOCKS

The laying of blocks created various problems, depending on the location of the blocks in the walls, roofs, tomb chambers, and pyramids and, of course, depending on the shape, size, and weight of the blocks and the material. The most common task must have been the building of a wall on a foundation of stone blocks or slabs. The normal procedure would entail a number of steps.

First, after the foundation blocks were laid, their upper surface was dressed completely flat. The extra stock was removed only *after* the building of the wall, and then a wide bed or socket for the wall was cut into it. For that purpose, a double line was measured and marked on the surface to be dressed, one for the foot line of the wall blocks and another perhaps a few centimeters in front of it, because the socket would have to be somewhat wider than the wall itself (fig. 4.7A).[34] There are cases, however, where so much extra stock was left on top of the foundation that in the end the wall would actually stand on top of a small step (fig. 4.7B).[35] With such a foundation, it would have been sufficient to flatten its surface and mark the front line of the wall. In both cases, the accurate horizontal level of the bed would have to be checked with the square level and boning rod.

Thick walls occasionally have a core of rough masonry. In that case, only

the bed for the casing blocks was leveled, and the emplacement of the core blocks was left standing,[36] indicating the original height of the foundation block.

Second, corner blocks and some stones in between, essential for keeping a straight line, were set first (fig. 4.8). Only their lower surface and the two side faces had to be completely dressed before setting. The rear, top, and front of the block were left undressed. The lower front edge would have to be clearly visible for an exact alignment on the front line of the wall.

Third, by stretching the cord again, this time on the level of the first course, the actual front alignment was measured and marked again, as it had been on the foundations. This procedure would have been more complicated when the actual corner of the wall was a torus, because the exact corner would be hidden by the extra stock for the torus.

Fourth, the normal wall blocks could now be maneuvered into place. The blocks were moved close to their destination on rollers in the direction of the wall. Moving the blocks the last few centimeters was achieved with levers (Figs. 4.10–4.11). For that purpose, mortises had been cut into the lower edge of the block being moved or into the surface over which it had to be pushed.[37] These strengthened the grip and effectiveness of the lever. The procedure could be further smoothed by using liquid mortar poured on the lower bed and in between the vertical joints. Reisner describes the action:

> The blocks of stone in the core walls, like those in the foundations, had been brought up on sledges from the adjacent quarry, still with the rough surfaces left by quarrying. Each stone had probably been turned over in loading on the sledge so that its strata ran vertically. Brought to its intended place in the wall, the exposed side which was to be the bottom and the end which was to fit the end of the stone already set were dressed flat. The block appears to have been then turned over on its long axis to fall into the place prepared and was

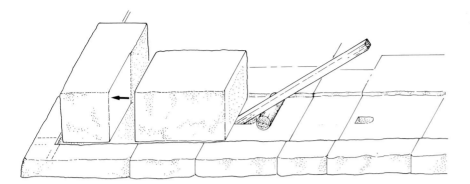

Fig. 4.9 Pushing wall blocks into position with the help of levers.

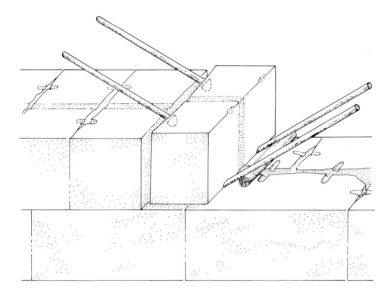

Fig. 4.10 Elaborate system of lever holes at the *chapelle rouge* of Hatshepsut at Karnak.

Fig. 4.11 A casing block of the Cheops Pyramid levered into position sideward. The lever hole was afterward sealed with plaster.

Fig. 4.12 When two working teams laid the blocks from two corners against the center, gaps could appear. They had to be closed with smaller blocks, as was the casing of the pyramid of Meidum.

Fig. 4.13 Grooves for inserting a keystone with the help of a rope, at the pyramid of Amenemhat III at Dahshur.

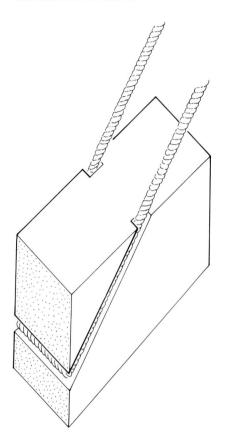

Fig. 4.14 Reused block at the pyramid of Senwosret I, originally dressed with grooves for positioning it with two ropes in upright position.

adjusted with wooden levers, probably having been "floated" on plaster. The place for the next block was then prepared by dressing the exposed end of the stone just set and the floor or the top of the course below.[38]

The last block to be set in a course had to be carefully dressed in order to fit into the remaining gap. Since the ancient Egyptians did not have the equipment (like lifting tongs or iron lewises), they could not lower this block into place from above but had to roll or lever it into place from the front (fig. 4.12).

In special cases, shifting into position could have been carried out from two sides, as indicated by lever mortises on opposite sides,[39] especially for larger blocks. In other places, it may have been necessary to lower a block from above with ropes (fig. 4.13). To sling the ropes around the blocks more safely and to prevent the ropes from being crushed or to enable their removal, two or three channels or grooves could have been cut for them around the block (fig. 4.14). But these grooves are known only from such pieces as sarcophagus lids,[40] pavement slabs,[41] and repair stones, not from regular wall blocks.

A fifth step may have involved the structural use of mortar. Although in Egyptian stone building stability was achieved by vertical pressure from the superpositioning of material, the use of mortar was not uncommon. In addition to the nonstructural use of mortar as lubrication between blocks when being positioned or "floated" into place, there are many examples of mortar filled into gapping joints in order to create a solid mass of masonry from the core masonry of pyramids, from the time of the building at Meidum on.

Blocks intended to be visible were occasionally set into mortar. We even find joints that were originally kept open by inserting pieces of wood until the mortar was filled in (Figs. 4.15, 4.16). The wood was fitted into shallow grooves cut into the touching surfaces.[42] Metal shims, which were frequently used in Greek, Roman, and medieval building, appeared only late in Egyptian architecture.[43]

Pointed stripes 10 to 30 centimeters wide made for the application of mortar to touching surfaces appear in the Twelfth Dynasty,[44] but are much rarer than in Ptolemaic and Roman buildings.[45] From measuring the length of these grooves, Golvin has shown that at each laying process, several blocks could be floated into position, as at Dendera, over distances of more than 3 meters. Vertical grooves for filling in mortar are rather rare in Pharaonic stonework.[46]

In general, one can see that the relatively minor role of mortar in Pharaonic stone masonry did not promote careful or complicated preparations for filling the joints between blocks, quite in contrast to the examples we know from Ptolemaic and Roman buildings.

Sixth, the laying of the following upper course required that the surface of the first course be completely leveled and dressed. Thereafter, the foot line for the lower front edge of the upper course was marked on the top face of the lower course. Typically for Egyptian masonry, the top face of a course was not brought to one level, but was dressed in steps in order to receive blocks of a greater height. This was done for reasons of economy of material.

Often, each course has a different height, even in pyramid casing (see the list on p. 167), suggesting that blocks of similar height had been arranged in the storage areas to permit speedy transport and setting in the walls. Without this preparation, builders would have received blocks of different dimensions, which would have required additional dressing and resulted in a waste of material. There are examples of leveling courses, however, as in the mastaba of Ptahshepses (fig. 4.87). They consist of thin slabs set on top of courses of uneven height. The top faces of these slabs were then carefully brought to the same level to create a fresh starting point.

The normal way to lift a block from ground level into position high up in the building, however, would have been by the help of a separate ramp or on the masonry itself, which could frequently have been used as a staircase.[47] This last method was not always feasible, as Reisner, for example, observed:

> For all the stones of the first course, the sledge was dragged on the surface of the rock or the foundation platform. For the second and third courses, construction planes of rubble packed with limestone rubbish were used, on which the sledges were dragged up to the higher levels.
>
> The condition in which the use of these construction planes left the spaces between the walls was clearly proved by the unfinished room. This was completely filled to the top of the second course with worn boulders and rubbish which formed the construction platform on which the stones of course three had been dragged to their places but this platform covered another platform at a lower level. The approach to these platforms was through a gap left in the western wall of the room, and I conclude that this gap was reached on the outside by an inclined plane.
>
> The effect of this method of construction was to leave the rooms of the temple completely filled with the material of the construction platforms when the core walls had been finished. It is obvious that this material had to be removed before the granite casing could be begun. Similar construction planes

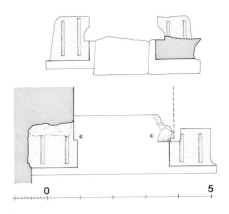

Fig. 4.15 Grooves under the door jambs of the Ramesseum for inserting wood to keep the space open for mortar.

Fig. 4.16 Grooves for inserting wood during the filling of the joints with plaster, at the causeway of Pepy II at Saqqara.

and platforms had to be built, at any rate for the granite courses, above the second course and for the roof, filling the rooms a second time up to the roof. This second set of platforms was removed gradually in dressing the surfaces of the granite casing from the top down.[48]

Thus for each course, the building operation actually took place on a kind of ground level. This method was essential because wooden falsework would not have permitted the Egyptians to handle the enormous stones that they used for their buildings, such as the architraves and roofing slabs of buildings like the Osireion at Abydos or hypostyle temple halls.

The laying of blocks of extraordinary size seems to have presented no real problems for Egyptian builders. Also, the lifting of core and casing blocks of the pyramids to great heights seems to have been routine work for them. Greater problems were certainly created by heavy blocks in awkward positions—for example, placing blocks underground in narrow caves and shafts, where the use of ramps, long levers, and crowds of workers would have been impossible. One such case was probably the setting of the roofing blocks on top of the burial crypt of some pyramids (fig. 4.17). Borchardt estimates that the roofing blocks on top of the chamber of Niuserra weigh about 90 tons,[49] and one of the roofing blocks of Djedkara Isesi weighs 24 tons.[50] Furthermore, sixty such blocks had to be built into the roof of the chamber of Niuserra. In the pyramids of Sahura and Neferirkara, the chambers were located aboveground, which certainly made the laying of the roof blocks easier. But in those of Userkaf, Niuserra, Djedkara, Unas, Tety, and Pepy II, the chambers were built into deep shafts underground, and some of the roofing blocks—perhaps all of them—had to be lowered accordingly. Borchardt thought that this was done with the help of huge brackets, an idea that we cannot substantiate. One would rather suppose that the blocks were lowered down the slope of the (then still-open) entrance cut. The first blocks, which were along the south side, had to be pushed against the short sides of the chambers in the east and west, with the following ones added in the center. A combination of levers and ropes anchored at the upper edge of the shaft would have been used to lift the blocks into their half-upright, half-sloping position until they could be supported by temporary masonry from below. In the same way, the row of blocks along the north side would have to be added, until the last block— the one in the axis of the entrance cut—could be fitted in. Thereafter, the lower end of the level of the sloping ramp of the entrance cut would have been lifted to the level of the gable of the first layer of the roofing blocks, so that the next layer could be brought in. Open gaps in some of the gables of these chambers indicate that these gigantic blocks could not always be joined perfectly.

JOINTS

The earliest real stone masonry, that of the Third Dynasty, was still influenced by brick architecture (fig. 4.18). The blocks were small, and the stones were square and brick-shaped. The side face of the blocks was still

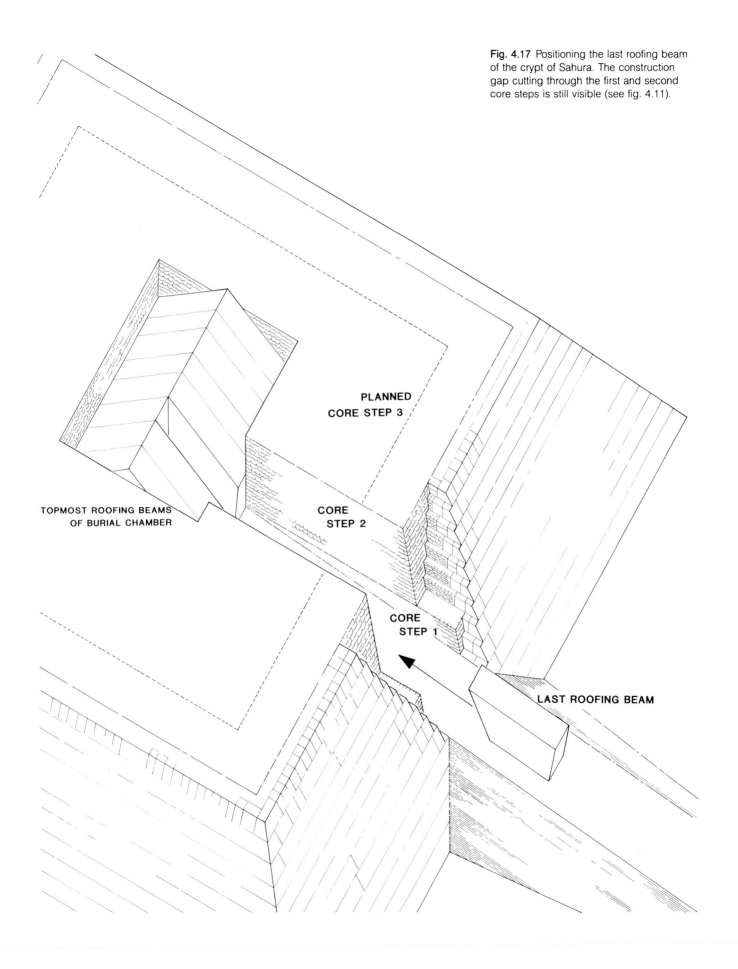

Fig. 4.17 Positioning the last roofing beam of the crypt of Sahura. The construction gap cutting through the first and second core steps is still visible (see fig. 4.11).

PLANNED
CORE STEP 3

CORE
STEP 2

CORE
STEP 1

TOPMOST ROOFING BEAMS
OF BURIAL CHAMBER

LAST ROOFING BEAM

Fig. 4.18 Masonry of the Third Dynasty.

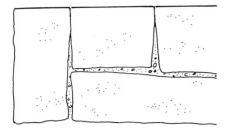

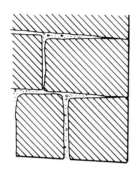

Fig. 4.19 Transferring the angle of an obliquely cut block to the following undressed block with a wooden instrument.

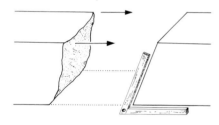

Fig. 4.20 Transferring the angle of an obliquely cut block to the following undressed block by measuring distances.

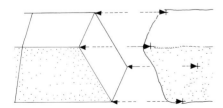

vertical, and the bedding joints were horizontal (if not inclined inward, as in the pyramids of the Third Dynasty).

The discovery that the use of larger blocks could reduce the number of trained masons probably led to their use in the Fourth Dynasty. Only in one later instance, during the Amarna period, were relatively small and more or less equally sized blocks used, the so-called *talatat*, measuring 3 × 3 × 7 palms. The reason for their use is not quite clear, but perhaps it was to speed up the building process. At all other times, building blocks were generally *not* based on a standard.

This practice, of course, had consequences for laying the blocks. After laying the first course of a wall, the top surface of the blocks—still uneven—was cut and dressed for the second course. Because the blocks of the lower course had different heights and it would have been a waste of stone to cut all of them down to the same height for each block to be laid, an individual stretch was measured and prepared. If necessary, a step or socket was cut into the lower blocks in order to accommodate the upper one.[51] Thus quite frequently rectangular masonry of stepped courses was the result, naturally with horizontal bedding joints.

These joints were not always horizontal. In inclined corridors, like pyramid passages,[52] or at raising ramps[53] or internal staircases,[54] the bedding joints normally follow the inclination, with the result that the raising joints are no longer vertical but are at a right angle to the slope. There are also examples where the roofing slabs on top of an inclined corridor are placed vertically, with only a sloping lower face.[55]

Frequently in architecture of the Old and Middle Kingdoms, and also in later buildings,[56] joint faces are not vertical. They are at a right angle to the front faces, but oblique in one or every other direction. In ancient Greek architecture, this masonry would be called trapezoidal and possibly isodomic if block heights are equal. This strange feature, which certainly meant more measuring and more time for the masons, can be explained only by economy of material. The cutting down of rough and irregularly shaped quarry blocks to rectangular building stones would, of course, have reduced the blocks considerably in size.

We do not know exactly how the masons achieved two corresponding and neatly fitted planes on two neighboring blocks. Clarke and Engelbach tried to show with the help of drawings and even models[57] that the blocks of one course had been assembled on chains of rockers (fig. 6.30). This temporary positioning on movable devices would have helped the masons to pull the joints closely together and to adjust the blocks, also in height, quite easily. This seems to be a possibility, but we have no proof that rockers of such size existed or that they were used for such a purpose.

In Greek architecture, polygonal masonry was used since Mycenaean times. The oblique joints were perhaps produced with the help of a stone angle, two connected laths that pivoted so that an existing oblique angle could easily be transferred to a rough block, which could then be dressed accordingly (fig. 4.19).[58]

Stocks has also suggested another possible method.[59] The undressed block was pushed from the side against an oblique joint, but kept at a distance that still allowed work on the rough block. With the help of boning rods, the necessary distance between the four corners of the side faces could be checked, and the block could then be dressed. In truth, boning rods would not have been necessary for such an operation, as any string would have worked as well (fig. 4.20). After determining the four intended corners of the rough block, they would have to be connected by dressing the rough area in between, which could be checked by a straight edge or ruler. Thereafter, the extra stock between them could be removed. This procedure would have required turning over the block, since work along the lower edge would otherwise not have been possible. This work would probably not have been done on the wall but on the ground, which leads to the equally unpleasant assumption that block courses had already been arranged and prepared on the ground before being built into the masonry. For the joints it was somewhat easier, however, as the oblique joints fit exactly only at the front edge but were executed more carelessly farther in.

Since cutting oblique joints was troublesome, it was not carried out unless the size of the block or its material and quality (Tura limestone or granite) made it worthwhile. In pyramid casing, oblique joints are therefore more frequent in granite[60] than in limestone.[61]

The bedding joints, even of well-dressed blocks, often show traces of mortar, which was apparently not used to glue the blocks together, but to grease the upper block when it was being pushed into position. In irregular masonry—for example, fieldstone or core masonry—the blocks were bedded into heavy layers of mortar and the gaps filled with chip and stones. Grooves for filling in liquid mortar at the side faces of blocks can be observed, but are less numerous (fig. 4.21).[62] At a roofing block in the entrance corridor of the pyramid of Amenemhat III at Dahshur, a groove started with two vertical branches that united in the center below (fig. 4.22).[63] This unusual type of groove reminds us of the joints of drainage blocks that were quite common in the South Cemetery of Lisht and were made waterproof by U-shaped plaster grooves (fig. 4.6). Sometimes these grooves may not have been used for adding mortar but for releasing surplus mortar that would be caught at the lower edge of two blocks when they were being pushed together.[64]

Close joints could be achieved in several ways. Traces of saws along the front edge of the raising joint and saw marks at the foot line of a wall on the surface of the foundation indicate that saws were used to trim remaining irregularities at the front edge.[65] Lauer thinks that a sheet of copper with quartz sand would have been sufficient.[66]

Another labor-saving method to obtain accurate joining of blocks had been invented in the Old Kingdom—anathyrosis, later a common feature in Greek architecture.[67] Contact was not achieved over the whole surface but only along a contact band at the front edge, while the center of the joint face was left rough and slightly concave.[68] In examples from the treasury of Karnak-Nord, the contact was achieved by concave side faces and a slightly projecting edge (fig. 4.23).[69]

Levers had to be placed on the side faces of blocks because wall blocks were generally set from the side.[70] Along the foot of the side faces, one or

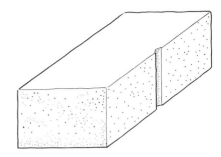

Fig. 4.21 Grooves for filling joints with liquid mortar, at the treasury of Thutmosis I at Karnak.

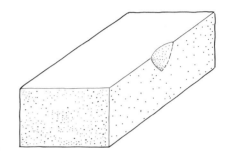

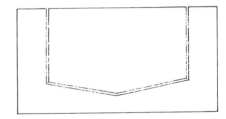

Fig. 4.22 U-shaped groove for filling in liquid mortar for insulation. Roofing blocks of the entrance passage of the pyramid of Amenemhat III at Dahshur.

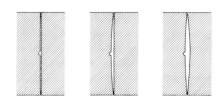

Fig. 4.23 Shapes of joints at the treasury of Thutmosis I at Karnak.

more mortises were cut (fig. 4.11).[71] In masonry of high quality, such as the casing of the Cheops Pyramid, these mortises were closed again with small stones and mortar.[72]

Close joining was frequently neglected, however, especially in the huge buildings of the New Kingdom, where the stone broke easily during handling or not enough time was left for more careful work. The results are gaping joints and crevices along the front faces of blocks, which had to be hidden by extensive use of mortar.[73] In buildings of such irregular and neglected joining, one cannot see how the builders could have planned the joint position. There are joints, however, that suggest that the builders intended not to interfere with essential features of the architecture[74] and decoration.[75] One guiding principle seems to have been to avoid cutting up the faces of the gods and the king.

Engelbach raised the interesting question of vertical joints separating two sections of a building.[76] For example, the doorway of a pylon sometimes is separated from the masonry of the two towers (Karnak Pylons VII and X; Medinet Habu I and Ethiopian pylon; Karnak Pylon I). In other buildings, the masonry of the doorway abuts the masonry of the towers (Karnak Pylons II, IV, V, VIII, and IX; Khonsu; Kalabsha; Philae; Edfu). The reason for the separation might have been that the doorways were constructed considerably earlier or were built of different material from the towers (granite in sandstone or sandstone in brick). The possibility that the separation was planned in order to prevent the doorway from being dragged down when the towers would sink somewhat by their own weight seems to be ruled out by the fact that the cornice of the doorway always passes into the masonry of the towers and was broken by the settling of the different pieces of masonry.

CONNECTING BLOCKS

Blocks that were thought by the ancient builders—sometimes without reason—to be under special stress were connected not only with mortar but sometimes with additional devices. The most common block connection is the dovetail cramp (or clamp). The first examples that we know were developed to connect the architraves with each other or with the pillar or column below (fig. 4.24). Copper cramps are found in the valley temple of Chephren, set into the underside of the architraves and into the top of the pillars, where they were fixed with an additional vertical pin.[77]

In the mortuary temple of Unas, the cramps were already placed in the positions that they would have from then on (fig. 4.25)[78]—the top surface of the architraves with a vertical pin under each tail. Additional dowels had to be added to connect the architraves to the top of the columns. They were cylindrical and vertical. Similar dowels for fixing architraves on columns can be observed in the mortuary temples of Userkaf,[79] Sahura,[80] Niuserra,[81] and Djedkara. Ordinary wooden dovetail cramps are used in all later architraves—for example, in the hypostyle hall of Karnak. In the same hall, the half-drums of the columns (or the smaller segments of them) were also connected by up to five cramps.[82]

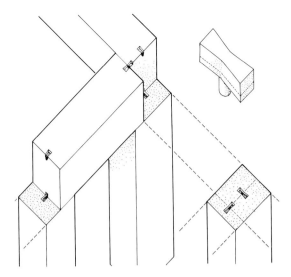

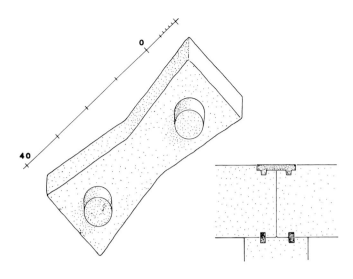

Fig. 4.24 Granite pillars and architraves of the Chephren valley temple connected with bronze cramps, reconstructed from the shape of the cramp slots.

Fig. 4.25 Bronze cramp from the mortuary temple of Unas, reconstructed from the shape of the cramp slot.

Other blocks under special lateral stress were the foundation blocks of obelisk bases, which were interconnected with several especially big dovetail cramps.[83] The longest cramps known are those of the colonnade of Shoshenq at Karnak, which measure about 1.5 meters in length.[84]

The more common use of cramps starts first in the Middle Kingdom—for example, in the temple of Mentuhotep Nebhepetera at Deir el-Bahari.[85] At the pyramids of the Twelfth Dynasty, all the casing blocks were already connected by cramps (figs. 4.26, 4.27).[86] In other buildings, only the corner blocks were secured in that way.[87] But special care was always taken for more delicate constructions, such as cornice blocks or roofing slabs (figs. 4.28, 4.29).[88]

In rarer cases, cramps were also affixed to vertical stone surfaces (fig. 4.30). Since the cramps could easily fall out and would be visible, this usage was restricted to less conspicuous blocks or to repairs of cracked blocks.[89] In general, cramps are not used in Pharaonic buildings as abundantly as in constructions of Ptolemaic and Roman times, in which all blocks were usually so connected and in all directions (fig. 4.31).[90]

In Pharaonic building, bronze cramps are known only from the monuments of Chephren, Unas, and Hatshepsut and at Tanis.[91] Those of Chephren were 30 centimeters long, 10 centimeters wide, and weighed about 20 to 25 kilograms. Those of Hatshepsut were cast directly into the cramp slots. Sometimes cramps are inscribed with the royal cartouches of the builder (figs. 4.26, 4.32). At the pyramid of Senwosret I, the two names of the king alternate from one cramp to the next.[92] The wood used for cramps is normally acacia, but sometimes precious imported woods such as ebony were selected.[93]

Since the cramps were slightly different in size, the grooves had to be cut to the individual size of the cramps after the setting of the blocks. Naturally,

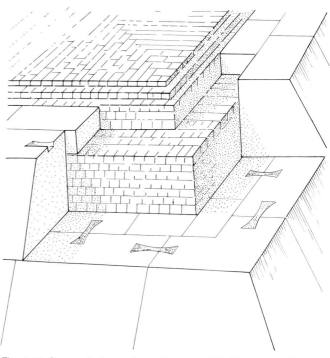

Fig. 4.26 Inscribed wooden cramps in the casing of the pyramid of Senwosret I at Lisht.

Fig. 4.27 Cramps in the casing of the pyramid of Senwosret III at Dahshur.

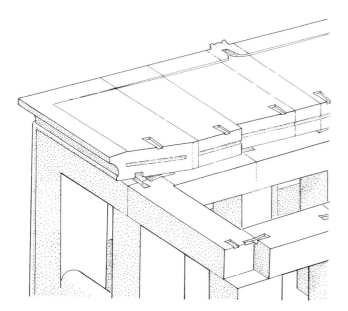

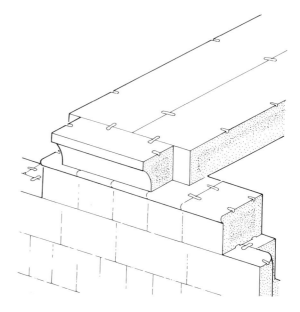

Fig. 4.28 Cramp slots in the roofing slabs of the *chapelle blanche* of Senwosret I at Karnak.

Fig. 4.29 Cramp slots in the *chapelle rouge* of Hatshepsut at Karnak.

the cramp mortises were slightly larger than the cramps, so there was room for gypsum and small flakes of stone. The plaster regularly shows a pink color, the origin and purpose of which has not yet been explained.

Stone dowels were used less frequently than cramps. They do occur, however, either in dovetail shape (fig. 4.33)[94] or as spherical dowels for the connection of architraves and columns in the Old Kingdom. The connection of the column shaft and the base could also be strengthened by a stone dowel or ball set into corresponding drill holes.[95] In the walls of the entrance corridor of the pyramid of Amenemhat III at Dahshur, quartzite cramps of roughly square shape connect the wall blocks (fig. 4.34).[96] Sometimes elongated pebbles are set into the cramp slots.[97]

Unusually cut block ends could serve for the connection of two to three architraves meeting on the same column or pillar (figs. 4.33, 4.35). As long as two architraves met, both oriented in the same direction, a simple straight joint was used. But when the two formed a right angle, different joints had to be cut. In order to avoid the architraves' meeting with their heads pointed at a 45-degree angle, the heads were cut at right angles (fig. 4.35).[98] When three architraves met on the same column, the end of the one arriving at a right angle was cut pointed, reaching into a V-shaped recess of the other two (fig. 4.33).[99]

Another, less common method to connect stones is the mortise and tenon. Lauer collected several interesting examples in the complex of Djoser, where some wall blocks but mostly column drums and the capstones of walls were fixed in that manner (fig. 4.36).[100] Other examples are from the Old,[101] Middle, and New Kingdoms (fig. 4.37).[102] This method was also frequently used to fix the pyramidion on top of the last one or two casing blocks of pyramids. The oldest examples known are from the secondary pyramids of the Fourth Dynasty (fig. 4.38).[103] There are round and square tenons (fig. 4.39)[104] and three examples where the lower edges of the pyramidion are chamfered to fit into a corresponding large socket.[105] Corner blocks of pyramids were frequently fixed in a similar way. The lower block has a groove on its top surface, and the upper block has a corresponding ledge along its underside. In one case, this method is combined

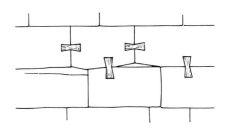

Fig. 4.30 Cramps in vertical position in a repaired wall at Medinet Habu.

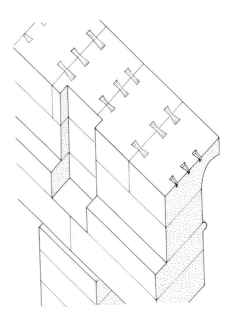

Fig. 4.31 Three parallel cramp slots in the architraves of the Roman kiosk of Philae.

Fig. 4.32 Acacia cramp of Sety I, probably from his mortuary temple at Thebes. (MMA acc. no. 41.2.1)

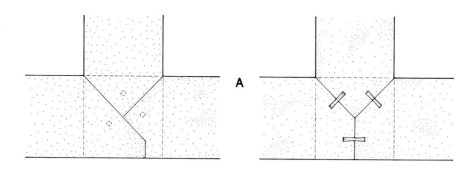

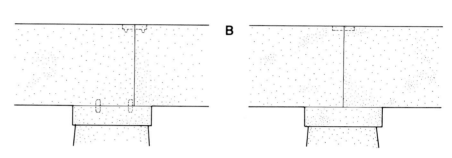

Fig. 4.33 Stone dowels in the architraves of (A) the mortuary temple of Niuserra and (B) the hypostyle hall at Karnak.

Fig. 4.34 Quartzite dowel in the entrance passage of the pyramid of Amenemhat III at Dahshur.

Fig. 4.35 Connecting two architraves on the corner column of the court of the mortuary temple of Sahura at Abusir.

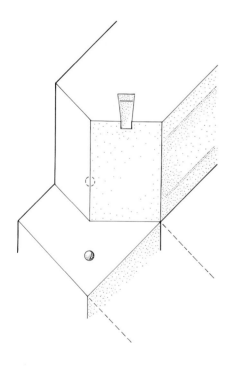

with mortises and tenons at the two side faces of the casing blocks (fig. 4.40).[106]

Another interesting way to fix a block is preserved on the last of the ten huge columns of Taharqa in the first court of Karnak (fig. 4.41). Here, not only is the capital of the column composed of five courses of blocks, but the topmost course consists of twenty-two thin segments, kept in place by the weight of the abacus, which is built from about twenty blocks.[107]

Finally, in rare cases stone casing slabs could be attached by ropes to brick masonry behind the stone slabs (fig. 4.42). Slings were pulled through drill holes at the rear upper corner of the slabs and built solidly into the brick-work. This method was necessary because the connection between brick-work and casing was rather loose, and the casing slabs were too thin to sit solidly on each other.[108] The method had originally been developed for the corner connection of stone sarcophagi, composed of single slabs.[109] Pairs of holes were drilled diagonally through both slabs. After their erection, a rope or wire was pulled through the holes.

CORNER CONSTRUCTIONS

A strong quoining of the outer corners of walls developed only after a period of trial and error in building. Lauer points out that the quoining in the Djoser precinct was a weak point in construction (fig. 4.43).[110] Bonded quoining appears but seems not to have been a main type. L-shaped corner blocks do exist, but very often the shorter branch of the L reaches only a few centimeters around the corner. Sometimes the corner is made up of a completely separate block that could easily fall out of the wall and could not function in keeping the two sides of the wall together. Another peculiarity of early stone building involves the corners of buildings (mostly pyramids)

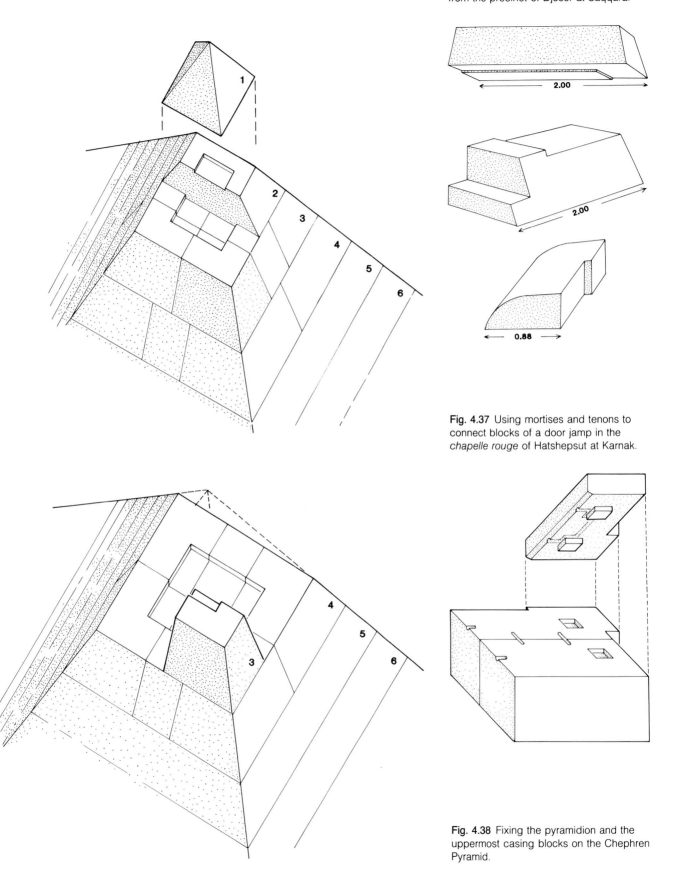

Fig. 4.36 Examples of block connections from the precinct of Djoser at Saqqara.

Fig. 4.37 Using mortises and tenons to connect blocks of a door jamb in the *chapelle rouge* of Hatshepsut at Karnak.

Fig. 4.38 Fixing the pyramidion and the uppermost casing blocks on the Chephren Pyramid.

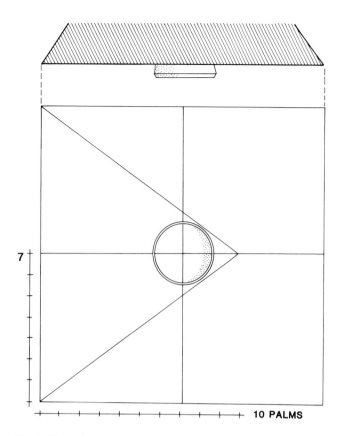

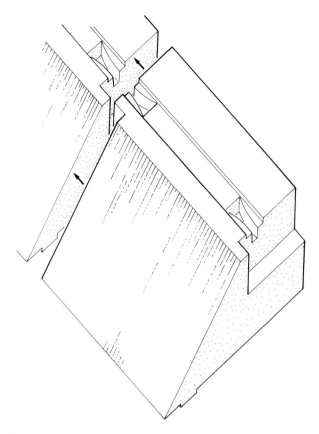

Fig. 4.39 The lower bed of the pyramidion of Khendjer, with a round tenon and construction drawing for the pyramidion.

Fig. 4.40 Using mortises and tenons and dovetail cramps to connect casing blocks of an unknown pyramid of the Middle Kingdom at Lisht.

Fig. 4.41 Securing the uppermost blocks of the columns of Tarharqa at Karnak by the weight of the abacus.

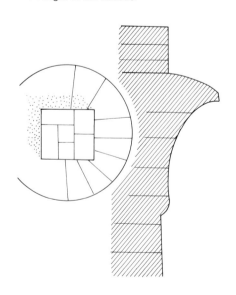

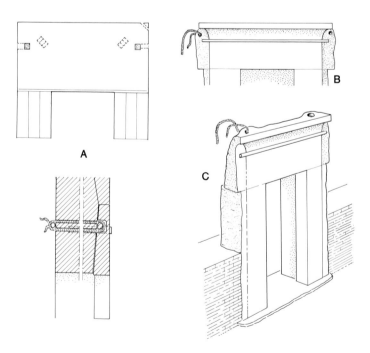

Fig. 4.42 Connecting facing slabs by ropes with the brick core of a wall from (A) the priests' houses at Karnak and (B,C) the *harim* at Medinet Habu.

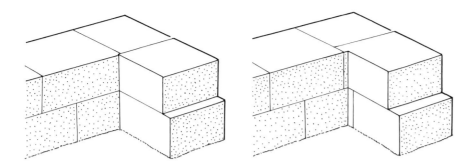

Fig. 4.43 Examples of corner connections from the Djoser precinct at Saqqara.

Fig. 4.44 Corner construction of buildings with inclined bedding joints from the Third Dynasty.

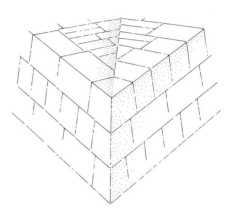

with inward-inclined layers. At the corner where the planes inclined in two directions meet, a pronounced angle is visible on the surface of the corner stone (fig. 4.44).[111]

The best example of a corner stone with its upper surface inclined in two directions is that of the Bent Pyramid. To avoid an eventual sliding toward the outside of the masonry that forms the edges of the pyramid, the corner blocks were thicker than the others and supported by foundation stones placed at a greater depth than the blocks along the faces.[112] Nobody seems to have studied how the blocks above the corner blocks were shaped and interconnected. The corner stones of the Cheops Pyramid were treated in a special manner, which has provoked some scholarly discussion, since the corner stones themselves are now missing and only their sockets are visible in the bedrock (fig. 4.45).[113] Possibly the upper corner stones were also linked with each other by mortises on the underside and corresponding sockets on the top surface, a system certainly known since it was used at the corners of the queen's pyramid Ic at Giza.[114] From the Fourth Dynasty on, sockets and mortises on corner blocks were generally used for pyramids of

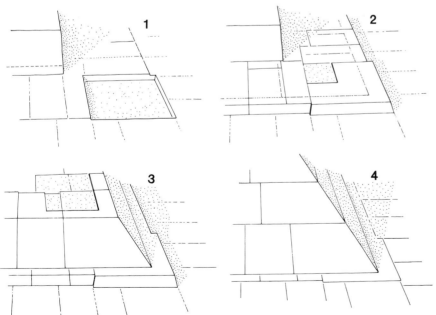

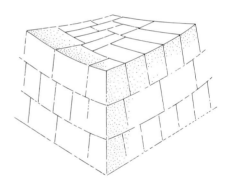

Fig. 4.45 Reconstruction of the laying of the corner stones of the Cheops Pyramid.

Building | 131

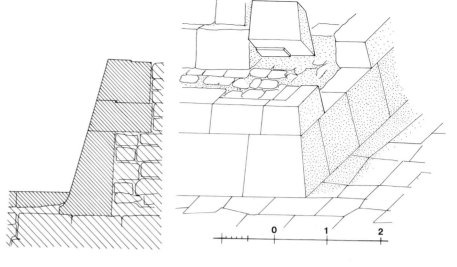

Fig. 4.47 Corner construction of the obelisk base of Niuserra at Abu Ghurab.

Fig. 4.46 Mortises on the corner blocks of the secondary pyramid of Pepy II at Saqqara.

the queens and some pyramids of the kings (figs. 4.46, 4.47).[115] Some examples are also known from the Middle Kingdom.[116] But from the pyramid of Senwosret I onward, corner blocks were also fixed with dovetail cramps.[117]

Bonded quoining was also used more or less regularly at the pyramids of the Old and Middle Kingdoms (fig. 4.48),[118] but examples with less regularly bonded corners are also known from the Middle Kingdom.[119] Quite systematic corner bonding can be observed at the corners of the pylons of the New Kingdom, which are also connected with dovetail cramps (fig. 4.49).[120] Corner blocks were set first in a course because their correct positioning determined the accuracy of the whole course.[121]

BOSSES[122]

Egyptian stone masonry in its finished state did not show pulvinated or bossed front faces. Bulging faces in Egyptian walls were considered unfinished, not decorative. Normally, building stones were set with extra stock at the front faces (fig. 4.50).[123] There are instances, however, where blocks were already dressed down before setting, and we do not always understand under what conditions this happened.

As a general rule, we can assume that at least the lower side and one side face of a block, and frequently the second side face as well, had to be dressed in the mason's workshop. If skew joints were to be cut, it could be done only with the neighboring block on hand—that is, probably at the foot of the wall to be built. The top surface in most cases was dressed only after the completion of a whole course, since the size and shape of the blocks of the following course had to be considered and the beds for these blocks prepared accordingly. The rear face of the blocks either was only roughly dressed or remained undressed, as normally happened with granite casing blocks of pyramids and walls. Considering the hardness of gran-

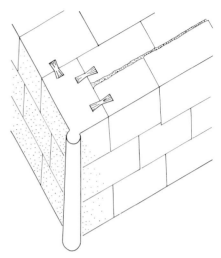

Fig. 4.48 Bonded quoining at the corner of the Meidum Pyramid.

Fig. 4.49 Bonded quoining of pylon corners of the New Kingdom.

ite, it was much easier for the masons to cut the softer limestone blocks behind the hard-stone casing in order to fit in the granite.

Since blocks with bulging front faces could not be exactly aligned, the front edge of the lower course as well as the lower edge of the next upper course of blocks had to be chamfered. The drafted margins enabled the masons to stretch the cord along the intended front face at the proper depth and to position the upper blocks accordingly. Less frequently, this was also done at the vertical joints. Another way to dress a bossed wall

Fig. 4.50 Bossed pavement blocks of the chapel of mastaba no. 17 at Meidum.

Fig. 4.51 Undressed granite casing of the pyramid of Mycerinus.

Fig. 4.52 Undressed casing blocks of the pyramid of Meidum.

surface was first to cut vertical channels, several meters apart, the bottoms of which were at the required batter. From these channels, the facing surfaces could easily be checked with the help of boning rods.[124]

Examples of unfinished walls are not frequent in ancient Egyptian architecture. The best known is probably the granite casing of the pyramid of Mycerinus (fig. 4.51) and the limestone blocks of the rear part of his mortuary temple. Another good example in limestone is the building phases E1 and E2 of the pyramid of Meidum, whose surface was dressed only in areas that would be visible (fig. 4.52),[125] with parts to be covered, the well-known ring bands, remaining undressed.

Bosses of another type are those for transport or handling, which are bulky knobs, similar to the handles of sarcophagus lids, protruding from the dressed or undressed surface (fig. 4.53). Most of these handling bosses were removed together with the rough block surface, but often their traces are still visible (fig. 4.54).[126] There are examples, however, where the handling bosses are still standing on the dressed surface or their traces can still be clearly seen, indicating that the blocks were dressed before setting and the handling bosses remained there to be used for lifting the block.[127] This

Fig. 4.53 Transport boss on a roofing beam of the crypt of Queen Neferuptah at Hauwaret el-Maqta.

Fig. 4.54 Remains and traces of transport bosses on the granite wall of the crypt of Mentuhotep Nebhepetra at Deir el-Bahari.

was probably not the rule, though, but was done only when the awkward position of a block or a wall necessitated it.

In general, the front face of blocks was dressed after the completion of the wall (fig. 4.55). At what moment in the construction process the surface of the pyramid casing was actually dressed is uncertain. Were the casing blocks delivered and positioned with a dressed front fact, or were they dressed after setting a block or a whole course? Or was the whole pyramid first erected and then the surface dressed down? The state in which we see the pyramid of Mycerinus today would suggest that the last was the case. But granite may have been treated differently from limestone, and we do not know how the limestone casing blocks of the same pyramid looked. The many patched joints of limestone casing blocks, which can be observed at several pyramids, seem to indicate that no protective bosses existed when these blocks were set and consequently the edges cracked.

On the casing of the pyramid of Meidum (E3), two conspicuous chisel marks run from the flattened surface of one casing block to the next (fig. 4.56). They were certainly made after the laying of the blocks and before the final dressing of the surface because they reach so deep that their grooves could no longer be removed when the surface was dressed flat. Why they were made is unknown, but their appearance seems to indicate that they were cut into an undressed rough surface. In any case, one might expect that essential parts, such as corner blocks and other guiding lines, were dressed during construction in order to enable accurate measuring.

A pyramid surrounded by an enveloping ramp could have been easily dressed when the ramp was taken down in steps. Without such a ramp, enormous quantities of wood would have been required for the construction of scaffolding to envelop the pyramid on all sides.[128] Putlog holes would have been necessary and would certainly have reached deep enough

Fig. 4.56 Chisel marks overlapping two casing blocks at the pyramid of Meidum.

into the surface to have left their traces even after dressing. No such holes are visible on the preserved parts of the casing of the pyramid of Meidum, the Bent Pyramid, and the pyramids of Cheops, Chephren, Unas, and Senwosret I. One should mention that the casing of pyramids was not ground smooth or polished, but only dressed flat with the regular small chisel.

In some special cases, the complete front face of a block was not left with extra stock, but only the edges. One good example is the black granite casing blocks in the rear part of the mortuary temple of Mycerinus (fig.

Fig. 4.57 Protective bosses on diorite blocks at the mortuary temple of Mycerinus.

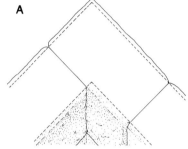

Fig. 4.59 Staircase block from the mortuary temple of Sahura, showing the original size of the block before the steps were cut.

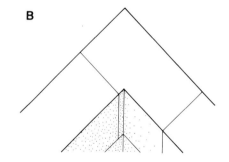

Fig. 4.58 Corner constructed of (A) undressed blocks and (B) blocks after dressing.

A

B

4.57).[129] Along all their edges, they have markedly raised ledges, apparently left undressed until after being positioned. And in the Osireion at Abydos, rough ledges appear along the upper front edge of blocks.[130] They were left to protect the edge when the following course was set on top. And the granite sarcophagus of Imhotep at Lisht shows 8-centimeter-high bands along the edges and corners that protrude slightly over the equally roughly dressed surfaces. Also the contrary is possible—a raised center of the stone with completely dressed upper and lower horizontal edges. In this case, the edges were unprotected.

The thickness of extra stock, which could occasionally have been considerable (up to 12 centimeters), can still be judged in certain cases, for quite frequently one can observe at inside corners what appears to be an L-shaped corner block with one vertical joint not far from the corner (fig. 4.58). This joint roughly indicates the former outline of the oversized block before its dressing.

The removal of bosses was carried out in two steps. A rough trimming of the surface, leaving sufficient stock for decorative elements—such as tori, cornices, and column capitals (fig. 4.59)—was apparently carried out by the masons. The next step was the final surface treatment and sculpting the decoration, work that was done by the sculptors.[131]

Examples of L-shaped corner blocks are frequent in the limestone-cased chambers of the pyramid of Amenemhat III at Dahshur. In these chambers are traces that suggest the technical procedure of dressing down the wall surfaces set in bosses (fig. 4.60). First of all, the middle axis of the room, scratched into the pavement, was used as a reference line. From the plumb bob suspended above this line, the masons could measure sideways with a cubit rod the amount of extra stock that had to be removed. The cooperation of a second person with mallet and chisel would have been necessary. With a

Fig. 4.60 Dressing marks on an unfinished wall in the pyramid of an unknown king of the late Middle Kingdom at Saqqara.

Fig. 4.61 Unfinished rock surface with dressing marks in shaft no. 5124 of the mastaba of Imhotep at Lisht.

few strokes, he cut a hole of the required depth and marked it in black. This was done repeatedly from the ceiling downward in lines 15 centimeters apart until the end of the wall was reached. The masons could now dress down the extra stock between the marks until the level of the black color was reached. This state of work is represented in many limestone cased tombs of the Middle Kingdom.

The same method was used for the final dressing of rock surfaces in underground chambers of the Middle Kingdom (fig. 4.61). It would have been followed by only a final grinding of the surface. In the pyramid of Amenemhat III, not even the dressing was carried out correctly so that one finds black marks still surrounded by extra stock.[132]

Decorative features (if this expression was permitted at all)—such as a torus, either horizontal or vertical, winged disks above doors, and the elaborate shapes of column capitals—required especially high and correctly measured bosses (fig. 4.62). Examples of these can be found frequently in Ptolemaic and Roman buildings, many of which were left unfinished.[133] Uvo Hölscher recorded such features from the unfinished Pylon I of Karnak (not before Nectanbebo I).[134] But we know that Pharaonic buildings in an unfinished state did look the same. The unfinished corner torus of Pylon IV of Karnak, for example, is not yet completely round but polygonal, thus preserving an intermediate step between the rectangular boss and the rounded torus.[135]

STONE PAVING

In Egyptian building, the pavement could be made of mud, mud brick, occasionally wood (in the crypts of the kings of the First Dynasty), or stone. The oldest known stone pavement was found in the Abydos tomb of King Den of the First Dynasty and consisted of hammer-dressed slabs of granite, 2.5 meters long and only 13 centimeters thick.[136] It must be regarded as an exception, however, for the next stone pavement in a royal tomb is found in the crypt of Khasekhemui at the end of the Second Dynasty.[137] From then on, we have innumerable examples of pavements in limestone, granite, basalt, alabaster, quartzite, and later, of course, sandstone.

In stone building, the uppermost course of the foundation is generally carried out as the pavement. Since the foundations are frequently built as a solid block of masonry, the topmost course does not reflect the position of

Fig. 4.62 Unfinished capitals in the Roman East Colonnade of Philae.

walls or columns.[138] Walls can stand well on separate foundations, the topmost course protruding slightly from the foot line of the walls. The actual pavement in the shape of thinner slabs is added later and pushed against that topmost course of the foundations.[139]

Occasionally, the paving slabs even cover the foot of the building, as at some pyramids where the pavement of the court is pushed over the first 2 palms of the inclined casing or against the vertical drop of the foot of the casing blocks.[140] In this case, the level of the pavement determined the level of the foot of the pyramid. The actual foot line of the pyramid was invisible, since it was buried by the pavement. In the funerary temple of Niuserra, the foot of the basalt orthostates of the walls were also hidden by the pavement slabs (fig. 4.63).

The shape and arrangement of the pavement slabs are mostly irregular and never produced the even but lifeless patterns that we are accustomed to see in monumental architecture of the nineteenth and twentieth centuries A.D. (figs. 4.64, 4.65). The Egyptian builders did not intend to create a visible joint pattern, but hoped to produce one uninterrupted stone surface. They worked backward from the farthest, most difficult area to reach, fitting in and cutting the slabs at hand, which resulted in a completely irregular mosaic.[141]

At the pyramid precinct of Senwosret I, one can see many examples of

Fig. 4.64 Sandstone pavement in the lower porticus of the temple of Mentuhotep at Deir el-Bahari.

slabs with pairs of vertical grooves on their opposite sides. These were the slabs that could no longer be pushed in from the side but had to be lowered vertically (4.66). In order to fit them in without injuring the hands of the workers, the slabs were lowered with slings of rope running through grooves, which permitted removal of the rope once the slabs were in place.[142] In the central court of the funerary temple of Senwosret I, the pattern of the paving slabs tells the sequence of setting the slabs (4.67). First, along the middle axis of the court a long row of rectangular slabs was set crosswise to the axis. At the same time, a ring of rectangular slabs was laid around the court. The space between the pillars was filled equally with one slab each. Then the two remaining halves of the court, north and south

Fig. 4.65 Pavement of irregular alabaster slabs in the valley temple of Chephren.

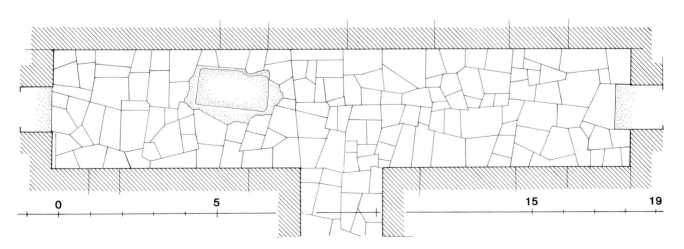

0   5   15   19

Building | 143

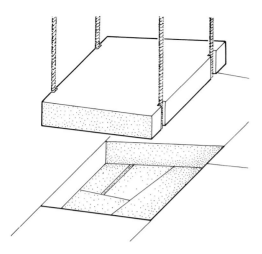

Fig. 4.66 Placing a paving slab with ropes drawn through vertical grooves.

Fig. 4.67 Limestone pavement in the court of the mortuary temple of Senwosret I at Lisht.

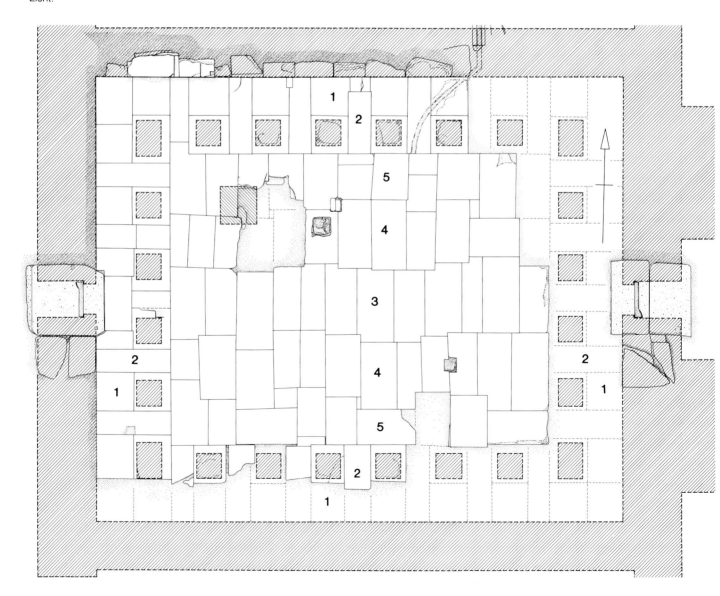

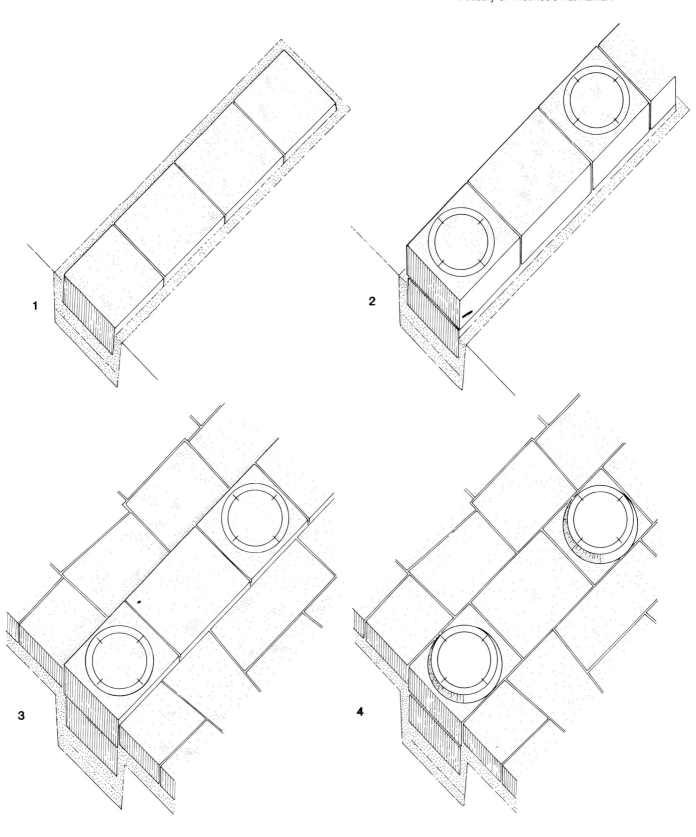

Fig. 4.68 Construction phases of pavement and column bases in the treasury of Thutmosis I at Karnak.

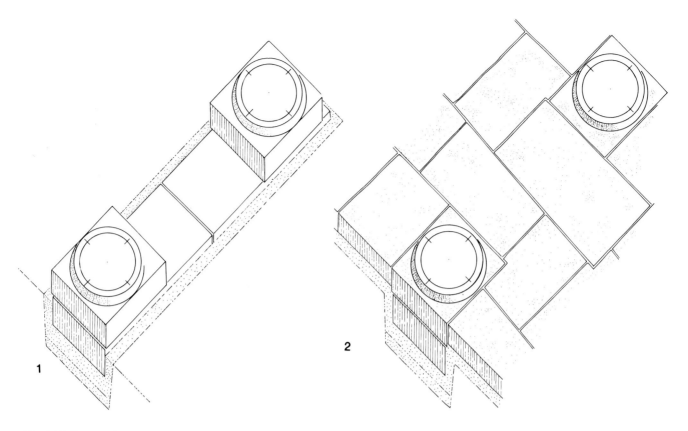

Fig. 4.69 Construction phases of pavement and column bases in the treasury of Thutmosis I at Karnak.

Fig. 4.70 Pillars in the lower porticus of the temple of Mentuhotep at Deir el-Bahari, indicating the height of bosses before dressing down to pavement level.

of the axial row had to be filled in. This was done with less regularly shaped slabs.[143]

Paving stones were often set with extra stock, especially those that would form the lower end or base of a column (figs. 4.68, 4.69). This procedure added to the stability of the columns insofar as the base was a solid part of the pavement (fig. 4.70).[144] Occasionally, the final size of the column base was underestimated so that not enough material was standing when the base had to be dressed. In that case, segments of the circular base were missing and had to be added with patches (fig. 4.71).[145]

Most paving slabs are of the same material that is found in the rest of the building, in the foundations and the walls. Thus most pavements in the Old and Middle Kingdoms are made of limestone and most in the New Kingdom, of sandstone. We have many examples, however, where the pavement was treated in the same way as the wall casing. Foundations considered to be of poorer quality were hidden under the pavement of better stone. In the huge limestone buildings of the Old Kingdom, a pavement of granite is not uncommon.[146] In a few cases, even basalt was used.[147] Since both stones were much harder to work than the underlying limestone, the undersurface of the pavement was often left rough and the upper surface of the limestone foundations was chiseled out in a way that allowed the protuberances of the pavement to fit into it. This could be done only by frequently setting and lifting the pavement blocks, a procedure that had to be carried out in any case to fit the mosaic-like blocks together. The builders used a system of marking the proper joints in which the edges of two blocks to be joined received the same hieroglyphic sign.[148]

For reasons of ritual purity, some special rooms, such as the offering halls of mortuary temples, were fitted out with a pavement of alabaster slabs.[149]

Fig. 4.71 Column base dressed from a block too small to cover the whole base, at the mortuary temple of the queen of Djedkara at Abusir.

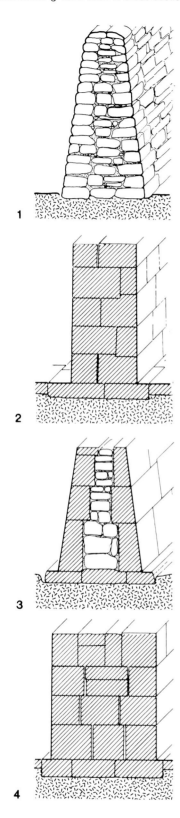

1

2

3

4

MASONRY CLASSIFICATION

The description and documentation of forms and types of Egyptian stone masonry in general would naturally not fall into the scope of this book. But construction methods cannot be fully understood without considering this subject. The fact that until now no such classification has been attempted is due to the way Egyptian builders constructed their walls. Quite frequently, several types of masonry were used in the same building, even in the same wall and especially in the core masonry behind the surface. The final surface treatment disguised all such differences either by filling all visible joints with mortar and rubbing the surface so completely smooth that it would resemble one solid block of stone or by decorating the surface with reliefs and paintings that covered all these differences. Hardly ever were features like bossed surfaces, trapezoidal block shapes, or the regular pattern of isodomic masonry accentuated into an artistic surface design, as was done in Greek masonry.

Another characteristic of Egyptian masonry, despite the monumentality of Egyptian building projects, is the apparent economy in the use of material. The reuse of older building material was common, as was the preference for dressing blocks into odd shapes in order to avoid wasting material. A third feature that can be observed throughout ancient Egyptian building history is the use of poorer material for the core of a structure that is being cased with stone of higher quality. This practice resulted in the construction of walls that consist of two coats of blocks or slabs, encasing a core of irregular masonry or even rubble. Golvin and Goyon stress the point that Pharaonic masons overcame this "malpractice" only from the time of Nectanebo I on.[150] But core blocks were often carefully dressed and fitted in much older buildings, such as the Mentuhotep temple at Deir el-Bahari or Pylons VII and VIII at Karnak. We may assume, therefore, that the builders knew how to construct true ashlar, but economic considerations often prevented them from doing so.

For the classification of masonry, two approaches are feasible: either the structure of a wall, whether freestanding or not, is seen in cross section, revealing core masonry and casing at the same time; or only the pattern of the blocks as seen on the surface is considered, and the internal structure of the wall is disregarded (fig. 4.72).

By Cross Section for Freestanding Walls · Fieldstone walls (fig. 4.73) were frequently built in all periods. Their rough and uneven shape restricted them to buildings of daily use without any artistic pretension, buildings that were not intended to last forever. The walls were built with rough or scarcely dressed stones, embedded into mortar, with smaller stones and chips between the joints. In general, the stones selected had rectangular flat shapes. As far as possible, they were set in horizontal courses, imitating regular ashlar. No patterns (such as herringbone) were aimed at. Occasionally, the surface was coated with mortar or mud. Such walls do not need special foundations and have a considerable inclination on both faces. The top is more or less rounded.[151] Real rubble walls composed of uncut stones bonded together with mud are of no importance in Egyptian building.

Walls that are one or two blocks thick (fig. 4.74) are used mostly for separating rooms and in buildings of moderate height. They are vertical and stand on foundations. Headers used as through stones connect the two rows of blocks.

Freestanding and high walls can consist of a coat of casing slabs that disguises a core built of fieldstones or roughly dressed stones, the joints filled with mortar and chips (figs. 4.75, 4.76). These walls are inclined, have a rounded top, and stand on stone foundations. Due to the strong inclination, the casing stones of both faces touch in higher courses or are replaced by blocks of the full thickness of the wall.

The last category includes thick walls with masonry cores (fig. 4.77). Stronger walls and more voluminous structures—such as pylons, massive statue bases, and obelisks—have a core of large, roughly dressed blocks arranged in courses that frequently but not always correspond to the courses of the outside blocks or casing. From the New Kingdom on, the core blocks are frequently reused material from the Old and Middle Kingdoms.

By Cross Section for Non-freestanding Walls (fig. 4.78) · Fieldstone retaining walls can be the outer coat of a core made of similar rough material or just rubble, chip, or sand. The joints are occasionally filled with smaller stones or chips.

Mastabas provide examples of block casing (fig. 4.79). Their cores, made of rough fieldstones or debris, are frequently cased with large blocks, set in slightly receding steps in order to be dressed down to a sloping surface. This last procedure was not often carried out,[152] if it was ever actually intended.

Fig. 4.73 Rough fieldstone wall of the forecourt of the Mentuhotep temple at Deir el-Bahari.

Fig. 4.74 Limestone enclosure wall of the Mentuhotep temple at Deir el-Bahari.

Building | 149

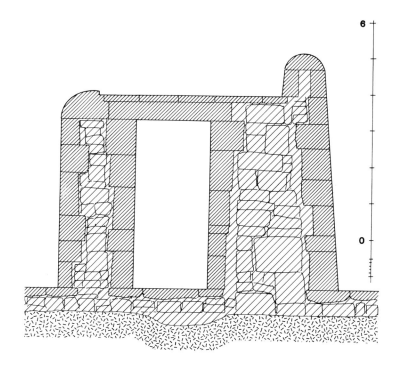

Fig. 4.75 Section through the ambulatory of the sun temple of Niuserra at Abu Ghurab.

6

0

Fig. 4.76 Section through the inner enclosure wall of the pyramid of Senwosret I at Lisht.

Fig. 4.77 Block masonry at Pylon III at Karnak (Horemhab/Ramesses I).

In enormous block structures, such as the valley and mortuary temples of the Old Kingdom, granite or limestone casing was added to core masonry of the same size.

Block-cased rock cores (fig. 4.80) are rare. One example comes from Giza, where cores of bedrock were left standing, to be cased with granite or limestone. Such solid constructions depend on the local conditions and are to be found at only a few pyramid sites, such as Giza, Illahun, and Deir el-Bahari (fig. 4.81).

By Surface Appearance (fig. 4.82)[153] · Rectangular blocks in stepped (broken) courses (fig. 4.83) were used by the Egyptian builders. In order not to waste material, they did not attempt to produce and work with blocks of exactly the same size. This stone-saving mentality led to structures with stepped, horizontal joints. The steps were cut into the top of the lower course according to the size and shape of the block on top.

Trapezoidal masonry (isodomic or pseudo-isodomic) (fig. 4.84) was also used in order to save material. Stonemasons often produced trapezoidal blocks whose lateral joints were askew from the front (cut at a slant) and sometimes from the top as well. These oblique joints were thought to be neither decorative nor structurally essential, since they do not occur regu-

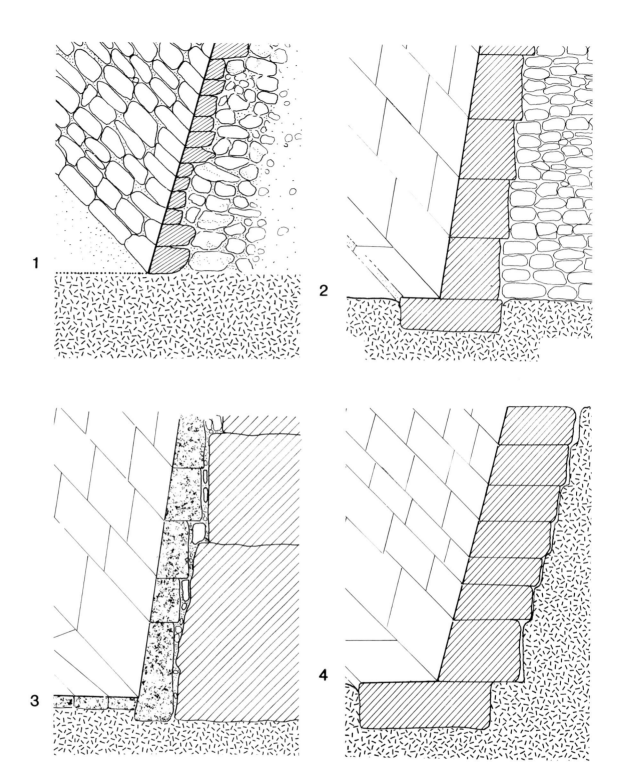

Fig. 4.78 Classification of masonry of
retaining walls seen in cross section.

Fig. 4.79 Block casing of the mastaba of Ptahshepses at Abusir.

larly but only occasionally in one course or another. It is remarkable that real polygonal masonry, which dominated Greek building until about 500 B.C. and played such a role in Inca stone masonry, was never carried out in Pharaonic Egypt.

Masonry of rectangular blocks set in isodomic, horizontal courses resembles brickwork (fig. 4.85). But a systematic change between headers and stretchers was not common, and the system is frequently interrupted by steps (as in the first method) or trapezoidal blocks (as in the second method). The blocks used were predominantly stretchers or blocks of quadrangular shape. This regular ashlar can also appear in variations: masonry of rectangular blocks of different frontal length, mixed with shorter, headerlike blocks; and masonry of rectangular blocks in pseudo-isodomic courses. Because the equal height of courses was not aimed at for optical reasons, the height of blocks and courses can easily change, sometimes considerably. The periodic change of height of courses at the pyramid of Cheops has been the subject of speculation. In some cases, the regular system of isodomic courses was interrupted by low leveling courses (fig. 4.87).[154]

Extremely irregular masonry (fig. 4.86) consisting of a mixture of small and large blocks randomly packed together is rare, since the stability of a structure was very important for Egyptian builders. Perhaps irregular masonry indicates a shortage of material.

Mixed masonry (fig. 4.87) is the final category. As has been explained, masonry of only one type scarcely appears in Egyptian building, and frequently masonry of predominantly regular blocks with isodomic courses may be mixed with blocks of trapezoidal shape or stepped horizontal beds.

For Pyramid Masonry (fig. 4.88) · With the exception of that of Zawiyet el-Mayitin, all Egyptian pyramids were erected on the west bank of the Nile.

Fig. 4.80 Rock cased with masonry, at the tomb of Khentkaues at Giza.

Fig. 4.81 Rock cased with masonry, at the Mentuhotep temple at Deir el-Bahari.

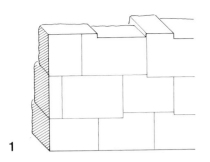

1

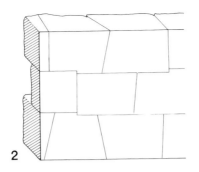

2

3a

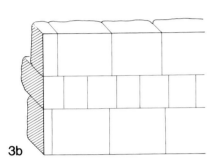

3b

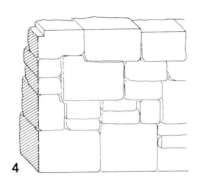

4

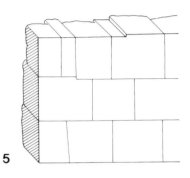

5

Fig. 4.82 Classification of masonry of freestanding walls, seen from the front.

Fig. 4.83 Broken course in the valley temple of the Bent Pyramid.

Fig. 4.84 Trapezoidal wall block in the temple Qasr el-Sagha.

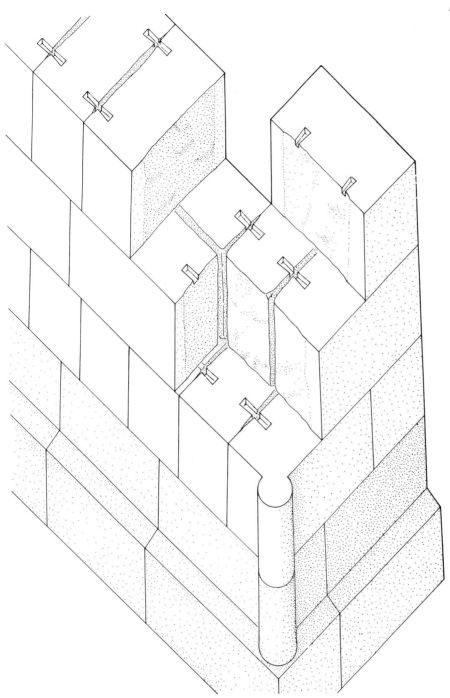

Fig. 4.86 Irregular masonry, at the temple of Karnak.

Fig. 4.87 Mixed masonry of the mastaba of Ptahshepses at Abusir.

In light of the availability of first-class limestone for building, they were constructed on the "wrong" side of the Nile because this stone was found only in the area of modern Moqqattam, Tura, and Ma'sara. It was used only for casing blocks and other visible parts of the buildings. The main bulk of material—that used for the core masonry—was built either with locally available, poorer limestone or, from the middle of the Twelfth Dynasty on, with bricks. This separation of casing and core was crucial in pyramid building and determined, together with the steplike shape of the casing construction, the structure of these buildings.

The earliest pyramids of the Third Dynasty were different from these buildings. Their sloping outer faces were not achieved by cutting the outer faces of casing blocks at an oblique angle, but by setting rectangular casing blocks at an inward slope (fig. 4.89). These early pyramids were "layered." This was done by surrounding a central core with up to thirteen or fourteen accretion layers with inclined faces, which were reduced in height from inside out in a steplike fashion. The visible faces were cased with well-dressed blocks, the material consisting of roughly dressed local fieldstones. Thus no distinction between core masonry and casing can actually be made.

The turning point in pyramid masonry came at the beginning of the Fourth Dynasty when at the Bent Pyramid the courses of the core were set horizontally for the first time and the casing blocks were set nearly so. At the same time, the stepped shape of a pyramid was either hidden in the core or given up altogether. Since the cores of the great pyramids of the Fourth Dynasty are difficult to study, discussions about their structure have led to no final conclusions.[155] The general opinion is that they consist of horizontally arranged blocks in the height of the casing course without further internal structure.[156]

For this type of construction in the Fourth Dynasty, one could suggest that the cores are still stepped and built with accretion layers. This feature could be disguised, however, by backing stones of the same height as those of the core and casing.[157] In the Fifth and Sixth Dynasties, this type of construction was either revived or continued, with the only difference being that the core no longer consisted of huge blocks but of smaller roughly squared stones or even just fieldstones (fig. 4.90).

A few Old Kingdom pyramids are considered to have a core of steps, not in inclined layers but in horizontal courses of rough masonry. This kind of core can be seen at the queens' pyramids Giza Ic, IIIb, and IIIc. Although the use of similar construction has been suggested elsewhere (at Mycerinus, Userkaf, and Djedkara), no observations of the joints have been made.

The Twelfth Dynasty provides two examples of stepped cores that apparently do not have a layered structure but consist of accumulated masses of rough blocks or fieldstones with a stepped outer face (Amenemhat I and Senwosret I). These steps are the beds for the backing stones of the casing (fig. 4.91). In both pyramids, the core steps are small. The core of the later pyramid has an additional system of walls radiating from the center so that the steps appear only between these walls.

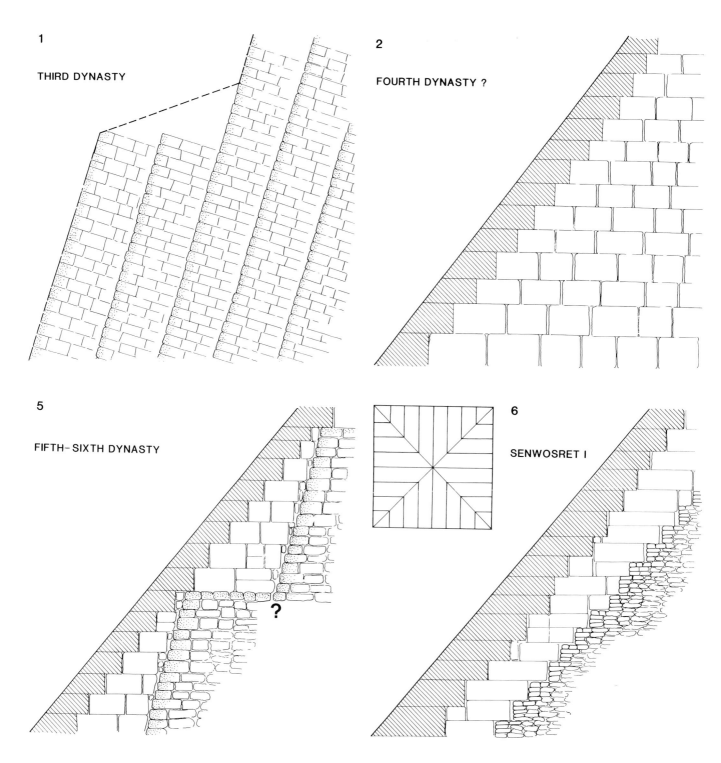

1 THIRD DYNASTY

2 FOURTH DYNASTY ?

5 FIFTH-SIXTH DYNASTY

?

6 SENWOSRET I

Fig. 4.88 Classification of masonry and structures of pyramids.

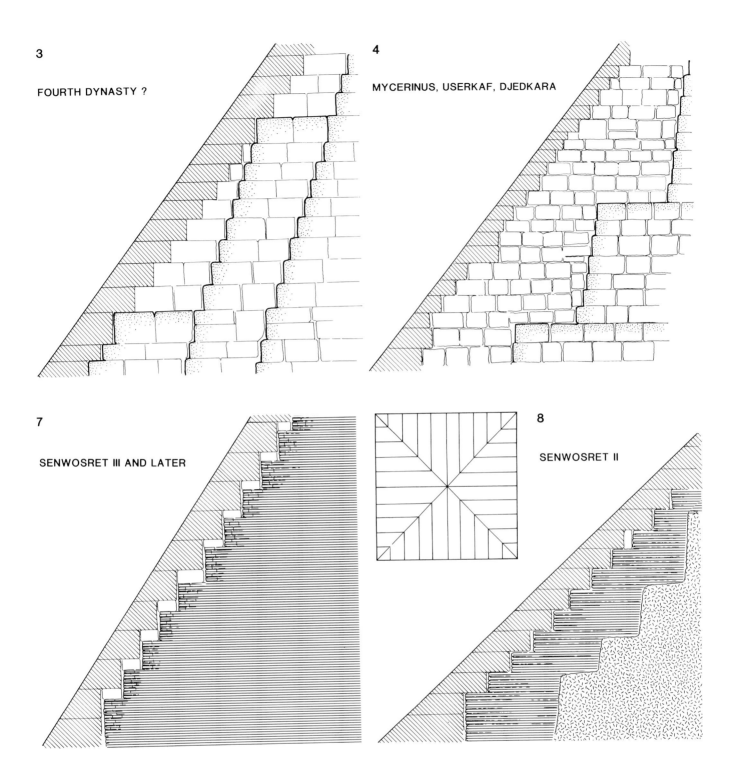

3

FOURTH DYNASTY ?

4

MYCERINUS, USERKAF, DJEDKARA

7

SENWOSRET III AND LATER

8

SENWOSRET II

Fig. 4.89 Inclined layers of roughly dressed fieldstones on the Step Pyramid.

Fig. 4.90 Rough fieldstone packing on the core steps of the pyramid of Neferirkara.

Fig. 4.91 Tilted backing stone (A) on the fieldstone core steps (B) of the pyramid of Senwosret I at Lisht.

Fig. 4.92 Skeleton wall on the rock core of the pyramid of Senwosret II at Illahun.

From the reign of Senwosret II on, all pyramids have a brick core. These cores are either stepped for only one backing stone (Senwosret III) or arranged in higher steps for four courses of casing and backing stones.

The pyramid of Senwosret II is an exception to using a rock-cut core dressed into the shape of a stepped pyramid (fig. 4.92). This rock core also carries structural walls like those of Senwosret I. The space between core and casing was filled with bricks.

CASING

During the Old and Middle Kingdoms, Egyptian builders used better quality Tura limestone and Aswan granite only for visible parts of their buildings. These stones were used for casing a core made of poorer quality stone of the kind that could be quarried nearly everywhere between Memphis and Esna. Since core masonry made up the greater percentage of the building volume, the transport efforts could be much reduced if only casing blocks had to be brought from greater distances.

From the New Kingdom on, when sandstone slowly replaced limestone in construction and the transport of this new building material from Aswan and Gebel Silsila to the construction sites became much easier, the necessity of casing gradually disappeared. Thereafter, there is no clear separation between core masonry and casing, and only a few examples are known where limestone and sandstone were mixed in the same construction.

Orthostats are a special form of casing, more common in Mediterranean architecture.[158] They are large and rather thin slabs with a smooth exterior and an irregular back face casing the lower part of walls. They do exist, however, in Egypt. A beautiful example is the basalt orthostats in the limestone walls of the ambulatory of the funerary temple of Sahura.

In the construction of underground apartments, poor bedrock frequently had to be cased, either for support or to provide a clean surface for decoration. In some of the crypts of the early cemeteries of Helwan, the walls are cased up to 3 meters high with thin limestone slabs. The wooden ceiling was not carried by the casing, but by brick walls behind the casing.[159] Technically more advanced than these crypts at Helwan is the crypt of King Khasekhemui at Abydos (fig. 4.93). Here the walls, which are constructed of regular ashlar blocks with plastered joints, seem to have directly carried the roofing beams.

Where large burial chambers with huge roof constructions and heavy walls were erected, as under the pyramids of the Old and Middle Kingdoms, the term *casing* seems inappropriate. Quite frequently, the tomb shaft had to be cased as a protective measure against collapse because it often had to penetrate layers of loose sand and desert conglomerate. Stone casing was common in the mastaba tombs of the Old Kingdom (fig. 4.79).[160] Later, brick walls were considered to be sufficient, and they were either plastered or at least whitewashed. A unique type of casing for shafts is so far known from only Middle Kingdom tombs at Lisht (unpublished). There the shaft walls are covered with a sandy, light-colored layer of plaster up to 12 centimeters thick in which potsherds were stuck, with their convex sides facing the shaft.

Fig. 4.93 Limestone casing of the crypt of King Khasekhemui at Abydos.

The most conspicuous use of casing can be observed in pyramid building (fig. 4.94). Two types of masonry were used. The first type of pyramid masonry—including the casing—consisted of inward-inclined courses and was prevalent during the Third Dynasty until the erection of the Bent Pyramid (fig. 4.95). The slope of the outer face of the pyramid was achieved by setting rectangular blocks sloping inward.[161] Only for the latest example, the Bent Pyramid, were the casing blocks not set perpendicularly to the faces. The blocks look in section like right-angled trapeziums (fig. 4.96).[162] In the early examples (Djoser P1, P2; Meidum E1, E2), a clear distinction between courses with blocks laid as headers and those with stretchers can be made. The tendency at the Bent Pyramid, however, seems to be to lay most of the casing blocks as headers. At the same time, a continual growth in the size of casing blocks can be observed. Djoser P1 has blocks up to 39 centimeters. Djoser P2 is cased with blocks about 1 cubit high. This size of 1 cubit was also used at Meidum. At the Bent Pyramid, heights of 74, 77, 92, and 114 centimeters can be measured.[163] At the pyramid of Cheops, the height of steps (which corresponds to that of the casing) starts with 1.49 meters from the ground (figs. 4.11, 4.97) and ends with 0.58, 0.56, 0.57, and 0.54 meters near the top. The second type of pyramid masonry consisted of horizontal courses. The change from inclined courses took place during the reign of Snofru. From the northern pyramid of Snofru and phase E3 of Meidum on, all pyramids have casing blocks with horizontal beds. One should remember, however, that the casing of the original Djoser mastaba M1-3 was already horizontal and not inclined.[164]

In the period from the Fourth to the Twelfth Dynasty, the shape and size of the casing blocks did not vary significantly (fig. 4.98). The lowest course usually has the highest step, starting with 2 to 3 cubits and slowly decreasing with every step upward until it measures about 1 cubit at the top (fig.

Fig. 4.94 Casing of the upper part of the
Chephren Pyramid.

Fig. 4.95 Inclined casing blocks of the
Bent Pyramid at Dahshur.

Fig. 4.96 Casing block of the Bent
Pyramid.

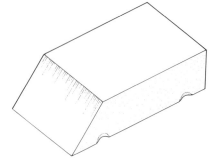

Fig. 4.97 Casing blocks of the Cheops Pyramid after the cleaning by Dow Covington in 1909.

4.99). This was clearly due to the problems of lifting. A block with a height of 1.5 meters and a base of 1 × 2.5 meters would weigh about 7 tons, whereas a smaller block of a height of only 0.5 meter and a base of 1 × 1 meter would be only 1 ton. The height, however, does not always regularly decrease, as can be seen from the measurements of casing blocks of the pyramids of Cheops, Unas (figs. 4.51, 4.100, 4.101), and Senwosret I:

		Cheops[165]	Unas[166]	Senwosret I[167]
Course	1	1.46–1.49 m.	1.50 m.	1.27 m.
	2	1.25–1.33	1.28	1.02
	3	1.15–1.22	1.35	0.91
	4	1.11–1.13	1.09	0.72
	5	0.99–1.03	0.92	0.96
	6	0.97–1.06	0.83	0.74
	7	0.99–1.12	—	0.66
	8	0.89–0.96	—	0.67
	9	0.87–0.93	—	—
	10	0.82–0.96	—	—

For the casing blocks of the Cheops Pyramid, Petrie noticed that the height decreases in general but that some courses in between are consider-

Fig. 4.98 Casing blocks of the tomb of Queen Khentkaues at Giza.

ably higher. Such courses appear in a completely irregular pattern in distances of 6, 7, 8, 9, 10, 12, 14, and 16 courses. A similar phenomenon can be observed at the Bent Pyramid. It is possible that these higher courses reflect the position of steps of the core masonry (fig. 4.102).[168] Since the last course of backing and casing stones on one core step may have been a small one (in depth as in height), the casing blocks in the following course may have been much deeper in order to better connect the casing with the core step. The greater depth might easily have led to a greater height. The existence of core steps in the pyramids of the Fourth Dynasty has not yet been attested well enough to support this theory. Since such core steps were built in all pyramids before and after the Fourth Dynasty, however, one should expect them in the Fourth Dynasty as well.

In general, only the front parts of the casing blocks rest on each other; the rear part rests on the backing stone below. This backing stone can fill the whole rear part of the step and reach back to touch the core masonry. In cases where the step is too wide—especially at the beginning of a core step—the backing stone could not completely fill the gap and was connected to the core either with another block of similar dimensions or with a fill of smaller blocks called packing stones.[169] The backing stones might have the same height as the casing blocks (fig. 4.103), but very often this is not the case. Sometimes two backing stones make up the height of one casing block, or sometimes the backing stone is higher so that a step at the upper front edge had to be cut to receive the rear of the casing block. In any event, the connection of the casing with the backing stones is very close and would have been carefully prepared. The best examples are the close joints between casing and backing stones at the three main pyramids of Giza. The backing stones were frequently dressed exactly to the shape of the rear face of the casing block, or larger gaps were filled with smaller stones and mortar.[170] There is no doubt that the casing, backing, and packing stones were treated as a structural unit to be built simultaneously. They are clearly separated from the core steps, which form another such unit, a unit that could well have been erected separately and perhaps even in advance. This discussion clearly refutes Petrie's erroneous conclusions based on Herodotus 2.125 that the casing blocks were set from the top to the foot of the pyramid, since that would have been technically impracticable.

Most pyramids were cased with limestone, but the following ones have one or more courses made of granite:

Djedefra	Possibly the whole casing?[171]
Chephren	First course[172]
Mycerinus	First sixteen courses[173]
Mycerinus IIIa	First course[174]
Shepseskaf	First course[175]
Neferirkara	First course or more?[176]

At the pyramid of Chephren, the granite blocks were set as headers, some of them 3 meters long (figs. 4.104, 4.105). Their rear faces were left undressed, as was normal when granite was used, and the backing stones were carved accordingly. The height of these blocks changes from 0.70 to 1.30 meters. The granite casing of the pyramid of Mycerinus is well preserved but left unfinished (fig. 4.51). Only the surfaces around the entrance and behind the offering chapel had been dressed and ground when the work was abandoned. All the other blocks still have their extra stock, some even with additional handling bosses. In order to facilitate the exact placement, the edges had been chamfered back to the intended sloping surface. The

Fig. 4.100 Casing blocks of the Unas Pyramid. The adjacent temple wall was carved from the same blocks.

great number of handling bosses preserved might well indicate that here the blocks had been pulled up to their place over a ramp on ropes because the pyramid is not very high and its top could easily have been reached by a ramp of some kind.

The limestone core walls of the valley and mortuary temples of Chephren and the mortuary temple of Mycerinus were completely cased with granite or at least the casing had been started. A long series of huge lever sockets in the bedrock in front of the walls shows that the granite casing blocks were levered into position from the front. For the Mycerinus temple, some blocks still show protective ledges along the front edges, which would certainly have been removed had the temple been completed.

Reisner thought that the top of the foundation platform of the mortuary temple of Mycerinus was individually dressed for each wall block.[177] The stones were dragged up and placed probably face down on beams opposite the place that they were to occupy in the wall. They had been roughly dressed on the sides and front. On the front, a low ridge, 5 to 10 centimeters wide and 3 to 5 centimeters high, had been left on the four outer edges. While lying thus, only the bottom of the stones was dressed flat with one side face. Then the crevices in the trench of the foundation platform were chinked with limestone chips and white plaster, and the core wall behind was hollowed out to take the bulging of the undressed back of the casing blocks. The granite blocks were then turned over on their lower edge as a fulcrum until they dropped into place in the wall on a layer of plaster. The final adjustment would be made by "floating" the stone by a few men. Some of the blocks had to be pushed with the help of levers into the shift cuttings, which had already been prepared.

Since casing blocks were visible, their surface had to be as smooth as possible. Therefore, after setting the stones and grinding the surface, the stonemasons had to make minor repairs. Flint inclusions and other disturbances of the surface had to be chiseled off, and the holes repaired with patches. Broken corners and edges often had to be replaced. The occasional cracks that resulted from the settling of the masonry also had to be disguised by patches. Early examples can be seen at the Bent Pyramid and

Fig. **4**.101 Core, packing stones, and restored casing of the Unas Pyramid.

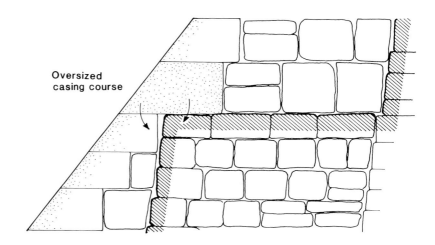

Fig. 4.102 Possible explanation for increased block heights at the beginning of a new core step.

Oversized casing course

Fig. 4.103 Changing heights of core steps, backing stones, and casing stones in the upper and lower parts of the Chephren Pyramid.

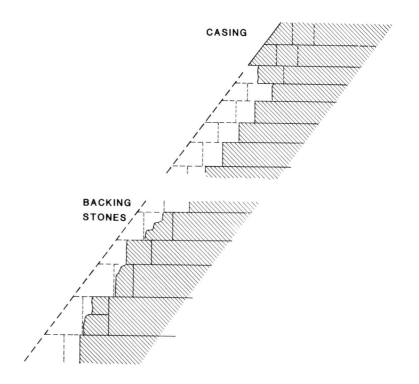

CASING

BACKING STONES

its secondary pyramid and at the pyramid of Senwosret I (figs. 4.106, 5.32);[178] later examples are abundant in the temple walls of the New Kingdom.

A different type of casing is found in rock temples and tomb chambers where bedrock had to be cased for stability or to provide the artists with a suitable background for their reliefs and inscriptions. This casing usually consists of thin slabs about 15 to 30 centimeters thick, which only mask the bedrock. Where such chambers had to be constructed like freestanding architecture and covered with stone roofs, this masonry can scarcely be called casing.

Fig. 4.104 Granite casing blocks of the Chephren Pyramid, with medieval wedge holes for splitting.

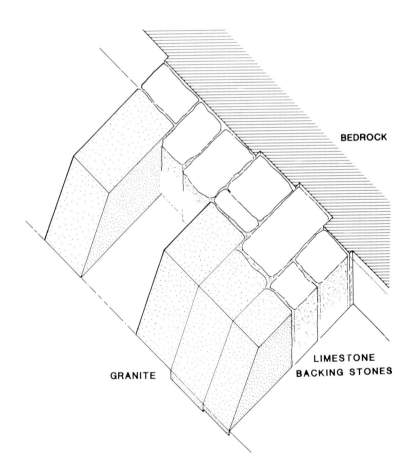

Fig. 4.105 Connection of the casing blocks with the backing stones and the rock core of the Chephren Pyramid.

BEDROCK

GRANITE

LIMESTONE
BACKING STONES

Fig. 4.106 Dislocated casing of the pyramid of Senwosret I, with numerous patches.

The earliest examples of burial chambers cased with limestone are tombs of the First Dynasty at Helwan,[179] certainly thought of as an alternative to the wooden timbering in contemporary tombs at Saqqara and Abydos.[180] The stones could be so large that they could cover a whole wall. One example at Helwan is $0.4 \times 2.0 \times 4.0$ meters.[181] In the somewhat later tomb of Khasekhemui at Abydos, the limestone wall casing was made of blocks only 25 to 33 centimeters high and set in six courses.[182] They were set in mortar, but their internal joints were frequently askew. Much advanced in refinement and careful execution is the limestone casing in the main tomb and in the southern tomb of Djoser.[183] Since the bedrock was ill-suited for decoration, eight courses of small blocks were set up in front and carved with decoration and reliefs in niches and prepared for an elaborate inlay of faience tiles. No exact documentation of these rooms was ever undertaken.

The actual burial chambers of Djoser and his successors in the Old Kingdom are built as gigantic granite constructions. A real casing was added in some of the pyramid burial chambers, where the gabled roofing beams were resting on top of a kind of backing stone, while the actual visible wall was built up in front as casing, which was relieved of bearing any weight and therefore safe from cracking (figs. 4.129, 4.130).[184] This was essential because the walls had to be inscribed with Pyramid Texts, which had to remain undamaged because of their magical value. In the Middle Kingdom, there are good examples of rock chambers cased with fine limestone slabs 15 centimeters thick, ready for decoration, such as the tombs of Neferu,[185] Khety,[186] Intef,[187] and Dagy.[188] Even the burial chambers of the Twelfth Dynasty that were never intended to be decorated were usually cased with limestone.[189]

In the New Kingdom, the more costly casing in limestone was restricted to a few royal tombs of the early Eighteenth Dynasty,[190] while most tombs

Fig. 4.107 The alabaster chapel (A) of the crypt of Mentuhotep at Deir el-Bahari, surrounded by the diorite casing (B) and the granite chamber walls (C) with a removed handling boss (arrow).

received only a coating of mud plaster. In some monumental Theban tombs of the Late Period, limestone casing for decoration was used to mask the fragile bedrock.[191]

In the Old and Middle Kingdoms, temple walls, especially those of the mortuary temples of the Fourth and Fifth Dynasties, were frequently cased with valuable stone. In general, either the limestone core walls were completely cased with granite[192] or at least the lower parts received a casing of orthostats made of granite[193] or, as in the case of Niuserra, of basalt.[194] In other temples, core walls were built of brick and cased with limestone or later with sandstone.[195]

An unusual casing of diorite slabs that measured 16 to 18 × 36 × 38 centimeters is found in the burial chamber of King Mentuhotep Nebhepetra (fig. 4.107).[196] These slabs fill the gap between the granite walls of the chamber and the alabaster shrine housing the wooden coffin of the king.

Fig. 4.108 Core masonry of the Mastabat el-Fara'un, with remains of packing stones and the white foundation of the casing.

The reason for the insertion of the diorite slabs—which was clearly not planned—is uncertain but may have been to protect the alabaster chamber against a threatening sideward thrust of the mountain.

CORE MASONRY

The core of walls, pyramids, mastabas, and other constructions from the Thinite period to the end of Pharaonic times were frequently built with roughly dressed or undressed fieldstones or quarry-dressed stones embedded in mortar. The outer faces of these core constructions were often smoothed with mortar to produce even faces and keep the stones from falling out of the wall.

Until the end of the Third Dynasty, core masonry was frequently set in inward-inclined layers. In pyramids, such layers surrounded a towerlike construction in the center. From the early Fourth Dynasty, the bedding joints became horizontal and the batter of the front face was produced by slightly setting back one course after the other. Even though the outer faces of cores were concealed behind a casing (figs. 4.78, 4.87), the front faces of cores were often built with larger blocks and in a more regular pattern.[197]

There are even examples for which one might doubt that the core was ever intended to be covered.[198]

In core masonry of the Third Dynasty and even in buildings of the Twelfth Dynasty, the size of the core material was so small that two people could carry one stone. During the Fourth Dynasty, however, there are examples of core blocks that surpass the casing blocks in size. In the mortuary temples of Chephren and Mycerinus, we see core blocks of up to $3 \times 5 \times 8$ meters that weigh about 220 tons.[199] The last example of excessively large core blocks is the Mastabat el-Fara'un, which is built in ten courses of limestone blocks 1.8 meters high (fig. 4.108).[200]

TABLE 4.1. CORE CONSTRUCTION OF MAJOR PYRAMIDS OF THE OLD KINGDOM

Pyramid	Layers	Steps
Djoser	12	6
Sekhemkhet		
E1	13	7
E2	14	7
Zawiyet el-Aryan	13–14	5?
Elephantine	?	?
Kula	3	3–4
Sinki	3	4
Zawiyet el-Mayitin	4	3–4
Seila	3 + x	4
Meidum		
E1	8	7
E2	9	8
Southern Pyramid	3	4
Bent Pyramid	12?	13?
Red Pyramid	?	?
Cheops	14–16?	15–17?
Djedefra	?	?
Chephren	?	?
Mycerinus	?	7
Userkaf	?	6?
Sahura	?	6
Neferirkara	?	8?
Neferefra	?	?
Niuserra	?	7
Djedkara Isesi	?	6
Unas	possibly 8	? (certain)
Teti	?	5
Merenra	?	? (certain)
Pepy I	? (certain)	? (certain)
Pepy II	8	8–9

Fig. 4.109 Reconstruction of the corner of the pyramid of Senwosret I, with radiating skeleton walls of the core.

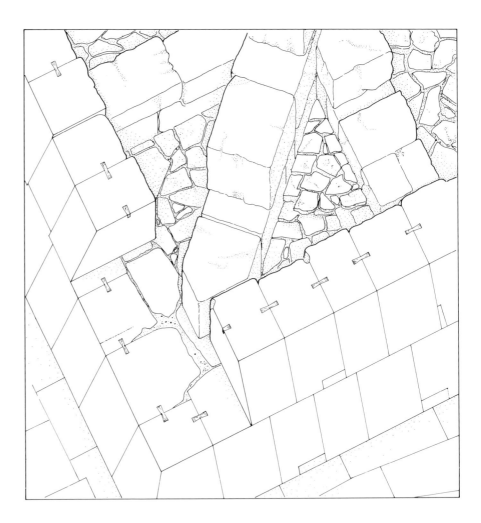

Since the core masonries of the pyramids of the Fourth Dynasty are still more or less intact, it is difficult to decide if they are constructed in horizontal courses running through the whole building or if they are structured in layers with horizontal courses that possibly run through the whole building (Table 4.1).[201] In the central core of the mortuary temple of Mentuhotep at Deir el-Bahari, the outer face is constructed of huge, practically undressed boulders and the fill behind consists of *tafl*.[202]

The cores of the pyramids of Senwosret I, Amenemhat II, and Senwosret II are reinforced by a system of walls radiating from the center toward the four cardinal points and four corners of the pyramids (fig. 4.109). The diagonal walls are flanked by several additional branches. The walls were made of huge, roughly shaped blocks, decreasing in size as they rose. The compartments in between were filled with rough fieldstones or brick. This method of core construction was used in a rudimentary manner in the base of the obelisk of Niuserra and in the core of the pyramid of Niuserra.[203] Perhaps the engineers of Senwosret I discovered the ancient method in these buildings.

In the New Kingdom, builders often made use of building material from demolished Middle Kingdom temples. This material was used mostly for foundations and cores. The fitting of such blocks of different sizes and shapes (even statues were used) into the surrounding masonry required some skill.[204]

Typical examples are Pylons II, III, and IX at Karnak (fig. 4.110). The cores are completely built from reused blocks arranged in long files and embedded into mortar with dividing walls of stronger masonry. For the much stronger casing, older blocks could be reused.[205] In rare situations, still-standing natural rock could also be used as the core for pyramids[206] and walls.[207]

Golvin and Goyon point out that from the Thirtieth Dynasty the distinction between core and casing is abandoned. Both now consist of closely connected blocks of equal dimensions, format, and quality.[208] This technique is already found in older buildings of the Late Period.

CONSTRUCTION GAPS

During the construction of a building, it was occasionally necessary to keep open temporary gaps or doors in the masonry in order to provide access for the workers and to permit the delivery of building materials. These gaps were closed only after completion of the work in the masonry that lay behind. Very often, these gaps can still be detected by the arrangement of joints in the core masonry, which clearly separate one block of masonry from the next. They can also be obscured in cases where the comblike

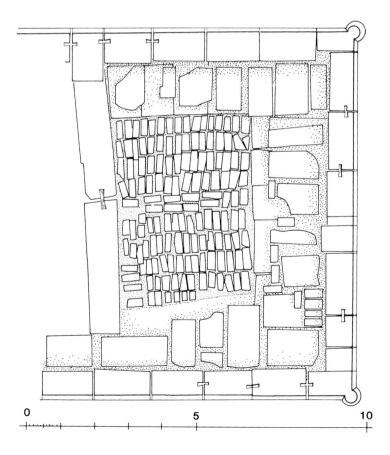

Fig. 4.110 Pylon IX at Karnak, with its core of reused blocks of the Aton temple.

0   5   10

Fig. **4.111** Construction gap above the entrance of the pyramid of Sahura at Abusir.

edges of the gaps could be used for closely interlocking the old with the new masonry.

Construction gaps are not of great interest in themselves, but they can teach us about the direction of the transport of material and the sequence of building phases. Generally, these gaps occur at the intersection of a construction road or ramp with already existing masonry, such as enclosure walls.[209] More interesting examples are in the core masonry of pyramids because they may give an indication of the direction of the construction ramps.

Unfortunately, such gaps have not yet been measured or studied. A few examples are visible. At the north side of the pyramids at Abusir, a huge gap opens in the center that was filled in later with rough fieldstones (figs. 4.17, 4.111, 4.112). Two rather narrow gaps in the core masonry of the south side of the pyramid of Pepy II can be observed. They certainly

indicated ramps or staircases leading up to the top of the first core step.[210] The huge trench in the core masonry above the entrance cut of the Mastabat el-Fara'un can also be considered as a construction gap. These trenches permitted the erection of the pyramids at an early phase when work in the underground corridor and chambers was not yet completed.

The entrance passage and probably also the ascending corridor and gallery of the Cheops Pyramid were constructed in such a trench (fig. 4.113). This trench had to remain open until the building of the roofs of the gallery and the upper crypt was completed and would have served as an interior access ramp not only for the construction of the gallery and crypt, but probably for the whole pyramid.

Construction gaps in the brick retaining walls of Saite tombs had to be kept open. They were protected by a brick arch and were occasionally closed rather carelessly, but hidden by the wall plaster.[211]

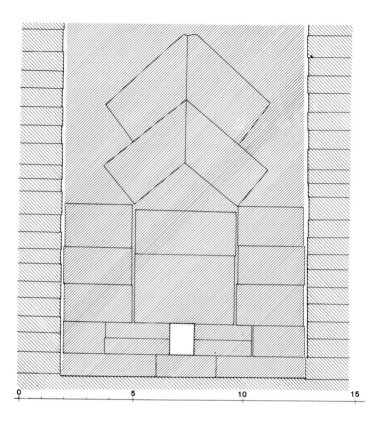

Fig. 4.113 The entrance passage of the Cheops Pyramid in its construction gap.

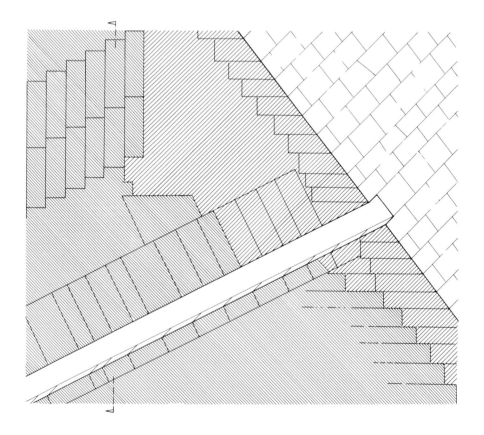

Since the main aim of this book is not the description of the architectural forms but of their construction, only the technical aspects of Egyptian stone roofing are considered here. In constructing stone roofs, the Egyptian builders were faced with choosing the right material, the correct proportions of the roofing beams, and the necessary type of roof. The conditions were, of course, different in a building whose roof had to carry only its own weight and in another whose roof was exposed to pressure either from masonry piled on it or from the natural rock of the mountain when the construction was underground. In principle, four types of roof were in use: the flat roof, the corbeled roof, the pointed or arched saddle roof, and the true vault.

The most natural solution, the flat roof, was the only known roofing type used during the Third Dynasty, and only at the end of that dynasty, in the pyramid of Meidum, was the corbeled roof introduced. Two thousand years earlier, corbeled domes had covered the burial chambers of megalithic cairns in western Europe. A few hundred years later, the tholos tomb makes its appearance in the Aegean world (Mesara). No bridge seems to connect these similar architectural phenomena, however.

In the Fourth Dynasty, there was an interesting development of the flat type in the pyramids of Snofru and Cheops. In the Cheops Pyramid, the pointed saddle roof was introduced. Arched saddle roofs also came into existence in the Fourth Dynasty, but were used mainly in the Middle and New Kingdoms. Only in the Twenty-fifth Dynasty was the true stone vault introduced, apparently a translation into stone of the brick vault, which was then more than 2000 years old. An outside influence cannot be established, since foreign builders worked with true arches and vaults of stone only 100 years later.[212]

Flat Roofs · The first flat limestone roof can be found in the complex of Djoser, in the entrance hall. Already in this early construction, the width of the rooms that could be roofed was enlarged by the introduction of engaged pillars, carrying architraves and reducing the span over the center to 1.3 meters. In the burial chamber of the king, which is only 1.65 meters wide, the strength of the roof is increased by setting the granite roofing beams upright, with a height of 1.1 meters (fig. 5.9).

After these rather modest beginnings, flat granite ceiling beams 2 meters thick cover the crypt of Cheops, which is 5.25 meters wide. But its builders—perhaps irritated by cracks that opened during the construction—distrusted its stability and added a fantastic system of five relieving chambers on top (fig. 4.114). The four lower ones were roofed with horizontal granite beams; the uppermost one, with a pointed saddle roof of limestone.

Since the stability of limestone was limited and granite in sufficient sizes and quantities was not available, it was not until the introduction of sandstone in the Eleventh Dynasty that the number of possibilities available to the architects of the Middle and New Kingdoms increased. This is felt

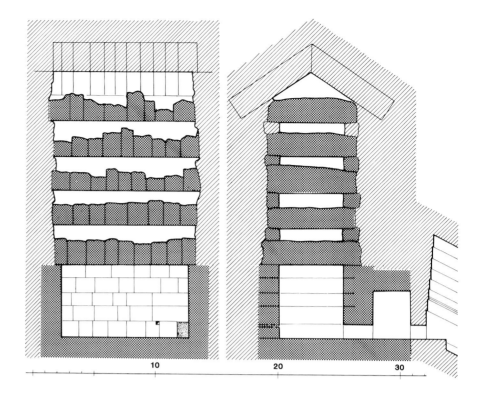

Fig. 4.114 The crypt of Cheops and its five relieving chambers. The left section is seen from south to north; the right section, from east to west.

10   20   30

already in the more lofty construction of the hypostyle hall and ambulatory of the Mentuhotep temple.[213]

But only in the New Kingdom were spans of 6 to 7 meters reached. The roofing slabs of the hypostyle hall of Karnak were 9 meters long and 1.25 meters thick, and bridged an aisle of 6.7 meters (fig. 4.115). The span of the gate of Pylon I measures 7.49 meters and of Pylon II 6.93 meters. They might, however, have been covered by a granite architrave. The sandstone architraves of the center aisle of the hypostyle hall are 7.25 to 7.35 meters long and span a distance of 4.72 to 4.82 meters (according to Richard Lepsius). One may assume, therefore, that the limit was approximately 7 meters, for either granite or sandstone (fig. 4.116). In buildings where longer distances were to be spanned, stone had to be replaced by wood. Most of these examples date from the Ptolemaic and Roman periods.[214]

To ease the problems of gaining sufficiently large blocks and transporting them, architraves were frequently combined from two or more beams. As long as two beams are placed together side by side, the strength of the construction is not considerably reduced.[215] But this was certainly the case when beams were resting on each other and architraves were made up of four pieces (fig. 4.117).[216] Egyptian builders never tried to hollow out architraves to reduce their weight, as was done in Greek architecture.[217]

Corbeled Roofs · A corbeled roof consists of a series of overhanging block courses that gradually approach each other from opposite sides until the gap in the center can easily be bridged by one stone.[218] The construction of corbeled roofs would have been done simultaneously with the rising of the surrounding core masonry in order to prevent the corbel blocks from falling in from their own weight.

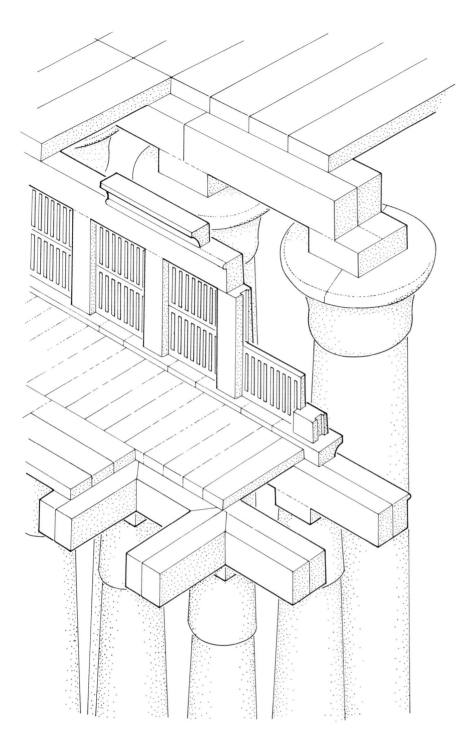

Fig. 4.115 The roof of the hypostyle hall at Karnak.

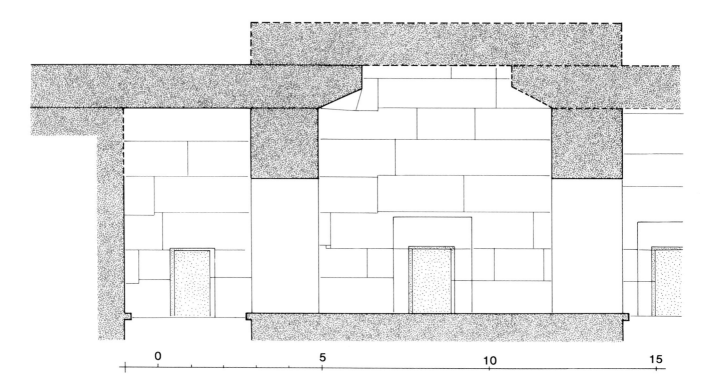

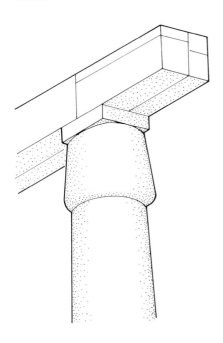

Fig. 4.116 Section through the center of the Osireion of Sety I at Abydos.

Fig. 4.117 Architraves of the hypostyle hall at Karnak, which are composed of several beams.

The earliest example is the burial chamber of the Meidum Pyramid (fig. 4.118). It spans a distance of 2.65 meters. Since this space could easily have been bridged by a flat ceiling, the purpose of the corbeling can only have been to relieve the pressure of the pyramid masonry on top. A religious meaning, however, cannot be ruled out.[219] This roof, which is only 5.05 meters high, is constructed of seven courses of irregularly wide and high overhangs.

After this modest beginning, the corbeled roofs of the following pyramids of Dahshur and Giza are quite impressive. In the Bent Pyramid, one burial chamber is 4.96 × 6.30 meters wide and 17.3 meters high; the other one, 5.26 × 7.97 meters wide and 16.48 meters high (fig. 4.119). In Snofru's Red Pyramid, the chamber is 4.18 × 8.35 meters wide and 14.67 meters high (fig. 4.120). They are corbeled from all four sides so that a kind of stepped cupola is produced, built in fourteen to sixteen steps. These magnificent roof constructions were surpassed in length only by the ascending gallery of the Cheops Pyramid, which is 46.71 meters long (fig. 4.121). Here the difficulties of the construction were considerably increased by the roof's slope at an angle of 26 degrees. Except for a few examples of Old Kingdom private tombs, no other corbeled roofs are known in Egypt with the same kind of roof construction.

Systems that were based on the same principle and that looked only slightly different were still being used in the New Kingdom. Two important examples are found in the Hatshepsut temple at Deir el-Bahari. The main sanctuary, with a width of 3.35 meters, actually has a corbeled roof (fig. 4.122). Its underside is dressed off in order to create a corbeled (false) arch.[220] To reduce the pressure of the mountain on top, a relieving cham-

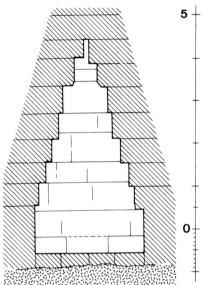

Fig. 4.118 The crypt of the pyramid of Meidum, with its corbeled roof.

Fig. 4.119 Looking up the the lower chamber (northern entrance system) of the Bent Pyramid, with the entrance to the upper chamber.

ber with a pointed saddle roof was added. The southern offering hall of the same temple also has a corbeled (false) vault consisting of only five courses, with a central joint on top separating the two blocks of the last course. Since this building was standing free, no relieving chamber was necessary (fig. 4.123).[221]

Constructed in the same way are the false vaults of the temple of Sety I at Abydos. They consist of only one corbel and the coping stone (fig. 4.124).[222] Another interesting example is found in the central part of the Osireion of the same temple at Abydos.[223] Here the roofing beams of the side wings reach over the architraves of the central part, producing a corbel that reaches 1.23 meters into the central part. These corbels carry the central roof slabs, the span of which is thus reduced from 6.96 to 4.50

Fig. 4.120 (overleaf) Looking at the entrance wall of the crypt of the northern pyramid of Snofru at Dahshur.

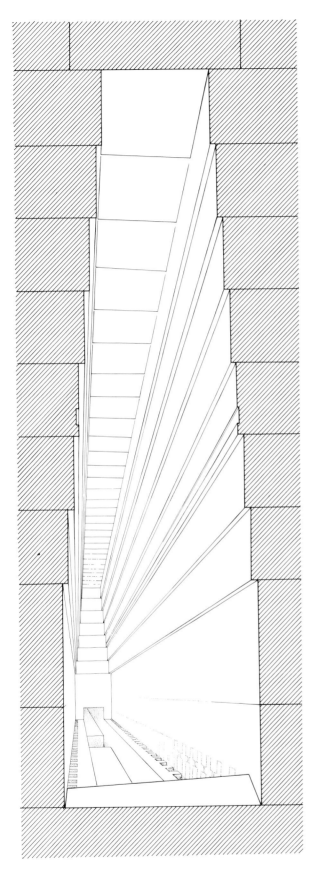

Fig. 4.121 Section through the ascending gallery of the Cheops Pyramid.

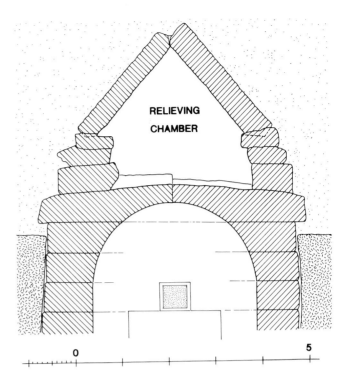

Fig. 4.122 Section through the relieving chamber of the Amun sanctuary in the Deir el-Bahari temple of Hatshepsut.

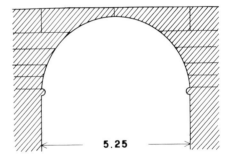

Fig. 4.123 Section through the southern offering hall of the Deir el-Bahari temple of Hatshepsut.

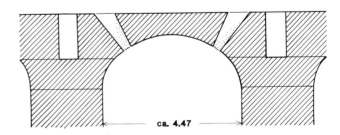

Fig. 4.124 Roof of the sanctuaries of the temple of Sety I at Abydos.

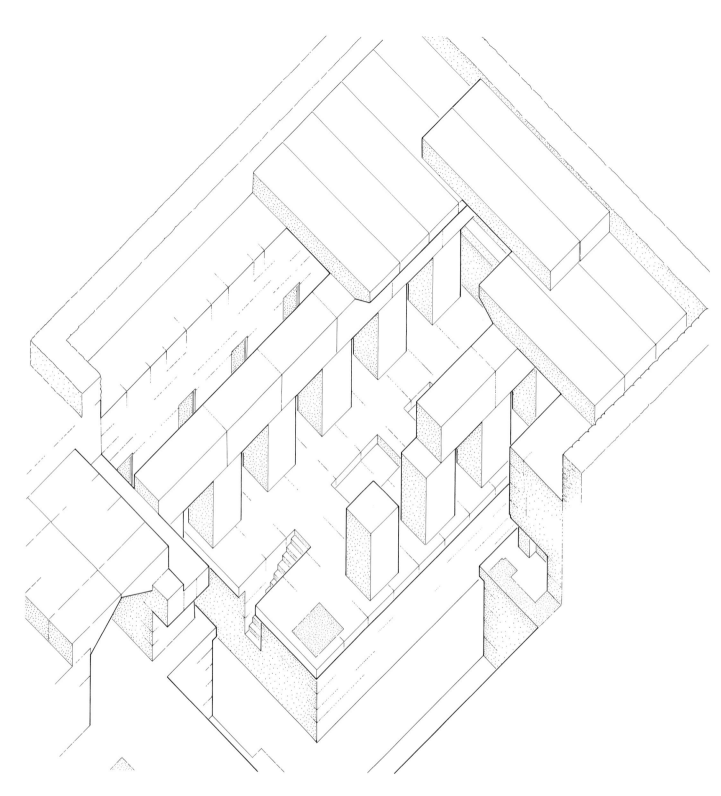

Fig. 4.125 Reconstruction of the Osireion
of Sety I at Abydos.

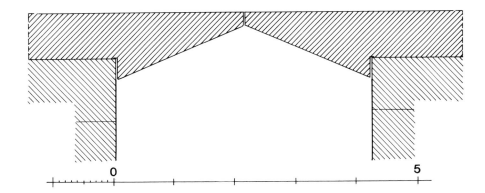

meters. The roofing slabs were long enough to rest above the architraves—that is, over 7 meters. The roofing slabs of the side wings are more than 10 meters long.

Also in the Osireion of Sety I (fig. 4.125), a kind of pitch roof was created, covering the 4.75-meter-wide sarcophagus chamber,[224] consisting of two beams pushed together against the center and cut out into the shape of a triangle. The blocks were 1.18 meters high and had a notch at the lower edge to prevent them from being turned downward (fig. 4.126). This system could actually be considered as a kind of saddle roof. Another example from this architecturally interesting temple complex is the roof of the staircase in the southern part of the temple (fig. 4.127).[225] Here one arch was made from a single slab, curved from below. The imposts are of different heights. The northern one is much higher up, resting on a kind of light corbel, whereas the southern one is deeper and protrudes considerably from the wall.

Saddle Roofs · Saddle roofs consist of pairs of roof beams or slabs leaning against each other at the top, thus directing the downward thrust into the side walls. The earliest examples, albeit of rather small scale, date from private tombs of the time of Snofru.[226] Only in the Cheops Pyramid were they used at a greater scale (fig. 4.114): the roof of the topmost relieving chamber of the royal crypt is made of eleven pairs of beams, 7 to 8 meters long and weighing about 36 tons each; and the roof of the "queen's chamber" is made of six pairs of beams set upright and at an angle of 30 degrees. The flat ceiling of the entrance passage of the pyramid is relieved by a double layer of enormous saddle stones, about 3 meters long and set with a pitch of 40 degrees.[227] They are the first examples of a roofing system that was in constant use for the burial chambers of all the pyramids of the Fifth and Sixth Dynasties (fig. 4.128). The lower ends of these beams are always at right angles to their slope, so that they are not resting on a horizontal impost but direct the thrust away from the chamber walls. Some of these beams are impressive in size and weight and must have created considerable problems for the builders.

In some cases,[228] the actual side walls of the chambers were set as a separate casing in front of the masonry that carried the thrust of the roof, so that these walls did not receive any pressure from above (fig. 4.129,

Fig. 4.127 Roof construction in the staircase of the temple of Sety I at Abydos.

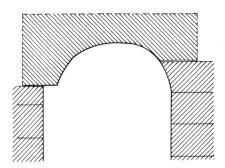

Fig. 4.128 The exposed roof of the crypt of Pepy I at Saqqara.

Fig. 4.128 The exposed roof of the crypt of Pepy I at Saqqara.

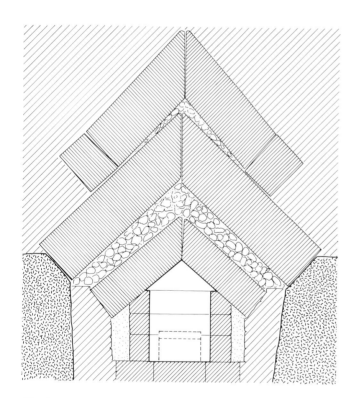

Fig. 4.129 The roof of the crypt of Niuserra at Abusir.

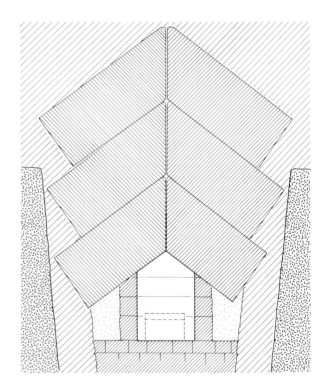

Fig. 4.130 The roof of the crypt of Djedkara at Saqqara.

Fig. 4.131 The crypt of Amenemhat I (?) at Thebes.

4.130). This was important because the walls were inscribed with Pyramid Texts that had to be protected from cracking.

Beams sitting on a horizontal impost were constructed from only the Eleventh Dynasty on.[229] In the burial chambers of Mentuhotep, Neb-hepetra, and Amenemhat I (fig. 4.131), however, a strange mixture with a corbeled roofing system was achieved by setting the inclined beams on a course of blocks overhanging the side walls and being chamfered according to the slope of the ceiling. Another combination of a saddle roof with corbeling (or a corbeled false arch) is found in the Anubis Sanctuary of the Hatshepsut Temple. Two blocks meeting in the center are rounded below and rest on corbel blocks.[230]

Experimentation with different kinds of impost systems shows that the Egyptian builders were aware of the possibility that the upper front edge of the side walls could easily be damaged by the pressure of the saddle beams. In some examples of the Middle Kingdom, the critical wall area had been replaced from the outset with separate patches. The saddle-roof construc-

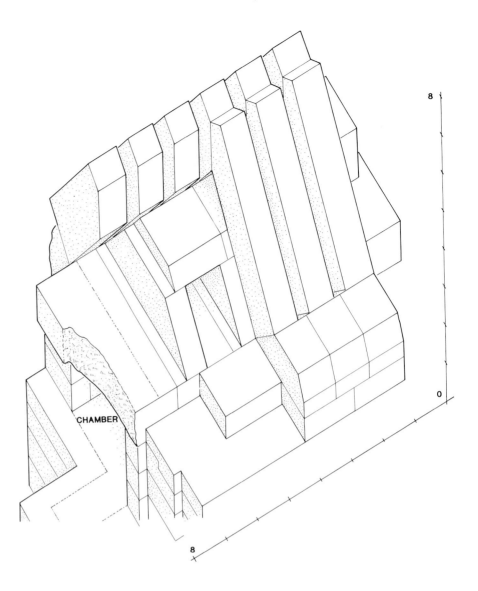

Fig. 4.132 The roof construction of the pyramid of Amenemhat II at Dahshur.

CHAMBER

8

0

8

tions of the Old Kingdom were exceptional due to their gigantic dimensions, but the smaller examples of the Middle Kingdom actually display greater technical refinement. Several interesting examples can be found in the royal burial chambers of Amenemhat II (fig. 4.132), Amenemhat III at Hawara (fig. 3.26), Awibra Hor (fig. 4.133), and Khendjer (fig. 3.27) and in private tombs of the great residential cemeteries.[231]

The builders of the burial chamber of Amenemhat II designed a peculiar roofing system that looks impressive but is to some degree ineffective (fig. 4.132).[232] The 2.8-meter-wide chamber is covered with horizontal beams, which were thought to be relieved by a saddle roof made of six pairs of sloping beams. They were—perhaps to ease their setting—positioned at intervals, which were later closed with smaller stones. Below this saddle roof, resting on the flat chamber roof, five crossbeams carried another intermediate stone roof. This unusual construction was apparently aimed at preventing the sloping beams from being pushed inward. The builders did not realize, however, that it also transferred the thrust of the sloping beams directly to the chamber roof. Because everything was overdimensioned, the roof resisted the pressure.

A building disaster in the pyramid of Amenemhat III at Dahshur induced the builders of the king to build a second pyramid at Hawara (fig. 3.26).[233] Here the chamber was carved out of one single stone, which was completely protected from any pressure from above. This was achieved by a huge saddle roof of sloping quartzite beams that did not rest on the side walls of the chamber but farther out. Here the cavity under the sloping beams was filled with two courses of blocks. They did not sit on the chamber roof, but on the walls surrounding it.[234] This principle prevailed from then on in the royal tombs of the later Middle Kingdom (fig. 3.27).[235]

Besides this common version of the pointed saddle roof, the Egyptian builders used the same architectural principle to create a kind of false vault by dressing the underside of the sloping beams into the shape of an arch. How this was achieved can be studied at the unfinished parts of the subterranean chambers in the pyramid of Amenemhat III at Dahshur (fig. 4.134).[236] After a preliminary, rough vault was cut into the underside of the sloping roofing beams, the height of the intended vault was measured

Fig. 4.133 The crypt of King Hor at Dahshur.

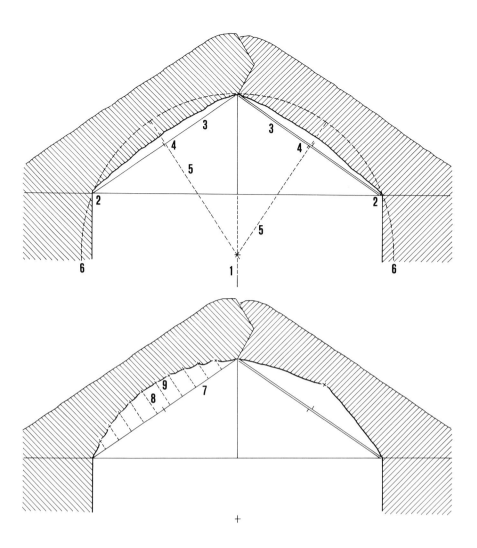

Fig. 4.134 The construction of a vault in the pyramid of Amenhemhat III at Dahshur.

and marked with a vertical line in the center of the end walls. In the height of the impost of the vault, a horizontal line was drawn across the end walls. The points of impost and the vertex of the arch were then connected by a line that was the hypotenuse of a triangle. This line was divided in half, and a builder's square was set at this point, one leg along the hypotenuse, the other one intersecting the vertical center line.

In this way, the center and the diameter of the intended arch were determined, being considerably below the level of the impost. On a plain surface, probably outside the pyramid, a full-size model of such an arch was drawn.[237] In this model drawing, the intended distance between the hypotenuse and the line of the arch could be measured and noted, perhaps on an ostrakon[238] that was carried into the pyramid. With the help of these notes, on the wall the real distances could be marked along the same line of measurements as on the model drawing. If the stone still had rough bosses, then small holes had to be cut in order to set the marks in their proper places.

This procedure not only was carried out at the end walls, but was repeat-

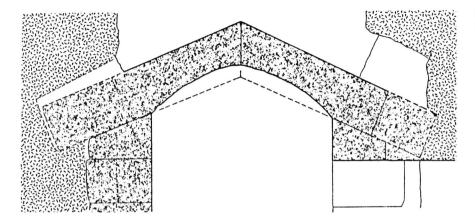

Fig. 4.135 The roof of the crypt of Mycerinus.

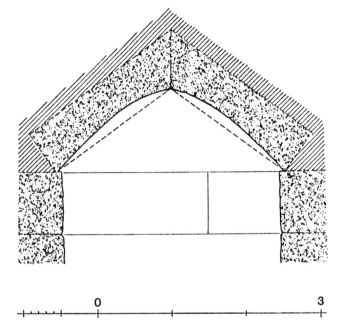

Fig. 4.136 The roof of the crypt of Shepseskaf at Saqqara (Mastabat el-Fara'un).

ed in a simplified manner all over the ceiling at distances of 15 centimeters, so that the rough vault was finally covered with hundreds of measuring marks that gave the sculptor the outline of the vault. In order to gain these points, a wooden frame[239] probably would have replaced the construction drawing and marks on the end walls. This method resembles that used by sculptors for transferring their measurements and reminds us of the fact that the building of stone chambers in Egyptian architecture had some similarity to carving or sculpting a cave.

From the reign of Sahura, the huge offering halls and the *pr-wrw*-halls of mortuary temples (5.25 meters wide, 21 meters long) were roofed with

Forerunners of this type of vault had been made for the crypts of Mycerinus (fig. 4.135)[240] and Shepsesptah (fig. 4.136),[241] both in granite. The impost of these "vaults" is not level but follows the slope of the roofing beams. The shape of the arch is irregular, and there is no circular segment at all.

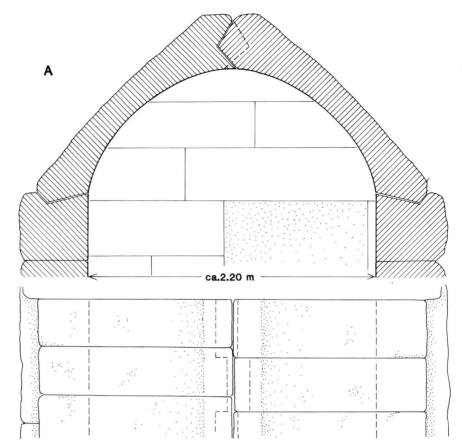

Fig. 4.138 The roofs of (A) one of the queens' crypts of the pyramid of Senwosret III at Dahshur and (B) the secondary tomb of the "Mastaba du nord" at Lisht.

Fig. 4.137 Section through the passage into the tomb of King Mentuhotep at Deir el-Bahari.

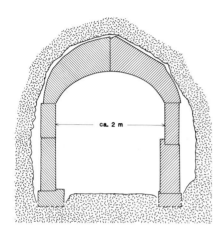

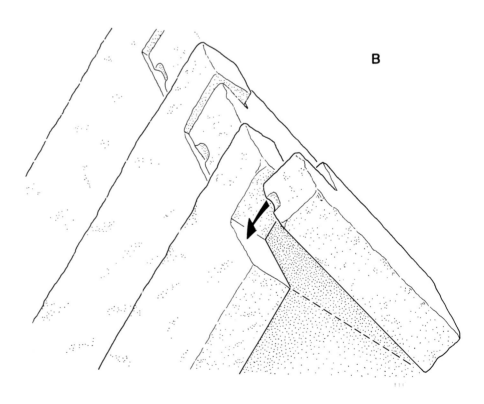

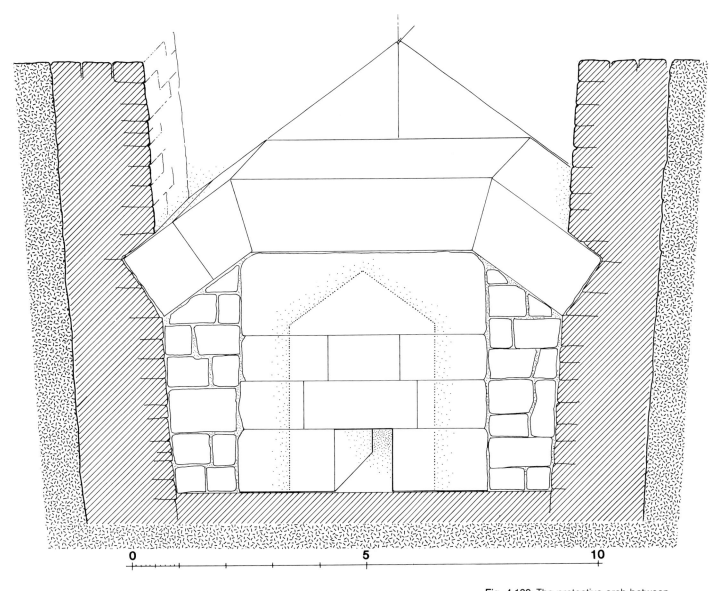

Fig. 4.139 The protective arch between antechamber and burial chamber in the pyramid of King Djedkara at Saqqara.

such false vaults. Unfortunately, all these gigantic constructions have been destroyed and are reconstructed from only a few fragments.[242] The imposts of these vaults are level. The roofing blocks must have been of enormous dimensions. There are many examples from burial chambers of the Middle Kingdom, starting with the entrance passage of the crypt of Mentuhotep (fig. 4.137),[243] which had sandstone roofing slabs. Good examples are also the vaults of the crypts of Senwosret III and Amenemhat III at Dahshur (with sixteen more rooms vaulted this way).[244] In the princesses' gallery of the pyramid of Senwosret III (fig. 4.138A)[245] and in the pyramid of Amenemhat III at Dahshur,[246] we also find examples of elaborate methods of joining the two sloping beams at the top. Here the joints are not straight but run in a zigzag line, with correspondent mortises and tenons on each block. The direction of the zigzag joint alternates from one block to the next. The system has prevented the saddle roof in the chambers of Amenemhat III from being pushed in, despite the heavy pressure from above.

An ingenious system of joining the roof slabs was used in the secondary

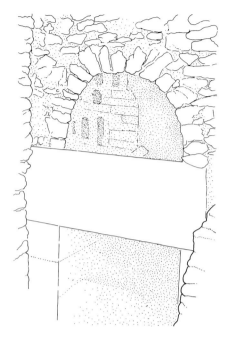

Fig. 4.140 The relieving arch in the tomb of vizier Hebsed-Neferkara of the Sixth Dynasty at Saqqara.

tomb of the "Mastaba du nord" at Lisht. A stepped projection on one slab fitted into a corresponding notch on the opposite block (fig. 4.138B).

One of the latest examples of a saddle roof has recently been discovered at Sharuna, covering the crypt of a huge Saite shaft tomb (S 14).[247]

True Stone Vaults · The variety of roofing systems available to the Egyptian builders and perhaps the rarity of timber necessary for its construction apparently prevented them from creating the true vault. It must have been considered too complicated to be carried out in stone, since it had been known in brick architecture from the First Dynasty.[248] In Pharaonic times, the vault was constructed in stone only in an emergency, perhaps due to a shortage of bricks[249] and never as a real breakthrough in construction methods. There is one curious example, however, from the roof of the crypt of Djedkara (fig. 4.139).[250] Here the separation between antechamber and crypt was relieved from above by a stone arch, constructed with three wedge-shaped blocks, with the central keystone (over 5 meters long) hanging suspended between the two side blocks. Had this construction not been hidden by masonry from below, we would have here a true stone arch with a span of about 5 meters.

There are a few more examples of true relieving arches from the Sixth Dynasty at Saqqara (fig. 4.140),[251] made to protect doorways below. These vaults are not made of wedge-shaped voussoirs but of roughly squared fieldstones, the joints opening against the extrados being filled with smaller stones or pebbles. These arches span a distance of only about 1 meter.

A change came only in the Twenty-fifth Dynasty (about 750 B.C.) when barrel vaults with wedge-shaped voussoirs were first developed at least at three places in Egypt. In the burial crypt of Shepenwepet I[252] and the chapels of Amenirdis, Shepenwepet II, and Nitocris,[253] the roofs were vaulted in this manner (fig. 4.141). The lower parts of the vaults of Amenirdis and Nitocris still consist of two to four corbeled courses with horizontal imposts and wedge-shaped voussoirs with radial joints in the upper parts of the vault. The vaults of the chapels are true semicircles (1.96 to 2.36 meters wide); that of the crypt of Shepenwepet I is still elliptical. These constructions do not give us any hint as to the method used for the vaulting. One assumes that no wooden framework was applied. Probably the chambers

Fig. 4.141 True vaults in the funerary chapels of the tombs of Amenirdis, Shepenwepet I, and Nitocris at Medinet Habu.

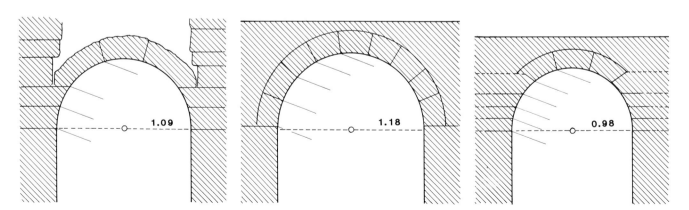

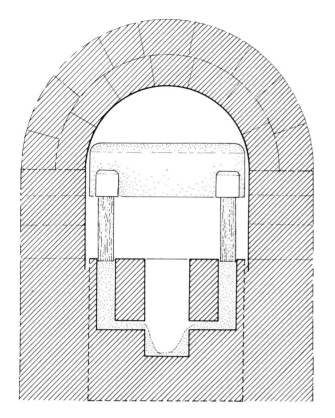

Fig. 4.142 The barrel vault over the sarcophagus of Neferibra-sa-Neith at Saqqara.

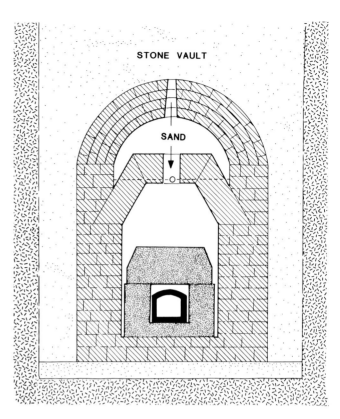

Fig. 4.143 The roofing system in "Campbell's Tomb" at Giza.

were filled with sand and debris, and on top a mound of stones and mud was piled up to carry the vault during its construction.

At Giza, three to four vaulted tomb structures with a span of 2.8 meters are known from the same period.[254] At Saqqara, the crypts of Neferibra-sa-Neith (fig. 4.142), Wahibra-men, and Hor are covered by barrel vaults constructed of two rings of blocks,[255] with a span of 1.8 meters. The so-called Campbell's Tomb at Giza shows a combination of a true barrel vault of three rings with a much more primitive vaulting system below, similar to that of Djedkara already mentioned (fig. 4.143).[256] Since the canon of shapes and forms of Egyptian architecture was already standardized at this later period, this technical improvement could no longer influence Egyptian building. Arches and vaults of greater dimensions were used in the Ptolemaic and Roman periods for buildings in Hellenistic style.[257]

NOTES

1. See, in general, *CEAEM,* 69–74. A rich source of information is the Karnak publications by the French–Egyptian expeditions (*Karnak-Nord* I–IV; *Karnak* I–V).

2. *CEAEM,* 69.

3. See the famous collapse of columns of the hypostyle hall of Karnak in October 1899 (G. Legrain, *ASAE* 1 [1900]: 121–140; Legrain, *Karnak,* figs. 158–162).

4. Lauer, *Pyramid à degrés* II, pls. 74, 87, 88, 90.

5. Ibid., pls. 10, 19–20.

6. Lauer, *Hist. Mon.*, figs. 61–63.

7. For Meidum, see Rowe, "Meydum," pl. 10; for the Red Pyramid, R. Stadelmann, *MDAIK* 38 (1982): 382, pl. 88a.

8. J. Dorner, *MDAIK* 42 (1986): 44, fig. 4.

9. Reisner, *Mycerinus*, 73–74.

10. The spreading of pure sand in the foundation trench was an important part of the foundation ritual, symbolizing the resting of the temples on a "primeval hill" (Golvin and Goyon, *Karnak*, 37 [4]; H. Ricke, *ZÄS* 71 [1935]: 110, n. 1).

11. Maragioglio, *Piramidi* VI, pl. 16.

12. Ibid., pl. 3.

13. Hölscher, *Chephren*, 73, fig. 61; Ricke, *Harmachis*, 20–22.

14. Maragioglio, *Piramidi* III, pl. 17 [8].

15. Borchardt, *Neuserre*, 99–100, p. 17.

16. Ricke, *Sonnenheiligtum* I, fig. 24.

17. Arnold, *Mentuhotep*, pl. 10.

18. See the assemblage of sections in Arnold, *Amenemhet III* I, pl. 41. Good examples from the Eighteenth Dynasty are in Jacquet, *Trésor*, pls. 13–17.

19. Hölscher, *Mortuary Temple* II, 31, fig. 32; D. P. Hansen, *JARCE* 6 (1967): 7, pl. 9, fig. 7.

20. *Karnak-Nord* III, pls. 26–37 (gate between temple of Amun and Montu at Karnak, Twenty-sixth to Thirtieth Dynasty: eleven courses of brick, 2 meters thick).

21. Arnold, *Senwosret I,* I, pl. 28c.

22. De Lubicz, *Temple* II, pl. 94c; *Temple* III, 130, fig. 222.

23. M. Pillet, *ASAE* 23 (1923): 110, pl. 1 [2]; H. Chevrier, *ASAE* 27 (1927): 140, fig. 2; *Karnak* IV, 93, fig. 10; *Karnak* V, 13, fig. 6; *Karnak* VII, 50–51, 62; *Karnak* VIII, 366–367; *Karnak-Nord* III, pls. 40, 41, 43; *Karnak-Nord* IV, pls. 30–32; De Lubicz, *Temple* II, pl. 94B; Golvin and Goyon, *Karnak*, 95.

24. H. Chevrier *ASAE* 46 (1947): 157, pl. 47.

25. Alexandre Varille, *Quelques caractéristiques du temple Pharaonique* (Cairo, 1946).

26. De Lubicz, *Temple* III, 355–363.

27. Jacquet, *Trésor*, 20, pls. 13, 15, 21.

28. H. Ricke, *ZÄS* 71 (1935): 110.

29. *CEAEM*, 76.

30. *Karnak* II, 265–267, figs. 13–15.

31. For the foundations of the Lateran obelisk, see P. Barguet, *ASAE* 50 (1950): 272, figs. 2–6.

32. Mortuary temple of Mycerinus and lower temple of Userkaf at Abu Ghurab, as previously noted.

33. Henry G. Lyons, *A Report on the Temples of Philae* (Cairo, 1908), pl. 13.

34. Examples of these setting lines are preserved (Jacquet, *Trésor*, pl. 44B; Arnold, *Mentuhotep*, pls. 8c–d, 17a–c, 19a; Arnold, *Qasr el-Sagha*, fig. 2, pl. 11a; Arnold, *Senwosret I* I, pls. 25d, 86).

35. For example, see Jacquet, *Trésor*, pls. 44B, 47A; for columns, see fig. 9.

36. Arnold, *Senwosret I* I, fig. 19.

37. A graphically clear reconstruction of the procedure (involving more complicated Ptolemaic-Roman lever hole-systems) is given in Golvin and Goyon, *Karnak*, 110; Lacau and Chevrier show lever mortises also at the upper edge for imposing a second pair of levers from the top (*Hatshepsout* I, fig. 1).

38. Reisner, *Mycerinus*, 75.

39. *Karnak-Nord* III, pls. 43, 44. The great number of lever mortises is difficult to explain. The end blocks have such cuttings from three sides.

40. *CEAEM*, fig. 80; tomb T near Theban Tomb no. 386 (unpublished data).

41. Petrie, *Kahun*, 22 (lid for foundation deposit in valley temple of Kahun); Arnold, *Senwosret I* I, pl. 91.

42. Good examples are in Borchardt, *Amonstempel*, 17, fig. 13 (here, fig. 4.15); Jéquier, *Pépi II* III, fig. 7 (here, fig. 4.16).

43. Winlock, *Hibis*, pl. 26H.

44. *Karnak-Nord* IV, figs. 7a, 33, 37, 39, 40b, 41a. Similar grooves can be seen running horizontally along the side and rear faces of the roof slabs of the *chapelle blanche* (Lacau and Chevrier, *Sésostris Ier*, pl. 8).

45. J.-C. Golvin and J. Larronde (*ASAE* 68 [1982]: 180, fig. 4 [9]) and Golvin and Goyon (*Karnak*, 111) assume that such shallow grooves appear only in the period after the Thirtieth Dynasty.

46. Jacquet, *Trésor*, figs. 21, 25; for casing of the pyramid of Amenemhat III, see fig. 4.22, p. 123.

47. Also proposed by J.-C. Golvin and J. Larronde, *ASAE* 68 (1982): 184, fig. 6.

48. Reisner, *Mycerinus*, 76.

49. Borchardt, *Neuserre*, 103. The blocks measure 1.75 × 2.5 × 9(!) meters, or 40 cubic meters.

50. Maragioglio, *Piramidi* VIII, 70–72, with a useful discussion of the roofing system of the crypt of Djedkara Isesi. The blocks are 27 cubic meters.

51. For examples, see fig. 4.82 (1–3a, 5), p. 155.

52. Arnold, *Amenemhet III* I, pls. 42, 43, 45, 48, folding map 2; Arnold, *Mentuhotep*, pls. 20a–b, 37; Maragioglio, *Piramidi* III, pls. 4, 11, 16; Reisner, *Mycerinus*, plan II [4], with inclined construction line.

53. Lipinska, *Tuthmosis III*, 56, fig. 49; Jéquier, *Architecture* I, pl. 36 [1].

54. De Lubicz, *Karnak*, pl. 395.

55. Arnold, *Amenemhet III* I, pls. 42, 43, 48, folding map 2.

56. Jacquet, *Trésor*, 123, where 30 percent of the blocks have oblique joints. For more examples, see *CEAEM*, figs. 100, 101, 103.

57. *CEAEM*, figs. 104–109.

58. Josef Durm, *Die Baukunst der Griechen*, Handbuch der Architektur (Darmstadt, 1881), 24.

59. D. Stocks, *Manchester Archaeological Bulletin* 2 (1987): 49–50.

60. For the casing of the pyramid of Mycerinus, see *CEAEM*, fig. 100.

61. Arnold, *Qasr el-Sagha*, pls. 2–3.

62. Jacquet, *Trésor*, 111–112, fig. 21; Arnold, *Amenemhet III* I, fig. 39; Winlock, *Hibis*, pl. 16D.

63. Arnold, *Amenemhet III* I, pl. 6c.

64. *Karnak* VIII, 199, fig. 3.

65. For details, see pp. 266–267.

66. Lauer, *Hist. Mon.*, 253.

67. Arnold, *Mentuhotep*, 41; Winlock, *Hibis*, pls. 15, 16, 24, 48.

68. For example, at the column bases in the mortuary temple of the queen of Djedkara Isesi (unpublished data).

69. Jacquet, *Trésor*, 124, fig. 25.

70. D. Arnold, in *Pyramid Studies and Other Essays Presented to I. E. S. Edwards*, ed. J. Baines, T. G. H. James, A. Leahy, and A. F. Shore (London, 1988), 54–56.

71. Lacau and Chevrier, *Hatshepsout* I, 9, fig. 1.

72. Maragioglio, *Piramidi* IV, 18

73. Many examples are in Jéquier, *Architecture* I, pls. 33, 60; II, pls. 29, 59.

74. See, for example, the position of the horizontal joints in the temple Qasr el-

Sagha, which results in beautiful blocks for the architraves of the chapels (Arnold, *Qasr el-Sagha*, pls. 25, 26).

75. De Lubicz assumed that a close correlation existed between the decoration scheme and the joining of blocks, even from the front face of a block to its rear. But such a system seems too sophisticated for practical use (*Temple* II, pls. 99, 100; *Temple* III, 114–138). See also H. Senk, *ASAE* 49 (1949): 175–182, who collected examples for a canonical arrangement of joints in tombs and temples.

76. *CEAEM*, 165.

77. Hölscher, *Chephren*, 43, fig. 26. The same type of cramps appears much later at Bogazkoy and Zinçirli (Naumann, *Architektur*, 104, figs. 90, 91).

78. Lauer, *Ounas*, pl. 12B.

79. Unpublished data. Round mortises for the connection of superimposed blocks are quite common in Anatolia (Naumann, *Architektur*, 105–107). Many of them were used, however, to fix wooden constructions on masonry.

80. Borchardt, *Sahure*, 45, pl. 9

81. Borchardt, *Neuserre*, 55, figs. 35, 36, pl. 13.

82. G. Legrain, *ASAE* 5 (1904): 4–8.

83. Cramps in the base of the Lateran obelisk are 83 centimeters long (P. Barguet, *ASAE* 50 [1950]: 272, fig. 2).

84. *CEAEM*, fig. 123. Peter Grossmann informs me that he observed cramp slots at least 80 centimeters long in the rear part of the temple of Hibis. They were added later when the temple was repaired, and they are arranged vertically.

85. Arnold, *Mentuhotep*, 41.

86. Arnold, *Senwosret I* I, 18, 59 n. 200, 62, 65, 81; Arnold, *Senwosret I* II (forthcoming). See also Arnold, *Amenemhet III* I, 12, 37, 80, fig. 38, pl. 2.

87. Arnold, *Qasr el-Sagha*, 17, pls. 7d, 11c, 24; Arnold and Winlock, *Mentuhotep*, pl. 20a.

88. Lacau and Chevrier, *Sésostris I*er II, pls. 4, 8.

89. Lacau and Chevrier, *Hatshepsout* I, 257, fig. 21; Gorringe, *Obelisks*, pl. 40; De Lubicz, *Temple* III, figs. 294E–F, 295; H. Chevrier, *ASAE* 53(1955): 17, figs. 4, 5; Hölscher, *Eighteenth Dynasty*, pl. 2.

90. Note, however, the exceptional number in Medinet Habu (*CEAEM*, fig. 124; Hölscher, *Mortuary Temple* I, pls. 16, 22, 23). Late examples are discussed in Borchardt, *Tempel mit Umgang*, pl. 6; J.-C. Golvin and J. Larronde, *ASAE* 68 (1982): pls. 1a, 2b. In Mediterranean architecture, cramps have been common since Minoan times (Shaw, *Minoan Architecture*, 157–161; Naumann, *Architektur*, 105).

91. Hölscher, *Chephren*, 43, fig. 26; Lacau and Chevrier, *Hatshepsout* I, 9–11; Tanis (*L' Or des pharons* [exhibition catalogue] [Paris, 1987], no. 53). Copper cramps of Nectanebo II were found at Behbet el-Haqar (Valentia, *Voyages and Travels* II [1809], pl. 23 [2]).

92. Arnold, *Senwosret I* I , 65.

93. Hölscher, *Mortuary Temple* II, 31, n. 21.

94. Frankfort, *Cenotaph*, pl. 8 [1]; Vyse, *Pyramids* III, 61. Also, the cramps in the base of the obelisk in Paris were of stone (De Lubicz, *Temple* III, fig. 294G).

95. Those of Sahura were of basalt and had a diameter of 7.5 centimeters. Those of Niuserra were of gneiss. In the mastaba of Ptahshepses at Abusir, the columns were fixed with wooden pins (diameter of 11.5–12.5 centimeters and depth of 12.5–14 centimeters) on their base (*Ptahshepses*, 119, figs. 66, 67). For similar Minoan examples, see Shaw, *Minoan Architecture*, 121, 228.

96. Arnold, *Amenemhet III* I, pls. 5a–b.

97. Arnold, *Senwosret I* II (forthcoming).

98. *CEAEM,* fig. 170.

99. Ibid., fig. 171; Gustave Jéquier, *Les Éléments de l'architecture égyptienne,* Manuel d'archéologie égyptienne (Paris, 1924), 281–284; Lipinska, *Tuthmosis III,* figs. 12, 19; H. Chevrier, *ASAE* 37 (1937): 188, fig. 3.

100. Lauer, *Hist. Mon.,* 253, figs. 70, 71.

101. Capstone of Userkaf enclosure (J.-P. Lauer, *ASAE* 53 [1955]: 122, figs. 1–3).

102. *Karnak-Nord* IV, fig. 32; Lacau and Chevrier, *Hatshepsout* I, 304, fig. 23 (connection between granite and quartzite); *Karnak* VIII, 314, 319.

103. Maragioglio, *Piramidi* V, pl. 6 (Lepsius).

104. Jéquier, *Deux pyramides,* 19, figs. 16–20, pl. 6; Jéquier, *La Pyramide d'Oudjebten* (Cairo, 1928), 4, fig. 2; L. Habachi, *ASAE* 52 (1952): pls. 16–18.

105. Jéquier, *Deux pyramides,* 58, pl. 16; L. Habachi, *ASAE* 52 (1952): pl. 19; Arnold, *Amenemhet III* I, 14, fig. 4.

106. From an unidentified pyramid at Lisht (unpublished data). See also Borchardt, *Sahure,* 74, fig. 98.

107. H. Chevrier, *ASAE* 27 (1927): 141, fig. 3.

108. *Karnak-Nord* IV, fig. 59b; *Karnak* IV, 221, fig. 7; Spencer, *Brick Architecture,* 87, fig. 48; Hölscher, *Mortuary Temple* II, fig. 30.

109. Sarcophagi of Aaschit and Kawit of the Eleventh Dynasty.

110. Lauer, *Hist. Mon.,* 254, figs. 72, 73.

111. Ibid., 248, fig. 68.

112. Maragioglio, *Piramidi* III, 56.

113. Petrie, *Pyramids and Temples,* 38–39, pl. 11; Borchardt, *Grundkanten,* fig. 2; Maragioglio, *Piramidi* IV, 18, 106 [7], pl. 2.

114. Giza Ic (Maragioglio, *Piramidi* IV, 90, 180 [70]); Ka-pyramid of Sahura (Borchardt, *Sahure,* 74, fig. 98; Maragioglio, *Piramidi* VII, 76); unknown secondary pyramid of Senwosret I at Lisht (unpublished data); Ka-pyramid of Pepy II (unpublished data).

115. Major pyramids: probably Chephren, since the second but last course of the casing at the top of the pyramid has sockets to receive the mortises of the last course under the pyramidion (*LD* Text I, 27). Also Borchardt, *Neuserre,* 100; Borchardt, *Re-Heiligtum,* 38, fig. 26.

116. Arnold, *Senwosret I* II (forthcoming).

117. Ibid.

118. Bonded corners were already carefully carried out at Meidum, less so at the Bent Pyramid, where enormous corner slabs follow each other. The casing of the Chephren pyramid again shows regularly bonded corner blocks.

119. For example, the rather irregular masonry of the temple Qasr el-Sagha (Arnold, *Qasr el-Sagha,* pl. 7d).

120. Jéquier, *L'Architecture* I, pl. 79; De Lubicz, *Karnak,* pls. 393–395, 399, 421; Lacau and Chevrier, *Hatshepsout,* pls. 1–3, etc.

121. J. Fitchen describes how the corner blocks would have been pulled in after setting the four straight runs, with the help of twisted ropes (*Building Construction,* 236–237; *Journal of the Society of Architectural Historians* 37 [1978]: 10, fig. 4). But corner blocks with shift cuttings have been found, indicating that they were set with the help of levers, a maneuver that needed empty space on both sides of the corner blocks. This confirms that the corner blocks were set first and the remaining straight runs last.

122. The term *boss* or *bossed* seems to be uncommon in English and is frequently replaced by expressions such as *oversized, extra stock,* or *protecting crust.*

123. H. Chevrier, *RdÉ* 23 (1971): pl. 5; De Lubicz, *Karnak* I, 93, fig. 7.

124. Preserved at unfinished parts of the Luxor temple (R. Engelbach, *ASAE* 28 [1928]: 150).

125. The so-called ring bands (Borchardt, *Entstehung der Pyramide*, 4–5; Maragioglio, *Piramidi* III, 14–16).

126. *CEAEM*, fig. 81; Arnold, *Mentuhotep*, pls. 21b, d; Arnold, *Qasr el-Sagha*, pl. 2. For handling bosses in Inca architecture, see Graziano Gasparini and Luise Margolies, *Inca Architecture* (Bloomington, Ind., 1980), fig. 323.

127. Many instances—for example, Petrie, *Pyramids and Temples*, 78, 82–83, 92; for Hauwaret el-Maqta (pyramid of Neferuptah), see fig. 4.53, p. 136.

128. Such a scaffolding is reconstructed in David Macaulay, *Pyramid* (Boston, 1975), 58–59.

129. Reisner, *Mycerinus*, pl. 6; see fig. 4.57, p. 138.

130. Frankfort, *Cenotaph*, pl. 13 [2].

131. J.-C. Golvin and R. Vergnieux give excellent examples from Ptolemaic and Roman buildings (*Hommages à François Daumas* [Montpelier, Vt., 1988], 299–320).

132. Arnold, *Amenemhet III* I, 79–80. Also the chambers in two tombs (nos. 5117 and 5124) of Imhotep at Lisht show these black strokes, neatly sunk into sockets of the bossed surface.

133. *CEAEM*, fig. 229; H. Chevrier, *ASAE* 39 (1939): pl. 94; Golvin and Goyon, *Karnak*, 115, 118.

134. U. Hölscher, *MDAIK* 12 (1943): 139–149; *CEAEM*, figs. 234–239; H. Chevrier, *ASAE* 39 (1939): pl. 97; Golvin and Goyon, *Karnak*, 111 (top left), 115, 120.

135. Golvin and Goyon, *Karnak*, 120 (top right).

136. Petrie, *Royal Tombs* II, supplement, 9–11, pl. 56A.

137. Ibid., 13, pl. 57 [4–5].

138. For example, the pavement of the temple of Luxor (Hellmut Brunner, *Die südlichen Räume des Tempels von Luxor* [Mainz, 1977], pls. 1, 4, 8, 17, 26, 29).

139. For example, Hölscher, *Chephren*, pls. 6, 7, 9, 10.

140. For example, the pyramid courts of Chephren (Maragioglio, *Piramidi* V, 48), Mycerinus (Maragioglio, *Piramidi* VI, pl. 4, figs. 7, 8), and Senwosret I (Arnold, *Senwosret I* I, pl. 94).

141. For example, Hölscher, *Chephren*, pl. 17; Reisner, *Mycerinus*, plan I. For the New Kingdom, see Jacquet, *Trésor*, pl. 29; Brunner, *Die südlichen Räume des Tempels von Luxor*, pls. 1, 4, 8.

Schwaller De Lubicz and Robichon were even convinced that the strange patterns in the pavement of the Luxor Temple were intentionally made (De Lubicz, *Temple* II, pls. 34–38; *Temple* III, 129–142).

142. Arnold, *Senwosret I* I, pl. 91.

143. That the middle axis of a building or room was paved separately with crosswise arranged slabs can be seen from Reisner, *Mycerinus*, plan I; De Lubicz, *Temple* II, pl. 34; Arnold, *Mentuhotep*, plan.

144. Jacquet has shown how the blocks for the bases and the blocks in between were dressed down only after paving (*Trésor*, fig. 22).

145. Patching column bases (*CEAEM*, 133, figs. 140, 141).

146. Granite pavement (Borchardt, *Sahure*, 70).

147. Basalt pavement (ibid., 7, 15, 24, 32, 64, 93–97; J.-P. Lauer, *ASAE* 46 [1947]: 248); interior of the temple of Tanis.

148. Borchardt, *Sahure*, 93–96.

149. Alabaster pavement (Hölscher, *Chephren*, 19, 25–26, 29, 55, 58–59;

Borchardt, *Sahure,* 54; Ricke, *Harmachis,* 8; Lauer, *Téti,* 23, 25, pls. 6, 13; Arnold, *Mentuhotep,* pls. 22d, 39).

150. Golvin and Goyon, *Karnak,* 111–112.

151. Jean Vercoutter, *Mirgissa* I (Paris, 1970), 79, fig. 22.

152. Junker, *Giza* I, 16–17. For classifications of mastaba core masonry and casing, see G. A. Reisner, *ASAE* 13 (1913): 231–241; Reisner, *Giza* I, 39–56; Jacques Vandier, *Manuel d'archéologie égyptienne* II, part 1 (Paris, 1954), 260–262.

153. This method is normally used for the classification of Greek and Roman masonry (Martin, *Architecture grecque,* 378–409).

154. Albert M. Lythgoe and Caroline L. Ransom, *The Tomb of Perneb* (New York, 1916), figs. 8–11.

155. Petrie, *Pyramids and Temples,* 41, 52, pl. 8; Borchardt, *Dritte Bauperiode,* 2, fig. 1, pl. 1; J. Brinks, *GM* 48 (1981): 17–23.

156. Stadelmann, *Ägyptische Pyramiden,* 109.

157. For further discussion, see p. 168.

158. For example, Naumann, *Architektur,* 73–83. For Egypt from the Archaic Period on, see W. Wood, *JEA* 73 (1987): 59–70.

159. Petrie, *Royal Tombs* II, pl. 57; W. Wood, *JEA* 73 (1987): 59–70, figs. 1, 2, where it is correctly suggested that the Helwan tombs should be dated to the Second and partially to the Third Dynasties.

160. A beautiful example of shaft casing in the archaic mastabas of Helwan is shown in W. Wood, *JEA* 73 (1987): pl. 6.

161. Lauer, *Hist. Mon.,* pls. v, vi, xl, xlvii.

162. Maragioglio, *Piramidi* III, 56, otherwise unpublished.

163. Author's measurements.

164. Lauer, *Hist. Mon.,* pl. iv.

165. Petrie, *Pyramids and Temples,* pl. 8; Maragioglio, *Piramidi* iv, pl. 3. W. Hönig translated these figures into Egyptian measurements without leaving enough margin for irregularities common in practical work (*Discoveries in Egypt* 12 [1988]: 39).

166. Lauer, *Ounas,* 63–65, fig. 42.

167. Arnold, *Senwosret I* I, 65, pls. 93a, 96.

168. The idea, first offered by Borchardt (*Dritte Bauperiode,* 1–3, pl. 1) and then by J. Brinks (*GM* 48 [1981]: 17–23), that the Cheops Pyramid has a stepped core cannot be attested by the help of the so-called girdle stones.

169. For example, the Mastabat el-Fara'un (Maragioglio, *Piramidi* vi, pl. 16; Borchardt, *Neferirkere,* figs. 48, 49).

170. For example, Maragioglio, *Piramidi* v, pl. 6.

171. R. Lepsius suggested limestone casing in the upper parts, but nobody since has seen any traces (*LD* Text I, 22).

172. Maragioglio, *Piramidi* v, pl. 6.

173. Maragioglio, *Piramidi* vi, pl. 4; Lauer, *Mystère,* pl. xiib.

174. Maragioglio, *Piramidi* vi, pl. 12.

175. Ibid., 138, 152 [3], but apparently not quite certain.

176. Borchardt, *Neferirkere,* 39, fig. 45.

177. Reisner, *Mycerinus,* 74, 79.

178. Arnold, *Senwosret I* I, pls. 41, 93.

179. Zaky Y. Saad, *The Excavations at Helwan* (Norman, Okla., 1969), pls. 14–17.

180. Petrie, *Royal Tombs* II, pls. 62, 63; for Saqqara, numerous examples are in Emery, *Great Tombs* I–III.

181. Saad, *Excavations at Helwan,* 29.

182. Petrie, *Royal Tombs* II, pl. 57.

183. Firth and Quibell, *Step Pyramid*, pls. 13–17, 38–45; Lauer, *Hist. Mon.*, pls. VIII, IX, XXIII–XXVIII.

184. For example, Celeste Rinaldi, *Le Piramidi* (Milan, 1983), figs. 96 (Unas), 105 (Teti); Lauer, *Mystère*, pl. XVI (Merenra); Jean-Philippe Lauer, *Saqqara* (London, 1976), pls. 60 and XV (Unas), 150 (Pepy II), 156, 157 (Pepy I).

185. Winlock, *Excavations*, pl. 13.

186. Ibid., pl. 16.

187. Arnold, *Jnj.jtj.f*, pls. 6, 7.

188. Norman De Garis Davies, *Five Theban Tombs* (London, 1913), pl. 29.

189. Practically all the larger tombs of the Middle Kingdom in the cemeteries of Dahshur, Lisht, Illahun, and Hawara.

190. Theodore Davies, Edouard Naville, and Howard Carter, *The Tomb of Hatshopsitu* (London, 1906), 80.

191. For example, Kuhlmann and Schenkel, *Ibi;* Manfred Bietak and Elfriede Reiser-Haslauer, *Das Grab des Anch-Hor* II (Vienna, 1982), pls. 38–42; Eigner, *Grabbauten*, 84.

192. Mortuary temples of Chephren and Mycerinus.

193. Borchardt, *Sahure*, 12, 16, 22, 33, 40.

194. Ibid., 24, fig. 20; Borchardt, *Neuserre*, 56.

195. For example, el-Tod (D. Arnold, *MDAIK* 31 [1975]: 175–181).

196. Arnold, *Mentuhotep*, 48–49, n. 121, pls. 22a, b.

197. For example, the unfinished walls of the complex of Sekhemkhet or the ring bands of the pyramid of Meidum.

198. For example, the cores of the small pyramids of the Third Dynasty, such as that of Seila.

199. See Reisner, *Mycerinus*, 70.

200. Maragioglio, *Piramidi* VI, pl. 16.

201. The fact that not only the cores of the pyramids of the Third but also of the Fifth and Sixth Dynasties regularly consist of layered steps (as shown in Table 4.1) is a strong argument for layered cores. The idea that the Cheops Pyramid is built with internal steps has already been presented by Borchardt (*Dritte Bauperiode*, 1–4, pl. 1) and was recently reiterated by J. Brinks (*GM* 48 [1981]: 17–21), although with less convincing arguments. Stadelmann is strongly opposed to it (*Ägyptische Pyramiden*, 109–110).

202. Arnold, *Mentuhotep*, pls. 8a, 11a–c, 13a–c.

203. Borchardt, *Re-Heiligtum*, 36–37, fig. 20; Borchardt, *Neferirkere*, 41, fig. 49.

204. *Karnak-Nord* III, pls. 40, 41, 43; *Karnak-Nord* IV, pls. 8–15; *CEAEM*, fig. 128.

205. *Karnak* IV, 145–150, figs. 3–5; H. Chevrier, *ASAE* 53 (1955): 22–39, pls. 10–16.

206. Cheops and Chephren at Giza; Senwosret II at Illahun.

207. For example, the inner enclosure wall of the pyramid of Illahun (Petrie, *Lahun II*, pl. 23).

208. Golvin and Goyon, *Karnak*, 111–112.

209. Examples are Borchardt, *Re-Heiligtum*, 61–62; Borchardt, *Neuserre*, 149; Borchardt, *Sahure*, 96.

210. An access ramp from the south of the pyramid seems to be logical, since the direction of the nearby transportation roads of the Mastabat el-Fara'un indicate that the local limestone quarries have to be considered. They are about 1 kilometer south of the area (Jacques De Morgan, *Carte de la nécropole memphite* [Cairo, 1897], pl. 6).

211. Eigner, *Grabbauten*, 69, pl. 34B.

212. According to A. W. Lawrence, the earliest stone arches appear on Cyprus in

the sixth century B.C. (*Greek Architecture*, 4th ed. [New York, 1983], 228–229), whereas T. D. Boyd says that "there is no example which can be dated to a period earlier than the late fourth century B.C." (*AJA* 82 [1978]: 83). Brick vaults in Mediterranean countries are considerably older. True vaults of burned brick in the palace of Tell Atchana (northern Syria) are dated to 2500 B.C. (Naumann, *Architektur*, 116–117, figs. 100–104).

213. Arnold, *Mentuhotep*, pls. 15, 16.

214. For examples, see Winlock, *Hibis*, 29–31; Borchardt, *Tempel mit Umgang*, pl. 28.

215. For example, the architraves of the colonnade of the Luxor temple and the hypostyle hall of Karnak.

216. Hölscher, *Mortuary Temple* I, pl. 20B; De Lubicz, *Karnak* I, fig. 65; *Karnak* II, pls. 54, 254–256.

217. Coulton, *Greek Architects*, 145–149, figs. 63–65. One Egyptian example is discussed in Arnold, *Amenemhet III* I, 50, n. 104, pl. 51.

218. For the widespread use of corbeling in Syria and Anatolia, see Naumann, *Architektur*, 122–125, figs. 105–113, and Coulton, *Greek Architects*, 152–153, who observed that the maximum span there was 6.40 meters, with the exception of the tholos tombs of Mycenae running up to about 14.40 meters in diameter. For the structural mechanics of the tholos tombs and corbeled roofs in general, see W. G. Cavanagh and R. R. Laxton, *Annual of the British School at Athens* 76 (1981): 109–137.

219. N. Swelim considers logistical reasons for the replacement of the flat granite roofs of the Third Dynasty with corbeled limestone roofs in the early Fourth Dynasty (*JSSEA* 14 [1984]: 6–12). This seems, however, not quite convincing because we find flat granite roofs side by side with corbeled and pointed limestone roofs in the Cheops Pyramid.

220. *LD* I, 87; *CEAEM*, fig. 221.

221. *LD* I, 87; Jéquier, *Architecture* I, pl. 36 [2].

222. *CEAEM*, fig. 220.

223. Frankfort, *Cenotaph*, pl. 5.

224. Ibid., pl. 3. Also, the transverse hall of the Osireion seems to be roofed in this way (ibid., pl. 19).

225. Jéquier, *Architecture* II, pl. 20 [4].

226. For the mastaba of Iinefer (time of Snofru), whose roof has a span of 2.6 meters, see A. Barsanti, *ASAE* 3 (1902): 198–201, figs. 4–6.

227. Maragioglio, *Piramidi* IV, pl. 2.

228. Probably all pyramid crypts of the Fifth and Sixth Dynasties.

229. Arnold, *Mentuhotep*, pls. 40b, 43.

230. Drawing Metropolitan Museum of Art, AM 1411.

231. De Morgan, *Dahchour* I, 19, figs. 20, 21; Reginald Engelbach, *Riqqeh and Memphis* VI (London, 1915), pl. 4.

232. De Morgan, *Dahchour* II, 32–36, figs. 77–83. Also, the entrance corridor has a saddle roof, which relieves the horizontal roofing beams.

233. Arnold, *Amenemhet III* I, 83–86.

234. Petrie, *Kahun*, pl. 4.

235. Jéquier, *Deux pyramides*, pls. 17, 18.

236. Arnold, *Amenemhet III* I, 78–79, fig. 37.

237. Such a model drawing is preserved; see fig. 1.22, p. 22 (G. Daressy, *ASAE* 8 [1907]: 237–241).

238. See fig. 1.1, p. 9, and B. Gunn, *ASAE* 26 (1926): 197–202; *CEAEM*, 52–53, figs. 53, 54.

239. Perhaps similar to a wooden frame in a tomb of Deir el-Medina (Bernard Bruyère, *Les Fouilles de Deir el Médineh 1924–1925* [Cairo, 1926], 23, fig. 13).

240. Maragioglio, *Piramidi* VI, pl. 6.

241. Ibid., pl. 17.

242. Borchardt, *Neuserre*, fig. 40; Lauer, *Téti*, 11–15, figs. 1–3; Pepy I (unpublished data); Arnold, *Senwosret I* I, 42, pl. 105.

243. Arnold, *Mentuhotep*, pls. 36, 37.

244. De Morgan, *Dahchour* I, fig. 121; II, 90, fig. 133; Arnold, *Amenemhet III* I, pls. 46, 50.

245. De Morgan, *Dahchour* I, 55, fig. 121.

246. Arnold, *Amenemhet III* I, figs. 6–8, 37.

247. J. Brinks et al., *GM* 93 (1986): 78–79, fig. 5.

248. Emery, *Great Tombs* III, 102, pl. 116 (time of Qa'a). Later examples are discussed in Garstang, *Bet Khallaf*, pls. 6, 18. For brick vaults in ancient Egypt, see Spencer, *Brick Architecture*, 123–127; Choisy, *L'Art de bâtir*, 42–49; *CEAEM*, 181–183. The largest span that was bridged by the help of a brick vault is at Medinet Habu (8.6 meters), and the second largest in the temple of Amenophis Son of Hapu (7.7 meters) (Hölscher, *Mortuary Temple* II, 18). The relieving vault over the crypt of Amenemhat III at Hawara spans 12 meters; it is not freestanding, but is walled up from below.

249. Jéquier, *Pépi II* III, figs. 49 (plan 1), 58; E. E. D. M. Oates, *Early Vaulting in Mesopotamia: Archaeological Theory and Practice* (London and New York, 1973).

250. Maragioglio, *Piramidi* VIII, 72, pl. 11.

251. Jéquier, *Pépi II* III, 56–64.

252. U. Hölscher, *Post-Ramessid Remains, Excavation of Medinet Habu* 5 (Chicago, 1954), 29–30, fig. 34, pl. 11B.

253. Ibid., pl. 16, fig. 35.

254. *LD Text* I, 123.

255. J.-P. Lauer, *ASAE* 51 (1951): 470–479; Lauer, *ASAE* 52 (1952): 133–136.

256. Vyse, *Pyramids* II, pl. between 130 and 131.

257. *CEAEM*, figs. 224–227; *Description de l'Égypte* I, pl. 29; *Description de l'Égypte* IV, pls. 57–58. While Pharaonic examples of true stone vaults never have a span exceeding 2.8 meters, the Greek arches (outside Egypt) were up to 6.48 meters and the Roman bridge of Fabricius in Rome even reached a span of 24.5 meters. For a comprehensive bibliography on vaulting, see John Fitchen, *The Construction of Gothic Cathedrals: A Study of Medieval Vault Erection* (Chicago, 1961), 317–336.

CHAPTER V   *Other Building Activities*

DIGGING SHAFTS AND TUNNELS

Digging shafts and tunnels[1] in the bedrock was routine work for the Egyptian workmen, who were experienced with cutting underground tombs or quarrying stone from underground quarries since the Second Dynasty. Because working in sandstone and limestone presented no difficulties for Egyptian masons and all known tombs and shafts were dug in these relatively soft stones, the problem was actually not cutting the stone but preventing its collapse due to cracks or the presence of softer strata of desert conglomerate, shales, or even sand. In order to penetrate these dangerous strata, the upper sections of tomb shafts or entrance corridors had to be cased with brick walls and vaults.[2]

The caisson, a unique device for working safely through dangerous strata of sand and conglomerate, had been developed by the workers at the south cemetery at Lisht in the Twelfth Dynasty (fig. 5.1).[3] It is a monolithic stone box, open at the top and bottom, that is slowly sunk into the sand layers by extracting the sand from inside and building up brick walls on the brim of the box. At the four corners of the caisson, vertical beams could be inserted into sockets and then be connected by wooden boards. These boards would help to keep the sand from flowing in before the brick walls were set up. Thus the caisson traveled safely through the sand until it came to rest on the more solid bedrock. No other examples from ancient Egypt have been documented, but some may still exist in less well studied tomb shafts.

Another way to prevent the collapse of the mouth of a tomb shaft during construction was not to begin digging vertically from the surface but to excavate a sloping, open trench a few meters below the surface until the ground became solid enough to dig the shaft.[4] Where solid rock could not be reached (for example, in many places in the Theban necropolis or at Dahshur and Lisht), a stone casing had to be built in. Until this was achieved, the workers had to protect themselves by means of temporary

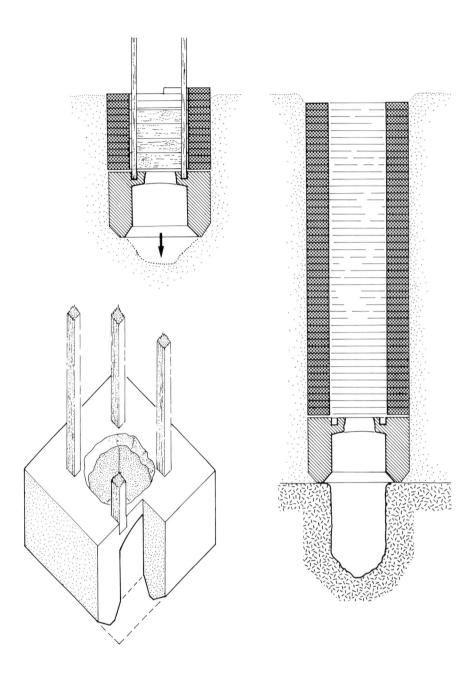

wooden props or brick walls. Such wooden constructions could be observed
in the pyramid of Amenemhat III at Dahshur, where a threatening collapse had to be prevented by hastily built wooden beams and brick walls
and vaults (fig. 5.30).[5] A similar measure had to be taken in the western
chamber of the Bent Pyramid, where cedar trunks 35 centimeters thick and
4.5 meters long were built in, but in this case only after the chamber walls
had been built.[6]

Cutting through bedrock was carried out by two methods. First, it could
be hacked off with stone mauls with pointed cutting edges. Such stone tools
were still in use for the rock tombs of the Middle and New Kingdoms and
even of the Late Period. Bedrock could also be cut with chisels, which have
left their marks quite frequently (fig. 2.10). The rock had to be quarried
away in block form, as was done in quarries. These methods resulted in a

steplike surface when tomb chambers were left unfinished, such as in the lower chamber of the Cheops Pyramid or some unfinished tombs of Beni Hasan and Amarna.[7]

The normal procedure for digging was to start, as in a quarry, with a narrow one-man tunnel at the level of the intended ceiling that was carried forward until the intended end wall of the tomb. The cutting of such tunnels must have been very tiresome because the tools could be used in only a very limited space and not with full force. The ceiling of this preliminary tunnel served as the axis of the tomb, and it was drawn in a red line.

From this line, offshoots were drawn to indicate the position of cross walls and pillars. The axial tunnel could be extended sideways and downward with more people working at the same time until the intended outline of the tomb was produced in rough shape. The axis of the tomb could then be marked on the floor; the height of the rooms indicated by leveling lines; and the shape of the vaults determined with methods like those described on pages 195–196. The final wall surface was measured and marked by brush marks set into mortises, which were cut through the extra stock of the rock, and the stonecutters or sculptors could dress down the bosses in between. When the ceiling height was higher than a man could reach with his arms, the process was repeated by lowering the floor in steps until the intended height was achieved. Naturally, the masons took advantage of the direction of the rock stratification, using cracks as ceiling or wall surfaces. But quite often, unsound material forced them to compromise in the shape and size of the rooms.

We do not know how the surveyors achieved correct orientations underground, since we have corridor systems that frequently change direction and level in a confusing manner. It was probably sufficient to work with a builder's square to construct the offshots from the main axis. At least it might have been used in the corridors of the pyramid of Amenemhat III at Dahshur, in which four turns of 90 degrees can be counted between entrance and crypt. The construction lines on the floor with their 90-degree offshoots are still preserved.[8] Pillars were frequently kept connected with the wall behind them until a later stage of work (fig. 5.2). Since the teams of workmen were often divided into a right and a left crew,[9] it may be that the work underground was carried out by different crews working along the right and left walls. Such a strange method, however, could be used only in rooms wide enough for separate chains of stonecutters and basket boys. But the division may have to be explained differently.

Underground work could be obstructed when two parties tried to connect tunnels by working from different ends. Very often, they might have succeeded in directly hitting the intended spot. Difficulties are disclosed, however, when corridors and shafts suddenly take a twisted course, indicating that several trials were made before both tunnels actually met. Some examples are the corridors connecting the two chamber systems in the Bent Pyramid (fig. 5.3),[10] the well shaft in the Cheops Pyramid,[11] the second entrance corridor of the Chephren Pyramid,[12] and the south tomb of the pyramid of Amenemhat III at Dahshur (fig. 5.4).[13]

Access to work underground was not always easy. Smaller shafts of even

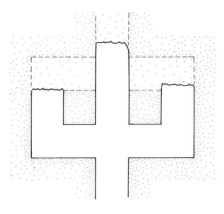

Fig. 5.2 Excavating a rock chamber with two pillars in the Eleventh Dynasty cemetery at El-Tarif.

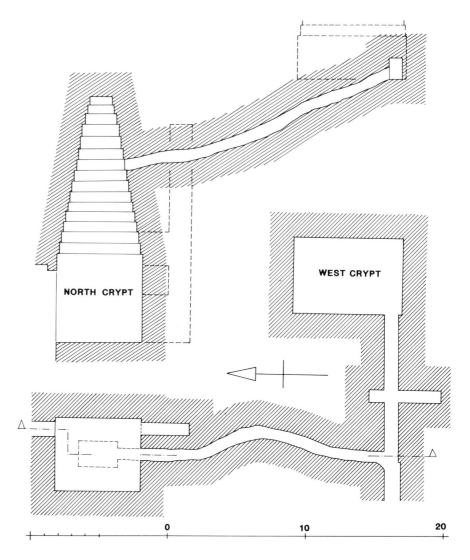

Fig. 5.3 The tunnel connecting the northern with the western burial systems of the Bent Pyramid.

greater depth were doubtlessly descended directly by clambering down the walls, perhaps with the help of a rope from above. Shafts too wide to be climbed in this way had footholds chiseled out in distances of about 40 to 65 centimeters. They were arranged either on opposite walls—if they could still be reached with the hands and feet—or at both sides of a corner, where the shaft was too wide.[14] The large shafts as they were built in Saite times were doubtlessly timbered with scaffoldings and ladders, as can still be seen from putlog holes cut into the side walls.

Ropes to lower material or use as a climbing device could be fixed at crossbeams inserted into the side walls or in a stone ring. Such a ring, made of a separate piece of pierced stone, was found set into the floor of an underground chamber in the Old Kingdom Cemetery of Lisht (unpublished). From this stone, a rope could be lowered into an adjacent 6-meter-deep shaft. Parts of a rope ladder (Third Intermediate Period?) were discovered in the tomb of Sety I.[15]

Waste material had to be pulled or carried up in baskets, certainly of a type similar to the *zambil* familiar to every archaeologist. A group of fifty

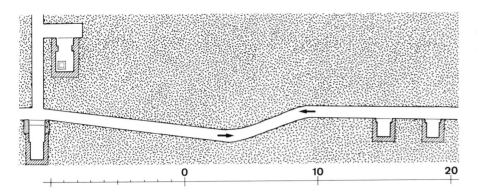

Fig. 5.4 The tunnel connecting two parts of the southern tomb in the pyramid of Amenemhat III at Dahshur.

such baskets were found, still filled, near the Mentuhotep temple where they were abandoned and covered after an interruption in work (fig. 5.5).[16] The workers of Deir el-Medina seem to have used leather bags instead for their work in the royal tombs of the New Kingdom.[17]

Most of the known shafts are not much deeper than 30 meters,[18] with the exception of the well shaft at Deir el-Medina, which reaches 40 meters,[19] and not much longer than about 200 meters.[20] Dust, heat, and shortage of air—problems that could not be solved, especially when the corridors disappeared under the mountain—all placed limits on the size of these shafts.

Tomb shafts such as those of the main and the southern tombs of Djoser and the pyramids of Abu Rawash and Zawyet el-Aryan (figs. 1.15, 1.16) demonstrate well the problems of shafts planned to be 30 meters deep (fig. 5.6). After a depth of 10 meters was reached, it proved to be too time-consuming to pull the debris out over the rim. A second shaft was dug 20

Fig. 5.5 Workers' baskets of the Eleventh Dynasty, abandoned at the Mentuhotep temple of Deir el-Bahari.

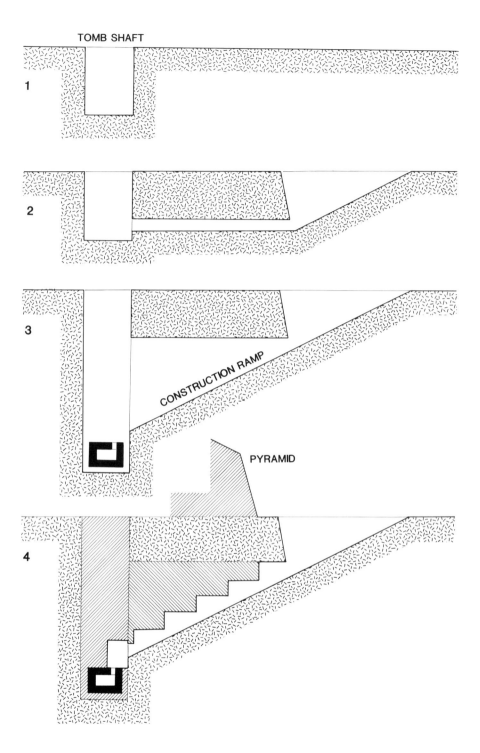

Fig. 5.6 Method of digging royal tomb shafts, with the help of a secondary access, in the Third and Fourth Dynasties.

TOMB SHAFT

1

2

3

CONSTRUCTION RAMP

PYRAMID

4

meters away and connected with the first one by a narrow tunnel. Through this shaft and tunnel, the debris could be removed more easily. In proceeding deeper, the floor of the tunnel was lowered accordingly and made a staircase leading directly to the surface. The enormous height of the staircase was reduced by the introduction of a stone roof. Above the entrance into the crypt a maneuvering chamber was erected, which kept the entrance clear when the main shaft was filled with debris. The burial could be introduced through the staircase, which was finally blocked with masonry.

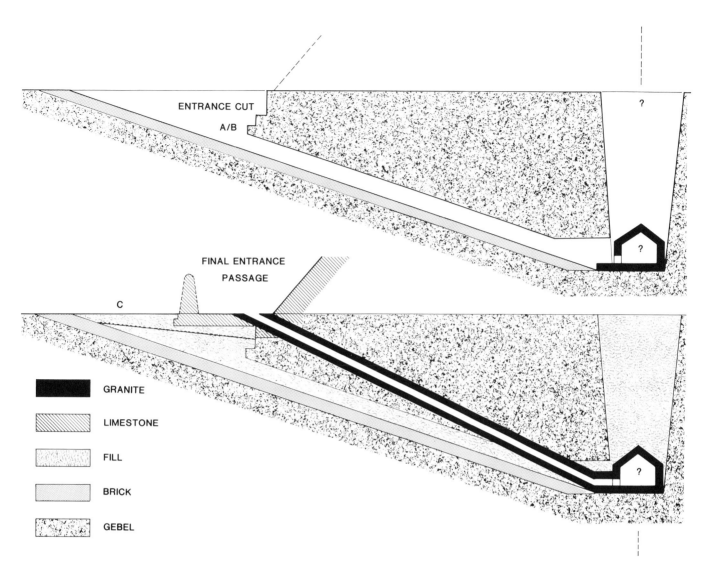

ENTRANCE CUT

A/B

FINAL ENTRANCE
PASSAGE

C

GRANITE

LIMESTONE

FILL

BRICK

GEBEL

Fig. 5.7 The construction access and the final entrance passage of the pyramid of Senwosret I at Lisht.

Numerous royal and private tombs of the Middle Kingdom have two shafts.[21] One of them is considered to be a construction shaft. It is normally situated under the mastaba core, which was later erected on top. Being wider than the burial shaft, it was apparently used for pulling up the waste material and for lowering casing blocks and sarcophagi. The second, smaller shaft starts from a place outside the mastaba and was kept open for the introduction of the burial.[22] The pyramid of Senwosret I had a preliminary entrance corridor for cutting out the cave for the burial chamber and for lowering the blocks for the crypt (fig. 5.7). This entrance cut was filled in when the final tomb passage was built at a much steeper slope and so narrow that only the mummy of the king could be moved in.[23]

An obvious question is why the construction shaft of private tombs was not built from the beginning far enough away from the mastaba so that it could be kept open until the burial. Digging a second shaft would thus have been unnecessary. Building was, however, not always carried out logically. For example, the crypt of Imhotep at Lisht was built with a sarcophagus pit. When the sarcophagus finally arrived, the builders realized that it could

Fig. 5.8 Limestone oil lamps found in the pyramid of Amenemhat III at Dahshur.

not be lowered into the narrow shaft. They then had to build a separate sloping passage.

The so-called air shafts of the Cheops Pyramid were certainly not intended as such, since the corridors and chambers were erected when the surrounding masonry was still flush with them and open air work was possible.[24]

Another problem was lighting, since methods of lighting underground work were insufficient. Egyptian oil lamps, which I once tested, produced only a dim light and many of them would have been needed for accurate work, such as decorating and inscribing walls (fig. 5.8). From distribution lists of linen wicks for lamps for the work in Biban el-Muluk,[25] we know that they played an important role in Ramesside tomb building. Occasionally, they were kept in small niches in the side walls. Wooden torches might also have been used for underground work, attested by the discovery of a huge number of wooden torches with handles and charred tops at Deir el-Medina.[26] There is no evidence, however, for the use of mirrors or other sorts of equipment for reflecting sunlight. Every archaeologist who has tried to use mirrors in excavation has to admit that it is not only difficult to keep track of the light beams, but also impossible to work with them; when people are moving up and down the corridors and shafts, they are dazzled by the light and at the same time prevent the light from reaching those working at the end of the tomb, who need it the most.

These problems of ventilation and lighting may explain why all ambitiously deep and long corridors and shafts are only poorly finished or were never finished at all. Pharaonic technology had reached its limits.

SECURING TOMBS

The blocking of tomb passages and burial chambers was an essential part of Egyptian stone building.[27] Even more important was the sealing of burials, which became a major focus of funerary architecture. Such procedures originated as soon as burial outfits became rich enough to attract robbers—that is, during the First Dynasty.[28] So from that early period, a contest began between builders and robbers. As soon as the architects had devised an apparently safe tomb construction, the tomb robbers learned how to surmount the obstacle, thus forcing the architects to increase their efforts.

The only considerable advantages that the builders had were that they could work with unlimited numbers of workmen and in the open. In those periods when governmental control was disrupted, however, tomb robbing could also be carried out in daylight and with a sufficient work force. As a result of these illicit activities, not a single blocking device remains intact; not one has managed to fulfill its purpose over time. A burial remained undisturbed not on the strength of its blocking system, but only if it became hidden and forgotten.

We cannot discuss here all precautions taken by the architects in designing security systems for tombs, such as prolonging the effort of the tomb robbers by hiding the tomb entrance or by merely deepening a burial shaft. We shall concentrate on the technical aspects of securing the entrance passages and doors to burial chambers, predominantly of the royal tombs, which, because of the much greater value of their burial equipment, were protected with much greater care than the private ones. There were five basic methods for securing a tomb with stone.

The most primitive (and rarely effective) system was to push large blocks or slabs of stone against the front of the door of the crypt or to wall up the whole corridor with stone masonry. In addition, the blocks could be set into an especially hard mortar. This system did not necessitate much technical preparation and would have required only some strong men with levers and ropes. The great disadvantage of the system was, of course, that it was only a question of time to undo it by breaking out stone after stone and finally smashing or pulling away the last blocking slab. Nevertheless, this method was used quite frequently, not only in private tombs that could not be protected by more refined systems,[29] but also in many royal tombs, mainly of the Middle[30] and New Kingdoms.[31] In the New Kingdom, there was greater reliance on the functioning of police control, huge amounts of masonry piled up in the corridors, and attempts to hide the tomb entrance. From the technical point of view, these constructions are not very rewarding.

The second method is a natural development of the first technique—the use of blocking stones that are either so large and numerous or made of such very hard material that they create serious obstacles for the tomb robbers, especially for those with limited resources and time. In no case could these plugs be pulled out of the way again when in position. They had to be chiseled through, a difficult task indeed with granite or quartzite, or else the robbers were forced to cut their way around the entrance through softer building material or nearby bedrock. The first important examples are the crypts of the southern and main tombs of King Djoser at Saqqara (fig. 5.9). Here the entrance into the crypt was a round hole in the granite ceiling beams through which the mummy or object to be buried had to be lowered in an upright position. These holes were closed after the

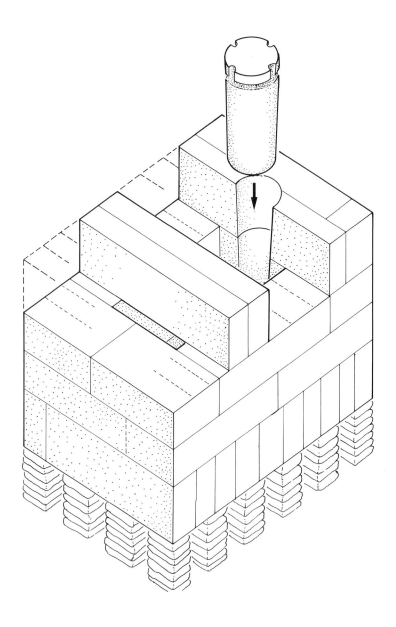

Fig. 5.9 The closing of the crypt of King Djoser's main tomb.

burial by inserting heavy granite plugs whose shape matched that of the entrance hole.[32]

Another interesting example is the entrance passage of the secondary pyramid of the Bent Pyramid (fig. 5.10).[33] The sloping passage was probably closed with several granite blocks, which have unfortunately vanished altogether. Behind, in the ascending part of the passage, we find for the first time a system that was later used in much grander style in the Cheops Pyramid.[34] Four granite plugs were built in during the construction of the passage, but kept in the uppermost part of the passage. This passage had a raised ceiling so that the traffic over the plugs during the construction and the burial was not hindered. The plugs were temporarily kept in position by a system of wooden beams, which we can no longer reconstruct, but which has left its traces in the floor and side walls. These beams could be removed from below in order to release the plugs, which by their own weight would slide down into their final position without trapping the workers who carried out the maneuver. The corridors of the Bent Pyramid

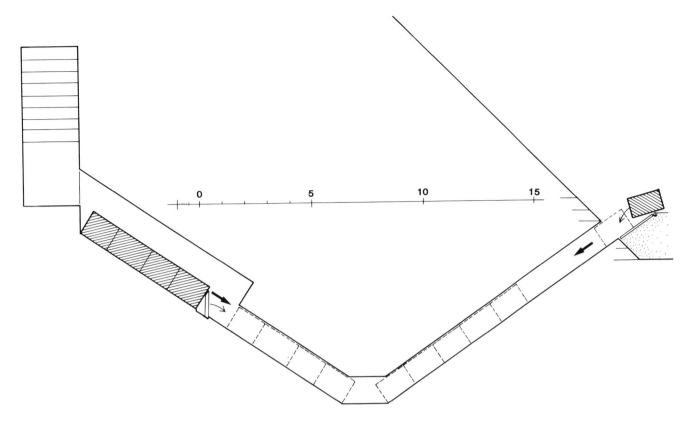

Fig. 5.10 The blocking of the secondary pyramid of the Bent Pyramid.

were probably only filled with masonry to judge from the western corridor, which had additional portcullises.

The sloping passage of the Cheops Pyramid, 105 meters long, either was completely blocked with masonry or was at least intended to be. Otherwise, the whole blocking scheme of the pyramid would have been substantially weakened.[35] All these blocks could be inserted from a ramp outside that led up to the pyramid entrance. But the blocking of the ascending corridor inside had to be prepared during the construction phase of the pyramid. As in the secondary pyramid of the Bent Pyramid, the granite plugs had to be shored up further in the huge ascending gallery (fig. 5.11), which was apparently built for this purpose only (fig. 4.121). They were held in position by an elaborate system of crossbeams housed in putlog holes of the side walls.[36]

There were two possible ways to close the ascending corridor. Either one block was released after the other, starting with the lowest one; this would have required the presence of workmen in the gallery. Or the blocks were released simultaneously by removing all the beams and somehow keeping the chain of blocks in position. To start the blocks moving, workmen would have been present in the ascending corridor. Were they quick enough to escape the avalanche of granite? In the first case, the presence of the well shaft would have ensured a safe escape for the workmen in the galleries. However, such a shaft would have negated the whole ingenious system of blocking the pyramid. Robbers would have used it as well to climb around the granite blocking of the ascending corridor. Could the pyramid builders

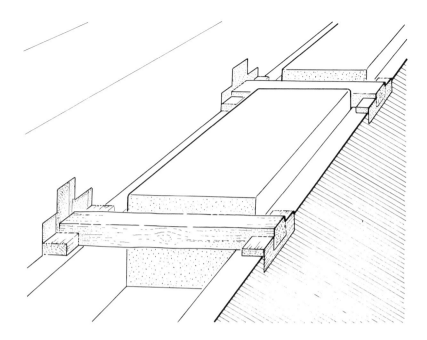

Fig. 5.11 The granite plugs stored in the ascending gallery of the Cheops Pyramid and held in place by crossbeams.

have overlooked this possibility? In any case, in all later pyramids ascending passages were avoided, and the blocking was more effectively concentrated on the sloping passages.

Interesting examples of blocking pyramid passages with granite appear again in the pyramids of Amenemhat I and of Senwosret I. In the first case, plugs that were 5 or 6 meters long were used.[37] Their insertion, however, must have been a difficult task because the corridor slope was not steep enough to get the blocks moving by themselves. This problem was avoided in the pyramid of Senwosret I, where the slope was increased so that the plugs, weighing up to 20 tons, crashed into one another and broke their ends. At the top end of one of the plugs, a huge groove was carved out that could have held a sandbag to soften the impact. In both pyramids, the granite filling the tunnels, which were 40 to 50 meters long, could not be penetrated by the tomb robbers. They chiseled their way along the side walls and even behind them and thus reached the crypts.[38]

The cenotaph of Senwosret III at Abydos was heavily secured (fig. 5.12).[39] The tomb robbers would first have had to empty an enormous shaft and construction corridor. After emptying the fill of the entrance hall, probably made of stone blocks, they would have discovered that the continuation of the tomb lay hidden above the far end of its ceiling. A further corridor—certainly intended to be filled with blocks—would have brought them to a dead end. Behind the rear wall opened a huge shaft. It could not have been bridged because there was no continuation of the corridor on the other side. Instead, at the bottom of the shaft, a small corridor led into another shaft of the same dimensions. Here the continuation was to be found at the top of the shaft. The continuation—a sloping passage—was, however, blocked by enormous quartzite plugs. The tomb lay not at the end of the passage but to the side of it, and was constructed in a way that it could not be discovered by destroying the plugs. Furthermore, the sarcophagus was not standing in the chamber but was hidden behind the wall casing. From there on, the tomb continued over a long distance, thus diverting the interest of the robbers to a faraway place, which was, of course, empty. In spite of that, the robbers succeeded.

Private tombs also occasionally had entrance corridors blocked by granite or limestone plugs. Again, in all cases the obstacles had either been chiseled through or circumvented by the tomb robbers.[40]

A third method involved portcullises, stone slabs that were lowered down from cavities above the passage where the slabs were stored until the final closing of the tomb. To simplify their construction, the portcullises were always set in horizontal parts of the passages. Their advantage over simple blocks pushed against the door was that they ran in grooves in the side walls, which prevented them from being turned round.

Predecessors of this blocking device can be seen in the slabs lowered from the top of the tomb into the staircase of mastabas from the First Dynasty (fig. 5.13).[41] Such stones, pierced by drill holes near their top to attach the ropes, were sometimes heavy, and their lowering through narrow channels must have been a hard work. But since portcullises of the first three dynasties were surrounded by only brickwork or bedrock, it was not a problem for the thieves to cut their way through.

The lowering of portcullises in pyramids was carried out in a different way. In the western corridor of the Bent Pyramid, an unusual arrangement is found (fig. 5.14).[42] Here the plug rests on a steep slope, kept in position by beams that had to be removed in order to let the stone fall. How this was done without endangering the workmen who carried out the maneuver is unknown. Perhaps they replaced the beams at the last moment by ropes and set them on fire. In any event, the method certainly functioned in this one pyramid, and the limestone plug successfully interrupted the passage.

The protective measure employed at the Bent Pyramid was apparently not considered very practical because portcullises of the Cheops Pyramid in front of the royal crypt were maneuvered by different means (fig. 5.15).[43] The portcullises were placed close together in a group of three, stored in a granite-lined chamber above the horizontal entrance passage, and probably held in position by wooden supports. They were lowered with ropes handled from above and slung around round beams that were inserted into half-round incisions in the side walls.[44] The system was rather naïve because the robbers could easily climb over the lowered portcullises through the maneuvering chamber and chisel off enough of the granite of the architrave over the entrance door.

Quite similar was the construction of the portcullises of the pyramid of Mycerinus.[45] The main difference from those of Cheops was the greater distance between the single slabs, bridged by granite architraves, and the higher placement of the beams for lowering the stones. The following royal tombs were regularly equipped with three portcullises, but even farther distant from one another and always in the horizontal part of the passage.[46] To prevent the thieves from chiseling around them, the whole section of the passage was surrounded by granite. The unfortunate position of the portcullises in the horizontal part of the passage allowed the

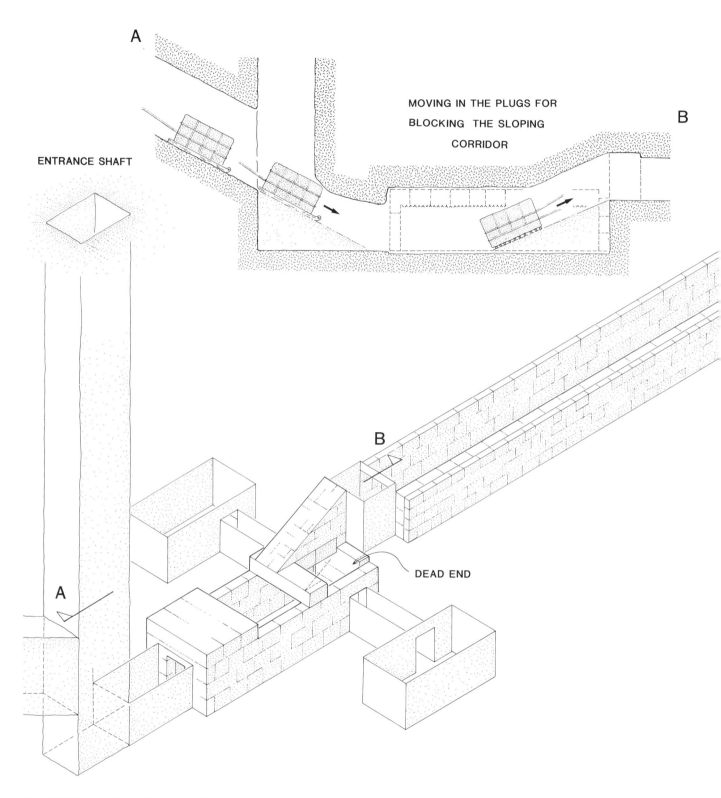

A

ENTRANCE SHAFT

MOVING IN THE PLUGS FOR
BLOCKING THE SLOPING
CORRIDOR

B

B

DEAD END

A

Fig. 5.12 The cenotaph of Senwosret III at
Abydos, with its blocking systems.

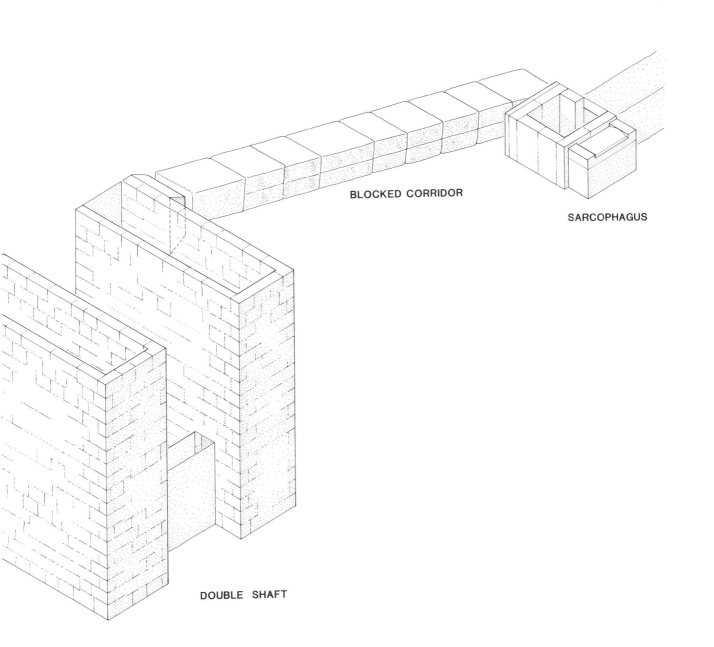

BLOCKED CORRIDOR

SARCOPHAGUS

DOUBLE SHAFT

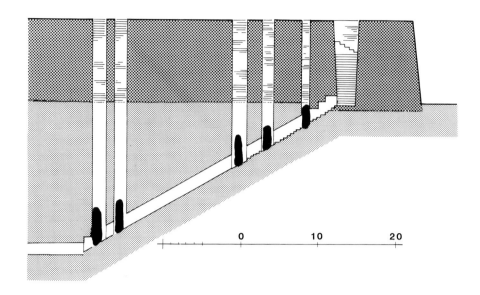

Fig. 5.13 The portcullises of the mastaba of King Djoser at Beit Khallaf.

robbers to set levers under them and lift them far enough up again to climb through below. To prevent this, the builder of the tomb of Senwosret-ankh at Lisht had prepared a pair of bolts in the side walls that glided out of their hole when the stone was lowered and prevented the portcullis from being pushed upward again (fig. 5.16).[47]

The system of portcullises was used less frequently later and was replaced by a fourth method, sliding blocks gliding from side niches (fig. 5.17). In the pyramid of Amenemhat II, a portcullis can be seen (probably one of the last examples) together with a sliding block.[48] The reason for the change may have been that sliding blocks could be made in much larger dimensions and therefore would be more difficult to break than a normal portcullis, which was limited in weight because of the problem of handling. The new system also had its disadvantages. In the same way that the

Fig. 5.14 The blocking of the western entrance passage of the Bent Pyramid.

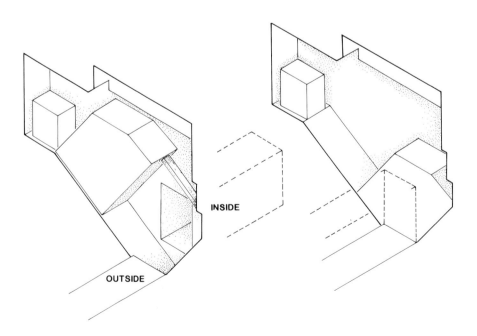

INSIDE

OUTSIDE

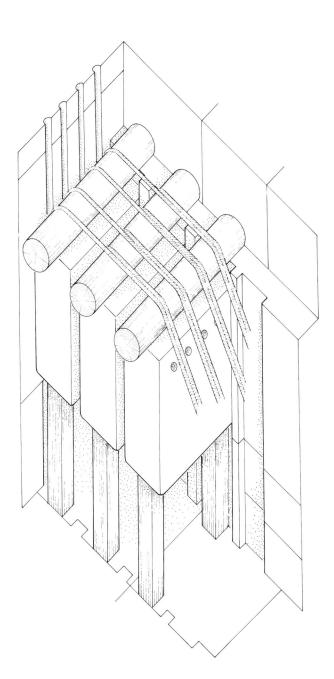

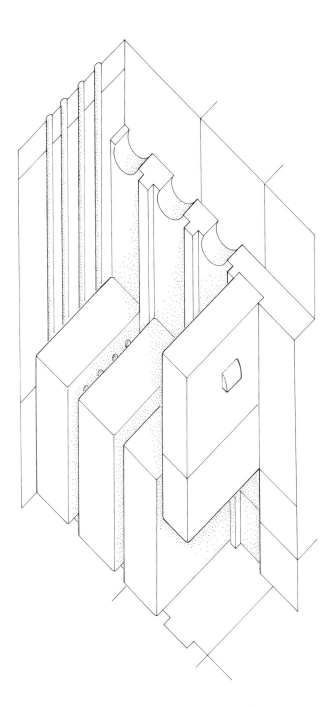

Fig. 5.15 The portcullises of the Cheops Pyramid before and after closing the tomb.

builders had the sliding block levered out of its niche, the robbers could lever it back again, even if they succeeded only in pushing a crossbar under its lower edge.

The builders improved their system by enormously enlarging the size of the sliding blocks and by setting them on inclined planes, which helped to bring the block down and prevented the robbers from levering it up again because of its weight (fig. 5.17).[49] Eventually, the closing maneuver became so complicated that in the pyramid of Amenemhat III at Hawara, only the first of the three gigantic quartzite portcullises could be closed.

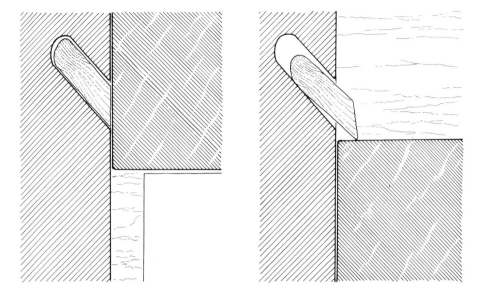

Fig. 5.16 Method to secure a closed portcullis in the mastaba of Senwosret-ankh.

Another method really prevented robbers from destroying or pushing back a sliding block. The level of the passage was changed so that the continuation was high up and could be reached only through an opening in the ceiling. This opening was to be blocked by a sliding stone of quartzite. Since quartzite could be broken only by pounding and this activity could not be carried out upward, it was indeed impossible to get through. As usual, the robbers avoided the quartzite and broke through softer parts of the corridor walls.[50]

There was one serious obstacle, however, which might indeed have saved some pyramid crypts. From Senwosret II on, the entrance to the pyramid was no longer located in the center of the north front. Furthermore, the interior systems of pyramids were so irregular and unpredictable that the robbers would not have known where to dig their tunnels, especially since the passages changed directions several times. The builders did not reckon with one event, which again destroyed all their efforts—the use of pyramids as quarries. In such cases, the pyramid masonry was dismantled stepwise until the roofing blocks were removed from the crypts. But rarely would the quarry workers have found very much. The pyramids of the Thirteenth Dynasty, which had those devices, were rarely finished or used for burials.

Finally, two additional devices should be mentioned. One, described further on page 75, is the combination of sarcophagus and crypt made of one huge and especially hard stone that is left without an entrance. The burial had to be lowered through a gap in the ceiling that could be closed by lowering a huge ceiling block from outside. This method was apparently invented—after the building disaster at the pyramid of Amenemhat III at Dahshur—for the pyramid of Hawara and used thereafter in the pyramids of the Thirteenth Dynasty (figs. 3.24, 3.25)[51] and the great tomb shafts of the Twenty-sixth Dynasty.

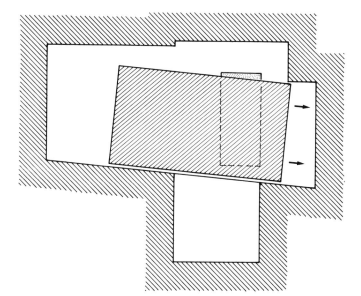

Fig. 5.17 Sliding quartzite block in the pyramid of an unknown king of the late Middle Kingdom at Saqqara.

The other device was developed only in tomb shafts of the Saite period (figs. 3.28, 5.18). Here the system of closing a huge sarcophagus of hard stone was combined with the system of drowning the sarcophagus in a sand fill in an exceptionally wide and deep shaft. To get near the sarcophagus, the whole sand fill would have to be emptied (about 2000 cubic meters), a task that would have taken several weeks and a considerable number of workers. The major device to flood the sarcophagus was the following. During the construction, round holes were cut into the stone vaults covering the sarcophagus. These holes were temporarily blocked with jars, so that the shaft on top could be filled with sand. At the moment of the closing of the tomb, the bottoms of the jars were smashed and the sand streamed in, thus covering the sarcophagus. It would continue to do so if the robbers started to dig a tunnel. In addition, the brick vault of the small corridor connecting the construction and the burial shaft could be broken so that the whole passage would be flooded.[52]

In the tomb of Senwosret-ankh at Lisht, a device was discovered that technically may have been the forerunner of such systems. Just in front of the four portcullises, a vertical shaft opened in the ceiling of the corridor and narrowed as it ascended. This shaft was found filled with loose material that would have collapsed over tomb robbers working their way toward the portcullises.[53] Clever tomb robbers could have avoided the sand by digging their tunnels through the bedrock and attacking the sarcophagus from below. To prevent this possibility, some tomb builders carved a cave below the sarcophagus and connected it with the sand fill on top by vertical shafts so that this part of the cave also would be filled with sand streaming down from above.[54]

A further step to increase the difficulties for tomb robbers can be observed in the Ptolemaic period.[55] The main, sand-filled shaft is surrounded by a large number of secondary shafts, equally filled with sand and con-

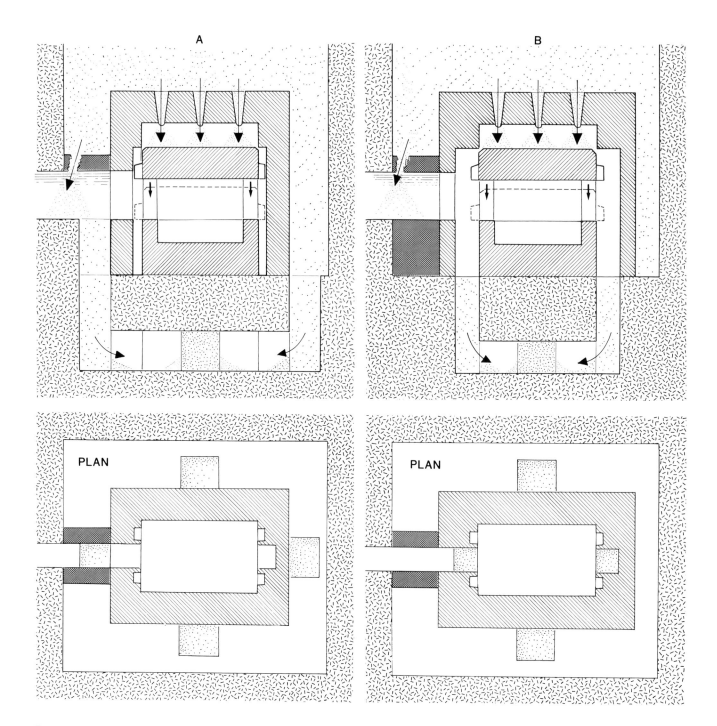

Fig. 5.18 Mechanism of sealing
sarcophagi with sand in Saite tomb shafts:
(A) all sand shafts outside the chamber;
(B) two shafts inside the chamber.

nected with one another and with the main shaft by large windows through
which the sand could flow in either direction. Therefore, not one of these
shafts could be emptied separately, but only all at the same time and with
the same speed. When the crypt is not set on bedrock but into heavy layers
of sand, this arrangement would even have prevented an approach by a
tunnel dug from below, for the sand would also have penetrated there. The
only two examples of this construction type have not yet been sufficiently
explored to judge the efficiency of the builders and their opponents.

Fig. 5.19 Light-pole scaffolding surrounding a colossal royal statue, as depicted in the tomb of Rekhmira. (MMA acc. no. 30.4.90)

Such gigantic installations are rare, and one has the impression that already in the New Kingdom, tomb builders had given up any hope of stopping tomb robbing with stone construction. Even high officials in the Theban and Memphite necropolises rarely did more to protect their burials than having their shafts filled with boulders and sand.

SCAFFOLDING

It is generally thought that the Egyptians erected their buildings with the help of inclined planes so that there was not much need for wooden scaffolding. In some cases, however, scaffolds were necessary—for example, for the final dressing of walls and their decoration, or for the work on freestanding sculpture. Such an activity is shown in the tomb of Rekhmira (fig. 5.19),[56] where sculptors are working on light-pole scaffolding that surrounds two colossal statues. The scaffolding consists of light poles, tied together by knots of rope, the primitive but efficient method also used in medieval cathedral building. The absence of putlog holes in the surface of

Fig. 5.20 Putlog hole in the core masonry of the pyramid of Pepy II at Saqqara.

walls—frequent in Roman and medieval architecture—shows, however, that scaffolding was not an essential part of construction.[57]

Difficult to explain is a series of putlog holes constructed like small niches in the core masonry of the south side of the pyramid of Pepy II, for core construction of pyramids did not require scaffolding (fig. 5.20). Nevertheless, putlog holes exist on flat ground, mostly cut in the shape of round holes (20 to 30 centimeters deep, 20 centimeters wide) in the bedrock underlying the foundations. Early examples were found in the court of the mortuary temple of Chephren (fig. 5.21).[58] These holes were arranged in a manner that may suggest scaffolding of three poles set at a distance of 2

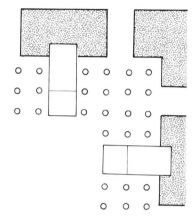

Fig. 5.22 Putlog holes for scaffolding in the ambulatory of the Mentuhotep temple of Deir el-Bahari.

Fig. 5.21 Putlog holes in the court of the funerary temple of Chephren.

cubits, apparently for sculpting the statues and decorating the granite passages between them.

In the temple of Mentuhotep at Deir el-Bahari (fig. 5.22), the temple of Ramesses III at Medinet Habu, and the tomb of Montuemhat,[59] similar deep and round holes suggest scaffolding for the sculptors decorating the ceiling and the columns. Putlog holes for scaffolding may also be represented by roughly squared limestone blocks found in the area of the pyramids of Senwosret I and of Amenemhat III at Dahshur (fig. 5.23). These blocks were pierced in the center by large round holes. Neither was found in position.[60]

Fig. 5.23 Putlog hole in a stone from the pyramid of Senwosret I at Lisht.

Fig. 5.24 System of the cedar beams that shore up the side walls of the western crypt of the Bent Pyramid.

Wooden poles and beams were also quite often inserted horizontally between two walls, either to keep them from falling in or as a means to fix ropes when heavy loads had to be raised or lowered, either at the upper end of sloping passages or near vertical shafts.[61] Such shores were discovered in great numbers in the underground apartments of the Step Pyramid,[62] most of them from the time of the construction. Also in the Meidum Pyramid[63] and the Bent Pyramid,[64] numerous examples of such wooden supports were found. In the Bent Pyramid, the upper burial chamber (western entrance) had to be protected against an enormous sideward thrust by erecting five beams vertically against each side wall and squeezing in two crossbeams or struts between each pair (figs. 5.24, 5.25).

In the grand gallery of the Cheops Pyramid, twenty-six opposing pairs of horizontal sockets, which supersede a system of vertical sockets, are cut into the side walls (fig. 5.11).[65] The sockets were certainly connected by beams

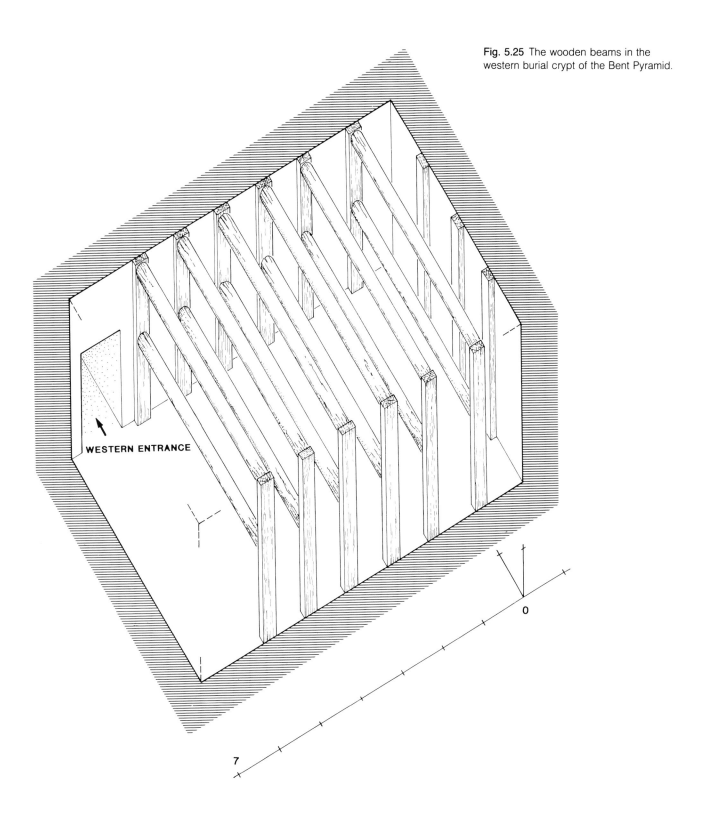

Fig. 5.25 The wooden beams in the western burial crypt of the Bent Pyramid.

WESTERN ENTRANCE

0

7

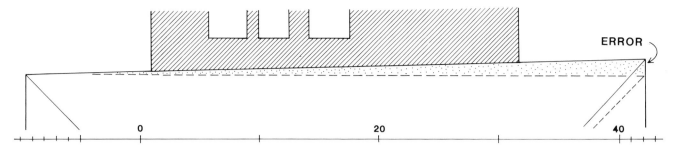

Fig. 5.26 The displaced eastern foot of the pyramid of Sahura and its correct alignment (dashed line).

that could have secured the granite plugs stored in the gallery, or perhaps carried a wooden staircase to facilitate the transport of the royal mummy and burial equipment over the granite plugs and into the burial chamber. Numerous sockets for the insertion of a heavy wooden construction were also found around the boat pit of Cheops.[66] This mechanism served to lower either the boat itself or the roofing blocks of the pit.

In the pyramid of Amenemhat III at Dahshur, which was threatened by collapse, the following system of supporting beams can be observed in two chambers. At the ends of the side walls, two beams 20 × 40 centimeters thick were put up on limestone slabs leaning against the corners. They carried upright horizontal beams of the same dimensions, not crossing the room but parallel to the side walls (fig. 5.30). These beams again supported flat-lying beams that carried the rock above. The space along the side walls, below these architraves, was walled up with bricks, which gave additional strength to the construction.[67]

Putlog holes around the sarcophagus pit of Mentuhotep at Lisht permit the reconstruction of the lowering procedure of the sarcophagus and its lid.

Hölscher suggested that in the temple of Medinet Habu hanging scaffolds were sometimes used[68] because small square openings in the roofs of the colonnades in the first and second courts were not necessary for light and ventilation and could have served for holding cords to raise and lower scaffolds. Real putlog holes for the insertion of woodwork exist, however, in the temple of Medinet Habu. They were used to fix the baldachin of the window of royal appearances. They even had holes for fixing beams with ropes.[69]

REPAIRING DAMAGES

In building, there is always the likelihood of problems and damage occurring during or after the construction work, including major disasters due to errors and miscalculations in planning or careless execution. In medieval building, cathedrals collapsed;[70] in modern construction, there are more and more disastrous collapses of ceilings, bridges, and skyscapers during construction.

In ancient Egyptian stone building, such accidents seem to have been less frequent as far as we can judge from archaeological observations. This is probably due to underestimating the actual strength of foundations, ceil-

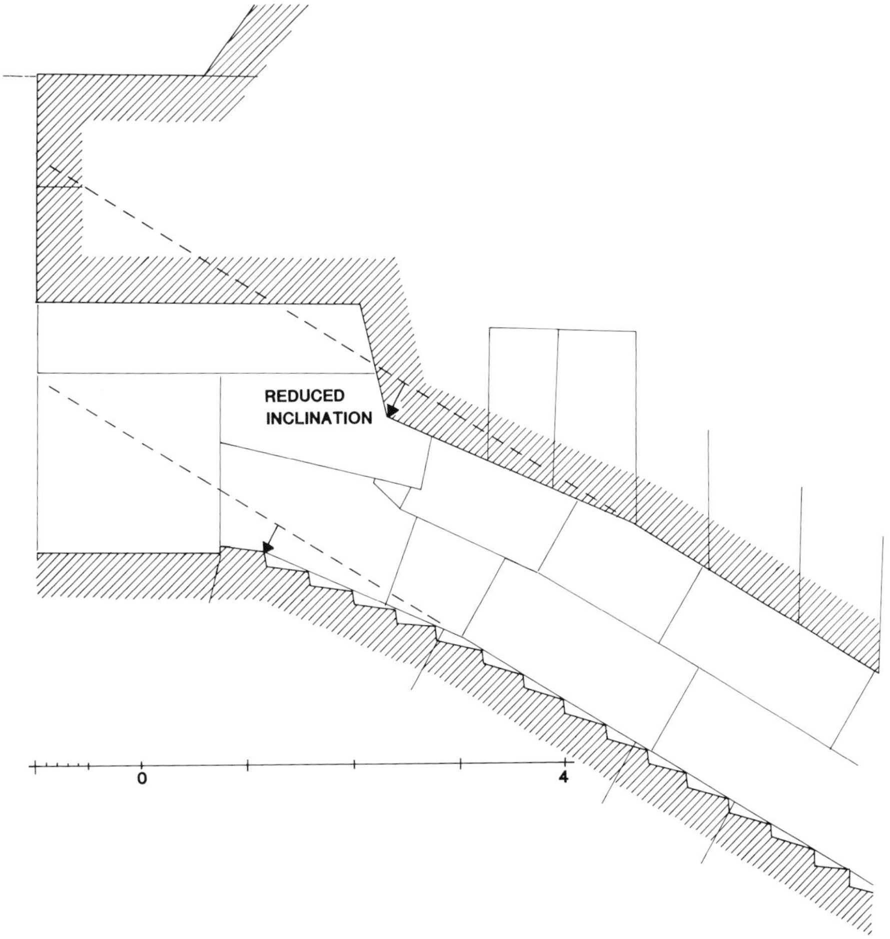

Fig. 5.27 Entrance passage of the pyramid of Amenemhat III at Dahshur, showing the original direction (dashed line) and its adjusted final execution.

REDUCED
INCLINATION

0   4

ings, and other elements, which were usually more solid than was necessary. There are, however, indications that in ancient Egypt building work could be hampered by such problematic occurrences due to minor errors and damage as well as serious mishaps.

During planning and surveying, errors could happen as at the pyramid of Sahura, where the eastern base line ran out of alignment by 1.88 meters (fig. 5.26).[71] In the pyramid of Amenemhat III at Dahshur, the slope of the two entrance stairs had to be considerably altered because the construction already begun would have brought the passage entrance to a place that was considered to be unsafe (fig. 5.27).[72] Petrie's measurements of the pyramid of Chephren seem to indicate that, due to faulty ancient measurements, the top of the pyramid was twisted in relation to the lower part.[73] The winding corridors in the Bent Pyramid (fig. 5.3)[74] and in the Ka-tomb of the pyramid of Amenemhat III at Dahshur (fig. 5.4) also indicate limitations in the Egyptian art of surveying.[75]

More serious were the problems encountered by overestimation of the strength of the ground when erecting a pyramid. At least four examples are known in which considerable structural damage occurred during the building of the pyramid. The least serious happened to the pyramid of Senwosret I.[76] It seems that a construction shaft under the center of the

Fig. 5.28 Long grooves for patches in the surface of the foundation of the pyramid of Senwosret I at Lisht, for repairing the foot of the casing blocks.

pyramid was not refilled enough and gave way so that the pyramid's masonry settled and caused the casing blocks to tilt in. The slight inward inclination of only 1 to 2 degrees was apparently sufficient to crack the lower edges of practically all the casing blocks, which had to be repaired by innumerable patches (fig. 4.106). For the insertion of the elongated patch stones, with their wedge-shaped cross section, deep grooves were cut. These grooves cut through the lower edge of the upper block and often continued deep into the upper edge of the lower blocks (fig. 5.28).

The art of patching stone was highly developed in Egypt. The corners of many sarcophagi, canopic chests, and statues were knocked off during handling and had to be replaced by patches of the same material. For that purpose, wedge-shaped repair stones had to be fitted in, frequently secured with an additional wedge-shaped tongue pushed into a corresponding slot.[77]

At the pyramid of Amenemhat III at Dahshur, the pressure of the weight of the pyramid on the underground apartments was so great that the apartments sank into the soft *tafl* below. The irregular settling caused so many dangerous cracks in the stone ceiling and architraves that the still partially unfinished corridors and chambers were threatened by collapse. Hastily erected wooden scaffolding and roofs bear witness to the perilous situation (figs. 5.29, 5.30). Finally, the pyramid had to be abandoned as a royal tomb and replaced by the more solid pyramid at Hawara.[78]

A similar event had happened 600 years earlier at the Bent Pyramid at the same place (fig. 5.31). Also here the soft *tafl* below gave way under the weight of the pyramid, probably causing damages in the casing. These are invisible today because another layer of casing was added to all four sides of the pyramid. Despite these measures, more damages occurred, causing cracks and deformation of the new casing (fig. 5.32), which was pressed 60

Fig. 5.29 Ceiling slabs in the pyramid of Amenemhat III at Dahshur that were broken during the construction.

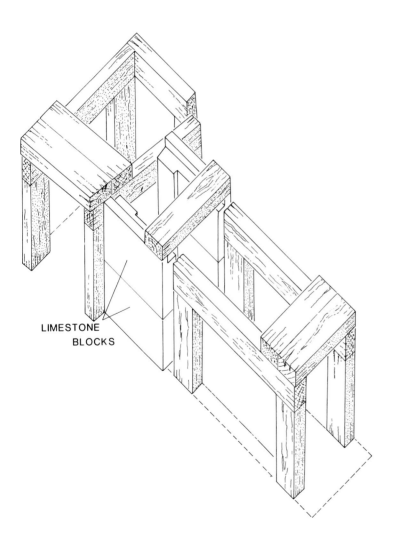

Fig. 5.30 Wooden struts in the unfinished galleries of the pyramid of Amenemhat III at Dahshur.

LIMESTONE
BLOCKS

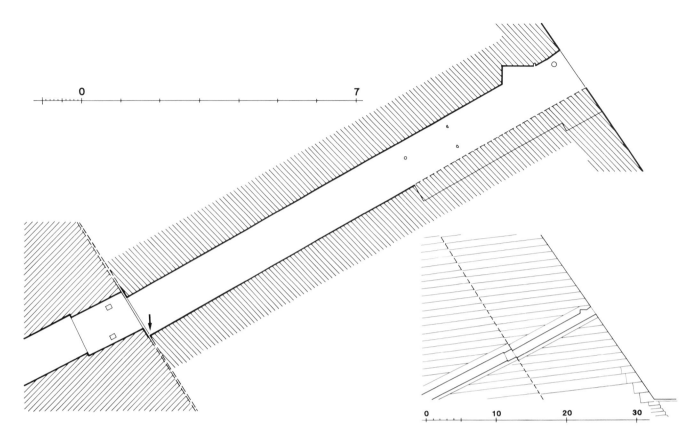

Fig. 5.31 The step in the entrance corridor of the Bent Pyramid caused by the sagging of the (later added) outer layer of the pyramid.

centimeters outward.[79] The new outer layer also slid down so much that in the entrance corridor a step of 23 centimeters appeared between the outer and the next inner layer. These damages were first repaired with patches and mortar. In the western burial crypt, a scaffolding of heavy wooden beams was put in to prevent the chamber from being crushed. But in the end, all these attempts to save the pyramid were given up and the unfortunate structure was completed with a much smaller top that was less inclined (from 54° 31′ 13″ to 43° 21′) than the original pyramid.[80] A second pyramid had to be built—the Red Pyramid of Dahshur.

The pyramid of Pepy II also seems to have suffered from some construction failure, perhaps again caused by the settling of the foundations. The foundations of the finished casing had to be surrounded by a three-course high and 6.5-meter-deep coat of limestone blocks intended to prevent the casing from falling apart.[81]

One major building disaster that has been imputed to the pyramid builders—at the pyramid of Meidum[82]—certainly never happened. Other accidents, such as earthquakes, cannot, of course, be blamed on the Egyptian builders. Apparently, the famous temple of Ramesses II at Abu Simbel was hit by such an earthquake either during or shortly after its construction; the damage was considerable but could be repaired.[83]

Another catastrophe was the breaking of the dam of a water reservoir built in the Fourth Dynasty in the Wadi Gerawi near Helwan,[84] apparently also during its construction. It may have been the result of a torrential rain

Fig. 5.32 Long vertical crack in the casing of the Bent Pyramid, originally hidden by patches.

and would have had devastating results for settlements at the mouth of the wadi.

Numerous were such minor disasters as collapsing walls and tombs, exemplified by the fall of a part of the tomb of Senenmut during its construction.[85] Countless are the smaller damages of masonry and its subsequent repair with the help of patches. Limestone and sandstone, the two major building stones, easily flaked off when put on edge or handled with levers. In addition, flint inclusions had to be removed frequently and replaced by repair stones, which were inserted into neat and well-prepared sockets.

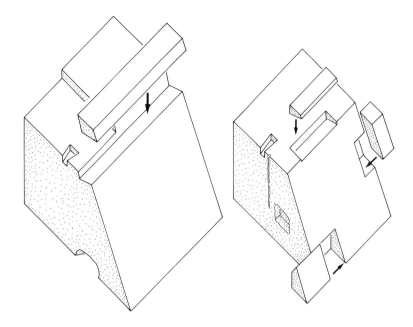

The sockets show an inwardly inclined lower edge that prevented the patching stone from falling out again (fig. 5.33). Of course, this also had to be fixed with mortar. In some buildings, such patches are so abundant that they cover whole block surfaces (figs. 5.34, 5.35).[86]

In the Eighteenth Dynasty Temple at Medinet Habu in the time of Hakoris (ca. 390 B.C.), a fluted column had to be put in to support the sagging roof slabs (fig. 5.36).[87] Other repairs were carried out in wood, as in the Bent Pyramid and the pyramid of Amenemhat III (as previously noted).

Wooden beams were also used to support a broken architrave in the temple of Karnak, where sockets were cut into the abaci of the columns to

Fig. 5.34 Patches in the front façade of the valley temple of the Bent Pyramid.

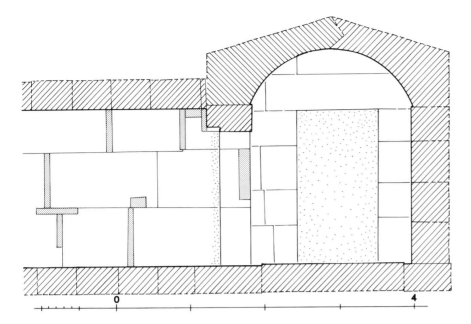

insert beams. Although the beams have perished long ago, the broken architrave is still in place.[88]

Naturally, such conservation work was carried out more frequently in later periods, when the older buildings started to decay. Such activities have a long tradition, however, and belonged to the duties of every pious Pharaoh. Written sources about the restoration of monuments found in ruins are abundant.[89] The actual execution, however, has not yet been thoroughly studied.[90]

BUILDING A COFFERDAM

The Egyptian culture was so dependent on artificial irrigation that the ancient Egyptians must have been experts in digging canals and constructing locks and dams.[91] The necessity of transporting heavy monuments such as obelisks by boat certainly required the construction of artificial waterways. None of these constructions, which must have been abundant in ancient times, has thus far been recognized. Perhaps none has survived. One may see reminiscences of such canals and dams represented in offering tables, such as the marvelous example in the Metropolitan Museum of Art, New York (fig. 5.37).[92]

The cofferdam Sadd el-Kafar in the Wadi Gerawi, southeast of Helwan, however, has recently been carefully studied and published (fig. 5.38).[93] The dam, 14 meters high and 98 meters deep at its foot, was intended to block the 110-meter-wide wadi at a narrow part of its lower end, preventing the torrential rainfalls from destroying settlements and fields and possibly harbor installations on the east bank of the Nile. How urgent the structure was can be deduced from its ill fate. The dam was still under construction when a sudden downpour produced a flood that carried away the uncovered core fill on the valley side. The center of the unfinished dam broke

Fig. 5.36 The ceiling of the temple of the Eighteenth Dynasty at Medinet Habu, supported by a column of the time of King Hakoris.

away, freeing a torrent that probably caused disastrous results. Only two side ends of the dam remain today.

The cofferdam actually consists of two dams separated by a rock fill, their outer slopes being cased with limestone blocks laid in steps like the backing stones of a pyramid. The core between the dams was a fill of sand, pebble, and fine sediments (silt), all material collected from the neighboring wadi terraces and dumped in from the two sides.

The block casing is made of roughly squared blocks of 30 × 45 × 80 centimeters set at a slight inward slope of about 6 to 12 degrees. This feature, characteristic of the Third and early Fourth Dynasties, suggests that the dam was constructed in the reign of the great builder Snofru. The

Fig. 5.37 Limestone altar of the First Intermediate Period from Lisht, representing a system of canals, dikes, and sluices. (MMA acc. no. 32.1.213)

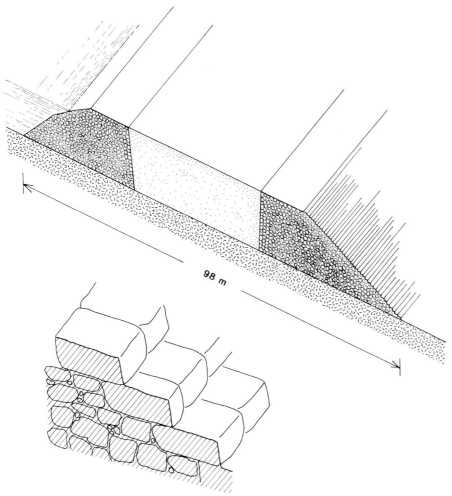

Fig. 5.38 The cofferdam in the Wadi Gerawi, and a detail of its block casing.

98 m

date is corroborated by the potsherds collected in workers' settlements nearby.

The dam was obviously designed by experts, and had it ever been complete would have served its purpose well. It would have held 600,000 cubic meters of water in a lake over 1 kilometer long. This lake, however, would have been full only every few years during heavy rainstorms. At other times, any precipitation in the lake would have either evaporated or leaked through the underlying bedrock.

NOTES

1. See, in general, S. Clarke, *Archaeologia* 55 (1896): 21–32; E. Mackay, *JEA* 7 (1921): 154–168; Frank Teichmann, in Erik Hornung, *Das Grab des Haremhab im Tal der Könige* (Bern, 1971), 32–37; Eigner, *Grabbauten*, 82–84. For work organization in the Biban el-Muluk in general, see Černý, *Community*; Černý, *Valley of the Kings*; Dominique Valbelle, *Les Ouvriers de la tombe, Deir el-Médineh à l'époque ramesside*, BdE, no. 96 (Cairo, 1985). For the famous tunnel on the island of Samos, see U. Jantzen et al., *Archäologischer Anzeiger* 3 (1973): 72–89.

2. Junker, *Giza* VII, 126, 143, 155, pl. 8a.

3. *BMMA* 28, part 2 (April 1933): 16–17, fig.13.

4. Lisht (unpublished data).

5. Arnold, *Amenemhet III* I, pls. 50, 52.

6. Fakhry, *Sneferu* I, 52–59, figs. 21–24, pls. 11–14.

7. Percy E. Newberry, *Beni Hasan* II (London, 1893), pl. 21; Ludwig Borchardt, *Allerhand Kleinigkeiten* (Leipzig, 1933), pl. 11[a]. For cutting tools in tombs, see H. W. Seton-Karr, *ASAE* 6 (1905): 176–184.

8. Arnold, *Amenemhet III* I, folding map 1.

9. Černý, *Community*, 101; Černý, *Valley of the Kings*, 19; Eigner, *Grabbauten*, 83.

10. Fakhry, *Sneferu* I, figs. 16–18, 36.

11. Maragioglio, *Piramidi* IV, pls. 3, 5.

12. Maragioglio, *Piramidi* V, 114.

13. Arnold, *Amenemhet III* I, 57.

14. Junker, *Giza* I, 41, 95; *Giza* VII, 184, fig. 76, etc.; Kuhlmann and Schenkel, *Ibi* II, 245, fig. 89; Reisner, *Tomb Development*, figs. 110, 111.

15. Ryan and Hansen, *Cordage*, 15–16.

16. Arnold and Winlock, *Mentuhotep*, 61–62, pls. 36c–d.

17. Černý, *Valley of the Kings*, 19.

18. For example, the shaft in the Bab el-Hosan is 31 meters below the floor of the crypt, which is already over 60 meters below ground; shaft in Beni Hasan, 31 meters (Newberry, *Beni Hasan* II, pl. 3); shaft at Deir el-Bersheh, 35.5 meters (A. Kamal, *ASAE* 2 [1901]: 206; Junker, *Giza* I, 143–144, fig. 21); construction shafts of the Step Pyramid and that of Zawyet el-Aryan; Saite tomb shafts; and so on.

19. Bernard Bruyère, *Rapport sur les fouilles de Deir el-Médineh 1948–1951* (Cairo, 1953), pl. 3. For ancient sources about the construction process, see R. Ventura, *JEA* 73 (1987): 149–160.

20. Lower corridor of Cheops Pyramid, 137 meters; Bab el-Hosan, 191 meters; cenotaph of Senwosret III, 180 meters; tomb of Hatshepsut, 213 meters; tomb of Sety I, 217 meters (or more?).

21. Cenotaph and pyramid of Senwosret III, Ka-pyramid and queens' pyramids

of Senwosret I, and mastaba of Senwosret-ankh at Lisht, and most of the larger Middle Kingdom tombs at Dahshur, Illahun, and Hawara.

22. Also, some of the Saite tomb shafts have a secondary entrance shaft to be used for the burial, because the main construction shaft had to be filled with sand.

23. Arnold, *Senwosret I* 1, 66–68.

24. For a discussion of the air shafts, see Maragioglio, *Piramidi* IV, pl. 2. For their purpose, see I. E. S. Edwards, in *Essays in Honor of Dows Dunham* (Boston, 1980), 55–57. The idea by Fitchen that they were for the provision of air for burning the beams under the portcullises has to be rejected, since a huge fire in front of the burial of a king is unthinkable (*Building Construction*, 207–211). Besides it would not explain the air shafts in the middle chamber, which has no portcullises.

25. Černý, *Valley of the Kings*, 43–54.

26. Bruyère, *Rapport sur les fouilles de Deir el-Médineh*, 67–68, pl. 19B. The torches are 25 to 40 centimeters long and are made of different kinds of wood; the tops are enveloped in linen soaked in resin. They may, however, actually have been used in Saite times for rituals or processions in the dark. For other kinds of lamps, see H. G. Fischer, in *LÄ* III, 914–918.

27. In general, see Alan J. Spencer, *Death in Ancient Egypt* (Harmondsworth, 1982), 74–111.

28. There is evidence that the royal tombs at Saqqara were already robbed during the First Dynasty (Emery, *Great Tombs* II, 7–12).

29. For example, Arnold, *Jnj.jtj.f*, pls. 33a, b.

30. The pyramids of Senwosret II and Senwosret III and that of Amenemhat III at Dahshur were blocked this way only. See also Arnold, *Mentohotep*, pl. 22c.

31. F. Abitz, *ÄA* 26 (1974): 41–45.

32. Firth and Quibell, *Step Pyramid*, pls. 21, 47.

33. Fakhry, *Sneferu* 1, 49.

34. Reconstructed in ibid., fig. 56.

35. This important question is discussed in detail in Peter Tompkins, *Secrets of the Great Pyramid* (London, 1971), 236–255.

36. G. Goyon, *Revue Archéologique* 2 (1963): 7–18; L. Borchardt once considered the possibility of a wooden scaffold standing high up in the gallery and carrying the plugs until the funeral procession had passed beneath (*Dritte Bauperiode*, 7, pls. 6, 7). This construction looks rather complicated and furthermore unnecessary, since the procession could easily have walked over the granite plugs being stored on the floor, perhaps being covered with a stepped board to enable walking up.

37. Arnold, *Senwosret I* 1, pl. 89.

38. Ibid., 69, fig. 26.

39. E. R. Ayrton, C. T. Currelly, and A. E. P. Weigall, *Abydos* III (London, 1904), pl. 41.

40. Gautier, *Licht*, 67, fig. 79.

41. For example, Walter B. Emery, *The Tomb of Hemaka* (Cairo, 1938), pls. 2, 5, 6. In the mastabas of Beit Khallaf, sets of six portcullises, weighing up to 20 tons, were lowered into shafts, the deepest being 32 meters (Garstang, *Bet Khallaf*, pls. 17, 18).

42. Vyse, *Pyramids* III, 69, pl. between 68 and 69; Fakhry, *Sneferu* 1, 49, 52, fig. 35; Maragioglio, *Piramidi* III, pl. 13 (2, 8).

43. Maragioglio, *Piramidi* IV, pl. 7 [8]; Borchardt, *Dritte Bauperiode*, 14–16, pls. 3–5.

44. There are four more vertical grooves in the south wall, apparently made for guiding the ropes behind the innermost portcullis. Since the grooves have a closed lower end, the ropes would have been cut by the descending block or would have

blocked the movement of the stone. No other explanation seems possible. Two similar grooves are preserved in the entrance shaft of the burial chamber of the Meidum pyramid, suggesting that already there a stone was inserted into the shaft hanging from ropes, but again the system is not quite clear.

45. Borchardt, *Dritte Bauperiode*, 18–20, pl. 12; Maragioglio, *Piramidi* vi, pl. 7.

46. The surveys are rather sketchy; however, the best example is Merenra (A. Labrousse, *Orientalia* 51 [1982]: pl. 8).

47. *BMMA* 28, part 2 (November 1933): fig. 25.

48. De Morgan, *Dahchour* ii, 34, fig. 81.

49. The sliding blocks in the pyramid to the south of the pyramid of Khendjer weigh about 36 tons (Jéquier, *Deux pyramides*, pls. 8 [G–H], 17, 18; Petrie, *Labyrinth*, pl. 48).

50. Petrie, *Kahun*, pls. 2, 3; Petrie, *Labyrinth*, pls. 39, 47, 48; Jéquier, *Deux pyramides*, 36, fig. 27, pls. 8, 17; V. Maragioglio, *Orientalia* 37 (1968): pl. 52.

51. Petrie, *Kahun*, pl. 4; Jéquier, *Deux pyramides*, pls. 8, 17, 18; Petrie, *Labyrinth*, pl. 40.

52. A. Barsanti, *ASAE* 1 (1900): 161–166, 230–234; Barsanti, *ASAE* 5 (1904): 69–73; Z. Saad, *ASAE* 41 (1942): 388–391; Vyse, *Pyramids* i, 216–218; *Pyramids* ii, 131–133.

53. *BMMA* 28, part 2 (November 1933): 19, fig. 25.

54. Z. Saad, *ASAE* 41 (1942): 383, fig. 76; J.-P. Lauer, *ASAE* 51 (1951): 469–478, pl. 1.

55. One is the so-called Campbell's Tomb at Giza (Vyse, *Pyramids* i, 216–218; *Pyramids* ii, 131–133 with pls.). The second, even greater example is the tomb being excavated by Miroslav Verner at Abusir (*ZÄS* 113 [1986]: 158–160).

56. *Rekhmire*, pl. 60. Workers on scaffolding may also be represented on two reliefs of the Eighteenth Dynasty (D. Wildung, *Münchner Jahrbuch für Bildende Kunst* 31 (1980): 260, 262; *Ägyptens Aufstieg zur Weltmacht*, no. 54.

57. I. E. S. Edwards kindly reminded me that putlogs were mentioned in connection with the pyramid of Senwosret III (Vyse, *Pyramids* iii, 61). But I think that they may have been patched repair holes, similar to those at other pyramids, because putlog holes on the surface of a pyramid would be unique. Real putlogs are visible, however, in the side walls of the huge Saite tomb shaft northeast of the pyramid of Unas. They indicate the system of scaffolding erected during the construction of the shaft.

58. Hölscher, *Chephren*, 76–77, figs. 68, 69.

59. Arnold, *Mentuhotep*, pls. 10a, c, d, 11d; Hölscher, *Mortuary Temple* ii, 32–33, fig. 36; Eigner, *Grabbauten*, 87–88, fig. 59.

60. Arnold, *Amenemhet III* i, pl. 61 [F]; *Karnak* viii, 164–165, pls. iii, iiii.

61. Arnold, *Amenemhet III* i, 22, 26, 37, 64; Bernard Bruyère, *Les Fouilles de Deir el Médineh 1924–1925* (Cairo, 1926), 23, fig. 13; A. Kamal, *ASAE* 2 (1901): 209. Holes for vertical poles were found around the tomb shafts of Montemhet and Pedamenophis (Eigner, *Grabbauten*, 143, figs. 59, 111, 112).

62. Firth and Quibell, *Step Pyramid*, pls. 12, 21 (Saite), 36 [1], 46 [3–4], 108 [3]; Lauer, *Pyramid à degrés* ii, pls. 32 [2], 33, 101, 102. Some show traces of ropes cutting into them.

63. Maragioglio, *Piramidi* iii, pl. 4; Rowe, "Meydum," pl. 25.

64. Maragioglio, *Piramidi* iii, 72, 108, pls. 12, 13; Fakhry, *Sneferu* i, 52–59, pls. 11–14. The meaning of the three beams against the north wall is not clear. Did the builders also plan to introduce north–south directed beams, which then proved to

be too long to be moved into the crypt? Equally unknown is the purpose of the three pairs of beams farther up in the corbeled roof.

65. Borchardt, *Dritte Bauperiode;* Maragioglio, *Piramidi* IV, pl. 6; N. F. Wheeler, *Antiquity* 9 (1935): 168–169; G. Goyon, *Revue Archéologique* 2 (1963): 10, fig. 4; J.-P. Lauer, in *Festschrift Ricke,* 133–141; Edwards, *Pyramids,* 116–117; Stadelmann, *Ägyptische Pyramiden,* 116. The sockets led to bizarre speculations on the "mysteries" of the Cheops Pyramid.

66. Zaki Nour, *Cheops Boats,* 24, pl. 24.

67. Arnold, *Amenemhet III* I, 46–47, pls. 19, 20, 50, 52.

68. Hölscher, *Mortuary Temple* II, 32–33, figs. 36, 37.

69. Hölscher, *Mortuary Temple* I, 42–43, figs. 20, 21.

70. For example, the collapse of the cathedral of Beauvais in 1573.

71. Borchardt, *Sahure,* 69–70, pl. 16.

72. Arnold, *Amenemhet III* I, 21, 38, 42, 48.

73. Petrie, *Pyramids and Temples,* 97.

74. Fakhry, *Sneferu* I, figs. 17, 18.

75. Arnold, *Amenemhet III* I, 57, pl. 37, corridor S6.

76. Arnold, *Senwosret I* I, 66, pls. 40, 41. For similar repairs at the Ka-pyramid of the Bent Pyramid, see Maragioglio, *Piramidi* III, pl. 16.

77. A capital at Tanis had been repaired by pegging the patches with metal pins (W. M. Flinders Petrie, *Tanis* II, The Egypt Exploration Fund 2 [London, 1888], 10).

78. Arnold, *Amenemhet III* I, 84–86, pls. 18d, 19c, 20a.

79. J. Dorner, *MDAIK* 42 (1986): 44.

80. Ibid., 55; Maragioglio, *Piramidi* III, 58, 60, pls. 9, 11; Stadelmann, *Ägyptische Pyramiden,* 89–96. The impact of the enormous pressure can be seen in the half-crushed masonry of the upper parts of the western burial chamber.

81. The architecture of this pyramid has never been properly studied; see only Jéquier, *Pépi II* II, 6, pl. 1.

82. The unfortunate theory by Kurt Mendelssohn (*The Riddle of the Pyramids* [London, 1974], 112ff; *JEA* 59 [1973]: 60–71) has been definitely refuted by I. E. S. Edwards (*JEA* 60 [1974]: 251) and C. J. Davey (*JEA* 62 [1976]: 174).

83. Louis-A. Christophe, *Abou Simbel et l'epopée de sa découverte* (Brussels, 1965), 206–207; K. A. Kitchen, *Pharaoh Triumphant: The Life and Times of Ramesses II* (Warminster, 1982), 135–136.

84. G. Garbrecht, *Antike Welt,* 2. Sondernummer (Antike Wasserbauten) (1965), 53; G. Garbrecht and H.-U. Bertram, *Der Sadd-el-Kafara: Die älteste Talsperre der Welt,* Mitteilungen, no. 81, Leichtweiss-Institut für Wasserbau der Technischen Universität Braunschweig (1983), 118.

85. Peter F. Dorman, *The Tomb of Senenmut,* vol. 1, *The Architecture and Decoration of Tombs 71 and 353* (forthcoming).

86. Good examples, besides the pyramid of Amenemhat III at Dahshur, are the valley temple of the Bent Pyramid, the alabaster shrine of Amenhotep I at Karnak (H. Chevrier, *RdÉ* 23 [1971]: 81, fig. 3, pl. 2), and the rock surface of the Theban Tombs (Kuhlmann and Schenkel, *Ibi* I, pls. 92, 93, 133, 134, etc.; *Ibi* II, 30, figs. 1, 130; Eigner, *Grabbauten,* 84). See also Jéquier, *Architecture* I, pl. 34; De Lubicz, *Temple* II, pls. 32, 33.

87. Hölscher, *Eighteenth Dynasty,* 20, pl. 19.

88. *CEAEM,* fig. 173.

89. For example, F. Gomaa, *ÄA* 23 (1973): 61–66, 76–77. More material is in *BAR* II, 157 (Thutmosis III), 612 (Sety I); *BAR* III, 31 (Haremhab); *BAR* IV, 276,

357–360 (Ramesses III), 627–630 (Smendes), 634 (Pinodjem), 659 (Mencheperra), 909–916 (Montemhat), 966 (Psametik I).

90. Golvin and Goyon, *Karnak*, 26; M. Azim, in *Mélanges offerts à Jean Vercoutter* (Paris, 1985), 27. See also V. Rondet and J.-C. Golvin, *MDAIK* 45 (1989): 249–259.

91. For artificial irrigation in ancient Egypt, see W. Schenkel, in *LÄ* I, 775–782, 1006; *LÄ* III, 310–312; E. Endesfelder, *ZÄS* 106 (1979): 37–51; H. Goedicke, in *LÄ* V, 657 (s.v. "Schleuse").

92. Hayes, *Scepter* I, 117, fig. 69. More examples are in C. Kuentz, in suppl. to *BIFAO* 81 (1981): 243–255, figs. 12–14.

93. Garbrecht and Bertram, *Der Sadd-el-Kafara*. The dam was discovered in 1885 by Georg Schweinfurth. For an ancient dam in Greece, see W. M. Murray, *AJA* 88 (1984): 195–203.

CHAPTER VI   *Tools and Their Application*

MEASURING TOOLS

Cubit Rods · Richard Lepsius—after a few less important predecessors—and Petrie were the first and last authors to study seriously the Egyptian cubit rod.[1] Lepsius collected information about fourteen more or less complete cubits. Most of these examples were not actually used as tools, but as votives, or were made for the funerary equipment and therefore made of hard stone. Some, however, are of wood, the material actually used for cubit rods by architects.

They resemble our yardsticks, being short (52.5 centimeters) and stout, with a quadrangular section and a fifth side produced by chamfering the front top edge (fig. 6.1). The front, the oblique, and the top faces were used for marking and numbering the single measurements. The rear and undersurface were often inscribed with the name of the owner. The measurements indicated consist of the 7 palms and digits and their subdivisions. Their lengths vary from 52.3 to 52.9 centimeters, reminding us that ancient measures were not so standardized as those of today and that such discrepancies have to be taken into account in our calculations of Egyptian buildings.

In the tomb of the architect Kha at Deir el-Medina,[2] two cubits were found. One was gilded and inscribed—apparently not made for daily use but as an honorary royal gift to the esteemed architect. The other one, of plain wood, could be folded in two parts by hinges and was probably used by its owner for actual work.

Another, more unusual cubit rod of "white wood" in the British Museum[3] is 2 cubits long (1.0489 meters or 2 × 0.52445) and shows that Egyptian architects had longer tools as well. In the settlement of Lisht North were found two primitive cubit rods made for daily use, one of them with marks for half- and quarter-cubits.

Apparently, stonemasons also used another measuring unit, the *nby*-rod,

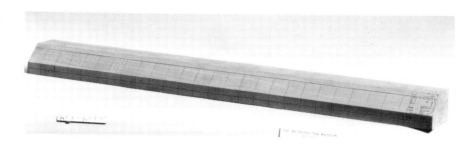

which might have been about 67 to 68 centimeters long, subdivided into seven spaces. Unfortunately, there is not much evidence for its application and exact dimension.[4]

Measuring Cords · For measuring great distances, ropes were certainly used, the predecessors of modern measuring tapes.[5] Since the number 100 is represented in hieroglyphs by a rope 🪢, one might suggest that measuring ropes of 100 cubits (52.5 meters) were used. Reisner once thought that the hieroglyph 𓏤 might represent a measuring cord, taking the end loops as handles and the side loops as tags marking the cubits.[6] Such ropes are shown in statuary of the Eighteenth Dynasty, held by kneeling officials who present their tools to the god.[7] These ropes were adorned with the ram head of Amun. In about eleven representations of the measuring of the wheat fields in Theban tombs,[8] we see surveyors working with such ropes, which have knots, apparently indicating subdivisions, probably cubits (fig. 6.2).

Dorner rightly suggests, however, that such ropes could have been used for only rough measurements, such as for fields.[9] A rope 52.5 meters long would have to be very thick, and the knots for its subdivision would have been so bulky that it could not have been used for accurate work. One might think, however, of different means of marking, such as the loops suggested by Reisner, fixed at a spot marked with red paint. By a practical test, Dorner also found that the length of a rope could be influenced by humidity, so the measuring tapes had to be treated with fat. Another interesting result of Dorner's calculations is that the famous base length of the pyramid of Cheops could have been achieved most accurately by using cubit rods 4 or 8 cubits long.

Fig. 6.2 Surveying fields with ropes, as depicted in the Theban tomb of Menna.

Fig. 6.3 A sculptor's cord on a reel from a Middle Kingdom tomb at Deir el-Bahari. (MMA acc. no. 22.3.72)

That ropes were actually used by builders is, however, shown by the method of producing the red leveling lines on the walls of buildings. The marks were made by dipping a cord into red ocher, stretching it over the surface, and lightly flinging it against the surface. Such cords were of course not necessarily measuring cords or ropes. A reel is preserved with a thin cord still attached and wound around a rotating axle (fig. 6.3).[10]

Plumbs · Plumbs consist of a plumb bob, suspended from a peg or a stick, which could also be used to reel up the cord. Many plumb bobs got lost during the actual work and have been recovered. They vary in material, shape, and size. Petrie collected a great variety,[11] with examples from the Third Dynasty on.

A more elaborate type of plumb was found in the tomb of the architect Senedjem at Deir el-Medina (fig. 6.4).[12] The board was held vertically against the wall to be tested, and the plumb bob was attached to a wooden crossboard so that the cord, if in a vertical position, would touch a second cross board below, which was the same size as the first. Plumbs were also used to put a square level in position. The string was fixed at the top of the two legs of the square, and the tip of the plumb had to touch the center mark on the cross board.

Builders' Squares · Egyptian builders and masons made use of the simple wooden device, the square, in order to lay off or check right angles, in building as well as dressing blocks. It is in principle the same instrument that is used today. Few squares have actually been found. The simplest version consists of two arms, connected at a right angle with pegs or with tongue and groove.[13] One of the two legs could be strengthened by a footboard, which allowed the square to stand upright by itself (fig. 6.5).[14]

There may also have been squares with a third piece of wood connecting the two legs in the shape of an *A*, similar to the square levels. In the tomb of Rekhmira, a square is shown lying in a carpenter's workshop,[15] reminding us that squares could be used by other craftsmen as well.

Square Levels · The square level not only was *the* leveling instrument of Pharaonic Egypt, but was used in Roman and medieval building as well. It was only later superseded by the water level, which was known to the Romans but was used by them for only special purposes.[16]

The oldest Pharaonic plummet known dates only from the Middle Kingdom. One can be sure that it existed much earlier. Although the medieval building square levels could have several shapes,[17] the Egyptian specimens

seem always to have had two legs of equal length, connected at a right angle with a cross lath, so that the tool was in the shape of the letter *A*. The legs were made in a way to make it stand. Near the connecting corner of the two legs was suspended a plumb bob, which could coincide—when the level was standing horizontally—with a mark in the center of the cross lath.

The shape of this instrument appears frequently in the hieroglyphic sign used for words connected with the activities of that instrument, such as *hh* or *sb³*.[18] But only three examples of the instrument itself have been discovered, two of them made for funerary purposes.[19] They were found in the tomb of the architect Senedjem (Nineteenth Dynasty) at Deir el-Medina (fig. 6.6). The specimen no. 58 in Petrie's *Tools and Weapons* has a base of 45.6 centimeters and legs 32.8 centimeters long; no. 59 has a base of 46.6 centimeters and legs 32.8 centimeters long. A third example, excavated near the pyramid of Senwosret I at Lisht, which probably dates to the Twelfth Dynasty, has not been adequately published.[20]

The object occurs quite frequently in the shape of an amulet.[21]

Fig. 6.5 Modern replica of a builder's square from the Theban tomb of Mektira. (MMA acc. no. 20.3.90)

Fig. 6.6 Modern replica of a square level (MMA), probably representing Cairo 27258.

Fig. 6.7 Reconstruction of the scene of men working with the boning rod and dressing a limestone block (chisel painted yellow) from the Theban tomb of Rekhmira. (MMA acc. no. 31.6.23)

Boning Rods · When dressing blocks, Egyptian masons used boning rods[22] in order to obtain completely flat planes, as shown in the representation of the tomb of Rekhmira (fig. 6.7).[23] Two people hold short pieces of wood; both pieces are the same length and are connected to each other at their tops by a string. One man is moving a third rod of the same length over the block surface between the two other rods. If there still are protruding parts, the third rod would show above the line of the string. This kind of boning would probably have been done crosswise over all four corners. It would not have been sufficient, however, to level the stones. This task was probably done with the help of two level boards,[24] a method used by masons even into this century.

Numerous sets of boning rods have been found all over Egypt, from the Old Kingdom on, and are practically all identical (fig. 6.8).[25] An L-shaped perforation is drilled into two rods, beginning at the top end and emerging

Fig. 6.8 Set of boning rods from the Hatshepsut temple at Deir el-Bahari. (MMA acc. no. 23.3.169)

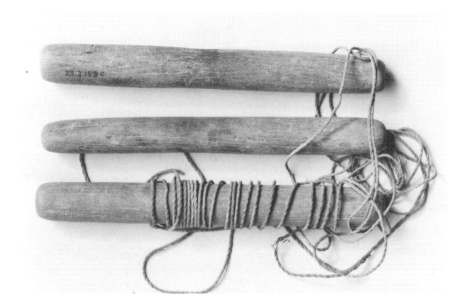

on the side. The string is fed through the holes in the sides and tied so that on each rod it emerges at the hole in the top. They are 10 to 13 centimeters long (fig. 6.9).

Stocks has suggested that boning rods could also have been used for the exact fitting of blocks with oblique rising joints to measure the constant distance between the corner points.[26] We have no actual evidence for this, and such measurements could have been carried out with any string of practical length or with other primitive instruments.

CUTTING TOOLS

Metal Tools · Egyptian metal tools[27] consisted of essentially unalloyed copper, arsenical copper, tin bronze, and leaded tin bronze.[28] A very high iron content is found occasionally and suggests that the tools were made from unrefined metal.[29]

The question of the date when iron tools came into general use in Egypt is much disputed.[30] Specimens of early iron are reported from predynastic dates on. Fragments supposedly of chisels from Saqqara are said to belong to the Fifth Dynasty, and pieces of a pickax found at Abusir and broken tools from Dahshur are said to be of the Sixth Dynasty. Since the circumstances of these finds are extremely vague, the dating of the tools may be questioned, and they could as well have been used by stonecutters of a much later period. A later date for these tools is also suggested by the fact that iron objects from the tomb of Tutankhamun were of poor quality and were considered to be so valuable that they were set in gold.

Only from the end of the Eighteenth Dynasty is there a gradual increase in the number of iron objects found in Egypt. In the Twenty-sixth Dynasty, iron became as common as bronze. At the same time, the first iron tools started to leave their traces on hard stones, and two tools of the seventh century B.C. are known to be of steel, their date being questioned, however.[31] The next step was the introduction of Roman types of iron tools, which differ considerably from the traditional Pharaonic tools.[32]

This development clearly shows that the tools of the Pharaonic period, with which we are concerned, were made primarily of copper or bronze. The question that must be considered, then, is to what extent metal chisels were used in comparison with stone tools.

Metal chisels were used for stoneworking, and many have been found. It seems not coincidental that the number of preserved metal chisels increases with the beginnings of monumental stone building in the Third Dynasty. Copper chisels (perhaps models) from tombs are known since the First Dynasty.[33] We have to suppose that they were used for woodworking. Some of the chisels from the Third Dynasty were certainly used for dressing stone, especially those from the Djoser precinct.

The two main types used for dressing stone were the round bar chisel (Petrie's type D) (fig. 6.10) and the flat mortise chisel (Petrie's type B) (fig. 6.11). Both are represented by dozens of specimens, ranging from the reign of Djoser to the New Kingdom. They were held in the hand and struck with a wooden mallet. They had to be a "handy" size, and therefore

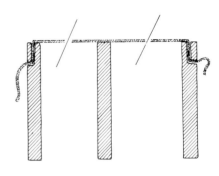

Fig. 6.9 Section through a set of boning rods.

Fig. 6.10 Round bar chisels of the Eleventh and Eighteenth Dynasties from Deir el-Bahari. (MMA acc. nos. 30.8.115 and 27.3.12)

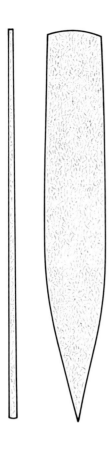

Fig. 6.11 Flat mortise chisel from a foundation deposit of the Mentuhotep temple at Deir el-Bahari. (Luxor Museum)

ranged from 16 to 25 centimeters long. Some were rather short and stout; others, more elongated.

The cutting edge of the round bar chisel is normally 1 to 2 centimeters wide, but sometimes more pointed, and it produces a cavity of corresponding width. In one operation, the successive cavities follow one another in the same straight or slightly curved line. Successive equidistant parallel lines are then repeated in the same manner until the tool has passed over the whole surface. Traces of this tool are quite frequent.

The flat mortise chisel is pointed and was not meant for flattening a surface but for cutting into it—that is, for producing features like mortises, ledges, and corners. It was probably not driven at an angle but more vertically.

From Petrie's rich collection, we learn about the existence of many more chisel types.[34] Most of them, however, were certainly not used for the production of building stones but for sculpting or for woodworking. Only one type might still belong to the tools of a stonecutter. It is the elongated, bare mortise chisel, which can be rather small—7 to 11 centimeters—or up to 52 centimeters long. The longer ones resemble a crowbar.[35] Such chisels were used for cutting small and deep mortises and holes or areas difficult to reach. Mortise chisels could also have been used by carpenters.

Many chisels were not held in the bare hand but inserted into wooden handles. Since a heavy blow would have driven the chisel deep into the handle and thus broken it, such instruments could have been used only for cutting soft material or would not have been used with a mallet at all. It is unlikely that such chisels were frequently used by masons. In fact, in representations they are shown in the hands of carpenters and leather workers.[36]

The list of examples in Table 6.1 is only a selection, with emphasis on the early representatives of each type.

Stone Tools · From the earliest times down to the New Kingdom and perhaps even later, stone tools played an important part in Pharaonic stoneworking (Table 6.2). Despite the existence of metal chisels since the Third Dynasty, stone tools certainly formed the majority. This is mainly

TABLE 6.1. EXAMPLES OF METAL TOOLS USED IN PHARAONIC STONEWORKING

Type	Provenance	Date	Length (cm)	Museum	Publication
Round bar chisel (Petrie's type D)	Djoser complex	Djoser	22.5–25	Cairo	Firth and Quibell, *Step Pyramid*, 232–233, fig. 234, pl. 96 [3]
	Abusimbel (desert)	Cheops	24	Cairo 68754	A. Rowe, *ASAE* 38 (1938): 391–393, pl. 59
	Pepy II pyramid	Pepy II	?	Cairo	Jéquier, *Pépi II* III, 48–49, fig. 47
	Deir el-Bahari	Mentuhotep	19.5	MMA 27.3.12	*BMMA* 23, part 2 (February 1928): 14, fig. 15
	Kahun	Twelfth Dynasty	14.6	University College, London 14240	Petrie, *Tools and Weapons*, 20, pl. 22 [80]

Type	Provenance	Date	Length (cm)	Museum	Publication
Round bar chisel (Petrie's type D)	Amarna	Amarna	24	Ashmolean	J. D. S. Pendlebury, *The City of Akhenaten* III (London, 1951), 82, pl. 72 [10.1]
	Memphis	Ramesses II	14.8	University College, London	W. M. Flinders Petrie, *Memphis* I (London, 1909), pl. 28 [30]
	Deir el-Bahari	Ramesses II	16.2	Royal Ontario Museum 907.18.26	Edouard Naville, *The XIth Dynasty Temple at Deir el-Bahari* III (London, 1913), 18, pl. 29 [7]
Flat mortise chisel (Petrie's type B), for levering pieces out	Beit Khallaf	Djoser	17	?	Garstang, *Bet Khallaf*, pl. 16 [13, 16–18, 23, 24, 30, 31]
	Djoser complex	Djoser	17	?	Firth and Quibell, *Step Pyramid*, 124–125, fig. 11 [8], pl. 93 [3]
	?	Userkaf	?	BM 66208–66209	*Introductory Guide to the Egyptian Collections* (catalogue of the British Museum) (London, 1969), 208, fig. 77
	Pepy II pyramid	Pepy II	?	Cairo 54478–54491	Jéquier, *Pépi II* III, 48–49, fig. 47
	?	Sixth Dynasty	12, 13	University College, London	Petrie, *Tools and Weapons*, 20, pls. 21 [23], 22 [71]
	Mentuhotep temple	Mentuhotep	18.8, 20.3, 20.5, 21	Luxor Museum	Arnold, *Mentuhotep III: Die Königlichen Beigaben* (Mainz, 1981), pls. 79, 87a
	Ghurab	New Kingdom	?	?	*CEAEM*, fig. 263b
Mortise chisel (Petrie's type A), for levering pieces out from distant parts (only for sculptors?)	Beit Khallaf	Djoser	7–10.6	?	Garstang, *Bet Khallaf*, pl. 23 [1–5]
	Djoser complex	Djoser	10–11	?	Lauer, *Hist. Mon.*, 237–238, fig. 66; Firth and Quibell, *Step Pyramid*, 124–125, fig. 11 [6–7], pl. 93 [3]
	Gebelein	?	52	Cairo	*CEAEM*, 263a
	Pepy II pyramid	Pepy II	?	Cairo	Jéquier, *Pépi II* III, 48–49, fig. 47
Wide chisel (Petrie's type C), for sculptors (?)	Beit Khallaf	Djoser	8–10	?	Garstang, *Bet Khallaf*, pls. 16 [27–28], 23 [27–28]
	Asyut or Meir	Middle Kingdom	?	Khashaba Collection	W. C. Hayes, "Selective Catalogue of Egyptian Antiquities from the Collection of Sayed Pasha Khashaba, Assiut" (Metropolitan Museum of Art, Typescript), pl. 45
	?	Ahmose	18.5	University College, London	Petrie, *Tools and Weapons*, 20, pl. 22 [68]

because the harder stones could be cut only with stone tools, not just in the earlier periods but even in Saite times when hard stones for sculpture, sarcophagi, and naoi were again highly esteemed.

Four main groups of tools can be established from the numerous objects found in nearly all Pharaonic construction, quarry, and mining sites: picks, pounders, two-handled rammers, and grinding stones.

The stone pick (ax or maul) (figs. 6.12–6.16) is an elongated implement of granite, chert, basalt, quartzite, or even hard, silicified limestone that is 30 to 50 centimeters long. It has a head more or less shaped, a contracted neck, and a pointed or wide cutting part. Representations (fig. 6.13),[37]

TABLE 6.2. EXAMPLES OF STONE TOOLS USED IN PHARAONIC STONEWORKING

Type	Provenance	Date	Size (cm)	Museum	Publication
Picks, axes, or mauls with narrow necks for handles	Djoser complex	Djoser	Up to 23	?	Firth and Quibell, *Step Pyramid*, 128, pl. 93 [6]
	Meidum	Snofru	21	University College, London	Petrie, *Tools and Weapons*, pl. 53 [74–86]
	Giza	Fourth or Fifth Dynasty	13–15	University College, London, and unknown	Petrie, *Tools and Weapons*, pl. 53 [75–77]; Junker, *Giza* IX, 18, pl. 6d; Reisner, *Mycerinus*, 236
	Thebes, Mektira	Eleventh Dynasty (?)	30	MMA 20.3.190	
	Thebes, Mektira	Eleventh Dynasty (?)	?	Cairo	*CEAEM*, fig. 266
	Beni Hasan	Middle Kingdom	18–25	University College, London	Petrie, *Tools and Weapons*, pl. 53 [83–86]
	Thebes	Middle or New Kingdom	35–43	Cairo 14737, 14749, 34118	H. H. Seaton-Karr, *ASAE* 6 (1905): 176–179
	Deir el-Bahari	Middle or New Kingdom	18.5–24	Cairo 64901–64906	Charles T. Currelly, *Stone Implements* (Cairo, 1913), 276, pl. 63
	Thebes	New Kingdom	?	?	Edouard Naville, *The XIth Dynasty Temple at Deir el-Bahari* III (London, 1913), pl. 29 [8]
Dolerite balls as pounders	Djoser complex	Djoser	Diameter, 10, maximum 40	?	Firth and Quibell, *Step Pyramid*, 128, pl. 93 [7]
	Giza	Fourth or Fifth Dynasty	?	?	Junker, *Giza* IX, 19, pl. 6d; *Giza* X, 16
	Lisht	Twelfth Dynasty	Maximum 30	Lisht/Saqqara	Unpublished
	Aswan	New Kingdom	20–46	?	Engelbach, *Aswan Obelisk*, 11–12; *CEAEM*, fig. 266
Rammers (two-handled pounders) (granite)	Saqqara	Old Kingdom (?)	?	?	Engelbach, *Aswan Obelisk*, pl. 4 [2]; Engelbach, *Problem of the Obelisks*, fig. 10
	Mycerinus complex	?	Height, 31	?	Reisner, *Mycerinus*, 236–237, pl. 20a–c

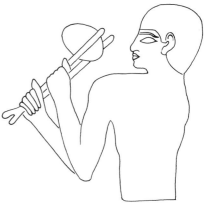

Fig. 6.12 Three limestone ax heads from Qurna, Eighteenth Dynasty. (MMA acc. nos. 09.183.5A–C)

Fig. 6.13 Sculptor dressing a statue with a stone hammer, as depicted in the tomb of Ti.

Fig. 6.14 Quartzite ax with original handle from the tomb of Mektira, Twenty-second to Twenty-sixth Dynasties, and diorite ax head from the site of the pyramid of Amenemhat I at Lisht, Middle or New Kingdom. (MMA acc. nos. 20.3.190, and 15.3.832)

Fig. 6.15 Gabbro hammer head from the site of the pyramid of Amenemhat I at Lisht, Middle or New Kingdom. (MMA acc. no. 22.1.819)

actual objects (fig. 6.14, 6.15),[38] and particularly the existence of the contracted neck indicate that the stone was not held in the hands but between two sticks attached to the stone at the neck with a leather strap. Most examples are only roughly shaped primitive tools, although others are more carefully made in regular shapes and even with smoothed surface.

This heavy tool was very effective in rough work, such as excavating tunnels and shafts for tombs or breaking the separation trenches for building blocks in quarries. The curved line produced by wielding the ax can still be seen on many unfinished surfaces, even on the surface of unfinished walls, indicating that skilled workers using this bulky tool could achieve a certain degree of flatness on the stone. One may even suggest that the completely flat and densely picked ("hammer dressed") surfaces of hard stones such as basalt were produced with such picks (figs. 6.12, 6.14).[39]

Bronze picks, quite common in Minoan Crete and in later Mediterranean cultures, seem not to have been used in Pharaonic Egypt.

Pounders are roughly or completely spherical balls, mainly of dolerite (fig. 6.16). They have a diameter of 15 to 30 centimeters and weigh about 4 to 7 kilograms and could only be lifted with two hands. The largest one known to me has a diameter of 40 centimeters.[40] They were found at most of the construction sites of the Old and Middle Kingdoms. Their appearance at the quarrying sites of the obelisks of the New Kingdom[41] attests that they were still in use. Pounding was the main method for working granite and perhaps other hard stones as well (not yet clarified).

Pounders could also be used with a helve. This is shown in ancient representations[42] as well as by the shape of the tools. Some have knobs for the leather strapping and are rather flat, resembling an ax.

Junker believed that these dolerite balls were actually used under heavy stones as rollers.[43] This method seems to have worked, as Junker's successful experiments proved. We may be sure that the Egyptians knew this method and made use of it. But it certainly was neither the only nor the main use of these dolerite balls. This is confirmed by their surfaces, which show clear marks of pounding, and also by the fact that they are found in areas that would not have provided the completely flat stone surface necessary for rolling a heavy monument on stone balls.

From two preserved examples[44] and a representation in the tomb of

Ti,[45] we know of the existence of a very heavy granite rammer with two handles (fig. 6.17), quite similar to a mighty ramming tool of wood, used in more recent times before the introduction of compressor rammers. Because pounding granite with dolerite balls leads to the gradual destruction of the tool, one wonders if such carefully made rammers were used for that kind of work at all. The tool may have been a kind of hammer, used, for example, to drive poles into the ground. This use might be suggested by the representation in the tomb of Ti, in which the rammer is used in shipbuilding, apparently to connect the boat timber with wedges. A devastating force was produced by a dolerite rammer used by late Middle Kingdom tomb robbers at Lisht. It had four knobs around which ropes had to be slung for lifting the heavy stone, but two men were needed to do that (fig. 6.17).

The final surface treatment of Pharaonic stone building was carried out with grinding stones.[46] In general, one has to differentiate between the initial, rougher work of grinding and the second step of finer surface polishing. Grinding could be done with all kinds of stone; only the hard ones, such as alabaster, marble, granite, diorite, graywacke, and basalt, could be polished.

Tools and Their Application | 263

For the grinding of limestone and sandstone, grinders made of sandstone could be used. The treatment of harder stones required the use of abrasive sand. Even the grinder itself would probably be of a harder substance. The sand could be dry, but dampened sand would have produced less dust and cleaner work. The fine polishing was probably carried out without water.

Grinding stones of many different materials have been found. The most common ones are sandstone or quartzite. Some grinders were carefully shaped; some even have a handle and were used for special purposes, such as sculpting. The grinding of large surfaces, such as the walls of temples, was carried out with hand-sized rough sandstones, which when used acquired a completely flat underside and were soon useless as tools. The remaining casing blocks of pyramids have been exposed to weathering so much that it is difficult to determine the degree to which they had originally been smoothed. At the pyramid of Meidum, large areas of the casing have recently been unearthed in quasi-original condition. The surfaces had been only flattened with stone picks and possibly chisels.

Isler studied the procedure of grinding the surface of the Luxor obelisks. Because two of their faces swell out, he assumed that this lateral convexity was due to the grinding motions, which disregarded the effect of gravity against the edges and produced slightly curved planes.[47] Grinding was also carried out after repairing a wall surface with patches or plaster in order to blend the repaired areas into their surroundings.

To achieve highly polished hard stone surfaces, several grinding and polishing phases with different grinders and grinding materials were necessary. One may assume that sculptors and masons developed their special private formulas for the procedure.

As discussed above, one would expect that stone chisels (flint, chert) were used for carrying out the finer surface work on limestone and sandstone. The great number of crescent-shaped flint tools found in the Djoser complex that probably date to the Third Dynasty is impressive. They were apparently used for cutting the fluting of columns.[48] Flint chisels whose shape seems to be suited for finer work in stone have rarely been found,[49] and their absence from the major construction sites of the Old and Middle Kingdoms is remarkable.[50] Thus although we should exclude the use of metal tools for cutting hard stone, we remain unable to present the alternative stone tools.

Mallets · Since the beginning of sculpting, the wooden mallet has been used by the sculptor to strike the chisel.[51] The Egyptian version consists of a rounded handle cut from the same piece of wood as the head of the mallet (fig. 6.18). The head is more elongated than the modern instrument and quite frequently shows a rough, ring-shaped groove that could have been carved for a metal band, which prevented the mallet from splitting. Apparently no mallet has preserved such a band, however, and one might suggest that the groove was caused by the impact of the chisel. Examples from Pharaonic Egypt are known in great numbers, and the larger museums are in possession of dozens of them.[52]

The most common type of mallet head has a bell-shaped or half-circle-shaped section. The older examples known—from the First Dynasty to the end of the Old Kingdom from Deshasheh (fig. 6.19) and depicted in many sculptors' and shipbuilders' scenes of the Old Kingdom[53]—are more slender and elongated.

One mallet has even preserved the owner's marks +⊕Å a mixture of invented signs and the hieroglyph of the square level.[54]

Drilling Tools[55] · In prehistoric times, the Egyptian craftsmen had developed great skill in drilling hard stone for the manufacture of vessels.[56] For a drilling tool, they used a forked axis that held a half-moon-shaped drilling stone of sandstone or flint; the drilling stone moved with a bow, and the movement was aided by pending weights. Drilling in architecture spread with the increase of stone building from the Third Dynasty on. The main tool seems to have been a tube attached to a long wooden staff, again driven by bows.[57] Since no actual drilling tube has ever been discovered in Egypt, the material used for the tubes remains unknown. The narrowness of the tubular-shaped slots and the greenish color of grains of quartz sand preserved in the drill hole of an unfinished alabaster vase suggest copper or bronze tubes. Wooden tubes are a possibility, but achieving a wall thickness of 1 to 5 millimeters in wood would have been difficult.

Shaw suggested that Minoan drills probably did not consist of bronze but of a section of reed or bamboo swiftly rotated with sand or emery and a lubricating agent such as water or oil.[58] Bamboo was unknown to the Egyptians, however. Whether the Egyptians used loose (wet?) quartz sand, fixed points of emery, or even diamond has been investigated in the practical experiments of Gorelick and Gwinnett. They found that the typical regular concentric lines on drilled cores of granite could be reproduced by a copper tube charged with emery only when used in a water slurry or in olive oil. Concentric cutting lines were also present after drilling with corundum and diamond. Sand and crushed quartz must therefore be ruled out as possibilities, since they do not produce concentric abrasion lines, when used either dry or wet.[59] These preliminary findings raise questions as to which one of the abrasives—emery, corundum, or diamond—was used, and also whether it came from some unknown source in the Egyptian deserts or was imported.[60] Drilling hard stone was carried out so frequently, however, that one has to assume that the abrasive material was easily available in sufficient quantities. This requirement does not favor emery, corundum, or diamond.

Stones that were drilled for architectural purposes were alabaster, limestone, sandstone, granite, basalt, amphibolite, and diorite, which shows that the hardness of stone placed no limits on the ingenuity of the Egyptian builders. A decision to drill was probably economic, since the consumption of metal would have been considerable. This consideration prevented the Egyptians from using drilling in the production of stones—for example, in separating blocks from the bedrock in the quarry.

Petrie observed that in Deir el-Bersheh a rock platform had been dressed down by cutting it away with gigantic tube drills 45 centimeters in diame-

Fig. 6.18 Wooden mallet, provenance unknown. (MMA acc. no. 10.130.1013)

Fig. 6.19 Elongated wooden mallet from Deshasheh, late Old Kingdom. (MMA acc. no. 37.4.65)

Fig. 6.21 Limestone block with ten boring sockets from the mastaba of Perneb at Saqqara. (MMA acc. no. 14.7.146)

Fig. 6.20 Drill hole with stump of the drill core from a Ramesside granite door jamb from the Asasif, diameter 7.5, depth 10.3 centimeters. (MMA acc. no. 13.183.2)

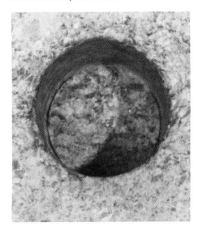

ter.[61] Drilling had to be used, however, for producing holes for pivots, door bolts (fig. 6.20), round cramps, nails for the application of sheet metal, and the insertion of emblems.[62] Alabaster and limestone slabs could be drilled with a pattern of round holes to produce "windows."[63] The only larger-scale activity with drilling was probably the production of the interior of sarcophagi in the Third and Fourth Dynasties (fig. 2.29).[64] It was probably carried out by a large number of closely set drill holes about 12 centimeters in diameter. The procedure had to be done in four to six steps because of the limited length of the drilling tubes and the need to break off the still-standing cores of stone.

As noted, no actual drilling tubes have so far been observed. Their use is definitely attested by the traces of the tool left on the stone and the drilling cones found mainly in Old Kingdom sites.[65] Unexplained are traces of drilling operations left on the rough surface of irregular limestone blocks in the enclosures of Djoser and Snofru (fig. 6.21).[66] They mostly appear in irregular groups, some so close that they overlap. They look as if the stones had been under an object that was drilled in a way that the drilling tube completely penetrated the object and then reached the underlying stone. This underlying stone was apparently used for several drilling operations.

Sawing Tools[67] · Lauer already suspected that the close joining of limestone casing blocks could have been achieved as early as the Third Dynasty by a method of sawing with a copper blade drawn through the front edge of the joints (fig. 6.22).[68] When the lower end of the joint was reached, the saw quite frequently cut into the foundation blocks, leaving a cutting line protruding an inch from the front line of the blocks. This method was certainly practiced for the casings of the Mastabat el-Fara'un (fig. 6.23) and of the pyramids of Unas and Senwosret I. We do not know the instrument that was used but suspect that it was a short, knifelike saw with a wooden handle.

Zuber confirms that the curved tool marks suggest the use of a saw, not a

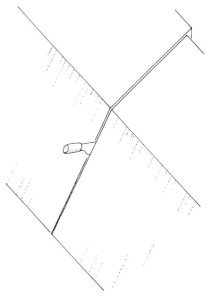

Fig. 6.23 Curved sawing marks in the stepped top face of a casing block of the Mastabat el-Fara'un.

Fig. 6.22 Use of a saw to plane the joint between two casing blocks.

cable. Since the cut never exceeds a width of half a centimeter, the use of an instrument with teeth of flint set into a metal frame is ruled out.[69] Sawing of softer stones was apparently not problematic and was carried out quite frequently; the sawing of harder rocks was, however, used only for special cases. The alabaster sarcophagus of Sekhemkhet (Third Dynasty) shows saw marks,[70] as do the alabaster altars in the sun temple of Niuserra.[71] Even harder stones could be completely cut by this method. The granite sarcophagus of Cheops[72] and two others of the Fourth Dynasty (fig. 6.24)[73] were definitely sawed, as were the granite portcullises of the Cheops Pyramid[74] and the basalt paving blocks in the mortuary temples of Cheops[75] and Niuserra.[76] Also the famous triads of Mycerinus made of graywacke show traces of sawing.[77]

Petrie estimated that the sawing blades used for the sarcophagus of Cheops must have been 2.4 meters long. They were probably toothless and used with sand as an abrasive. The experiments by Stocks[78] add to Petrie's ideas that the sawing power was not exercised so much by the saw itself as by the quartz sand. Nevertheless, the loss of metal must have been considerable and the method so expensive that it could have been carried out only on royal monuments.

Unfortunately, no saws of this size have been discovered in Egypt.[79] But smaller examples, especially in the form of tomb models (and intended to be used for sawing wood), are known from the Third Dynasty on.[80] Sawing stone has remained a method common in stonework from Roman times[81] until today.

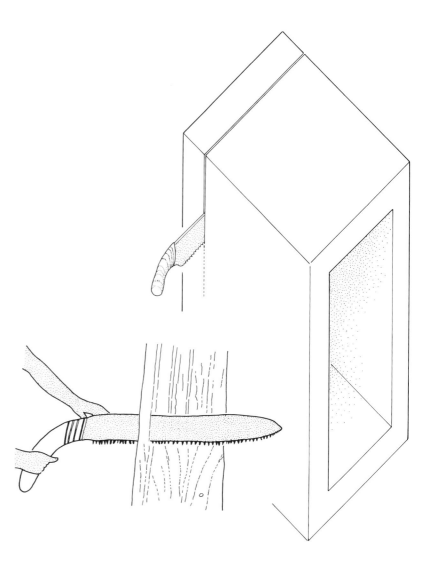

Fig. 6.24 Cutting wood with a heavy saw (tombs of Beni Hassan), and sawing the lid from the bottom of a granite sarcophagus.

MOVING IMPLEMENTS

Ropes · Handling building materials, especially stone, depends on the existence of ropes strong enough to permit all kinds of maneuvers (fig. 6.25). Unfortunately, our knowledge about ropes in ancient Egypt is restricted because few specimens have been collected and even fewer have been properly studied.[82] All examples known were made by the method of twisting and countertwisting fibers, each yarn being twisted in the same direction, and only very few were made by plaiting.[83]

As material of cordage, dom palm fibers (*Hyphaene thebaica*), reed, flax, grass, esparto grass, halfa grass (*Desmostachya bipinnata*), and papyrus (*Cyperus papyrus*) are mentioned. Ropes found with the boat of Cheops were made of halfa grass.[84]

Naturally, ropes of a small diameter are more frequent, but we also know of thick ropes. Papyrus ropes found in 1942 and 1944 in the Tura caves, presumably of Ptolemaic or Roman date, had a circumference of 20.3 centimeters and a diameter of 6.35 centimeters. They consisted of three strands of a number of split and twisted papyrus culms.[85] A rope made of five strands was recovered from the boat pit of Cheops.[86] A "mammoth piece of cordage" of the Nineteenth Dynasty was found at Deir el-Bahari; it had a diameter of 6.8 centimeters.[87]

There is no question that the Egyptian builders made use of even stronger ropes for the movement of such heavy monuments as colossal statues and obelisks. We have only literary sources, however, for evidence of such ropes; references are made to high-quality ropes 1000 and even 1400 cubits (525–735 meters) in length[88] to be used for the royal bark. Engelbach calculated:

> As to the size of the ropes required for the rolling out of the obelisk, all we can do is to obtain a very rough idea as to it. If they spread the men out slightly fanwise, I do not see how they could have used more than 40 ropes. The strain per rope will be, as we have seen, $2/9 \times 1170/40 = 6.5$ tons per rope.
>
> The rope used was probably the very best palm-rope, newly made. The safe load which can be put on coir rope, which is of about the same strength, is given by the formula: Load in cwts- (circumference in inches) divided by 4. Substituting, we have $6.5 \times 20 \times 4 = C^2$ which gives the circumference of 22.8 inches (58 cm) and a diameter of $7\,1/4$ inches (18.4 cm). If such a rope were used it would require handling loops on it.[89]

In contrast to the reconstruction of such heavy ropes are the calculations for the ropes used for lowering the obelisk of Thutmosis III in front of Pylon VIII at Karnak, which was removed by Roman engineers in A.D. 330.[90] The result of these calculations is that the ropes were about 85 to 90 meters long and had a circumference of 18 centimeters and a diameter of 5.7 centimeters, with a normal working strength of 6 to 7 tons and a breaking resistance of 20 tons. Such ropes were used in modern seafaring before the introduction of synthetic ropes.

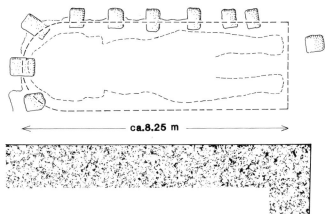

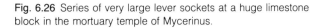

Fig. 6.26 Series of very large lever sockets at a huge limestone block in the mortuary temple of Mycerinus.

Fig. 6.27 Series of ten lever sockets in the rock in front of the Chephren valley temple, probably for positioning a sphinx.

Levers · The use of wooden levers to lift, shift, or turn over stone blocks was quite common in ancient Egypt.[91] Instruments that can be identified as levers, however, are rarely recognized in excavations because they would usually have looked like ordinary beams with an obliquely chopped or chamfered end. There are a few examples,[92] and even a bronze crowbar 67.2 centimeters long was discovered at Amarna.[93]

Levers have left unquestionable traces in the blocks themselves (figs. 4.10, 4.11). These traces are in the shape of shift cuttings and lever holes, frequently seen either on the side face of the blocks that were lifted or pushed or on the top surface of blocks that had stones moved over them. Sometimes both occur together.[94] There are also cases where the lever holes appear along the upper edge of a side surface just a few centimeters from the edge.[95] Such holes helped to place the blocks exactly against their adjacent blocks.

Ordinary blocks with bigger dimensions, such as the casing blocks of the pyramid of Senwosret I, were provided with only one hole, which was positioned at the lower edge of one of the side faces. It was always hidden by the adjacent block so it could not be seen when the building was finished. Even in such a concealed place, however, it was often carefully patched with mortar and small stones after the placement of the block.[96]

Larger blocks had to be moved with the help of more than one lever from one side. There are examples of blocks with up to seven lever holes along one side (fig. 6.26).[97] The supposed sphinxes in front of the valley temple of Chephren are surrounded by nine sockets from the front and the short sides in order to push the monuments against the temple façade (fig. 6.27).[98] The alabaster socle in the colonnade of Taharqa at Karnak was levered into place by two pairs of levers.[99] In order to allow room for the operation, trenches had to be dug for each lever around the block. The pedestal of the colossus of Amenhotep III in front of Pylon X weighs 90 tons and was moved with two levers on each side. Judging from the sockets, the levers were 20 × 30 centimeters thick.[100] A block from the entrance chapel of Senwosret I weighing 45 tons has three lever holes of 20 × 34, 27 × 27, and 22 × 25 centimeters.

The use of such gigantic levers, which were pulled downward with fixed ropes by a group of about ten men each, was demonstrated when Legrain had the upper part of one of the Hatshepsut obelisks moved.[101] Levers were also used for lifting. But did the Egyptian builders know how to raise blocks by rocking them up with the help of two supports near the center? Petrie calculated that by this method the fifty-six ceiling blocks of the crypt of Cheops weighing 54 tons each could be lifted by ten men with crossbars, since they would have to lift only 5 tons each time.[102] Levers were also used to push portcullises out of their wall niches in order to close tomb passages. For this purpose, a system of lever sockets had been prepared (fig. 6.28).

Rockers · In foundation deposits of the Eighteenth Dynasty are found little models of a wooden appliance that is usually called a rocker (fig. 6.29).[103] The model consists of two parallel boards with rounded undersides that are connected to each other by up to six cross sticks. Because no traces of the real instrument have ever been discovered and no representations of its use have been noticed, its original size and purpose are unknown. Nevertheless, Egyptologists and others have speculated much on this instrument. There are two main theories.

Tools and Their Application | 271

Fig. 6.29 Model of a rocker from a foundation deposit of the Hatshepsut temple, Deir el-Bahari. (MMA acc. no. 96.4.9)

The most common opinion is that rockers were large and could be used for "rocking up" a building block.[104] Loaded with a block, the rocker would have been rocked back and forth, and shims would have been positioned under the raised runners alternating left and right. In this way, a rather small team of workmen would have been able to raise a block with moderate effort and in good time. This theory naturally appears in connection with pyramid building and may even be called the backbone of most such theories. In general, one assumes that the pyramid steps produced by the backing stones would have functioned as a staircase to rock up the material for the courses above. One has to keep in mind, however, that in actual work, it might not have been so easy. One has to visualize that the steps are—depending on the angle of the pyramids (that is, 50 to 60 degrees)—high rather than wide. Also, only for the first one to ten courses of a pyramid are the steps wider than 50 centimeters. This space on a steep pyramid is not sufficient for the safe handling of a rocker loaded with a block 50 × 70 × 100 centimeters, which is a weight of nearly 1 ton. Furthermore, at the end of each rocking maneuver, the rocker would have stood on a pile of wooden shims or beams the height of a pyramid step. The fall of a loaded rocker would have wiped out all working teams below. The loss of life and equipment might not have concerned the pyramid builders, but the interruption of work certainly would have. Fitchen, recognizing this problem, stressed the need to stabilize the pile of shims. He suggested vertical timbers fixed in sockets on the surface of the underlying block course. No such sockets on pyramid casings or core blocks have ever been noticed. Another basic question is whether a heavily loaded rocker standing on shims or wedges could still be rocked at all.

One might suggest, therefore, that rockers could have been used only on particularly wide and specially equipped steps—that is, on a staircase that was never provided by the pyramid itself, but only by masonry added at a lesser angle from outside the pyramid slope.

Engelbach presented another theory, based on tests with a model (fig. 6.30).[105] Arranged in a long line, many rockers would carry a whole course of wall blocks when they were dressed. The rockers would have permitted

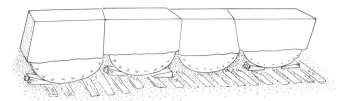

Fig. 6.30 The use of rockers as proposed in *CEAEM*, figs. 107–109.

the stone masons to test, fit together, or move about the blocks, especially in cases where oblique joints had to be produced. Thus the whole course could have been assembled beforehand. Engelbach's theory is not convincing, however. The preparation of whole courses of blocks for larger projects—such as temple walls, pylons, and pyramids—on the ground in front of the building would have required too much organization to be really useful. Instead, one might follow Petrie's suggestion that "for shifting large building stones the Egyptians seem to have placed them on a cradle of wood, so that they could be readily twisted round, drawn along, or rocked up an inclined plane."[106]

Another possible interpretation of the model rockers is that they represent in a simplified way nothing other than ordinary sledges. This would explain why no real rockers have been discovered. Perhaps real rockers never existed.

Rollers · In Pharaonic Egypt as in technologically similar cultures,[107] the use of wooden rollers was quite common (they are even used today), and many rollers have been excavated in Egypt (fig. 6.31).[108] They are short and have rounded ends, to prevent their catching. They have a diameter of about 10 centimeters, indicating the range of weights that could be moved by this method. Rollers are not easy to operate on uneven or soft ground, so clearly the most suitable surface would have been flat stone or a double row of beams arranged as tracks in the direction of movement.

Such skid poles were still found in position (or at least the grooves cut for them) in several places, mostly near or under sarcophagi (figs. 6.32, 6.33)[109] or at the entrance of pyramid corridors, where they obviously served to roll the closing block into position (fig. 6.34).[110] In the secondary tomb of the "Mastaba du nord" at Lisht, the closing blocks of the crypt ran

Fig. 6.31 Pair of sycamore rollers from Thebes. (MMA acc. nos. 28.3.3, 4)

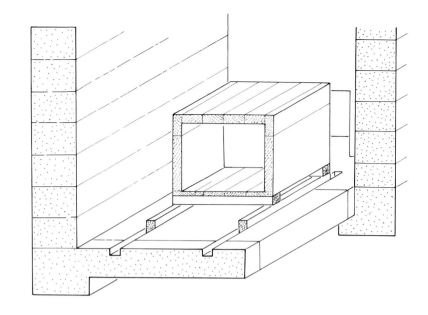

Fig. 6.32 Placing a sarcophagus with rollers on guiding beams, at the Middle Kingdom tombs of Qattah.

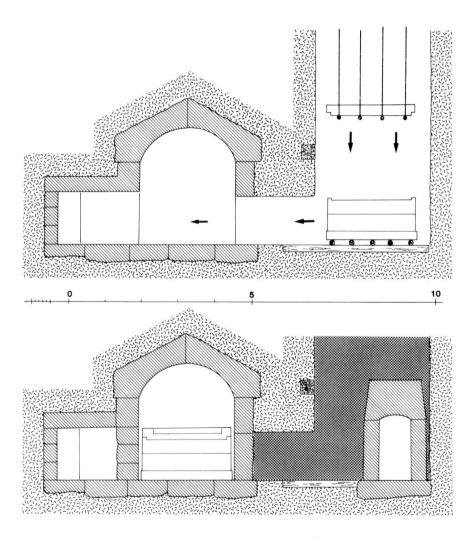

Fig. 6.33 Moving the sarcophagus of Senwosret III from the construction shaft into the burial chamber on rollers and guidance beams.

on a pair of parallel poles that are still in position. In both cases, neither the sarcophagus nor the sealing stone could be pulled with ropes from the front but had to be pushed from behind, which was enormously simplified by the use of rollers. No skid poles or their grooves were noticed in other places, suggesting that the use of skid poles and rollers was restricted to work under such special conditions. But one would assume that building blocks were rolled in position whenever transport sledges had to be left behind—for example, on top of walls or pyramid stumps under construction. That blocks could also be moved on rollers in quarry caves is attested by the discovery of a limestone block in one of the Tura caves that was still resting on rollers. Unfortunately, the discovery was made under unfavorable conditions and never recorded.[111]

There is a painting of a burial procession in which a coffin canopy standing on a sledge is pulled over rollers.[112] This combination might occasionally have eased transport problems, but was certainly not the rule. The handling of rollers may also have been depicted in the tomb of Rekhmira, but the damaged representation no longer shows if the rollers were put under building blocks or under a sledge.[113] For heavy monuments, such as obelisks and colossal statues, weighing hundreds of tons, the rollers would have been complete tree trunks of the hardest available wood. Otherwise, they would have soon been squashed, and the consumption of trees would have been enormous. In an actual experiment to move a block of 32 tons, which was carried out in 1979 in France (see n. 21, p. 102) trunks of oak 40 centimeters thick were used. During the operation, the block was constantly rolling on four to six such trunks, arranged at close distances. Bronze rollers would have better sustained such weights. The only ones I know were found in the royal tombs of Tanis.[114] They may have been exceptional.

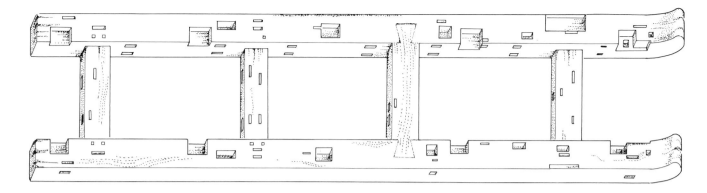

Fig. 6.35 Sledge found south of the pyramid complex of Senwosret III at Dahshur.

Sledges · To move heavy loads on sledges appears to us, who now use them only in snow, a hopelessly outdated technology. But the days when such sledges were still commonly used are not really so long ago. For example, we know that in the quarries of Carrara, heavy blocks of marble were lowered on a *lizza* in 1929.[115] These sledges carried well over 25 tons. They were constructed of oak, holm-oak, or beech; were 6 to 12 meters long; and were pulled by as many as fourteen pairs of yoked oxen.

Based on the great number of representations, the frequent use of the hieroglyph (from *tm.t* [sledge]), and a few objects found, sledges were the main instrument for moving heavy loads in Pharaonic Egypt, as in other countries of similar technological level.[116] Three real sledges have been excavated in Egypt. The biggest one, 4.2 meters long, was buried near the pyramid of Senwosret III at Dahshur, apparently after having served for the transport of some heavy burial equipment (fig. 6.35).[117] It consists of two runners with a diameter of 12 × 20 centimeters, connected by four crossbeams, attached with tongues and grooves. All the beams have slotted holes that could be used to fix ropes for securing the load or for pulling. But no hole for the main pulling rope at the front of the sledge is visible.

A smaller sledge, made of cedar wood, was excavated south of the pyramid of Senwosret I at Lisht (fig. 6.36).[118] It is only 1.73 meters long and 0.78 meter wide and has only two crossbeams. An additional round pole attached in front of the front crossbeam was used for fixing the pulling ropes. A number of slots would have secured the object to be moved with the help of dowels. This sledge was made to carry a shrine or a similar

Fig. 6.36 Sledge for a shrine, from a deposit south of the pyramid of Senwosret I at Lisht. (MMA acc. no. 24.1.84)

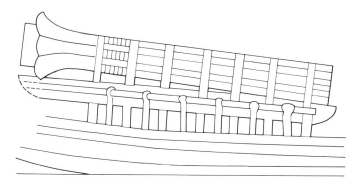

Fig. 6.37 Granite column on a sledge traveling in a boat from Aswan to the pyramid temple of Unas, as depicted in the Unas causeway.

object but was never used for real transport, since the undersides of its runners show no traces of wear. Remains of color indicate that the sledge was painted pink.[119] Petrie excavated a portion of a large sledge for dragging stones that was lying in the debris of the pyramid of Hawara and was made of reused boat timber.[120]

Most of the Egyptian representations of sledges show the transport of funerary equipment, such as Ka statues, coffins, canopic boxes, and other shrines.[121] They are pulled by men, oxen, or both. But there are also representations of the transport of building materials. The oldest scene, in the causeway of Unas (fig. 6.37)[122] shows granite columns and architraves on their boat trip from Aswan to Saqqara. The architraves and the 6-meter-long columns are tied up on sledges, which would therefore have been about 7 meters long.

Another famous transport scene is that in the tomb of Djehutihotep at Bersheh (fig. 6.38).[123] It shows the seated alabaster figure of the monarch tied to a huge sledge, which is pulled by 172 men walking in four columns. The ground immediately in front of the sledge is watered for ease in gliding. There are no indications of the use of rollers for road construction. The statue may have been 7 meters high and weighed about 58 tons. It is amazing that the four pulling ropes radiate from one point, since four ropes fixed to a draw bar might have been expected. To increase the number of men, as was necessary for large monuments, this draw bar would have projected on both sides of the sledge so that many more parallel ropes could be pulled at the same time. To the side, a heavy beam with a side with teeth is carried. We may suppose that it was used to block a backward movement of the sledge when pulled over uneven ground.

From the New Kingdom, we know three important transport scenes with sledges. The first is a rock relief from the quarries of Ma'asara-Tura, which probably dates from the time of King Ahmose and is now in the Egyptian Museum, Cairo (fig. 6.39).[124] It represents the hauling of a block, the size of which may be estimated to have been 1 × 1 × 2 meters (about 5 tons). It is on a sledge pulled by three pairs of yoked humpbacked oxen, guided by

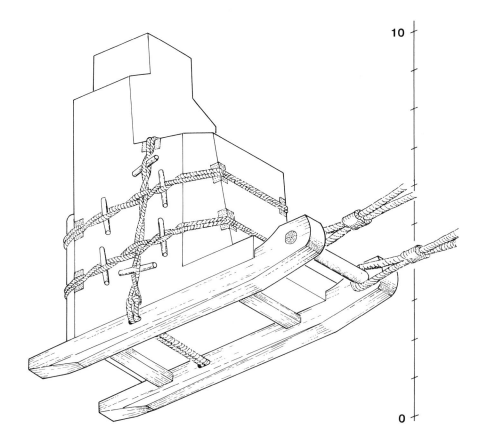

Fig. 6.38 Reconstruction of the sledge for transporting the colossus of Djehutihotep.

10

0

three drivers. The first could be a Semite; the third, a Libyan. These people and the oxen may indicate the use of prisoners and booty of war from the early Eighteenth Dynasty onward.

The next example is provided by the obelisks of Queen Hatshepsut loaded on sledges traveling from Aswan to Thebes on huge boats (fig. 6.40).[125] The sledges must have been about 31 meters long and would have been composed of complete tree trunks. The obelisks rest on crossbeams and are fixed with ropes. One of the obelisks weighs 320 tons.

In the building representations of the tomb of Rekhmira, apparently two scenes depict the hauling of blocks on sledges,[126] but both scenes are much damaged. Besides the remains of foremen and the men pulling, one can still recognize three workmen giving additional help with levers from behind the sledge. For that purpose, Egyptian (and Assyrian) sledges have a chamfered lower rear edge. In the upper of the two scenes, the workers are handling poles, which could indicate the use of additional rollers.

Fig. 6.39 Transport of a block of limestone on a sledge, early New Kingdom, as depicted in rock relief from Ma'asara. (Cairo 62949)

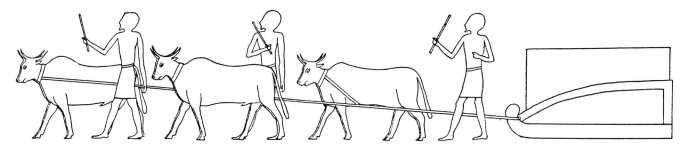

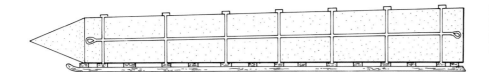

Fig. 6.40 One of the obelisks of Hatshepsut on a sledge traveling by boat from Aswan to Thebes, as depicted in the Queen's temple Deir el-Bahari.

One should recall here the famous representations of the transport of winged bulls from the palace of Sennacherib at Nineveh (about 700 B.C.) (fig. 6.41),[127] which show that in Mesopotamia, some 700 years later, exactly the same transport methods were used. The Assyrian bulls are lying on huge wooden sledges (one bull is standing), which are being pulled over short rollers. From the front, prisoners of war are pulling on four heavy double ropes, to which they are attached by cords pulled over their shoulders. From behind, others are helping with enormous levers, which are pulled down with ropes by several men at each rope. The levers are set on wedge-shaped fulcrums, which can be raised with additional wedges. Other men are forced by guards to carry the rollers from behind the sledge to the

Fig. 6.41 A human-headed winged bull for the palace of Sennacherib being dragged on a sledge, as depicted on a relief from his palace at Nineveh.

front to be reused there. The rollers seem to be short pieces that could be put under only one runner of the sledge and that could not reach from one side to the other.

Since a heavy sledge would get stuck in sand and dust, it could be hauled over only solid ground, stone chips, or specially prepared roads. From the boat glide of Mirgissa, representations of workers pouring out water in front of sledges, and the experience transmitted by Chevrier,[128] we know that a road surface of mud or lime treated with water would considerably reduce the friction. Chevrier found that six men could easily pull a sledge loaded with a 4.8-ton stone on a horizontal plane covered with watered mud. The relation would thus be one man per ton.

The pulling force could be increased by the use of oxen, as it was still done in the nineteenth century.[129] Not only were such animals represented in the early Eighteenth Dynasty relief just mentioned, but carcasses of four strong bulls that apparently died from exhaustion during construction work were actually excavated by H. E. Winlock in the temple of Mentuhotep at Deir el-Bahari.[130]

The stone quarried in Roman times in the Mons Claudianus area was apparently transported with the help of cattle.[131] The route stations along the Wadi Qena were equipped with huge stables that could accommodate 300 to 400 animals. Whether the stones were moved on sledges or wagons here is unknown.

To what extent animals could be used for pulling sledges is also unknown. The examples from the quarries of Carrara show that twenty-eight animals could be properly arranged and guided. They would easily have had a pulling force of 150 to 200 tons.[132] One can imagine, therefore, that a sledge loaded with a weight of 1000 tons would have needed 200 animals.

Compared with the method of using rollers to move monuments, the sledge has the great advantage of being more easily controlled, especially for keeping the correct direction of movement. The monument itself is also much better protected against the impact of ropes, levers, and rollers. One would assume, therefore, that the transport of heavy and precious monuments was carried out on sledges and that rollers were used only for ordinary building material and rough work.

Wedges · An essential tool for every mason who handles blocks of any size is the wooden wedge. Its main purpose is to keep a block aloft during work so that hands or a lever can easily be put under the edge to move the stone. Such wedges must have existed in great numbers in Egypt, but because they are little valued, few have been noticed in excavation and even fewer have been published.[133]

In order to facilitate the pulling out of the wedge from its position under a stone, some were made with a handle, carved from the same block of wood (figs. 6.42, 6.43). The old and still often cited statement that wooden wedges were inserted into wedge slots in order to break stones with the help of the swelling power of water was shattered in 1965 by Röder.[134] Metal wedges were not known in Pharaonic Egypt.

Iron wedges for splitting blocks of stone have been found in the

Fig. 6.43 Wooden hand wedge from the pyramid of Senwosret I at Lisht. (MMA acc. no. 34.1.35)

Ramesseum. Petrie dated them to about 800 B.C.,[135] but they could be of a much later date as well.

Wagons · We assume that wheels and carriages were introduced into Egypt only in the Second Intermediate Period, when Egypt was involved with its northeastern neighbors, who possessed horses and chariots. From then on, chariots became an essential part of the equipment of the Egyptian army and were also used as prestigious toys of the nobles of the New Kingdom. The picture of the Old and Middle Kingdoms without the knowledge of wheels and carriages is shaken, however, by the discovery of two wall paintings of the late Old Kingdom and the Eleventh Dynasty depicting siege towers that were moved on wheels (fig. 6.44).[136] It would be strange if transport wheels were restricted to only military purposes and not used for moving other heavy weights as well.

There are indications that the carriage of the New Kingdom was used not only for fighting and hunting, but also for transporting goods. In the tomb of Ahhotep (early Eighteenth Dynasty), a wood and bronze model of a four-wheeled wagon was found,[137] on which funerary barks were deposited. In the tomb of Sobeknakht at el-Kab (also early Eighteenth Dynasty), a funerary bark is represented being pulled by two oxen on what seems to be a four-wheeled carriage (only two wheels are shown, of course).[138] In the funerary papyrus of Maiherperi of a later date in the Eighteenth Dynasty, a funerary bark on a sledge is being pulled on rollers or wheels.[139]

Some representations of Late Period date show that four-wheeled carriages were frequently used in temple processions for displaying barks and shrines. Remains of such a wooden temple carriage were excavated in the temple of Medinet Madi.[140] The only reference to large-scale transport in wagons is from the Ramesside period, in the report on the expedition of Ramesses IV to the Wadi Hammamat, which mentions: "There were transported for them supplies from Egypt in ten wagons, there being six yokes of oxen to [each] wagon, drawing [them] from Egypt to the mountain of Bekhen."[141] One might suppose, however, that this was not the first expedition to use ox carts. Still, there is no evidence that the ox wagons of Ramesses IV were also used for the transport of the *bekhen* stone back to the Nile Valley. The size of the work force in connection with that expedition (although the number may be misinterpreted) seems to indicate that workers were also used for hauling stones. Carts drawn by oxen may have been used much later to bring the material from the Mons Claudianus and Mons

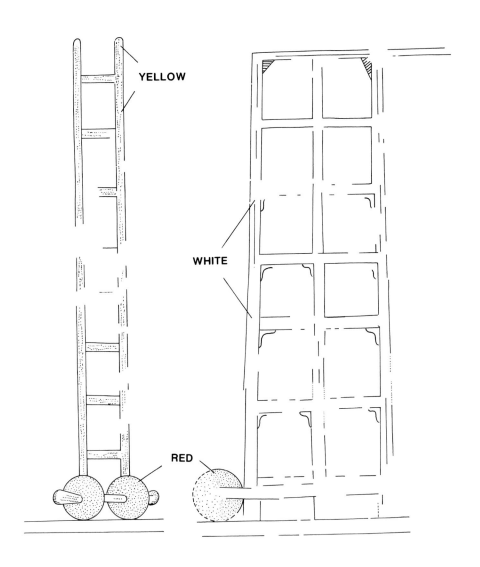

Fig. 6.44 Siege towers moved on wheels, as depicted in the tomb of Kaemheset at Saqqara and Intef at Qurna, Sixth and Eleventh Dynasties.

YELLOW

WHITE

RED

Porphyrites down to the Nile Valley—for example, the sixteen columns of tinted granite for the Pantheon in Rome, each of which was 12.5 meters long and weighed 48 tons.

Bearing Stones for Ropes · At Giza were found two stone implements, apparently of Old Kingdom date, that were part of an unknown device to pull or lower three parallel running ropes over an edge or around a corner. The first one, of basalt (24 centimeters long, 18 centimeters wide), was found in the pyramid city of Khentkaus (fig. 6.45).[142] Its head has grooves for three thick ropes and was inserted with an elongated mortise like a bearing into some device—probably not in stone, for it was fixed with a round peg or tenon. The second one, from the valley temple of Mycerinus, is of dark slate (37 centimeters long, 16 centimeters wide) and is broken (fig. 6.45).[143] Its mortise is longer and has room for two pegs to be fixed.

By the shape of the head of the stones, one may conclude that they were made to change the direction of the ropes by 45 to 90 degrees. The object into which the stones were inserted must have been a pole, the head of a scaffold, or a kind of trestle.[144] The shape of the head and the way it was fixed to a shaft prevent it from being used for vertical lifting or lowering.

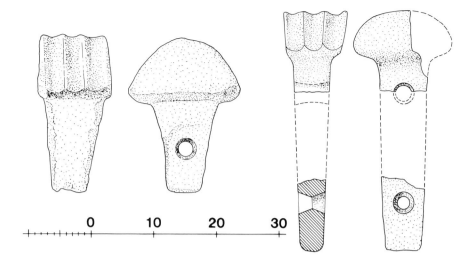

Fig. 6.45 Bearing stones of the Fourth Dynasty found in the pyramid city of Khentkaus (A) and the valley temple of Mycerinus (B).

Fig. 6.46 Possible use of a bearing stone to change the direction of the pull of ropes.

This could have been achieved only by putting it into an oblique shaft or crane (fig. 6.46). In a vertical position, the weight pulled could have been moved only at an angle of 45 degrees. It could have well served, therefore, to lift or lower heavy weights—for example, a pillar or a colossal statue.

We have here a primitive forerunner of a pulley, or a so-called fast pulley, firmly attached to a shaft. The existence of this device seems to indicate that real pulleys made of a wheel with a grooved rim did not yet exist. M. Isler has suggested to me that bearing stones would have been superior to even wooden pulleys because the wooden pulley axles would have been too fragile to bear heavy loads.

NOTES

1. Richard Lepsius, *Die alt-aegyptische Elle* (Berlin, 1865); W. M. Flinders Petrie, *Ancient Weights and Measures* (London, 1926), 38–41; Petrie, *Kahun,* 27; Petrie, *Illahun, Kahun and Gurob 1883–1890* (London, 1891), 14. See also Erik Iversen, *Canon and Proportions in Egyptian Art,* 2nd ed., ed. Yoshiaka Shibata (Warminster, 1975), 14–19, pl. 33; A. Schwab-Schlott, *MDAIK* 28 (1972): 110–111.

2. Ernesto Schiaparelli, *La Tomba intatta dell'architetto Cha: Relazione sui lavori della missione italiana in Egitto, anni 1903–1920* (Turin, 1927), 168–173, figs. 154–156, and 80, fig. 47.

3. BM 6025 = Lepsius no. 14.

4. The *nby* is mentioned on Theban ostraka (William C. Hayes, *Ostraka and Name Stones from the Tomb of Sen-Mut (No. 71) at Thebes.* Publications of the Metropolitan Museum of Art Egyptian Expedition 15 [New York, 1942], 36). The *nby* may be identical with the units on two (incomplete) rods discovered by Petrie at Kahgun (Petrie, *Kahun,* 27; Petrie, *Illahun, Kahun and Gurob,* 14). There is no need, however, to interpret them as foreign units.

5. L. Borchardt, *ZÄS* 42 (1905): 70–72; W. Schenkel, in *LÄ* IV, 115. The cord was called *nwḥ* (P. C. Smither, *JEA* 27 [1941]: 74–76).

6. Reisner, *Mycerinus,* 78, n. 1. For early representations of the hieroglyph, see Petrie, *Royal Tombs* I, pls. 9 [1–5], 11 [6, 16], 21 [28], 31 [46]. Generally understood as a "looped cord serving as hobble for cattle" (Alan Gardiner, *Egyptian Grammar* [London, 1973], 523 [V 16]).

7. Statues of Senenmut, Penuris, and Amenemhat-Surer (L. Borchardt, *ZÄS* 42 [1905]: 70–72; Jacques Vandier, *Manuel d'archéologie égyptienne* III, Plates (Paris, 1958), pl. 164 [1, 3, 6].

8. *CEAEM*, fig. 62; S. Berger, *JEA* 20 (1934): 54–56; Norman De Garis Davies, *The Tombs of Mencheperrasomb, Amenmose and Another* (London, 1933), pl. 17; Charles Wilkinson and Marsha Hill, *Egyptian Wall Paintings* (New York, 1983), fig. 46.

9. Dorner, "Absteckung," 94–95. See also W. Meyer-Christian, *MDAIK* 43 (1987): 197.

10. *CEAEM*, fig. 265a = MMA 22.3.72; Hayes, *Scepter* I, fig. 192 (center).

11. Petrie, *Tools and Weapons*, 42, pl. 48 [B64–89].

12. *CEAEM*, fig. 264; Petrie, *Tools and Weapons*, 42, pl. 47 [B57] (Cairo 27280).

13. Petrie, *Tools and Weapons*, 43, pl. 49 [94]; Gautier, *Licht*, 61, fig. 72 (Cairo 31044); Alexander Badawy, *Ancient Egyptian Architectural Design* (Berkeley and Los Angeles, 1965), 40–43.

14. Petrie, *Tools and Weapons*, pl. 47 [60] (burial of Senedjem, Nineteenth Dynasty, Cairo 27259). A model from the tomb of Meketra is in the Metropolitan Museum of Art, New York (MMA 20.3.90, measuring 15.1 × 11.5 centimeters). For a model from a Twelfth Dynasty tomb at Nag' ed-Deir, see William K. Simpson, *Papyrus Reisner* II (Boston, 1965), frontispiece. See also J. E. Quibell and A. G. K. Hayter, *Teti Pyramid, North Side: Excavations at Saqqara* (Cairo, 1927), 41.

15. *Rekhmire*, pl. 55.

16. Vitruvius, *The Ten Books on Architecture* VIII.5; see also *Paulys Real-Encyclopädie der classischen Altertumswissenschaft* III (Stuttgart, 1899), 2439–2440 (s.v. "Cherobates").

17. Günther Binding and Norbert Nussbaum, *Der Baubetrieb nördlich der Alpen in zeitgenössischen Darstellungen* (Darmstadt, 1978), 93, 99, 133.

18. *WB* III, 331/12; *WB* IV, 86/15, 261/10–13.

19. Petrie, *Tools and Weapons*, 42, pl. 47 [58, 59] (both in Cairo 27258). For the discovery, see E. Toda, *ASAE* 20 (1920): 154.

20. Gautier, *Licht*, 60, fig. 71 (Cairo 31045, CG 1931).

21. W. M. Flinders Petrie, *Amulets* (London, 1914), pl. 4.

22. See, in general, *CEAEM*, 105–106, pl. 265e; D. Stocks, *Manchester Archaeological Bulletin* 2 (1987): 42–50.

23. *Rekhmire*, pl. 62. A model of this scene was displayed in the Egyptian Museum, Cairo.

24. Krauth, *Steinhauerbuch*, 186–188, figs. 243–245.

25. Jéquier, *Pépi II* III, 47, fig. 46 (Cairo 52347); *CEAEM*, fig. 265e; Petrie, *Tools and Weapons*, 42, pl. 49 [B44–50]. The set B from Beni Hasan (Middle Kingdom) is square. *Egypt's Golden Age*, no. 27 (New Kingdom [from Deir el-Bahari]).

26. D. Stocks, *Manchester Archaeological Bulletin* 2 (1987): 49–50, fig. 25.

27. For metal tools in general and their application, see R. Anthes, *MDAIK* 10 (1941): 79–121; W. Barta, in *LÄ* IV, 19–20. For Minoan Crete, see Shaw, *Minoan Architecture*, 44–61, figs. 35–48.

28. R. Michael Cowell, in W. V. Davies, *Tools and Weapons*, vol. I, *Axes* (catalogue of the Egyptian Antiquities in the British Museum) (London, 1987), 96–101, with more references on recent surveys and analyses of Egyptian metalwork.

29. Ibid., 98; see also Zaki Nour, *Cheops Boats*, 34–39.

30. Lucas and Harris, *AEMI*, 235–243.

31. A. R. Williams and K. R. Maxwell-Hyslop, *Journal of Archaeological Science* 3 (1976): 283–305. A foreign origin of the tools cannot be ruled out.

32. See the articles by J. C. Golvin in *ASAE* 68 (1982): 165–190; *ASAE* 70 (1984–

1985): 371–381; and *Hommages à François Daumas* (Montpelier, Vt., 1988), 299–329.

33. Petrie, *Royal Tombs* II, 24, 28, pls. 6, 9A, 38 [94], 41.

34. Petrie, *Tools and Weapons*, pls. 21, 22. The variety of tools used by stonemasons of the nineteenth century A.D. is illustrated in Krauth, *Steinhauerbuch*, 176–185, figs. 233–242. Eigner seems to have noted the traces of droves or boasters (4.5 to 7 centimeters wide) and of a 1.1-centimeter-wide toothed claw with seven claws (necessarily of metal) (*Grabbauten*, 84). This concerns the tomb of Pedineith (Theban Tomb no. 197), which dates, however, only from the period of Amasis (about 550 B.C.). A true metal hammer in the Metropolitan Museum of Art, New York (MMA acc. no. 30.8.113), is certainly too small to be used for stoneworking.

35. *CEAEM*, fig. 263a, said to be from Gebelein.

36. *Rekhmire*, pls. 52–55.

37. Henri Wild, *Le Tombeau de Ti* III (Cairo, 1953), pls. 120–124, 133; Norman De Garis Davies, *The Rock Tombs of Deir el Gebrawi* (London, 1902), pl. 16.

38. F. Debono, *ASAE* 46 (1947): 265–285. Two examples were found at Qurna, probably dating from the Twenty-second to Twenty-sixth Dynasty (*CEAEM*, fig. 266; Petrie, *Tools and Weapons*, pl. 53). Engelbach believed in the existence of metal mason's picks (*ASAE* 29 [1929]: 19–24). His suggestions are based, however, on traces on a sarcophagus of Persian or Ptolemaic date (H. Abou-Seif, *ASAE* 24 [1924]: 91–96).

39. R. Klemm is convinced, however, that the tool marks in quarry walls were not produced by picks but by pointed chisels (personal communication).

40. Firth and Quibell, *Step Pyramid*, 128, pl. 93 [7].

41. Engelbach, *Aswan Obelisk*, 11–13.

42. Henri Wild, *Le Tombeau de Ti* II (Cairo, 1953), pls. 97, 129.

43. Junker, *Giza* X, 16.

44. Engelbach, *Aswan Obelisk*, pl. 4 [2]; Reisner, *Mycerinus*, 236–237, pls. 20a–c.

45. Wild, *Tombeau de Ti* II, pls. 97A, 129.

46. For representations, see Gustave Jéquier, *Les Frises d'objets des sarcophages du Moyen Empire* (Cairo, 1921), 279.

47. M. Isler, *JEA* 73 (1987): 137–147.

48. J.-P. Lauer and F. Debono, *ASAE* 50 (1950): 1–18.

49. Possibly some of the specimens in Petrie, *Kahun*, pl. 16; Petrie, *Illahun, Kahun and Gurob*, pl. 7. One example from Giza (Zaki Nour, *Cheops Boats*, pl. 15A).

50. Petrie mentions flints in the builder's debris thrown over the cliffs of Giza; he does not consider them to be tools, but thinks that they originated from clearing the desert surface (*Pyramids and Temples*, 213). Large numbers of flakes broken from stone tools have been found, however, in the stonecutters' debris around the pyramid of Senwosret I at Lisht (unpublished data). They are enclosed in layers of granite dust.

B. Vachala and J. Sroboda observed large quantities of hammerstones and flint tools around limestone buildings at Abusir (*ZÄS* 116 [1989]: 178) and suggest the use of stone tools for dressing limestone.

51. Krauth, *Steinhauerbuch*, 180, fig. 238.

52. Petrie, *Tools and Weapons*, 40, pl. 46; *CEAEM*, fig. 264; De Morgan, *Dahchour* II, 105, fig. 153; *Egypt's Golden Age*, no. 25; Arnold and Winlock, *Mentuhotep*, 60–61, pls. 34b, 35a–b.

53. Emery, *Great Tombs* II, fig. 69, pl. 30; W. M. Flinders Petrie, *Deshasheh* (London, 1897), pl. 34.

54. Edouard Naville, *The XIth Dynasty Temple at Deir el-Bahari* III (London, 1913), 18. For more examples of mallets, see ibid., pl. 29 [3].

55. See, in general, *CEAEM*, 194, 202–204; Lucas and Harris, *AEMI*, 42–44, 66–71, 423–426; Petrie, *Pyramids and Temples*, 173; Hölscher, *Chephren*, 77–79; Borchardt, *Neuserre*, 142–143; Zuber, "Travail des pierres dures," 205–215; D. Stocks, *Popular Archaeology* (April 1986): 24–29; Jéquier, *Frises d'objets sarcophages du Moyen Empire*, 275–277.

56. Ali El-Khouly, *Egyptian Stone Vessels of Predynastic Period to Dynasty III* (Mainz, 1978).

57. D. Stocks, *Popular Archaeology* (April 1986): 24–29.

58. Shaw, *Minoan Architecture*, 69–70, figs. 61–63.

59. L. Gorelick and A. J. Gwinnett, *Expedition* (1983): 40–47. Their result contradicts Stocks's experiments, which seem to have achieved striations on stone cores with dry quartz sand. Stocks also notes that A. Lucas found a mass of quartz sand in a drill hole of an alabaster fragment (*Popular Archaeology* [April 1986]: 24–29).

60. Lucas and Harris doubt that emery was found in Egypt and suggest its being imported from the Greek Islands. G. Schweinfurth seems to have located a findspot near Aswan; however, see Borchardt, *Neuserre*, 142. Pliny mentions that for sawing stone, sand had to be imported to Rome from India, Egypt, and Nubia (*Natural History* XXXVI. 9–10).

61. Petrie, *Pyramids and Temples*, 176.

62. Numerous examples are in the Djoser complex (Firth and Quibell, *Step Pyramid*, pls. 64 [1], 86 [6], 93 [1]; C. M. Firth, *ASAE* 25 [1925]: pl. 5 [2]). For a later example, with 36-centimeter-deep drill holes in granite slabs, see Ricke, *Sonnenheiligtum* I, fig. 9.

63. Junker, *Giza* III, 190, fig. 34.

64. D. Stocks, *Popular Archaeology* (April 1986): 26, fig. on p. 28. Apparently, the sarcophagi of Sekhemkhet (Lauer, *Hist. Mon.* I, 195) and of Cheops (Petrie, *Pyramids and Temples*, 176) were drilled that way. How common the method was, however, is not established.

65. Firth and Quibell, *Step Pyramid*, pl. 94 [5]; Hölscher, *Chephren*, 77–79; Borchardt, *Neuserre*, 142, fig. 122 [1]; Petrie, *Pyramids and Temples*, 173. Hölscher mentions, without further details, "the end of a bronze drill which had broken off deep in the boring" (*Mortuary Temple* II, 37). Tiny bronze fragments can also be seen in the drill hole in a doorpost of Ramesses II in the Metropolitan Museum of Art (acc. no. 13.183.2).

66. Firth and Quibell, *Step Pyramid*, pls. 86 [6], 93 [1–2]. Petrie cites a slightly later example, which he explains as a "pivot block to turn heavy blocks on in moving stone" (*Meydum and Memphis*, 5, pl. 20).

67. See, in general, *CEAEM*, 203–204; Junker, *Giza* X, 82; Jéquier, *Frises d'objets des sarcophages du Moyen Empire*, 271–273; Zuber, "Travail des pierres dures," 202–205.

68. Lauer, *Hist. Mon.* I, 253.

69. Zuber, "Travail des pierres dures," 202–205.

70. Lauer, *Hist. Mon.* I, 195, 235; Anna Maria Donadoni-Roveri, *I Sarcofagi Egizi dalle origini alla fine dell'antico regno* (Rome, 1969), A1.

71. Borchardt, *Re-Heiligtum*, 44.

72. Petrie, *Tools and Weapons*, pl. 52 [53]; Petrie, *Pyramids and Temples*, 174.

73. Donadoni-Roveri, *Sarcofagi Egizi dalle origini alla fine dell'antico regno*, B10 and B31; from the tomb of Djedefhor (Cairo CG 6193) and from mastaba Giza G 7270 (Kunsthistorisches Museum, Vienna), see Junker, *Giza* X, 82.

74. Petrie, *Tools and Weapons*, pl. 52 [57].

75. Ibid., pl. 52 [52, 54, 56].

76. Borchardt, *Re-Heiligtum*, 44, gives only "Abusir."

77. Reisner, *Mycerinus*, 116.

78. D. Stocks, *Popular Archaeology* (April 1986): 28–29.

79. One example of iron from the seventh century B.C. could be of foreign origin (A. R. Williams and K. R. Maxwell-Hyslop, *Journal of Archaeological Science* 3 [1976]: 283–305). Numerous Minoan saws are preserved, the largest being 1.7 meters long and 21 centimeters wide (Shaw, *Minoan Architecture*, 55–69, figs. 43–46). Most of them have teeth along the entire length of their cutting edges. The mason's saws were toothless, however. They have small round holes in one end. These holes were intended for the attachment of wooden handles. Saw marks are recorded on hard limestone, conglomerate, green schist, and speckled basalt. The width of saw cuts ranges from 1 to 2 millimeters. Frequently, saw cuts were used only as a "guide line" in order to produce a clean break when the stone was struck with a hammer.

80. Garstang, *Bet Khallaf*, pl. 23 [35].

81. Vitruvius (*Ten Books on Architecture* II. 7.1) and Pliny (*Natural History* XXXVI. 9–10) mention cutting stone with toothless saws. For modern usage, see *Marble*, 136–142, figs. 157–169. The author's remarks on ancient Egypt are completely misleading, however.

82. Lucas and Harris, *AEMI*, 134–136; Ryan and Hansen, *Cordage*.

83. Carefully studied from representations of rope-making scenes by E. Teeter, *JEA* 73 (1987): 71–77.

84. Zaki Nour, *Cheops Boats*, 42, pls. 12, 63–65.

85. E. A. M. Greiss, *BIE* 31 (1949): 271–272. Apparently, six ropes were found, one of which was 56 meters long.

86. Zaki Nour, *Cheops Boats*, pl. 38.

87. Ryan and Hansen, *Cordage*.

88. J. J. Janssen, *Commodity Prices from the Ramessid Period* (Leiden, 1975), 439; Janssen, *Two Ancient Ship's Logs* (Leiden, 1961), 87.

89. Engelbach, *Aswan Obelisk*, 25.

90. B. Catoire, in *Karnak* VII, 181–202.

91. *Rekhmire*, pl. 58.

92. G. Daressy, *ASAE* 1 (1900): 28.

93. J. D. S. Pendlebury, *The City of Akhenaten* III (London, 1951), 45, pl. 74 [1]. Is the 52-centimeter-long copper instrument depicted in *CEAEM*, fig. 263a, a crowbar or a long chisel?

94. For late examples, see Winlock, *Hibis*, pl. 48.

95. Lacau and Chevrier, *Hatshepsout* I, 9, fig. 1.

96. For example, the casing blocks of the Cheops Pyramid and core blocks of the mortuary temple of Chephren. See also Zaki Nour, *Cheops Boats*, pl. 32.

97. On core blocks of the mortuary temple of Chephren. Good examples are in Hölscher, *Chephren*, pl. 8. Reisner observed up to five mortises along the lower edges of the core blocks of the mortuary temple of Mycerinus, 10 to 15 × 20 to 30 centimeters wide and 10 to 15 centimeters deep (*Mycerinus*, 75).

98. Hölscher, *Chephren*, pl. 17.

99. *Karnak* v, 79–82, figs. 2, 3, pl. 31.

100. Ibid., 163, fig. 3.

101. Golvin and Goyon, *Karnak*, 130. The application of huge levers pulled down with ropes is also shown in the reliefs of Sennacherib at Nineveh (Julian Reade, *Assyrian Sculpture* [Cambridge, Mass., 1983], figs. 51, 51).

102. Petrie, *Pyramids and Temples*, 212. It is not certain, however, that the relieving chambers were already planned when the blocks could be loaded on one of the lower courses in order to "travel" upward.

103. Many have been found. A photograph at the Metropolitan Museum of Art,

New York, shows thirty-six rockers from foundation deposits of Hatshepsut excavated by Edouard Naville (E. Naville, *The Temple of Deir el Bahari* VI [London, 1908], pl. 168; Hayes, *Scepter* II, 85–86, fig. 47; *Ägyptens Aufstieg zur Weltmacht*, no. 69a).

104. For example, Choisy, *L'Art de bâtir*, 80–86; Borchardt, *Re-Heiligtum*, 62; J. Fitchen, *Journal of the Society of Architectural Historians* 37 (1978): 3–9.

105. *CEAEM*, 102–103, figs. 107–109.

106. Petrie, *Tools and Weapons*, 41 [B37].

107. On the road to the Inca fortress Ollantaytambo, building blocks still lie along the roadside, one on rollers of adder wood (J. Ogden Outwater, in *Tecnologia Andina* [Lima, 1978], 581–589, fig. 3). At Nuri (Sudan), two short thick granite rollers were found in Pyramid VIII (Engelbach, *Aswan Obelisk*, 38).

108. *CEAEM*, fig. 267, from the pyramid of Pepy II (= Jéquier, *Pépi II* III, 47–48, fig. 44, in Cairo 51432); Petrie, *Tools and Weapons*, pl. 49 [B38, 39]; Guy Brunton, *Lahun* I (London, 1920), pl. 20A; MMA 24.1.77 and [24.1.78] (unpublished).

109. De Morgan, *Dahchour* II, 90, fig. 134; E. Chassinat, *Fouilles de Qattah*, MIFAO 14 (Cairo, 1906), 22, fig. 8; Gautier, *Licht*, figs. 77, 78, 90; Arthur Mace and Herbert E. Winlock, *The Tomb of Senebtisi at Lisht* (New York, 1916), 14, figs. 5, 6. Burial pit of vizier Mentuhotep at Lisht with a network of short poles (60 to 80 centimeters) in front of the sarcophagus. Poles for rolling roofing slabs (Arnold, *Qasr el-Sagha*, fig. 9, pl. 7c). Poles for sliding coffin lid in position (Maragioglio, *Piramidi* VIII, pl. 10).

110. Arnold, *Amenemhet III* I, 22, pl. 44b; Jéquier, *Deux pyramides*, pls. 8, 17; Maragioglio, *Piramidi* V, pl. 8 [4, 6]; Gautier, *Licht*, 72, fig. 90; queen's pyramid 3 of Senwosret I at Lisht (unpublished data); P. Montet, *ASAE* 46 (1947): pl. 79, with a granite plug on four rollers blocking the crypt of King Psusennes at Tanis.

111. N. Charlton, *JEA* 64 (1978): 128. From observations made in the quarries of Carrara, one would expect instead crossbeams for transportation on such uneven ground (Mannoni, *Marble*, fig. 245).

112. Saleh and Sourouzian, *Kairo*, no. 142a (Eighteenth Dynasty papyrus of Maiherperi).

113. *Rekhmire*, pl. 58.

114. G. Goyon, *Revue Archéologique* 2 (1963): 5, n. 1.

115. Mannoni, *Marble*, figs. 129–132, 248, 256.

116. As it was certainly done in Mesopotamia. Compare the representations of the transport of winged bulls on sledges (with rollers!) from the palace of Sennacherib (Reade, *Assyrian Sculpture*, figs. 50, 51).

117. De Morgan, *Dahchour* I, 83, fig. 204; *CEAEM*, fig. 85; George A. Reisner, *Models of Ships and Boats* (Cairo, 1913), 88–89.

118. *BMMA* 15 (July 1920): 10–11, fig. 7 (MMA no. 24.1.84); Hayes, *Scepter* I, fig. 118.

119. A similar sledge from the tomb of Tutankhamun symbolically carried the gilded Ka shrine of the king.

120. W. M. Flinders Petrie, *Seventy Years in Archaeology* (London, n.d.), 100. The present location of the sledge is unknown.

121. H. G. Fischer, *JEA* 67 (1981): 166, fig. 1. Many examples are in Marianne Eaton-Krauss, *The Representations of Statuary in Private Tombs of the Old Kingdom* (Wiesbaden, 1984).

122. G. Goyon, *BIFAO* 69 (1971): 11–41, pls. 3–5; H. G. Fischer, *JEA* 61 (1975): 33–34, fig. 2.

123. Percy E. Newberry, *Bersheh* I (London, 1895), pl. 15; J. Vandier, *CdE* 18 (1943): 185–190; A. Badawy, *MIO* 8 (1963): 325–332. Model made by R. Engelbach in 1933 (H. Chevrier, *RdÉ* 22 [1970]: 22–23, pl. 1).

124. Vyse, *Pyramids* III, 99, no. 6; G. Daressy, *ASAE* 11 (1911): 263–265; Saleh and Sourouzian, *Kairo*, no. 119.

125. Naville, *Temple of Deir el Bahari* VI, pl. 154.

126. *Rekhmire*, 55, pl. 58.

127. Austen Henry Layard, *The Monuments of Nineveh* II (London, 1849), pls. 13–17; Archibald Paterson, *Assyrian Sculptures: Palace of Sennacherib* (Haarlem, 1915), pls. 110–123. Mulloy suggests that the Easter Island statues were moved on one-piece sledges made of tree forks ("Easter Islands," 9–12). They would have been moved forward with the help of a bipod seated above the sledge.

128. H. Chevrier, *RdÉ* 22 (1970): 20.

129. Mannoni, *Marble*, figs. 129, 134–137, 245, 248. For the role of oxen in medieval church building, see Ian Dunlop, *The Cathedrals' Crusade* (London and New York, 1982), 52.

130. Arnold and Winlock, *Mentuhotep*, 62, pl. 37.

131. J. Röder, *MDAIK* 18 (1962): 89–91.

132. Mannoni shows a block weighing about 40 to 50 tons pulled by fourteen oxen (*Marble*, fig. 129).

133. Jéquier, *Pépi II* III, 47, fig. 45, and *CEAEM*, fig. 267 (Sixth Dynasty, Cairo 51433); Hayes, *Scepter* I, 290, fig. 192 (MMA 34.1.35, made of hard tamarisk wood).

134. J. Röder, *Archäologischer Anzeiger* 3 (1965): 467–551.

135. Petrie, *Tools and Weapons*, 41 [B16–17], pl. 13.

136. Quibell and Hayter, *Teti Pyramid, North Side*, frontispiece; H. Senk, *ASAE* 57 (1954): 207–211; Brigitte Jarŏs-Deckert, *Das Grab des Jnj-jtj.f: Die Wandmalereien der XI. Dynastie* (Mainz, 1984), foldout 3.

137. Saleh and Sourouzian, *Kairo* no. 123. For another example from the Nineteenth Dynasty, see Guy Brunton and Reginald Engelbach, *Gurob* (London, 1927), pl. 52.

138. N. De Garis Davies, *JEA* 12 (1926): 111.

139. Saleh and Sourouzian, *Kairo*, no. 142a.

140. K. H. Dittmann, *MDAIK* 10 (1941): 60–78.

141. Jules Couyat and Pierre Montet, *Les Inscriptions hiéroglyphiques et hiératiques du Ouadi Hammamat* (Cairo, 1912), 38, lines 19–21.

142. Selim Hassan, *Excavations at Giza IV, 1932–1933* (Cairo, 1943), 44 [23], pls. 18A–B.

143. Reisner, *Mycerinus*, 272, pl. A [6].

144. A relief from the tomb of Apui at Saqqara might suggest that the bearing stones could also have been inserted into the tops of masts of sailing boats (*CEAEM*, fig. 45).

APPENDIX *Mortar and Plaster*

MORTAR[1]

Mortar fulfills mainly two functions in Pharaonic architecture. One is that of a binding material between blocks of stone, either in the horizontal joints as a means to guarantee the stable and level bedding of a block or as a connection of blocks in the vertical joints (fig. A.1). It is assumed, however, that Pharaonic gypsum mortar had little actual adhesive power.

There are cases in which mortar was used as a sliding or lubricant material to reduce friction when heavy blocks were pushed in position (fig. A.2). This may have been the case when mortar appears only in the center of the surface of the lower blocks.[2] In brick construction, the mortar used is clay (Nile alluvium), sand, or a mixture of both, often with an addition of powdered limestone, chopped straw, or other material.[3] The color changes accordingly. Lauer gave the following analysis of samples taken from phase M1-3 of the Step Pyramid:[4]

	Whitish	*Yellowish*	*Reddish*
Clay	54.0%	38.5%	3.0%
Powdered limestone	11.0%	53.0–55.0%	14.0%
Quartz sand	35.0%	8.0%	83.0%
	100.0%	100.0%	100.0%

In stone construction, gypsum mortar was used at least since the Second Dynasty. It consisted of burned gypsum and sand and very often chipped limestone. But we still do not know if the Egyptians of Pharaonic times knew the use of lime or if lime found in mortar was of natural origin, as impurities derived from the raw material.[5] Lucas also quotes unusual mixtures such as resin mortar, which may have been used only for special purposes.[6] More research seems necessary. One also has to reckon with ad hoc inventions made by imaginative builders. For example, in Pylon IX at Karnak the *talatat* were embedded into a mortar consisting of gypsum and sandstone dust.[7]

Gypsum mortar was also frequently used to repair the surface of limestone walls, to fill mortises for levers and cramps, and to model relief figures that were damaged or where the surface of the stone did not provide the needed quality.[8] Fine gypsum mortar was successfully used to tighten the joints between the roofing blocks of the Cheops boat pit.[9]

PLASTER[10]

In brick architecture and for plastering rock-cut tomb walls, the normal plaster used was a mixture of clay, sand, and chopped straw. The plaster was usually applied in two qualities, a coarse one below and a fine one on top. The better quality can also be a natural mixture of very fine clay and

Fig. A.2 Gypsum plaster used as lubricant between building blocks in the temple Qasr el-Sagha.

limestone dust found at the foot of the desert hills, nowadays known under the name of *hib*.[11]

Gypsum plaster could also be applied directly on the walls of temples and tombs, where it was often used to fill irregularities and cracks before the surface was smoothed.[12] In this use, both mortar and plaster seem to appear.

Pure gypsum was also used for the ceiling of houses and palaces, where it was thrown against the reed attached to the beams.[13] Fine plant fibers were found mixed into such ceiling plaster at the pyramid site of Amenemhat III at Dahshur in order to increase its cohesiveness.

The Egyptian term for plaster was *qd*,[14] which is thought to be a loan word from the Akkadian *gassu,* still surviving in our own *gesso* and *gypsum.* But since gypsum as a material was known in Egypt before the introduction of its Akkadian name, another Egyptian word, which has not yet been identified, must have existed.

The plasterers used tools quite similar to those of the present time. A large float with a cylindrical grip was used for the rough coat. It had a beveled end in order not to disturb the coat in the corner of an adjoining wall. The smaller float, which was lighter and smoother, was made for the facing coat. The floats were often carved in one block.[15]

Gypsum and probably mortar as well were often prepared or carried in bottoms of broken beakers and bottles. Such containers, partially filled with gypsum and showing the fingerprints of the workmen, are frequently found at construction sites. In the Middle Kingdom tombs of Beni Hasan, a wooden plasterer's dish was discovered with ropes to suspend it from the shoulders of the workmen or a scaffold. Its interior still showed traces of plaster or mortar.[16] The dish was used during the construction of the tombs.

1. In general, see Lucas and Harris, *AEMI*, 74–76; Junker, *Giza* I, 90; Jacquet, *Trésor*, 125–126; Zaki Nour, *Cheops Boats*, 31–34, with analyses.

2. Arnold, *Mentuhotep*, pl. 13c; Reisner observed that "the stones appeared to have been adjusted in place by 'floating' on plaster as was certainly done in the case of the granite blocks" (*Mycerinus*, 74).

3. Spencer, *Brick Architecture*, 133.

4. Lauer, *Hist. Mon.* I, 245–246.

5. A. Lucas, *ASAE* 7 (1906): 4–7; Z. Iskander, *ASAE* 52 (1954): 272–274; Maragioglio, *Piramidi* III, 92.

6. Lucas and Harris, *AEMI*, 75. Junker mentions grinded potsherds (*Giza* III, 126).

7. *Karnak* II, 143, n. 3.

8. Junker, *Giza* VII, 74, 210; *Giza* X, 118.

9. Zaki Nour, *Cheops Boats*, 31–33.

10. See, in general, Lucas and Harris, *AEMI*, 76–79. For a detailed study of Minoan lime and clay plaster, see Shaw, *Minoan Architecture*, 207–226.

11. A similar plastering technique is recorded from the early palace of Phaistos: "A thick layer of clay and straw, two or three centimeters thick, was first applied to the rubble walls; a final coating of monochrome greyish-yellow plaster was smoothed on over it" (Shaw, *Minoan Architecture*, 209).

12. In the mortuary temple of Mycerinus, the joints of the core blocks had been closed with a pink plaster "made of sulphate of lime and sand" (Reisner, *Mycerinus*, 74).

13. Barry Kemp, *Amarna Reports* III (London, 1986), 18–19, fig. 1.13.

14. W. Spiegelberg, *ZÄS* 58 (1923): 51–52; Černý, *Valley of the Kings*, 35–41.

15. Examples are in Petrie, *Tools and Weapons*, pl. 47 [B53, 54]; Petrie, *Kahun*, 26, pl. 9 [9, 10]; *Egypt's Golden Age*, 56, 57, no. 28; *Ägyptens Aufstieg zur Weltmacht*, no. 56; *CEAEM*, fig. 263 [f], made of copper. Quite similar are a float and a trowel from Gournia (Crete) (Shaw, *Minoan Architecture*, 210, figs. 238–239).

16. John Garstang, *The Burial Customs of Ancient Egypt as Illustrated by Tombs of the Middle Kingdom* (London, 1907), 132, fig. 130.

Glossary

Abacus Square, flat upper member of the capital of a column that connects the column capital to the architrave (fig. 1.19).

Anathyrosis Labor-saving method of creating a precise joint by smoothing the contact surfaces of two blocks along a narrow border around the edges of the stones. The center was either left rough or made concave and filled with mortar (fig. 4.23).

Architrave Horizontal structural member that connects pillars, columns, and door frames (lintel) to one another. It also carries the roofing slabs (figs. 4.24, 4.33).

Ashlar masonry Masonry in which all stones are square and have the same size and proportions. They are arranged in courses of the same height with horizontal joints that are continuous along the length of the course (fig. 4.85).

Backing stones Stones between the casing blocks and core masonry that support or carry the casing blocks (figs. 4.88, 4.99, 4.105)

Barrel vault Simple vault with a semicircular cross section (fig. 4.142).

Bed Depression cut into the surface of the foundation course or bedrock in order to join it to the lower face of a block (fig. 4.7).

Bonded quoining Construction that uses the method of headers and stretchers to secure the corner blocks (figs. 4.48, 4.49).

Boning (boning rods) Sighting with one eye along the surface of a block in order to test its flatness (fig. 6.7). For the use of boning rods, see pp. 256–257.

Boss (extra stock) Rough, undressed front face of a block that projects from the wall surface (figs. 4.50–4.52).

Broken course Course with stepped, not continuous, horizontal joints (fig. 4.83).

Cavetto (Egyptian cavetto or cornice) Hollowed molding used in cornices (figs. 4.28, 4.29, 4.55).

Chamfer Beveled corner and the method of cutting a right-angle slope or bevel.

This glossary of terms used in Egyptian architectural history is partly based on Joseph Gwilt, *The Encyclopedia of Architecture* (1842; reprint, New York, 1982).

Column Vertical cylindrical support.

Corbel, corbeling Range of stones in which each projects beyond the front face of the stone below, thus reducing the span over a room. Corbeled ceilings create a vertical, but not a lateral, thrust (figs. 4.119–4.121).

Cornice Molded projection that crowns a building, usually in the form of the Egyptian cavetto.

Cramp (more rarely, **clamp**) Dovetail-shaped dowel that is usually made of wood or bronze, rarely of stone, and connects two blocks of stone (figs. 4.24–4.35).

Cubit Measure of length that equals 52.5 centimeters, subdivided into 7 palms (7.5 cm each) of 4 digits (1.875 cm).

Dowel (cramp) Wood or bronze peg fitted into corresponding sockets in two adjacent blocks (fig. 4.33).

Extrados Rounded upper surface of an arch or a vault.

Header Wall block placed lengthwise across the thickness of the wall and showing only its "head."

Impost Upper surface of the structure (in Egyptian architecture, a wall), which carries the vault.

Isodomic (masonry) Wall construction with horizontal courses of equal height (fig. 4.82[3a]).

Keystone Topmost, central voussoir of an arch or a vault (figs. 4.141, 4.142).

Lintel Horizontal structural member that spans a door or window and supports the superincumbent weight.

Orthostats Tall, upright slabs of stone that form the lowest course of a wall, ordinarily used to case poor-quality masonry (fig. 4.63).

Packing stones Smaller stones that fill the gaps between backing stones and core masonry (figs. 4.88[5], 4.90).

Pillar Vertical, rectangular support or cross section created by chamfering the corners of the rectangle (octagonal, sixteen-, or thirty-two-sided pillar). Sixteen- or thirty-two-sided pillars are practically cylindrical and are often called columns.

Portcullis (portcullises) Stone slab lowered vertically from a recess in the ceiling in order to block a passage (figs. 5.13–5.15).

Putlog hole Hole in the face of a wall used to attach the ends of horizontal beams or putlogs. It is ordinarily used to stabilize scaffolding (figs. 5.20–5.23).

Pylon Towering structure in the form of a truncated pyramid. One or two pylons serve as a gateway to a building.

Pyramidion Apex block of a pyramid in the shape of a small pyramid.

Quoins External corner stones interlocking two walls that meet at a right angle so that a header block of one wall becomes a stretcher of the other wall and vice versa (figs. 4.48, 4.49).

Quoining Connecting two walls that meet at a right angle with corner blocks set in a comblike manner (figs. 4.48, 4.49).

Ring bands Courses of blocks with bossed faces visible only on the masonry of the pyramid of Meidum (fig. 3.31).

Sill In stone construction, a horizontal slab that supports the frame of a door or window. Door sills have an elevated front ledge with the stop face for the door wing.

Stretcher Block laid (stretching) with its longer face parallel to the face of the wall.

Subfoundation Course of rough stones laid under the foundation blocks.

Tafl Arabic term for the layers of marly clay that frequently underlie the desert conglomerate.

Torus Semicircular or three-quarter-circular moldings along the edges of a building (vertical along the corners, horizontal along the upper edges). The horizontal torus is the origin of the cavetto (fig. 4.85).

Trapezoidal (masonry) Walls composed of blocks with oblique, rising, and horizontal bedding joints (fig. 4.82[2]).

Vault Ceiling construction based on the arch system, and composed of wedge-shaped stones (voussoirs) in which the stones remain in position because of their shape.

Voussoir Wedge-shaped block of an arch or a vault (figs. 4.141, 4.142). The central voussoir is called the keystone.

Chronology of Dynasties and Rulers

	J. V. Beckerath (1984)	R. Krauss (1985)	Cambridge Ancient History (1962–1965)
Early Dynastic Period	3000–2600	2965–2640	3100–2613
First Dynasty	3000–2820	2965–2815	3100–2890
Second Dynasty	2820–2670	2860–2750	2890–2686
Khasekhemuy			
Third Dynasty	2670–2600	2750–2640	2686–2613
Djoser			
Sekhemkhet			
Old Kingdom	2600–2195	2640–2195	2613–2181
Fourth Dynasty	2600–2475	2640–2520	2613–2494
Snofru			
Cheops			
Djedefra			
Chefren			
Mycerinus			
Shepseskaf			
Fifth Dynasty	2475–2345	2520–2360	2494–2345
Userkaf			
Sahura			
Neferirkara Kakai			
Niuserra Iny			
Djedkara Isesi			
Unas			
Sixth Dynasty	2345–2195	2360–2195	2345–2181
Tety			
Pepy I			
Merenra			
Pepy II			
First Intermediate Period			**D. Franke (1988)**
Eighth to Eleventh Dynasties	2195–2040	2195–1987	2168/2198–1990/1970

Middle Kingdom	2040–1781	1987–1759	1990/1970–1759
Eleventh Dynasty	2160–1994	2081–1938	2081–1938
Mentuhotep Nebhepetra	2065–2014	2008–1957	2008–1957
Unification	2040	1987	1990/1970
Mentuhotep Seankhkara	2014–2001	1957–1938	1957–1945
Twelfth Dynasty	1994–1781	1938–1759	1938–1759
Amenemhat I	1994–1964	1938–1908	1939/1938–1909
Senwosret I	1974–1929	1918–1875	1919–1875/1874
Amenemhat II	1932–1898	1876–1842	1877/1876–1843/1842
Senwosret II	1900–1881	1844–1837	1845/1844–1837
Senwosret III	1881–1842	1836–1818	1837–1818
Amenemhat III	1842–1794	1818–1772	1818/1817–1773/1772
Amenemhat IV	1798–1785	1772–1762	1773–1763
Thirteenth Dynasty	1781–1650	1759–1640	1759–1630
Auibra Hor			
Khendjer			
Hyksos Period			
Fourteenth to Seventeenth Dynasties	1650–1550	1630/1626–1522/1518	1630–1550
			Helck (1988)
New Kingdom	1550–1075	1540–1075	1530–
Eighteenth Dynasty	1550–1291	1539–1292	1530–1293
Ahmose	1550–1525	1539–1514	1530–1504
Amenhotep I	1525–1504	1514–1493	1504–1483
Hatshepsut	1479–1458	1479–1458	1467–1445
Thutmosis III	1479–1425	1479–1426	1467–1413
Amenhotep II	1428–1397	1426–1400	1414–1388
Thutmosis IV	1397–1387	1400–1390	1388–1379
Amenhotep III	1387–1350	1390–1353	1379–1340
Akhenaten	1350–1333	1353–1336	1340–1324
Tutankhamun	1333–1323	1332–1323	1319–1309
Haremhab	1319–1291	1319–1292	1305–1293
			Kitchen (1988)
Nineteenth Dynasty	1291–1185	1292–1190	1295–1186
Ramesses I	1291–1289	1292–1290	1295–1294
Sety I	1289–1278	1290–1279	1294–1279
Ramesses II	1279–1212	1279–1213	1279–1213
Merenptah	1212–1202	1213–1204	1213–1203
Twentieth Dynasty	1185–1075	1190–1075	1186–1070/69
Ramesses III	1184–1153	1187–1156	1184–1153
Ramesses IV	1153–1147	1156–1150	1153–1147
Third Intermediate Period	1075–664	1075–716	
Twenty-first Dynasty	1075–945	1075–944	
Twenty-second Dynasty	945–718	944–716	
Twenty-third Dynasty	820–718	823–732	
Twenty-fourth Dynasty	730–712	722–716	
Late Period	710–332	716–332	
Twenty-fifth Dynasty (Kushite)	775–656	750–656	

Twenty-sixth Dynasty	664–525
Psametik I	664–610
Necho II	610–595
Psametik II	595–589
Apries	589–570
Amasis	570–526
Twenty-seventh Dynasty (Persian)	525–404/401
Twenty-eighth Dynasty	404–399
Twenty-ninth Dynasty	399–380
Hakoris	393–380
Thirtieth Dynasty	380–342
Nectanebo I	380–362
Nectanebo II	360–342
Second Persian Period	343–332
End of the Pharaonic Period	332

Bibliography

ABBREVIATIONS OF PUBLICATIONS

ÄA	*Ägyptologische Abhandlungen* (Wiesbaden)
ÄgAbh	Ägyptologische Abhandlungen (Wiesbaden)
ÄgFo	*Ägyptologische Forschungen* (Glückstadt)
AJA	*American Journal of Archaeology* (Baltimore)
ASAE	*Annales du Service des Antiquités de l'Égypte* (Cairo)
BdE	Bibliothèque d'Étude (Cairo)
Beiträge Bf	Beiträge zur Ägyptischen Bauforschung und Altertumskunde (Cairo)
BIE	*Bulletin de l'Institut Égyptien*
BIFAO	*Bulletin de l'Institut français d'Archéologie orientale* (Cairo)
BMMA	*Bulletin of the Metropolitan Museum of Art* (New York)
CdE	*Chronique d'Égypte* (Brussels)
FIFAO	Fouilles de l'Institut français d'Archéologie orientale (Cairo)
GM	*Göttinger Miszellen* (Göttingen)
JARCE	*Journal of the American Research Center in Egypt* (New York)
JEA	*Journal of Egyptian Archaeology* (London)
JSSEA	*Journal of the Society for the Study of Egyptian Antiquities* (Toronto)
MDAIK	*Mitteilungen des Deutschen Archäologischen Instituts Abteilung Kairo* (Cairo)
MIFAO	Mémoires publiés par les membres de l'Institut français d'Archéologie orientale du Caire (Cairo)
MIO	*Mitteilungen des Instituts für Orientforschung* (Berlin)
OIP	Oriental Institute Publications (Chicago)
OLZ	*Orientalistische Literaturzeitung* (Berlin)
RdÉ	*Revue d'Égyptologie* (Paris)
SAK	*Studien für Altägyptische Kultur*
UGAÄ	*Untersuchungen zur Geschichte und Altertumskunde Ägyptens*
ZÄS	*Zeitschrift fur Ägyptische Sprache und Altertumskunde* (Berlin)

Ägyptens Aufstieg zur Weltmacht *Ägyptens Aufstieg zur Weltmacht.* Exhibition Catalogue, Roemer- und Pelizaeus-Museum, Hildesheim. Edited by Arne Eggebrecht. Mainz, 1987.

Arnold, *Amenemhet III* Dieter Arnold. *Der Pyramidenbezirk des Königs Amenemhet III. in Dahschur.* Vol. 1. Mainz, 1987.

Arnold, *Jnj-jtj.f* Dieter Arnold. *Das Grab des Jnj-jtj.f.* Vol. 1, *Die Architektur.* Mainz, 1971.

Arnold, *Mentuhotep* Dieter Arnold. *Der Tempel des Königs Mentuhotep von Deir el-Bahari.* Vol. 1, *Architektur und Deutung.* Mainz, 1974.

Arnold, *Qasr el-Sagha* Dieter Arnold and Dorothea Arnold. *Der Tempel Qasr el-Sagha.* Mainz, 1979.

Arnold, *Senwosret I* Dieter Arnold. *The Pyramid of Senwosret I.* Publications of the Metropolitan Museum of Art Egyptian Expedition 22. New York, 1988.

Arnold and Winlock, *Mentuhotep* Dieter Arnold. *The Temple of Mentuhotep at Deir el-Bahari: From the Notes of Herbert Winlock.* Publications of the Metropolitan Museum of Art Egyptian Expedition 21. New York, 1979.

BAR James Henry Breasted. *Ancient Records of Egypt.* 5 vols. Chicago, 1906. (Quoted by sections)

Borchardt, *Amonstempel* Ludwig Borchardt. *Zur Baugeschichte des Amonstempels von Karnak.* Leipzig, 1905.

Borchardt, *Dritte Bauperiode* Ludwig Borchardt. *Einiges zur dritten Bauperiode der grossen Pyramide bei Gise.* Berlin, 1932.

Borchardt, *Entstehung der Pyramide* Ludwig Borchardt. *Die Entstehung der Pyramide an der Baugeschichte der Pyramide bei Meidum nachgewiesen.* Berlin, 1928.

Borchardt, *Grundkanten* Ludwig Borchardt. *Längen und Richtungen der vier Grundkanten der grossen Pyramide bei Gise.* Cairo, 1926.

Borchardt, *Neferirkere* Ludwig Borchardt. *Das Grabdenkmal des Königs Nefer-ir-ke-Re.* Ausgrabungen der Deutschen Orient-Gesellschaft in Abusir 1902–1908, no. 5. Leipzig, 1909.

Borchardt, *Neuserre* Ludwig Borchardt. *Das Grabdenkmal des Königs Ne-user-Re.* Ausgrabungen der Deutschen Orient-Gesellschaft in Abusir 1902–1904, no. 1. Leipzig, 1907.

Borchardt, *Re-Heiligtum* Ludwig Borchardt. *Das Re-Heiligtum des Königs Ne-woser-Re' (Rathures).* Vol. 1, *Der Bau.* Berlin, 1905.

Borchardt, *Sahure* Ludwig Borchardt. *Das Grabdenkmal des Königs Sahu-Re.* Vol. 1, *Der Bau.* Ausgrabungen der Deutschen Orient-Gesellschaft in Abusir 1902–1908, no. 6. Leipzig, 1910.

Borchardt, *Tempel mit Umgang* Ludwig Borchardt. *Ägyptische Tempel mit Umgang.* Cairo, 1938.

CEAEM Somers Clarke and Reginald Engelbach. *Ancient Egyptian Masonry.* Oxford, 1930.

Černý, *Community* Jaroslav Černý. *A Community of Workmen at Thebes in the Ramesside Period.* BdE, no. 50. Cairo, 1973.

Černý, *Valley of the Kings* Jaroslav Černý. *The Valley of the Kings.* BdE, no. 61. Cairo, 1973.

Choisy, *L'Art de bâtir* Auguste Choisy. *L'Art de bâtir chez les Égyptiens.* Paris, 1904.

Coulton, *Greek Architects* J. J. Coulton. *Ancient Greek Architects at Work.* Ithaca, N.Y., 1977.

De Lubicz, *Karnak* R. A. Schwaller De Lubicz, G. Miré, and V. Miré. *Les Temples de Karnak.* 2 vols. Paris, 1982.

De Lubicz, *Temple* R. A. Schwaller De Lubicz. *Le Temple de l'homme: L' Apet du sud à Louxor.* 3 vols. Paris, 1957.

De Morgan, *Dahchour* I Jacques De Morgan. *Fouilles à Dahchour, Mars–Juin 1894.* Vienna, 1895.

De Morgan, *Dahchour* II Jacques De Morgan. *Fouilles à Dahchour en 1894–1895.* Vienna, 1903.

Description de l'Égypte Commission des monuments d'Égypte. *Description de l'Egypte.* Plates, 10 vols. Text, 9 vols. Paris, 1809–1828.

Dorner, "Absteckung" Josef Dorner. "Die Absteckung und astronomische Orientierung ägyptischer Pyramidem." Ph.D. diss., University of Innsbruck, 1981.

Edwards, *Pyramids* I. E. S. Edwards. *The Pyramids of Egypt.* Harmondsworth, 1985.

Egypt's Golden Age *Egypt's Golden Age: The Art of Living in the New Kingdom 1558–1085 B.C.* Exhibition Catalogue, Museum of Fine Arts, Boston. Boston, 1982.

Eigner, *Grabbauten* Dieter Eigner. *Die monumentalen Grabbauten der Spätzeit in der thebanischen Nekropole.* Denkschriften der Gesamtakademie, Österreichische Akademie der Wissenschaften, no. 8. Vienna, 1984.

Emery, *Great Tombs* Walter B. Emery. *Great Tombs of the First Dynasty: Excavations at Saqqara.* 3 vols. Cairo, 1949; London, 1954, 1958.

Engelbach, *Aswan Obelisk* Reginald Engelbach. *The Aswan Obelisk.* Cairo, 1922.

Engelbach, *Problem of the Obelisks* Reginald Engelbach. *The Problem of the Obelisks: From a Study of the Unfinished Obelisk at Aswan.* London, 1923.

Fakhry, *Sneferu* Ahmed Fakhry. *The Monuments of Sneferu at Dahshur.* 2 vols. Cairo, 1959, 1961.

Festschrift Ricke *Aufsätze zum 70. Geburtstag von Herbert Ricke.* Beiträge Bf, no. 12. Wiesbaden, 1971.

Firth and Quibell, *Step Pyramid* Cecil M. Firth and J. E. Quibell. *The Step Pyramid.* Cairo, 1935.

Fischer-Elfert, *Anastasi I* Hans-Werner Fischer-Elfert. *Die satirische Streitschrift des Papyrus Anastasi I.* ÄgAbh, no. 44. Wiesbaden, 1986.

Fisher, *Minor Cemetery* Clarence Fisher. *The Minor Cemetery at Giza.* Philadelphia, 1924.

Fitchen, *Building Construction* John Fitchen. *Building Construction before Mechanization.* Cambridge, Mass., and London, 1986.

Frankfort, *Cenotaph* Henry Frankfort. *The Cenotaph of Seti I at Abydos.* Egypt Exploration Society Memoirs, no. 39. London, 1933.

Garstang, *Bet Khallaf* John Garstang. *Mahasna, and Bet Khallaf.* London, 1902.

Gautier, *Licht* Joseph-Etienne Gautier and Gustave Jéquier. *Mémoire sur les fouilles de Licht.* MIFAO, no. 6. Cairo, 1902.

Golvin and Goyon, *Karnak* Jean-Claude Golvin and Jean-Claude Goyon. *Les Bâtisseurs de Karnak.* Paris, 1987.

Gorringe, *Obelisks* Henry H. Gorringe. *Egyptian Obelisks.* New York, 1882.

Goyon, *Khéops* Georges Goyon. *Le Secret des bâtisseurs des grandes pyramides "Khéops."* Paris, 1977.

Hayes, *Scepter* William C. Hayes. *The Scepter of Egypt.* 2 vols. Cambridge, Mass., 1953, 1959. Reprint. 1990.

Hölscher, *Chephren* Uvo Hölscher. *Das Grabdenkmal des Königs Chephren.* Veröffentlichungen der Ernst von Sieglin Expedition in Ägypten I. Leipzig, 1912.

Hölscher, *Eighteenth Dynasty* Uvo Hölscher. *The Temples of the Eighteenth Dynasty (Excavation of Medinet Habu 2).* OIP, no. 41. Chicago, 1939.

Hölscher, *Mortuary Temple* Uvo Hölscher. *The Mortuary Temple of Ramses III (Excavation of Medinet Habu 3–4).* 2 vols. OIP, nos. 54, 55. Chicago, 1941, 1951.

Jacquet, *Trésor* Jean Jacquet. *Le Trésor de Thoutmosis Ier: Étude architecturale (Karnak-Nord V).* 2 vols. Cairo, 1983.

Jéquier, *Architecture* Gustave Jéquier. *L'Architecture et la décoration dans l'ancienne Egypte.* 3 vols. Paris, 1911, 1920, 1924.

Jéquier, *Deux pyramides* Gustave Jéquier. *Deux pyramides du Moyen Empire.* Cairo, 1933.

Jéquier, *Le Mastabat Faraoun* Gustave Jéquier, with the collaboration of Dows Dunham. *Le Mastabat Faraoun.* Cairo, 1928.

Jéquier, *Pépi II* Gustave Jéquier. *Le Monument funéraire de Pépi II.* 3 vols. Cairo, 1936, 1938, 1940.

Junker, *Giza* Hermann Junker. *Giza.* 12 vols. Vienna and Leipzig, 1929–1955.

Karnak Cahiers de Karnak. 8 vols. Cairo, 1968 (Kemi 18), 1969 (Kemi 19), 1970 (Kemi 20), 1971 (Kemi 21), 1975, 1980, 1982, 1987.

Karnak-Nord I Alexandre Varille. *Karnak* I. FIFAO, no. 19. Cairo, 1943.

Karnak-Nord III Louis A. Christophe. *Karnak-Nord* III. FIFAO, no. 23. Cairo, 1951.

Karnak-Nord IV Paul Barguet and Jean Leclant. *Karnak-Nord* IV. FIFAO, no. 25. Cairo, 1954.

Klemm, *Steine der Pharaonen* Rosemarie Klemm and Dietrich Klemm. *Die Steine der Pharaonen.* Munich, 1981.

Krauth, *Steinhauerbuch* Theodor Krauth and Franz Sales Meyer. *Die Bau- und Kunstarbeiten des Steinhauers.* Leipzig, 1896.

Kuhlmann and Schenkel, *Ibi* Klaus P. Kuhlmann and Wolfgang Schenkel. *Das Grab des Ibi.* 2 vols. Mainz, 1983.

LÄ Lexikon der Ägyptologie. 6 vols. Edited by Wolfgang Helck and Eberhard Otto. Wiesbaden, 1975–1986.

Lacau and Chevrier, *Hatshepsout* Pierre Lacau and Henri Chevrier. *Une Chapelle d'Hatshepsout à Karnak.* 2 vols. Cairo, 1977, 1979.

Lacau and Chevrier, *Sésostris Ier* Pierre Lacau and Henri Chevrier. *Une Chapelle de Sésostris Ier a Karnak.* 2 vols. Cairo, 1956, 1959.

Lauer, *Hist. Mon.* Jean-Philippe Lauer. *Histoire monumentale des pyramides d'Egypte.* Vol. I, *Les Pyramides à degrés (IIIe Dynastie).* BdE, no. 39. Cairo, 1962.

Lauer, *Mystère* Jean-Philippe Lauer. *Le Mystère des pyramides.* Paris, 1974.

Lauer, *Observations* Jean-Philippe Lauer. *Observations sur les pyramides.* BdE, no. 30. Cairo, 1960.

Lauer, *Ounas* Audran Labrousse, Jean-Philippe Lauer, and Jean Leclant. *Le Temple haut du complexe funéraire du roi Ounas.* Mission archéologique de Saqqarah II. BdE, no. 73. Cairo, 1977.

Lauer, *Pyramid à degrés* Jean-Philippe Lauer. *La Pyramid à degrés: L'Architecture.* 2 vols. Cairo, 1936, 1939.

Lauer, *Téti* Jean-Philippe Lauer and Jean Leclant. *Le Temple haut du complexe funéraire du roi Téti.* Mission archéologique de Saqqarah I. BdE, no. 51. Cairo, 1972.

LD Carl Richard Lepsius. *Denkmaeler aus Aegypten und Aethiopien.* Plates, 12 vols. Berlin, 1849–1859. Text, 5 vols. Leipzig, 1897–1913.

Legrain, *Karnak* Georges Legrain. *Les Temples de Karnak.* Brussels, 1929.

Lipinska, *Tuthmosis III* Jadwiga Lipinska. *Deir el-Bahari II: The Temple of Tuthmosis III. Architecture.* Warsaw, 1977.

Lucas and Harris, *AEMI* A. Lucas and J. R. Harris. *Ancient Egyptian Materials and Industries.* London, 1962.

Mannoni, *Marble* Luciana Mannoni and Tiziano Mannoni. *Marble: The History of a Culture.* New York and Oxford, n.d.

Maragioglio, *Piramidi* Vito Maragioglio and Celeste Rinaldi. *L'Architettura delle Piramidi Menfite.* 7 vols. Turin, 1963–1975.

Martin, *Architecture grecque* Roland Martin. *Manuel d'architecture grecque.* Vol. 1, *Matériaux et techniques.* Paris, 1965.

Mulloy, "Easter Islands" William Mulloy. "A Speculative Reconstruction of Techniques of Carving, Transporting and Erecting Easter Island Statues." *Archaeology and Physical Anthropology in Oceania* 5 (1970): 1–23.

Naumann, *Architektur* Rudolf Naumann. *Architektur Kleinasiens von ihren Anfängen bis zum Ende der Hethitischen Zeit.* Tübingen, 1955.

Petrie, *Antaeopolis* W. M. Flinders Petrie. *Antaeopolis.* Publications of the Egyptian Research Account and British School of Archaeology in Egypt, no. 51. London, 1930.

Petrie, *Kahun* W. M. Flinders Petrie. *Kahun, Gurob and Hawara.* London, 1890.

Petrie, *Labyrinth* W. M. Flinders Petrie, Gerald A. Wainwright, and Ernest Mackay. *The Labyrinth, Gerzeh and Mazghuneh.* British School of Archaeology in Egypt and Egyptian Research Account, no. 21. London, 1912.

Petrie, *Lahun II* W. M. Flinders Petrie, Guy Brunton, and Margaret A. Murray. *Lahun II.* British School of Archaeology in Egypt and Egyptian Research Account, no. 33. London, 1923.

Petrie, *Meydum and Memphis* W. M. Flinders Petrie, Ernest Mackay, and Gerald Wainwright. *Meydum and Memphis III.* British School of Archaeology in Egypt and Egyptian Research Account, no. 18. London, 1910.

Petrie, *Pyramids and Temples* W. M. Flinders Petrie. *The Pyramids and Temples of Gizeh.* London, 1883.

Petrie, *Royal Tombs* W. M. Flinders Petrie. *The Royal Tombs of the Earliest Dynasties (1900–1901).* 3 vols. Egypt Exploration Society Memoirs, nos. 18, 21, 21 suppl. London, 1900–1901.

Petrie, *Tools and Weapons* W. F. Petrie. *Tools and Weapons.* British School of Archaeology in Egypt and Egyptian Research Account, no. 22. London, 1917.

PM B. Porter and R. Moss. *Topographical Bibliography of Ancient Egyptian Hieroglyphic Texts, Reliefs, and Paintings.* 7 vols. Oxford, 1934–1981.

Ptahshepses *Preliminary Report on Czechoslovak Excavations in the Mastaba of Ptahshepses at Abusir.* Prague, 1976.

Reisner, *Giza* I George A. Reisner. *A History of the Giza Necropolis.* Vol. 1. London, 1942.

Reisner, *Mycerinus* George A. Reisner. *Mycerinus, the Temples of the Third Pyramid at Giza.* Cambridge, Mass., 1931.

Reisner, *Tomb Development* George A. Reisner. *The Development of the Egyptian Tomb down to the Accession of Cheops.* Cambridge, Mass., 1936.

Rekhmire N. De Garis Davies. *The Tomb of Rekh-mi-Re' at Thebes.* Publications of the Metropolitan Museum of Art Egyptian Expedition 11. New York, 1943.

Ricke, *Harmachis* Herbert Ricke. *Der Harmachistempel des Chefren in Giseh.* Beiträge Bf, no. 10. Wiesbaden, 1970.

Ricke, *Sonnenheiligtum* Herbert Ricke. *Das Sonnenheiligtum des Königs Userkaf.* 2 vols. Beiträge Bf, no. 7. Cairo, 1965.

Rowe, "Meydum" Alan Rowe. "Excavations of the Eckley B. Coxe, Jr., Expedition at Meydum, Egypt, 1929–30." *University of Pennsylvania Museum Journal* 22 (1931).

Ryan and Hansen, *Cordage* Donald P. Ryan and David H. Hansen. *A Study of Ancient Egyptian Cordage in the British Museum.* British Museum Occasional Paper, no. 62. London, 1987.

Saleh and Sourouzian, *Kairo* Mohamed Saleh and Hourig Sourouzian. *Die Meisterwerke im Ägyptischen Museum Kairo.* Mainz, 1986.

Shaw, *Minoan Architecture* Joseph W. Shaw. *Minoan Architecture: Materials and Techniques.* Annuario della Scuola Archeologica di Atene, vol. 49, n.s. 33, 1971. Rome, 1973.

Spencer, *Brick Architecture* A. J. Spencer. *Brick Architecture in Ancient Egypt.* Warminster, 1979.

Stadelmann, *Ägyptische Pyramiden* Rainer Stadelmann. *Die ägyptischen Pyramiden: Vom Ziegelbau zum Weltwunder.* Mainz, 1985.

Urk *Urkunden des aegyptischen Altertums.* Edited by Georg Steindorff. 22 vols. Leipzig, 1903–1957.

Vyse, *Pyramids* Howard Vyse. *Operations Carried on at the Pyramids of Gizeh in 1837.* 3 vols. London, 1840, 1842.

WB Adolf Erman and Hermann Grapow. *Wörterbuch der ägyptischen Sprache.* 5 vols. Leipzig, 1925–1931.

Winlock, *Excavations* Herbert E. Winlock. *Excavations at Deir el Bahri 1911–1931.* New York, 1942.

Winlock, *Hibis* Herbert E. Winlock. *The Temple of Hibis in el Khargeh Oasis.* Part I, *The Excavations.* Publications of the Metropolitan Museum of Art Egyptian Expedition 13. New York, 1941.

Zaki Nour, *Cheops Boats* Mohammad Zaki Nour and Zaky Iskander. *The Cheops Boats.* Cairo, 1960.

Zuber, "Travail des pierres dures" Antoine Zuber. "Techniques du travail des pierres dures dans l'Ancienne Egypte." *Techniques et Civilisations* 29, vol. 5, no. 5 (1956): 161–178; *Techniques et Civilisations* 30, vol. 5, no. 6 (1956): 196–215.

ILLUSTRATION SOURCES

Chapter 1 *1.1 ASAE* 26 (1926): 198–199; *1.2* Arnold, copy from original; *1.3*
MMA photo; *1.4 Ancient Egypt* (1917): 22; *1.5 CEAEM*, fig. 49; *1.6* Cairo photo;
1.7–1.14 Arnold; *1.15* MMA photo; *1.16, 1.17* Arnold; *1.18 MDAIK* 12 (1943):
149, fig. 8; *1.19 CEAEM*, fig. 155; *1.20* Arnold; *1.21* Lisht Expedition photo;
1.22 ASAE 8 (1907): 241, fig. 1.

Chapter 2 *2.1* R. Stadelmann; *2.2 CEAEM*, fig. 9; *2.3–2.6* Arnold; *2.7–2.9*
R. Klemm and D. Klemm; *2.10* Adela Oppenheim; *2.11* Arnold; *2.12*
CEAEM, fig. 15; *2.13* Arnold; *2.14* R. Klemm and D. Klemm; *2.15* Engelbach,
Aswan Obelisk, pl. 16; *2.16* Engelbach, *Aswan Obelisk*, fig. 6; *2.17* M. Isler, *JEA* 73
(1987): 138; *2.18 CEAEM*, fig. 31; *2.19 CEAEM*, fig. 32; *2.20 Rekhmire*, pl. 62;
2.21 Arnold; *2.22* Lisht Expedition photo; *2.23* Arnold; *2.24 MDAIK* 12 (1943):
146, fig. 5; *2.25 MDAIK* 12 (1943): 147, fig. 6; *2.26 Description de l'Égypt* IV,
pl. 64 [3–5]; *2.27* MMA photo; *2.28* Arnold; *2.29 Popular Archaeology* (April
1986): 28; *2.30* Arnold.

Chapter 3 *3.1* MMA photo; *3.2* Lauer, *Hist. Mon.*, 240, fig. 67; *3.3, 3.4* Arnold;
3.5 Percy E. Newberry, *El-Bersheh* I (London, 1895), pl. 15; *3.6* DAI photo; *3.7*
MMA photo; *3.8* Felix Arnold; *3.9* Reisner, *Mycerinus*, 85, figs. 15, 16; *3.10*
Engelbach, *Problem of the Obelisks*, figs. 27–33; H. Chevrier, *ASAE* 52 (1954): 312,
fig. 2; Chevrier, *RdÉ* 22 (1970): 34, fig. 26; *3.11, 3.12* Arnold; *3.13* Borchardt,
Amonstempel, 15, fig. 11; *3.14 LD* IV, 48a; *3.15, 3.16* MMA photo; *3.17* Bernard
Bruyère, *Les Fouilles de Deir el Médineh 1933–1934* (Cairo, 1937), 122, fig. 54;
3.18 Lauer, *Pyramid à degrés*, 52, fig. 26; *3.19* MMA photo; *3.20* Kuhlmann and
Schenkel, *Ibi*, 247, fig. 90; *3.21* Arnold; *3.22* Arnold; sarcophagus from Richard
A. Fazzini et al., *Ancient Egyptian Art in the Brooklyn Museum* (New York, 1989), 10;
3.23–3.25 Arnold; *3.26* Petrie, *Kahun*, pls. 3, 4; *3.27* Jéquier, *Deux pyramides*,
pl. 18; *3.28* Arnold; *3.29 MDAIK* 38 (1982): 84, figs. 2, 3; *3.30 MDAIK* 37
(1981): 16, fig. 7; *3.31* Arnold; *3.32* Borchardt, *Entstehung der Pyramide*, fig. 4;
3.33 Arnold; *3.34* Junker, *Giza* IX, 5, fig. 2; *3.35* L. Borchardt, *ZÄS* 39 (1901):
98, fig. 7; *3.36* Cecil M. Firth and Battiscombe Gunn, *Teti Pyramid Cemeteries:
Excavations at Saqqara* (Cairo, 1926), fig. 19; *3.37* MMA photo; *3.38* Lisht
Expedition photo; *3.39* MMA photo; *3.40* Arnold; *3.41, 3.42* MMA photos; *3.43*
Arnold; *3.44* Petrie, *Lahun II*, pls. 13, 15; Petrie, Notebook 43a Illahun, 1–4;
3.45 Arnold, *Qasr el-Sagha*, 14, fig. 9; *3.46* Arnold; *3.47* Hölscher, *Chephren*,
fig. 59; *3.48* Engelbach, *Problem of the Obelisks*, 60, fig. 22; *3.49, 3.50* Arnold; *3.51*
MDAIK 12 (1943): fig. 2; *3.52 Rekhmire*, pl. 60; *3.53* Arnold; *3.54* Arnold, from
MDAIK 37 (1981): 25, fig. 4; *3.55* Arnold.

Chapter 4 *4.1* Arnold, from *MDAIK* 42 (1987): 42, figs. 1, 2; W. M. Flinders
Petrie, *A Season in Egypt, 1887* (London, 1888), 30–31, pl. 24; *4.2* MMA photo;
4.3 De Lubicz, *Temple* II, pl. 94; *4.4 CEAEM*, 65; *4.5 Karnak* II, fig. 14; *4.6–4.9*
Arnold; *4.10* Lacau and Chevrier, *Hatshepsout*, 9, fig. 1; *4.11–4.14* Arnold; *4.15*
Borchardt, *Amonstempel*, 17, fig. 13; *4.16–4.18* Arnold; *4.19* Josef Durm, *Die
Baukunst der Griechen*, Handbuch der Architektur (Darmstadt, 1881), 24; *4.20*
Arnold; *4.21* Jacquet, *Trésor*, fig. 21; *4.22* Arnold; *4.23* Jacquet, *Trésor*, fig. 25;
4.24 Arnold, from Hölscher, *Chephren*, fig. 26; *4.25* Arnold; *4.26 Popular
Archaeology* (April 1986): 28; *4.27* De Morgan, *Dahchour* I, fig. 108; *4.28* Lacau
and Chevrier, *Sésostris I*er, pl. 8; *4.29* Lacau and Chevrier, *Hatshepsout*, 257,
fig. 21; *4.30 CEAEM*, fig. 124; *4.31* Arnold, from Borchardt, *Tempel mit Umgang*,
pl. 6; *4.32* MMA photo; *4.33* Borchardt, *Niuserre*, figs. 35–37; *4.34* DAI photo;
4.35 Arnold; *4.36* Jéquier, *Le Mastabat Faraôun*, 10, fig. 4; *4.37* Lacau and
Chevrier, *Hatshepsout*, fig. 23; *4.38* Arnold, from *LD* Text I, 27; *4.39* Jéquier,
Deux pyramides, 20, fig. 16; *4.40* MMA drawing; *4.41 CEAEM*, fig. 156;
4.42 (A) *Karnak* IV, fig. 7; (B) Hölscher, *Mortuary Temple* II, fig. 30; *4.43, 4.44*
Lauer, *Hist. Mon.*, figs. 72, 73, 68; *4.45* Borchardt, *Grundkanten*, 15, fig. 2; *4.46*
Arnold; *4.47* Borchardt, *Re-Heiligtum*, 38, fig. 26; *4.48–4.53* Arnold; *4.54* DAI

photo; *4.55* *MDAIK* 12 (1943): 148, fig. 7; *4.56–4.59* Arnold; *4.60* Jéquier, *Deux pyramides*, pl. 20; *4.61* Lisht Expedition photo; *4.62*, *4.63* Arnold; *4.64* MMA photo; *4.65* Hölscher, *Chephren*, pl. 17; *4.66*, *4.67* Arnold; *4.68*, *4.69* Jacquet, *Trésor*, fig. 22; *4.70* DAI photo; *4.71*, *4.72* Arnold; *4.73*, *4.74* MMA photos; *4.75* Borchardt, *Re-Heiligtum*, 30, fig. 16; *4.76* Arnold; *4.77* MMA photo; *4.78–4.80* Arnold; *4.81* MMA photo; *4.82–4.84* Arnold; *4.85* Arnold, from Lacau and Chevrier, *Hatshepsout;* *4.86–4.92* Arnold; *4.93*, *4.94* MMA photos; *4.95*, *4.96* Arnold; *4.97* MMA photo; *4.98* Arnold; *4.99* MMA photo; *4.100–4.102* Arnold; *4.103* Maragioglio, *Piramidi* v, pl. 6; *4.104–4.106* Arnold; *4.107* DAI photo; *4.108*, *4.109* Arnold; *4.110* *Karnak* IV, 148, fig. 3; *4.111–4.113* Arnold; *4.114* Maragioglio, *Piramidi* IV, pl. 3; *4.115* Georges Perrot and Charles Chipiez, *Histoire de l'art dans l'antiquité* I (Paris, 1882), 614, fig. 410; *4.116* Frankfort, *Cenotaph*, pl. 5; *4.117* CEAEM, fig. 172; *4.118* Maragioglio, *Piramidi* III, pl. 4; *4.119* BMMA photo; *4.120* DAI photo; *4.121* *Description de l'Égypt* v, pl. 13; *4.122* *MDAIK* 39 (1983): 248, fig. 2; *4.123* CEAEM, fig. 221; *4.124* CEAEM, fig. 220; *4.125* Arnold, from Frankfort, *Cenotaph;* *4.126* Frankfort, *Cenotaph*, pl. 3; *4.127* Jéquier, *Architecture* II, pl. 20 [4]; *4.128* Arnold; *4.129* Maragioglio, *Piramidi* VIII pl. 2; *4.130* Maragioglio, *Piramidi* VIII, pl. 12; *4.131* Arnold; *4.132* Arnold, from De Morgan, *Dahchour* II, 32–36, figs. 77–83; *4.133* DAI photo; *4.134* Arnold, *Amenemhet III*, fig. 37; *4.135* Maragioglio, *Piramidi* VI, pl. 6; *4.136* Maragioglio, *Piramidi* VI, pl. 17; *4.137* Arnold, *Mentuhotep*, pls. 36, 37; *4.138* De Morgan, *Dahchour* I, 55, fig. 121; *4.139* Maragioglio, *Piramidi* VIII, pls. 11, 12; *4.140* Jéquier, *Pépi II* III, 56, fig. 58; *4.141* U. Hölscher, *Post-Ramesside Remains: Excavations of Medinet Habu* 5 (Chicago, 1954), 30, fig. 35; *4.142* ASAE 51 (1951): 490, pl. 2; *4.143* Georges Perrot and Charles Chipiez, *Histoire de l'art dans l'antiquité* I (Paris, 1882), 317, fig. 200.

Chapter 5 *5.1*, *5.2* Arnold; *5.3* Arnold, from Fakhry, *Sneferu* I, figs. 16–18, 36; *5.4* Arnold; *5.5* MMA photo; *5.6* Arnold; *5.7* Arnold, *Senwosret I*, fig. 24; *5.8* DAI photo; *5.9* Arnold, from Firth and Quibell, *Step Pyramid*, pls. 21, 47; *5.10* Fakhry, *Sneferu* I, 49, fig. 56; *5.11* G. Goyon, *Revue Archeologique* 2 (1963): 10, fig. 4; *5.12* Arnold, from E. R. Ayrton, C. T. Currelly, and A. E. P. Weigall, *Abydos* III (London, 1904), pl. 41; *5.13* Garstang, *Bet Khallaf*, pls. 17, 18; *5.14* Maragioglio, *Piramidi* III, pl. 13; *5.15* Borchardt, *Dritte Bauperiode*, pls. 3–5; *5.16* MMA drawing; *5.17* Jéquier, *Deux pyramides*, pl. 18; *5.18* Arnold, from ASAE 1 (1901): 161–163, figs. 1–3; 230–233, figs. 1–4; *ASAE* 2 (1901): figs. 1–4; *ASAE* 5 (1904): 70–72, figs. 1–4; *ASAE* 51 (1951): 476–478, pls. 1, 2; *5.19* MMA photo of color copy; *5.20* Arnold; *5.21* Hölscher, *Chephren*, figs. 68, 69; *5.22* DAI photo; *5.23* Lisht Expedition photo; *5.24* Arnold, from Maragioglio, *Piramidi* III, pls. 12, 13; Fakhry, *Sneferu* I, pls. 11–14; *5.25* MMA photo; *5.26* Arnold, from Borchardt, *Sahura*, 69–70, pl. 16; *5.27* Arnold, *Amenemhet III*, foldout 2; *5.28* Arnold; *5.29* DAI photo; *5.30* Arnold, *Amenemhet III*, pl. 50; *5.31* Arnold, from *MDAIK* 42 (1986): 56, fig. 4; *5.32–5.34* Arnold; *5.35* Arnold, *Amenemhet III*, pl. 47; *5.36* DAI photo; *5.37* MMA photo; *5.38* Arnold, from G. Garbrecht and H. U. Bertram, *Der Sadd-el-Kafara: Die älteste Talsperre der Welt*, Mitteilungen, no. 81, Leichtweiss-Institut für Wasserbau der Technischen Universität Braunschweig (1983).

Chapter 6 *6.1–6.3* MMA photos; *6.4* Cairo photo; *6.5*, *6.6* MMA photos; *6.7* MMA photo of color copy; *6.8* MMA photo; *6.9* Arnold; *6.10* MMA photo; *6.11* DAI photo; *6.12* MMA photo; *6.13* Arnold, from Henri Wild, *Le Tombeau de Ti* III (Cairo, 1966), pl. 173; *6.14–6.16* MMA photos; *6.17* A. Oppenheim; *6.18–6.21* MMA photos; *6.22–6.24* Arnold; *6.25* Lisht Expedition photo; *6.26* Arnold; *6.27* Hölscher, *Chepren*, pl. 17; *6.28* Arnold; *6.29* MMA photo; *6.30* CEAEM, figs. 107–109; *6.31* MMA photo; *6.32* Arnold, from E. Chassinat, *Fouilles de Qattah* (Cairo, 1906), 22, fig. 8; *6.33* Arnold, from De Morgan, *Dahchour* II, 89–90, figs. 132–134; *6.34* DAI photo; *6.35* Arnold, from George A. Reisner, *Models of Ships and Boats* (Cairo, 1913), fig. 326; *6.36* MMA photo; *6.37* *BIFAO* 69

(1971): pl. 3; **6.38** Choisy, *L'Art de bâtir*, 118, fig. 90; **6.39** *ASAE* 11 (1911): 263; **6.40** Edouard Naville, *The Temple of Deir el Bahari* VI (London, 1908), pl. 154; **6.41** Austen Henry Layard, *The Monuments of Nineveh* II (London, 1849), 16; **6.42** Jéquier, *Pépi II* III, 47, fig. 45; **6.43** MMA photo; **6.44** J. E. Quibell and A. G. K. Hayter, *Teti Pyramid, North Side: Excavations at Saqqara* (Cairo, 1927), frontispiece; Brigitte Jaroš-Deckert, *Das Grab des Jnj-jtj.f: Die Wandmalereien der XI. Dynastie* (Mainz, 1984), pl. 3; **6.45** Arnold, from Selim Hassan, *Excavations at Giza IV, 1932–1933* (Cairo, 1943), pl. 18A–B; Reisner, *Mycerinus*, pl. A [6]; **6.46** Arnold.

Appendix A.1, A.2 Arnold.

The following objects and copies of Egyptian wall paintings
are reproduced by courtesy of the Metropolitan Museum of Art, New York.

96.4.9 (**fig. 6.29**)	Gift of Egypt Exploration Fund, 1896
09.183.5A–C (**fig. 6.12**)	Gift of the Egyptian Research Account and British School of Archaeology in Egypt, 1909
10.130.1013 (**fig. 6.18**)	Gift of Helen Miller Gould, 1910
11.151.733–735 (**fig. 6.16**)	Rogers Fund, 1911
12.182.6 (**fig. 2.27**)	Rogers Fund, 1912
13.183.2 (**fig. 6.20**)	Gift of Edward S. Harkness, 1913
14.7.146 (**fig. 6.21**)	Gift of Edward S. Harkness, 1914
14.108 (**fig. 1.3**)	Gift of N. de Garis Davies, 1914
15.3.832 (**fig. 6.14**)	Rogers Fund, 1915
20.3.90 (**fig. 6.5**)	Rogers Fund and Edward S. Harkness Gift, 1920
20.3.190 (**fig. 6.14**)	Rogers Fund and Edward S. Harkness Gift, 1920
22.1.751 (**fig. 6.6**)	Rogers Fund and Edward S. Harkness Gift, 1922
22.1.819 (**fig. 6.15**)	Rogers Fund and Edward S. Harkness Gift, 1922
22.3.30 (**fig. 1.2**)	Rogers Fund and Edward S. Harkness Gift, 1922
22.3.72 (**fig. 6.3**)	Rogers Fund and Edward S. Harkness Gift, 1922
23.3.169 (**fig. 6.8**)	Rogers Fund, 1923
24.1.84 (**fig. 6.36**)	Rogers Fund and Edward S. Harkness Gift, 1924
27.3.12 (**fig. 6.10**)	Rogers Fund, 1927
28.3.3,4 (**fig. 6.31**)	Rogers Fund, 1928
30.4.44 (**fig. 6.2**)	Rogers Fund, 1930
30.4.90 (**fig. 5.19**)	Rogers Fund, 1930
30.4.115 (**fig. 3.15**)	Rogers Fund, 1930
30.8.115 (**fig. 6.10**)	Theodore M. Davis Collection, Bequest of Theodore M. Davis, 1915
31.6.23 (**fig. 6.7**)	Rogers Fund, 1931
32.1.213 (**fig. 5.37**)	Rogers Fund, 1932
34.1.35 (**fig. 6.43**)	Rogers Fund, 1934
37.4.65 (**fig. 6.19**)	Rogers Fund, 1937
41.2.1 (**fig. 4.32**)	Rogers Fund, 1941

Reproduction based on

41.160.102 (**fig. 6.1**)	Bequest of W. Gedney Beatty, 1941

Index